Computer Programming Fundamentals

ANARCHISM

Computer Programming Fundamentals

Herbert D. Leeds

Product Administrator, Large Scale Systems
IBM Data Processing Division

Gerald M. Weinberg

Senior Staff Member, IBM Systems Research Institute

Second Edition

McGraw-Hill Book Company

New York   St. Louis   San Francisco   London   Toronto   Sydney

Computer Programming Fundamentals

1 2 3 4 5 6 7 8 9 0 (HD) 7 2 1 0 6 9 8 7 6

PREFACE

Preparing a second edition of a book is sometimes a painful task for authors, especially if they find that the material of the first edition did not stand the test of time and use. This pain could be particularly acute if the authors had set themselves the task of extracting and presenting the *fundamentals* of their subject, for the fundamentals should not change over a period of a few years. We feel fortunate, then, that no such pain accompanied this revision, which has in no way modified the basic objectives of the original edition. What has been modified, and modified extensively, is the expansion upon these fundamental concepts as presented to the reader. Our initial objectives thus still are meaningful.

We are extremely grateful and indebted to the many people who have used "Computer Programming Fundamentals" and who have suggested to us a number of ways in which the book could be improved. Most of their suggestions have been incorporated in this revised, enlarged, and—we hope—thereby improved second edition. The major changes are the following:

1. The addition of FORTRAN as an example of a higher level language, developed right alongside the corresponding discussions of symbolic machine-language programming.
2. The addition of new concepts, including operating systems, man-machine communication, multiprocessing, and those concepts related to the use and abuse of higher level languages such as FORTRAN.
3. The addition of numerous problems illustrating the points of the text. There are more than twice as many problems as in the original edition, and most of the new problems have been sug-

gested by teachers who have used them with the text in classroom
work.

4. The addition of an annotated bibliography to help the reader
   move on to more advanced stages of his computer education.

There have also been numerous corrections, small additions, re-
phrasings, and some deletions. Naturally, we hope that we have kept
everything that is good, eliminated everything that is bad, and added
only the most relevant material. These goals, though, we know to be
impossible. Perhaps we should only wish that we have managed some
kind of general improvement and that our new readers will be as co-
operative and generous as others have been in helping us create this
new edition.

In writing this book and its revision, we have set ourselves the task
of filling a long-felt need in the computing industry, namely, the
preparation of an adequate, truly introductory text on digital computing. Although the advanced literature in this field has been growing explosively, this primary need is still inadequately represented.

After studying this book, we hope that the reader will have accomplished one or more of the following objectives:

1. He will be able to read general computing literature such as is
   published by The Association for Computing Machinery, the
   Society for Industrial and Applied Mathematics, and various
   commercial automation and control magazines.
2. If he has problems of his own, he will be able to communicate
   with the programmers who can assist him.
3. By reading the literature on specific systems, he should be able
   to make an intelligent assessment of their power and applicability.
4. He will be better able to learn the coding for a particular machine
   from reference manuals and classes.

We hope to provide the reader with a broad, but not nebulous, base
from which to depart on his particular course in the computing field.
At the same time, we have attempted to make the book self-contained
and of interest to people who will not be taking an additional course.
We realize that the average reader will raise many questions that could
not be answered in a book of this size. Those concepts that we felt
to be most difficult for the beginner have been treated with extreme
thoroughness.

In general, the structure, emphasis, and tone of the book constitute a summary of the authors' experiences in working with computers and in teaching various courses, especially introductory courses. We have attempted to write the textbook that our students have wanted. We did not intend to write a reference book—an encyclopedia of computing. Our objective was to supply a pedagogical tool for other teachers in similar situations, and the omissions and commissions in the text—that is, those which were consciously made—have been largely determined by that objective.

For example, we have rearranged topics from the "conventional" form—especially by the delaying of arithmetic as long as possible and by the early introduction of input-output so that "complete" problems could be coded—in order to conform to the most successful teaching sequence we have yet found. To keep the book from becoming "topic bound," we have tried to introduce subjects at natural times, to reintroduce them later so that the reader may then reinterpret familiar ideas, and to vary the pace and depth so as to prevent both prolonged plodding and habitual skimming.

One particular arrangement of topics deserves special note. The chapter on "The Language Barrier" is particularly necessary when the book is used in a course where actual machine practice is included; for without a relatively clear understanding of these concepts, the student may become so involved in mechanics that his progress in the course will cease. When using the book in a nonlaboratory course, the instructor may wish to treat these topics more lightly, repeating them after the students have made one traversal of the book.

We have attempted to keep the level of the book such that the reader need have no special technical training. (The *only* mathematical knowledge assumed is high-school algebra.) Consequently, we hope that the book will be suitable as an introductory text for students in business administration, economics, and other nontechnical fields, as well as the physical sciences and mathematics courses. In fact, since the use of computers is spreading to so many diverse fields, we have endeavored to use examples from relatively common experiences which do not depend on specialized training. This should allow the book to be used in courses where the students are of mixed backgrounds. The instructor may wish to furnish examples and problems of his own to supplement those in the text.

The book was organized somewhat on the basis of material covered in a 90-hour course. About 40 per cent of this time was spent in working problems under supervision so that as a text, this book should be suited to a one-semester course. No attempt was made to force the book into a course pattern. The intention was rather to have a book that would be of value to the reader proportional to the distance he read into it. Each chapter is intended to present some new concept and develop it into the over-all scheme.

The first section brings the student into contact with the fundamentals that provide him with an understanding of the relative significance of what follows. Flow diagramming and coding for a specific machine (IBM 7090) are explored in the longer second section. No attempt is made to present a picture of all the details of the machine, but the student should gain an appreciation of the source of power and difficulties of computers.

Perhaps a few words on the choice of computers for the text examples is in order. The first question was whether or not we should "invent" a machine, so as to supply a more perfect pedagogical instrument than any actual computer might present and at the same time give academic purity to the book. We decided against this for the following reasons:

1. An actual machine would give the student recourse to information other than that covered directly in the book.
2. In an effort to gain purity, we would probably have attained sterility. We felt that the naming of an actual machine would lend authenticity to the book and give the student some feeling for the compromises that often have to be made in the design and use of a real computer.

Having settled the question of a real versus an imaginary machine, we were faced with the problem of which real computer to choose. Of the several computers with which we have had experience, we at first favored one of the "medium-scale" decimal machines, but after some study, we concluded that the 7090 and associated systems offered a more representative view of the many types of programming features available on recent machines.

We were presented with a similar decision in preparing our revision. Many new computers have emerged since our book was published originally.   However, it was our conclusion that the 7090 and its associated systems was still representative of the developments of the past several years.   Again, the fundamentals remain consistent with the new developments.   We therefore wish to give particular thanks to the International Business Machines Corporation for permitting us to use the 7090 as our example.

It would be impossible to give proper credit to the many people, especially students and other teachers, who have contributed indirectly to the organization and content of this book.   We hope that the book itself, if it succeeds in bringing their insights to others, will be sufficient thanks to them.

Herbert D. Leeds   **Gerald M. Weinberg**

CONTENTS

Computer Programming Fundamentals

CHAPTER 1

WHAT IS A COMPUTER?

Without doubt, much nonsense has been written about computers and their effect upon the human society. As a result of such nonsense, there are undoubtedly a number of people who actually lose sleep worrying about a computer coming into their bedrooms and choking them in their beds. More realistically, other people worry that computers are going to take away their jobs or make robots out of them. But for every reasonable fear about the effects of computers on human life, there are ten or a hundred fears that would be dispelled with the eradication of the fundamental lack of understanding most people have about the part computers can and do play in their everyday lives. In only a decade or two, computers have proved so useful a tool for human well-being that no modern society could function without them. It is no longer a question of whether we want computers or not—unless we think we can return to the innocence of the Garden of Eden—but of how we can make sensible use of computers to better the lot of the whole human race. The first step in this process is to acquire a fundamental knowledge of what computers are and what role they play in modern technology.

How much are computers involved in our everyday life? To illustrate their pervasiveness, let us look into a suburban community where John Jones is preparing to go shopping. He calls the store to see if it is open, never considering the computer that assigned all the telephone numbers and prepared the directory, or the computer that handles the call from start to finish. He turns out the light and shuts off the electricity which comes from a power plant designed with the aid of a computer and controlled by another computer. A computer addressed the magazine and renewal notice in his mailbox, another computer calculated the electric bill, and yet another computer set the type and layout of the newspaper on his doorstep. He drives to the store in an automobile which was designed and built with computer direction at almost every stage. He stops at a traffic signal which is controlled by a computer. He turns on his radio (whose circuits were designed by a computer) and listens to a computer-calculated weather forecast. He enters a new freeway, which was laid out by a computer and had a computer calculating the cost of its construction as it was built. He pulls into a gas station where he buys gasoline produced according to computer-planned specifications in a computer-controlled refinery, and he charges his purchase with a credit card which provides an entry to a computer system for centralized billing of all his gasoline purchases. He drives to the shopping center and admires the flowers growing there, a new variety bred with the help of a computer. The developers of his shopping center used a computer to plan its location. The architects used a computer to help design the structure. The shipping order for a truckload of groceries being delivered was written by a computer which forecast that certain items would soon be out of stock. The lighting in the store, the height of the shelves, the position of the meat department were all planned with computer assistance. The brand of tooth paste he buys was named by a computer. As he walks up to the check-out counter, he takes out his pay check and thinks, "How complex these machines must be which can calculate my pay with all these deductions." Yet these machines are not too complex for John Jones to understand. Just as their effects manifest themselves (mostly unnoticed) in our daily living, so do their basic principles exhibit themselves in much of our common experience. Even as John stands in the check-out line, he is completely unaware that he is observing a device which has many of the characteristics of the automatic digital computer—the cash register.

A simple digital computer, the cash register is a device which, in addition to being a drawer for money, keeps a total of the costs of each of the items we purchase. The cash register is fundamentally an adding machine. On the cash register, each piece of data (price) is entered when the operator depresses the keys representing the dollars-and-cents price. Another key is pressed which causes this price to be added to the previous total. How does this adding take· place, and how is the total represented inside the cash register? Actually, the operator does not need to know the internal mechanics of the machine in order to operate it. (The operator of a more complex computer also does not need to know its internal mechanism.) The cash-register operator needs to know only two things: (1) how to enter each number, and (2) how to cause the total to be shown at the top of the machine or on the paper tape.

In other words, we enter digits into the register and get digits out as a result, but this is *not* the reason for classifying the cash register as a type of digital computer. We can, in fact, build a digital computer which will accept analog (*un*digital) information. We classify a computer on the basis of how the *input* information to the computer is transformed into its *output* information. In the cash register this transformation is basically accomplished through the rotation of gears which can take only several discrete positions, each representing a *digit*. Thus we call it a *digital* machine. We shall consider only digital computers in this book.

In order to look more closely at the use of the cash register, we must consider the relationship between the machine and its operator. Part of the work at the check-out counter is done by the operator and part by the machine. The operator furnishes numbers to the machine; the machine calculates and furnishes a printed record of the numbers and results. The operator, moreover, is in control of the operation. He may enter any numbers he wishes, and he may take totals at any time. Apparently, then, the machine cannot get along without its operator. The operator, however, can do quite nicely without the machine. We know, in fact, that many stores today operate without cash registers. Why, then, do we have them at all? We immediately think of speed. Few people can, with pencil and paper, keep up with an average checker at a cash register. Nevertheless, the difference in speed is not so great as to account for the wide use of these machines. Only when we consider the relative accuracy of the two methods do we find *striking* differences.

Errors

Let us examine the question of accuracy: What are the possible errors—and what can be done about them? In the cash-register operation three major sources of error exist:

1. The checker may enter a number incorrectly.

2. One of the cash-register gears can fail to function within necessary tolerance.

3. The checker could read the total incorrectly.

The type 1 error is concerned with the process of introducing to the computer the quantities with which it will compute. How subject to error is this process? An hour or so of careful observation at a check-out counter should demonstrate the answer.

How much, then, do these errors limit the effective use of the cash register? If you have been watching the checker and *see* him make an error, you can certainly inform him. The checker can also correct his own errors. Once he becomes aware of his error, is it a great problem in setting it right? Not at all. It seems, then, that we have a way of entirely eliminating type 1 errors on the register. This is only an illusion, however. It is still possible that both you and the checker will overlook a mistake. What then can be done to prevent undetected errors? We might add another observer—but it is still possible that three people could overlook the same error. No matter how many people are watching (not even considering the cost of such an operation), there is always some chance of everyone's missing the error.

We see that there is definitely no *perfect* system, although somehow we feel that the more people we have watching, the smaller the chance of an undetected error. Let us approach this problem more analytically. We shall make the following assumptions:

a. People will make errors, or fail to recognize errors, for one number out of each one hundred (a conservative figure arrived at through much time in long check-out lines).

b. Any number is as likely to cause an error as any other.

c. Errors made by different people are unrelated.

Using our assumptions, if one person is watching the checker, he will miss one error in a hundred. But the checker will make one error for every hundred numbers. Therefore, once every $100 \times 100 = 10,000$ times, an error may slip through. If two people watch, one error in a million might escape detection, and so forth. It seems that we could reduce the errors to an arbitrarily small number, but this is a place for caution. If we examine our assumptions (*b*) and (*c*), we find they are not precisely true. Certain numbers *are* more likely to cause errors than others (3,245 than 1,000, for example); and people do tend to overlook each other's errors (have several of your friends try copying a list of 15-digit numbers and check each other's work). Nevertheless, this principle of double checking is still good, and we shall have much use for it with computers.

When we examine the type 3 errors, we find that they are quite similar to the type 1 errors and that they can be reduced by similar methods.

Computers are a good medium for learning some of the important lessons of life. Error detection, for example, provides a fine demonstration of the fact that you always pay for what you get. If we have two people watching for each other's errors, any time either detects an error, he stops to examine it and correct it. Since both make errors, however, the second will often think that the first made an error, when in reality he did not. Thus the error detector can cause "errors" to be detected which are only his own mistakes. The designers of the computer must decide just how many false errors they can afford in their quest for true-error detection.

We are not in a position to examine the origins of the type 2 errors in the machine, but we can gain some idea of the average error of this type. For this answer we shall have to do some calculation. By far the most common error will be of one in any decimal place, that is, 5 instead of 6, 9 instead of 8, etc. Such an error might occur once in each position in 100,000 additions. Since most of our amounts will not be over $9.99, we could say that our error would be $1.00 plus $0.10 plus $0.01, or $1.11, in 100,000 computations, yielding an average error of about 0.00001 dollar, or one-thousandth of a cent.

Actually, this whole procedure reminds one of the statistician who drowned crossing a river with an average depth of 3 ft. For an average does not tell us what our extremes or exceptions are. The river could well be only ½ ft deep in some places while 15 ft deep at others. Therefore, what is really important in checking groceries is that 99.99 per cent of the customers will have no error in their bill, and those who do have an error can find it by checking their paper tape. In fact, we should prefer that the actual error were larger. If, when the machine made an error, it never was wrong by less than $10, we should have no difficulty; for few people would fail to notice when a jar of pickles and a box of marshmallows cost $10.84.

This, then, demonstrates one of the first principles of digital computing:

Make no errors; but when you do, make them big. (This is by no means easy to do!)

You may wonder at this point why so much emphasis in this first chapter has been placed on the subject of errors. There are three reasons:

First, we shall soon pass from simple machines like the cash register to larger machines capable of thousands of calculations per second. Assume that we have a machine which can add 10,000 numbers in one second (there are much faster machines than this). If this machine were as reliable as our cash register (one error in 100,000 additions), it would, on the average, make one error *every 10 seconds*, or six errors every minute. Without reliability many times greater than this, we should find little use for computers. Historically, the theoretical knowledge necessary to design modern computers has existed for decades, but only the last few years have produced the components necessary for such reliability. Mechanical components, such as the gears in the cash register, could not be made reliable (or fast) enough, but electronic devices such as vacuum tubes and transistors have made possible the largest computers. We shall find that when various mechanical or electromechanical devices must be attached to the computer they generally become the slowest and least reliable elements in the system.

The second reason for emphasis on errors is to dispel some common notions. Among people recently acquainted with computers, two opposite feelings seem prevalent. They are about equally distributed and equally dangerous. The first notion is that the computer is omnipotent and thus cannot make a mistake. The second, based on a consideration of the enormous complexity of the electronic circuitry of the computer, is that the computer cannot really work. One notion seems to go with an undying faith in whatever "science" produces, the other with an equally undying rejection of all new things. The first idea usually begins to weaken with increasing experience, but unfortunately is often lost in a single "catastrophic" incident involving the computer which would never have occurred had less been expected of the machine. Too often people forget that a computer operation requires *hard work*. The second idea is sometimes never given up. Every once in a while, someone will insist to us that, if a machine has a million parts and each part is 99.9 per cent sure to work, the machine is almost sure to fail. We can only agree with the plausibility of this statement, while patiently pointing out that he may be overestimating the number of parts in a computer, underestimating the reliability of the components (drastically), and not taking account at all of the ability of the computer designers. A word about design is in order. There is a popular saying that "a chain is no stronger than its weakest link." Actually, it does not require much thought to design a chain which is considerably stronger than its weakest link. For example, one solution is to connect a stronger link in parallel with the weakest link. Likewise, by careful design, it is possible to build computers which are far more reliable than their least reliable component. We shall not, however, attempt to show how the circuits of such a machine would be built (nor shall we discuss circuits at any time).

The reader should take two statements on faith; he can confirm them by his own experience later:

1. Computers are reliable enough to do useful work—much useful work.

2. Computers are not reliable enough that we need *never* consider the possibility of error.

And so we come to the third reason for this lengthy discussion of errors. Having made statements 1 and 2, we shall not always refer to them explicitly in every problem we discuss. This will serve the interests of simplicity and clarity. To serve the interests of truth, however, you must always be prepared for the consequences of errors, and you will be reminded of that fact from time to time.

Multiple Operations

We started this chapter by showing that the automatic digital computer, as employed today, is a machine capable of performing a multitude of tasks. When discussing our cash register, however, we purposely kept its description as simple as possible. Our machine simply added the figures which were entered into its keyboard and presented us with a total (as a bell rings and the drawer opens) after the last item was rung up. Even this simple machine has two operations it can perform—adding an amount and displaying the total. How does the register decide which of these two things it should do? Clearly, once we give our machine the ability to perform other than a single operation, we must also provide it with a means of choosing —deciding—which of the operations to perform. As we know, the register chooses its operation according to which operation key is pressed by the checker. There is an ADD key and a TOTAL key. The ADD key is depressed after each number is set in the keyboard; the TOTAL key is depressed after the last item has been added.

Of course, there are many other features which we often see on cash registers. These features may require special operation keys of their own or may be designed to operate automatically when some other function is being performed. One device may calculate change. Another may provide a separate total of the sales-taxable items, so that the checker may compute the tax without sorting the groceries. A common device is one which keeps daily totals for each type of item sold in the store—for example, meat, produce, groceries, drug items, and beverages. Each of these features increases the value of the cash register, but each one also adds to the cost. To decide which register to buy, you must measure the *value* against the *cost*. The cost is quite easily determined, but the value involves many variable and elusive factors. As we use computers, we shall always be called upon to make such measurements. In planning computer applications, people often pick sledge hammers for cracking peanuts, while others are tempted to try smashing boulders with nutcrackers.

Another factor in adding functions to a cash register is the change in the operator's task. The first two devices mentioned probably make his job easier. The third (for accumulating separate daily totals) adds an extra decision to his responsibility without simplifying his job. The device provides valuable information for managing the store and thereby makes the checker's job more important, more responsible. This too is characteristic of computers. Though they do much for us, they demand from us much more skilled and responsible efforts.

Some Words of Encouragement

Digital computers are not new to any of us. In this volume, we shall see how the principles of simple computing devices, such as the cash register, can be utilized in larger machines, rendering them capable of carrying out complex tasks seemingly unrelated to the simple principles involved. As you study the use of computers (and especially after you have passed the studying phase), keep several thoughts circulating in your mental stream:

1. You do not have to understand the internal computer mechanism in order to make profitable use of the machine.

2. Computers can make errors, but people are sure to make them. If an error occurs the odds are at least 100 to 1 it is a human error.

3. Think about errors: the *cost* of avoiding them and the *loss* in ignoring them.

4. Consider the effect on the people involved when planning for a computer. Do not ask for impossible performance, but do not be afraid to ask for quality. Do not forget: A smooth-running computer results *only* from hard work!

5. Never lose track of the cost-value relationship. Through the use of computers it will usually be easier to increase value than to decrease cost.

6. Remember that, if the computer will not do a better job or do the same job for less cost, it should not be used; but do not be discouraged by difficulties in starting, once you are sure of the value of your results.

PROBLEMS

1-1. What other devices could be added to a cash register to make it do a better job?

1-2. Would any of these devices or the devices mentioned in the chapter make a really *major* change in the performance of the cash register? Try to think of a device which would make a major change in performance.

1-3. What other digital-computing devices are you familiar with? What types of errors are these devices subject to?

1-4. Why can we not make an absolutely perfect computer?

1-5. If we could build such a machine, how would we use it?

1-6. Suppose we had a computer which was 1,000 times as fast as the cash register, 10,000 times more reliable, and had the ability to perform many other functions such as multiplication, division, and subtraction. How could it be used?

1-7. What would limit the usefulness of the machine described in Prob. 1-6?

What Computers Do

Now that we have a glimpse of what computers *are*, perhaps we should pause to examine in more detail some of the things computers *do*. The range and variety of applications which a given computer can perform are not necessarily apparent, even to its designers. When automatic digital computers were first introduced to the mass market, most users were application-ignorant. They were able to use the machines—that is, keep them running and producing output of measurable value. But too often they used the computer only to do the things they were previously doing, never realizing the wider fields of application which the computer's unique abilities opened to them. It sometimes required years of experience before these people were able to utilize their computers properly. We shall try to make you more aware of this most important area of computers—their *use*. In order to make our presentation more meaningful we can think of an interesting analogy between the class of computers and a much better-known class of items, namely, trucks.

Let us start by listing some of the things trucks do:
1. Transport produce from farm to market.
2. Carry cement to building sites.
3. Deliver groceries to individual homes.
4. Carry flowers from a florist.
5. Deliver clothing from a laundry.
6. Transport gasoline from a refinery.

What do all these tasks have in common? They all involve carrying some commodity from one place to another. That is the *general function* of trucks; in fact, trucks are often referred to as carriers.

Is there a general function of computers? Let us try to determine one, if there is one, by listing some of the areas where digital computers have been used:
1. Calculate and write payrolls.
2. Keep track of checking accounts in a bank.
3. Evaluate formulas dealing with various airplane designs.
4. Keep track of all airplanes flying over the United States at any time.
5. Predict where an earth satellite will be many weeks in the future.
6. Analyze sales in a lumberyard.

This list certainly is much more varied than our truck list, and the tasks certainly seem far more complex than those of our cash register. Probably no immediate similarity, or underlying principle, is so apparent as the principle of carrying goods was for trucks. Of course, most of these computer tasks are less familiar to us than those of the truck list. Perhaps we should try to examine these computer applications in more detail, in order to find some underlying principles. Let us outline, therefore, what is specifically involved in each of these jobs:

1. Payroll
   a. Gather data on employee's name, hours worked, rate of pay, number of deductions, earnings, and taxes so far this year.
   b. Calculate current earnings, taxes, and other deductions.
   c. Write checks, earnings statements, company payroll, and tax records.
2. Checking accounts
   a. Gather data on each account, all checks written, deposits made, service charges, balance in account.
   b. Calculate new balance, balance transactions against cash, calculate service charges.
   c. Print out statements, note all accounts out of balance, send overdraft notices.
3. Evaluating airplane designs
   a. Gather data on the various dimensions and materials of the airplane as well as the conditions under which it will operate.
   b. Evaluate formulas which describe the behavior of the airplane under different conditions.
   c. Indicate which sections will fail to perform satisfactorily given specified conditions and specified materials. Also indicate what combinations give the best performance.
4. Tracking airplanes
   a. Receive information on all known flights, commercial, military, and private; receive radar sightings on all craft in the air.
   b. Calculate positions and speeds from radar data; compare results with known flights.
   c. Issue notification of all planes not identified, giving position and speed.
5. Predicting satellite orbits
   a. Take in data from radio and optical tracking stations, data on earth's shape and mass, position of moon and sun.
   b. Evaluate formulas giving orbit of satellite; compare results with more data; make corrections to predictions.
   c. Print out predictions showing speed and position of satellite at various times; indicate when satellite will be visible from different locations.
6. Analyzing sales
   a. Gather data on each purchase and return: type of item, quanti-

ties, amount of money, date, type of customer, cash or charge sale.

b. Distribute amounts and quantities by type of item, by type of customer, and by date.

c. Report this information showing best and worst items, seasonal fluctuations, most profitable kinds of customers.

Of course these descriptions are not complete, nor could they be, for each application has many variations. Nevertheless, in reviewing this extended application list, we should be able to approach some general principles that exist in all the specific cases. Each application seems to break naturally into three parts, or phases:

a. The gathering of information or data.

b. The combining, comparing, and calculating with these data in various ways.

c. The presentation of other data which results from step b operations.

(Which of these aspects did the cash register present?)

It is possible for us to simplify this list. The general function of computers is to *transform* certain *information,* or data, into other information derived from it. In fact, computers are often called data-processing machines or information machines.

We have now discovered part of the function of computers. Perhaps we can derive more information from our analogy with trucks. Even though we can find a common denominator for the jobs that trucks do, they still are *different* jobs. A flower truck would not be well suited for carrying cement, even though it is similar in many ways to a cement truck. We therefore have different trucks to do different jobs. But a flower truck *could* be used to deliver groceries, or laundry. In fact, a flower truck could be used to haul cement—in small quantities. Thus we have special-purpose trucks and general-purpose trucks, though the distinction between them is not always easy to make. A panel truck is general-purpose as far as flowers, groceries, and laundry are concerned but is not suited for petroleum transport. A gasoline truck is certainly special-purpose but could be used for the transport of certain other liquids.

The classifications of *special-purpose* and *general-purpose* are useful in describing computers. Normally, a computer designed for one specific job, such as tracking airplanes, is called special-purpose but nevertheless could quite likely be used for calculating payrolls if its operators so desired. General-purpose computers often are designed for a certain class of problems, such as those found in a bank or in a scientific laboratory. Often they are intended for use by a firm which has such diverse uses as payroll, design of products, scheduling of production, and analysis of sales. Obviously, such a machine must have amazing versatility. Where does such versatility come from?

Let us look again to our analogy for a clue. A panel truck is general-purpose in that objects of a similar size, weight, physical condition, temperature, and fragility can be transported economically over relatively short distances. A semitrailer may be similarly general-purpose but for longer-distance transport. How are these distinctions made? Further, how do we cause these trucks to transport different items to different places? Simply by giving different instructions to the driver. We say that the driver *controls* the truck, even though he may be acting under the instructions of his employer. Thus different sets of instructions will result in different utilizations of the truck.

Control

Computers must also be controlled in their performance of different tasks. In the case of the cash register, the primary control rests with the operator. He enters the amounts, selects the categories in which they belong, and causes them to be added. When the last item has been entered, he causes a total to be taken. The machine does one step at a time, and each step is explicitly motivated or caused by the operator. One fundamental limit of this operation is the skill of the operator. We could build a cash register which could add an amount in one-thousandth of a second (we call one-thousandth of a second a millisecond, abbreviated msec); but if the operator could enter only one amount every second, this machine would not really be faster than one which could add in 10 msec (or even 100 msec). Likewise, if the machine made one error in a million operations while the operator made one every hundred operations, we could do as well with a machine only one-tenth or one-hundredth as accurate.

Our computers are therefore dependent upon our human operators. We see then that, if we wish to utilize the full powers of machines which are faster and more accurate than humans, we must somehow make the *control* of these machines, as well as their calculating ability, independent of the speed and accuracy of humans. When this is done (and it is done to many different degrees), the machines are called *automatic* computers. In this book, we shall mean automatic computers when we speak of computers though we shall be referring only to a certain, though rather large, degree of automatic operation. This type of computer will usually have an operator, but he does not have too much to say about the control of the machine. His job is to bring the correct data (generally in a special form and usually in selected groups) to the machine, start the computer, and watch for obvious malfunctioning. The computer control is built into the machine. That is, once the operator furnishes a set of instructions, the machine follows them automatically. (For example, think of an automatically piloted truck!) If the operator wishes to have the computer do a different job, he simply supplies it with a different set of instructions.

The set of instructions which tell the machine to perform a given job is called the *program* for that job. The task of preparing this set of instructions is called *programming*. Programming enables us to prepare the computer to perform a certain task. We do not even need to be present when the task is performed. Once a program is written, it may be used over and over again. Programming also allows many people to prepare problems simultaneously for the same machine. Actually, this is usually necessary if we are to keep the computer busy—some of the larger computers need staffs of 100 or more programmers to supply them with problems.

It is through programming that the general-purpose computer takes on special functions. In fact, special-purpose computers also require programming; but we have already observed that the distinction between general and special purpose is one of *degree,* not of kind. For the remainder of this book we shall restrict ourselves to the *most general* of the general-purpose machines, though many of the things we learn will be applicable to the most specialized computers. Schematically, we have now narrowed our field of interest to a single branch of the tree in Fig. 1-1.

From now on, when we say "computer," we shall mean "general-purpose automatic digital computer."

One more look at our truck analogy will exhaust its usefulness. We observed that a change in the capacity of a truck could effectively change its function. That is, we would not be likely to use panel trucks to haul 1,000 refrigerators across the country if we had semi-

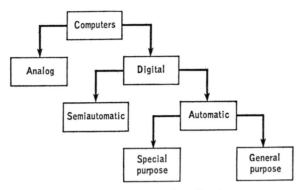

Fig. 1-1. Computer classification.

trailers available. On the other hand, we would not ordinarily use a semitrailer to deliver one refrigerator to a house 12 blocks away. As you may have imagined, a similar distinction exists among computers. The smallest computers are about the size of a desk, can do several operations (e.g., additions, subtractions) in a second, and can be bought for around $25,000 (well out of the reach of the average workingman). The largest occupy most of the floor space in a large room, can do *several million* operations in a second, and cost millions of dollars. Although the small computer can theoretically do anything the large one can do, given enough time, practical considerations preclude this. In fact, it is often stated that human beings could theoretically do all the calculations which even the largest machine could do—given enough time.

How much time is enough? A machine capable of adding 500,000 twenty-digit numbers in a second could do as much computation in one hour as a man could do in 1000 years working 12 hours a day. One fallacy in such comparisons lies in the fact that in that hour the machine would probably not make a single error, while the man would undoubtedly make millions of errors in performing the same computation! This comparison indeed points out the importance of our emphasis on the question of errors. Of course, time itself is enough of a limiting factor in most cases. If the computer is being used to forecast the weather, for example, we cannot wait for 1000 years for the morning forecast, nor even 1000 hours. Although it will be useful to examine the way human beings calculate, we must not forget this ability of computers to change function with changing capacity. The computers are *not* human beings; they are far better at doing certain things, infinitely worse at doing others.

What Are Computer Applications?

Computers are often classed as large-scale, medium-scale, and small-scale, but for this book there is little use in such vague and often misleading labels. The size of a machine should properly be measured only relative to the job it is to do. This type of measurement we shall always try to keep in mind, for it is not difficult to present problems to the computer which are far beyond its capacity—no matter what its size. It is also possible—in fact it happens frequently—that a given problem is too small or not of the type to be solved economically by using a computer. It is indispensable to be able to recognize which problems are suited to computers. How can we do this? There are no simple, sure rules. In most cases it will be easier to recognize problems which are *not* suited. First we must gain a clear idea of the problem. (This is a simple sentence hiding a topic worthy of many volumes.) Then we must look for an element of repetition.

"Repetition" is a key word in evaluating applications. If a problem has no repetitive aspects, we can solve it much more quickly by manual methods than we can program it for a computer! If nothing else, we would need at least one hand computation to compare with the computer's results. (How else could we know if our program is correct?) But this computation itself would provide the needed solution for a single use of the program. For example, it would be no benefit to calculate one's income-tax return on the computer. Why then does the Treasury Department use a computer? Repetition! Once the necessary instructions have been given to the computer to check a tax return, it can proceed automatically to do 10 or 10 million. This type of repetition—*repetition of data*—is easy to recognize in many applications. Payrolls, checking accounts, tracking airplanes, analyzing sales all display this type of repetition. A company with 10 employees, a bank with 10 checking accounts (each writing one check a day), a country with 10 airplanes flying over it at any time, or a shop which makes 10 sales a week has no need for this type of automatic information processing. In these problems, the information is relatively easy to extract; only sheer volume of work makes manual methods unattractive.

The other type of repetition is not so easy to illustrate in everyday terms. In the tracking of satellites, for example, it is necessary to find just the orbit which will fit all the observations. Several techniques are available to do this, but one of them involves a kind of trial-and-error approach. The computer is supplied with a "guess," and it proceeds to apply a formula which improves this guess. Thus it makes a guess of its own. The formula is now applied to this guess, and new guesses are *repeatedly* obtained by the same formula until a good enough answer is found. Here, with a relatively small amount of information, a great deal of computation is performed.

The guessing aspect of these methods does not cast any doubt on the final result, which can ordinarily be demonstrated to be a valid solution. For example, you are looking up a name in the telephone directory, say "Thomas C. Jones." You try to guess where to open the book, and you find the name "Painter" on the page. You know you have gone too far; so, keeping your finger in that page, you guess at a page farther to the front. You find the name "Hughes." Too far. Turn toward the back. "Lloyd." Too far that way. Back again. "Kelly." Not far enough. "Johnson." Too far. "Jones, C." Not far enough. "Jones, Mary." Not far enough. Next page. "Jones, Thomas C." Success! But you had no doubt that you would find the name, even though you used a guessing technique all along. Of course, Thomas C. Jones might not have been in the directory. But your method would have told you that, too; and sometimes that is more valuable information than finding the name.

This type of procedure is called an *iterative* procedure. We say that we perform an iteration, or iterate. There are a number of iterative procedures. Some always find an answer or come as close to it as one wishes. Some do not always find an answer but indicate clearly that they have failed. Others have the possibility of giving false answers which look correct—one of the great dangers of the computing business. Errors plague us, but *hidden* errors make our job impossible. One of our recurring problems lies not in finding errors but in *not* finding errors. We must always be alert for them; we can never be complacent about our results.

We have seen two types of repetition—data repetition and iteration. Either or both may be present, but if neither is present to any great extent, we do not have a computer problem. When both types are present, problems can become extremely large. For example, if we have 10,000 observations of a satellite and each observation requires 100 iterations of the steps in a program to compute the orbit, a total

Iteration Data repetition	Small	Large
Small	Non-computer problems	"Computing" problems
Large	"Data-processing" problems	Large computer problems

Fig. 1-2. Types of computer problems.

of $100 \times 10,000 = 1$ million repetitions of the program will be made. In general, the total number of times a program will be repeated equals the number of sets of data times the number of iterations per set. Thus if we double the amount of data *and* double the number of iterations, we make the problem *four* times as large.

Problems are often characterized as "computing" problems and "data-processing" problems. This classification, carelessly applied, may tend to obscure the fact that some problems are not computer problems at all while the most challenging problems combine the best and worst qualities of both types (Fig. 1-2).

There is also a tendency to associate the word "data-processing" with the type of problem found in a "commercial" establishment and the word "computing" with the problems found in a "scientific" or "engineering" laboratory. Although there is some usefulness and truth in these classifications, it will be well for us to consider each problem for what it is and not try to pigeonhole it without adequate examination. In the design of certain computers, greater emphasis has been placed on one aspect or the other—data repetition or iteration. As these computers come into use, however, their users often come to regard these imbalances as deficiencies, for the use of the computer usually leads to other uses, not thought of or necessary before and not falling into easy categories. Thus the tendency seems to be toward true general-purpose machines or true special-purpose machines.

PROBLEMS

1-8. Study the method outlined for looking up names in a directory. Try it several times. Write explicit instructions which would enable anyone who knows alphabetical order to learn the method. Do you think a computer could be used to look up names by this technique?

1-9. Describe another iterative method for using the directory. (Write explicit instructions for using this method.) Could a computer use this method?

1-10. Which method is faster, on the average?

1-11. Which method is easier to describe?

1-12. Do both methods indicate when a name is not in the directory?

1-13. Could either of these methods be used to find a name if we only knew the telephone number? Why?

1-14. Describe a method for finding the name corresponding to a given telephone number. Is the method practical? Could a computer use this method?

1-15. If your job was to look up telephone numbers and find the names of subscribers, how would you like to have your directory arranged? How would you use it?

1-16. Consider some job you are familiar with, or perform yourself. Is this job applicable for a computer? If so, what type of problem is it?

CHAPTER 2

HOW THE COMPUTER IS USED

In this chapter we shall examine in more detail the over-all organization of computers. We shall then determine what requirements this organization places on the programmer. That is, we shall develop how he must proceed with the preparation of a problem for machine solution.

What functions should a computer be capable of performing? Let us make a tentative list:

1. Since this is to be an information-processing machine, it should have the ability to perform certain operations on that information. These operations might include—but not be limited to—the various arithmetic operations which we know—addition, subtraction, multiplication, division, rounding, taking square roots, and others. (We shall call this the *processing* ability.)

2. Having the ability to process information, the computer must also have the ability to bring new information to the processing unit when needed. (The sections of the machine related to this ability will be termed *input* sections.)

3. In order for the computer to be useful, it must be able to furnish, in a form suitable for human use, the results of its processing on the information supplied to it (through the *output* devices).

4. The ability to coordinate these first three activities—that is, to see that the instructions in the program are executed in the proper sequence—will certainly be a vital function (the function of *control*).

5. Another desirable feature would be the ability of the machine to detect and indicate whenever it makes an error. Since we cannot prevent it from making errors, the best thing we can try to do is make it tell us whenever it does (referred to as *error checking*).

Schematically a possible arrangement of these functions and their interrelations is shown in Fig. 2-1.

The lines represent the following:

a. Flow of information into the processing unit.

b. Flow of information out of the processing unit.

c. Flow of information to the various units controlling their operation.

d. Influence of the error detection on the control. (For example,

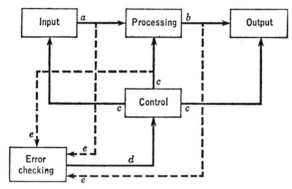

Fig. 2-1. Computer organization—a first arrangement.

this feature could cause the machine to stop or signal the operator when an error was detected.)

e. Communication of checking information to the error-detection mechanism. Notice that the checking system is used to detect errors in information moving from one part of the system to another. (In future schematics, we shall not specifically represent the error detection but shall assume that it might be present for any functions.)

This arrangement of components is quite limited in the types of information processing it can do. It must read a single piece of data from the input, process it, and write it on the output before the processing unit is available for more work. It cannot perform duties which require it to compare one item with another or to use data in any order but that in which it is introduced. In order to improve this system, we should like to provide it with a facility for saving data until no longer required. This facility is called the *storage* or *memory* of the computer—because of its resemblance to that phenomenon.

The storage of a computer is not unlimited; it holds some maximum quantity of data. These data may be in the form of characters—usually the digits 0 to 9, letters A to Z, and a number of special characters, such as * , . − + () \$ @ # and /. The capacity of these memories is often used as a measure of the power of the computer; but as with human beings, impressive memory capacity is not always joined with corresponding abilities to utilize that memory. Storage devices are also rated by the speed with which data can be withdrawn from them. After all, an ability to remember telephone numbers would be of little

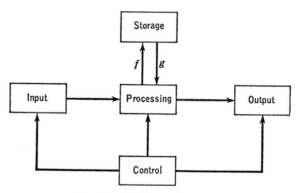

Fig. 2-2. Addition of storage.

use if it took twice as long to recall a number as to look it up. Also, many computers have several types of storage, of different speeds and capacities. The storage might be connected to the system as in Fig. 2-2.

Compare this diagram with Fig. 2-1 (remember we are not indicating error detection). The relationship of input, output, processing, and control remains the same, but we have added the storage and two lines of communication. These lines indicate that the processing unit can store information in the memory (f) and retrieve information from the memory (g). Note that the control does not communicate directly with the storage but causes the processing unit to make such communication. Also note that data enter storage from the *input* through the processing unit and become output data by passing through the same unit. With this design, then, the processing unit is involved in all transfers of information (other than control information). We now can cause data to be held for rearrangement or comparison with other data.

PROBLEMS

2-1. In Fig. 2-1, the lines marked e carry information from one part of the machine to another (to the error-checking mechanism). Since the error-checking mechanism is supposed to check all information moving from one part of the machine to another, these lines should also be checked. Redraw Fig. 2-1, showing the lines necessary to check the *e* lines, and mark these new lines *x*.

2-2. In Fig. 2-1, the line marked *d* also carries information from one part of the machine to another. Make the necessary additions to the diagram of Prob. 2-1 to check information transfer along line *d* (and mark any new lines *x*).

2-3. In the drawing of Prob. 2-2, do the lines marked *f, g* carry information from one part of the machine to another? Is it possible to build a machine in which every transfer of information is checked?

2-4. Suppose that some facility were available for saving the information output from the computer in Fig. 2-1 in a form suitable for reentering through the input devices. In this manner, information could be "stored" for later use by the computer. Would this "storage" be any different logically from the storage scheme shown in Fig. 2-2? Would there be any practical difficulties in using such a storage?

A Typical Problem

Of course, it is all very well to talk about "comparison and rearrangement of data," but do we have any idea just how we would go about causing the computer to do these things? What do we even mean by "comparison" or by "rearrangement"? Let us examine one of the applications mentioned in Chap. 1 in order to explain these terms. As we do this, we can also watch how the stages of the programming process naturally develop from one another. Perhaps we shall gain an over-all picture to which we can refer as we later examine individual parts in greater detail. In a payroll, we receive information from basically two sources: the employee's cumulative, or master, record and the employee's current payroll information, such as timecards. The first thing we must do is associate each employee's record with the correct current information. This might be accomplished by arranging all the timecards in alphabetical order and comparing them with the master records which are *kept* in alphabetical order.

On a machine organized as in Fig. 2-2, this might be done in the following way:

1. *Read all the timecards (input) and store the information on them in storage.* Of course, the timecards must be prepared in some form which the computer can "read." Present-day computers cannot usually read written information such as we might read. They can

read information in the form of holes punched into cards or paper tape or written as magnetized spots on special magnetic tape.

2. *Arrange (sort) this information in alphabetical order.* This procedure will require some abilities we have not yet explicitly discussed.

3. *Read the master records in sequence, one at a time.* These records might be kept, in order, on magnetic tape, for example.

4. *Compare the name on this record with the name on the first timecard stored in the memory.* Since the timecard information is now in order, too, three possible conditions can arise from this comparison:

> *a.* The names are the same. The computer would then proceed with the regular payroll computation for this man.
>
> *b.* The timecard name comes alphabetically before the name on the master record. Because of the order of both sets of information, this means that this man had not worked before— he is a new employee. Therefore, the computer would have to undertake special procedures such as creating a master record for this man, before performing the regular payroll calculation as in step 4*a*.
>
> *c.* The master-record name comes alphabetically before the timecard name. This means there is no timecard for that master record. This could be caused by absence or because the man no longer works for the company. In either case, this man is not to be paid; so step 4*a* is by-passed.

Flow Diagramming

Note how we have successfully established an initial approach to a given application without concerning ourselves about what computer will be used. Any computer solution eventually requires the statement of the problem in some such logical sequence of steps—an arduous task, because such a statement implies a true understanding of the problem.

To help in the planning of problems for the computer—that is, in programming—it is most useful to have a shorthand way to represent these sequences of operations which must be performed. The desired technique is to draw a series of blocks, each containing a brief description of the step to be taken, connected by arrows, showing the sequence in which the blocks are to be used. This technique is often called *block diagramming* or *flow diagramming* (because the arrows show the *flow* of control). Let us try to develop a flow diagram for this payroll calculation as we have outlined it so far. Step 1 might be represented by a block stating: "Read and store timecard information."

We might include in the block a list of the information we were to read from the timecard in the following form:

1. Read and store
   Timecard
   Information:
      Name
      Hourly rate
      Hours worked
      Overtime hours

The next block might say: "2. Sort to alphabetical order by name."

Of course, both blocks 1 and 2 (as well as succeeding blocks) only summarize a procedure which will require a series of instructions to the machine. In other words, each of these blocks might be broken down further into a sequence of more detailed flow diagrams. This logical breakdown would ultimately lead to a set of simple, basic machine instructions. These are the instructions which will be given to the machine in order to cause it to calculate this payroll.

Blocks 1 and 2 are connected by an arrow to show that the procedure outlined in 2 must follow the procedure outlined in 1. These blocks, in turn, are followed by block 3, as shown in Fig. 2-3.

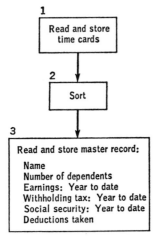

When we come to step 4, we find some difficulty representing it in the same way as the others. Why? Because step 4 is not *one* step but *three* steps. Furthermore, these three steps are not to be done in sequence (as were steps 1, 2, and 3) but as alternatives to one another. That is, the flow of control divides at this point, like a fork in a road. The machine can take only one path of the three—it must *make a choice.*

Fig. 2-3. Flow diagram—the operation box.

The ability to choose alternative paths, depending upon the outcome of some comparison, multiplies the power of the computer almost infinitely. On the flow diagram, we represent this ability to choose by the *alternative box*. (The other type, as used in steps 1, 2, and 3, is called an *operation box*.) Whereas an operation box has one flow line (arrow) leaving it, the alternative box has two or more flow lines leaving it, depending on the number of alternatives. Step 4, then, would be represented by an alternative box, followed by *several* operation boxes, as shown in Fig. 2-4.

In looking at the diagram, several features draw our attention. In the first place, we now have the program proceeding along three different courses. These will have to be brought together again at some time. Second, we seem to have completed our program in that the payroll calculation is finished. In fact, box 4c has nothing to do (and will therefore be eliminated as we proceed). But we have treated only one man, and we must continue our flow diagram for the next man.

We now encounter a situation that is extremely common to the development of many programs. We find that the procedure followed for any subsequent input data may well be dependent upon which alternative was used with the previous input (employee, in this instance). The sequences of events for all alternatives may be quite independent. We find ourselves, therefore, at different points in the program.

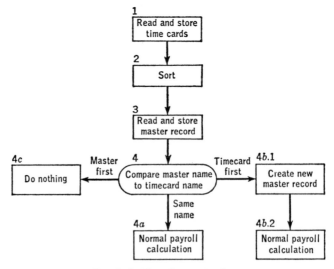

Fig. 2-4. The alternative box.

Thus, if we are at block 4a, we must replace the first name from our timecard list by the second name. We may do this by deletion of the first name so that the second name *becomes* the first name. Then we must read the next master record and follow a procedure similar to that used with the first man.

If we are to proceed after step 4b, we again must delete the first timecard. But this time we do not want to read another master

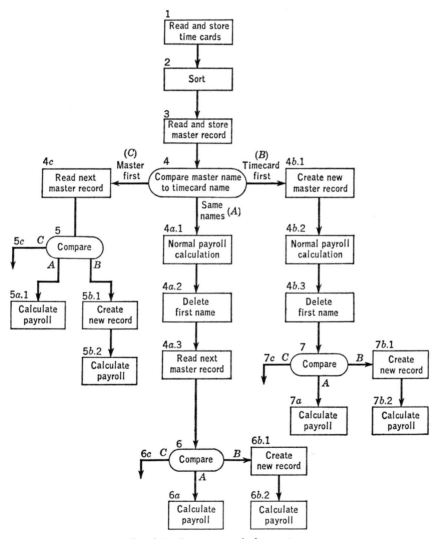

Fig. 2-5. Expansion of alternatives.

record, because we have not yet used the one we have already read. Thus we can resume our regular procedure with the same master record.

After step 4c, we do not want to delete the first timecard because it has not yet been used. We must, however, read a new master record before we proceed, because the previous one has no timecard and therefore is no longer needed. Our flow diagram now might look like Fig. 2-5.

Now we have nine possible paths in the flow diagram. This is because each of the three possible outcomes of the comparison is followed by three possibilities on the next comparison. It is important to note that the flow diagram indicates only all the *possible* flow paths. Which of the paths becomes the actual path taken depends upon the data.

Let us make this point more lucid by examining some possible cases of data. For all these cases, let us assume the master file begins with the names ADAM and BAKER. We shall look at what happens with different sets of timecards. Assume steps 1, 2, and 3 have taken place, that is, we have readied the program for its first comparison.

Case I   Timecards: ADAM, BAKER
           Program path: 4a, 6a
Case II   Timecards: ADAM, ARNOLD
           Program path: 4a, 6b
Case III   ADAM, COOPER
           Path: 4a, 6c
Case IV   ABEL, ADAM
           Path: 4b, 7a
Case V   COOPER, DUNN
           Path: 4c, 5c

Altogether there are nine cases (nine paths), and the reader may find it worthwhile to construct the other four.

If we were to continue with the flow diagram, we would soon have 27 paths, then 81, then 243, and so on. Clearly, it would soon become physically impossible to draw the diagram, not to speak of writing the basic machine instructions to which each block is broken down. Perhaps this, then, is the time for us to examine our flow diagram more carefully and to do some thinking. Look at blocks 5, 6, and 7 and the operation blocks which follow them. Are they similar? Are they identical? If you examine the nine cases, you will see that,

·once the program reaches block 5, 6, or 7, it really makes no difference what was the previous path.

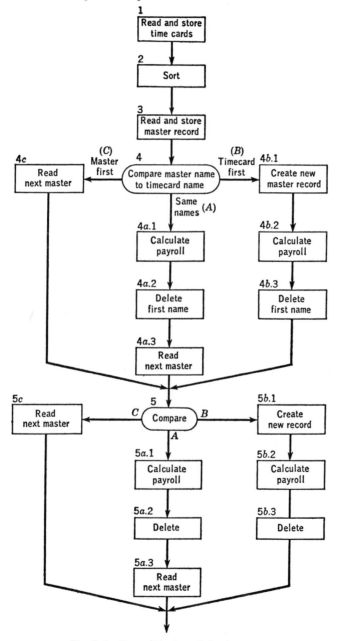

Fig. 2-6. Consolidation of duplication.

In other words, we have properly "generalized" our program. By this we mean that, once we finish dealing with a *particular* data case, we make whatever adjustments are necessary so that the next case may be treated independently (steps 4c, 4a.2, 4a.3, and 4b.3). Thus, in our illustration, the program simply compares the master record now in storage with the "first" timecard in storage. When each man's payroll is calculated, it makes no difference whether the previous man was a new employee or was on vacation or was simply a regular employee working regular hours. Proper generalization also means, therefore, that our diverging paths may converge before the next data case is begun.

Since blocks 5, 6, and 7 and *all following blocks* are identical, we can make them into the same block, as shown in Fig. 2-6. The convergence of the different paths after they have accomplished their separate tasks cuts the flow diagram down to manageable size (at least temporarily). Can we apply this technique to any part of our new flow diagram? We can as long as we are properly generalized. Look at blocks 4c and 4a.3, or 5c and 5a.3. Are they identical? Are they both followed by the same set of blocks? Since the answer to both these questions is "yes" we have further generalization and thus we can consolidate these blocks to improve the diagram further, as shown in Fig. 2-7.

Since this technique has been so fruitful, perhaps we should look for other places in our diagram to apply it. Blocks 4a.1 and 4b.2 are identical, but they do not lead to the same sequence of blocks. Likewise for blocks 4a.2 and 4b.3. Blocks 4b.3 and 4a.3 are followed by the same set of blocks, but they are not identical. We seem to have exhausted all the possibilities for consolidation. All that remains, then, is to continue the diagram down the page. How far shall we continue it? The processing should continue until all the timecards and master records have been used.

Looping

Let us assume we have approximately 1,000 men on the payroll and ignore for the moment the exact method of ending the process. We would then have to repeat blocks 5, 5a.1, 5a.2, 5a.3, 5b.1, 5b.2, 5b.3 about 1,000 times to complete our work. Our flow chart would be enormous! But why repeat? If we do repeat these blocks they will be identical. If we repeat, each set will be *followed* by an identical

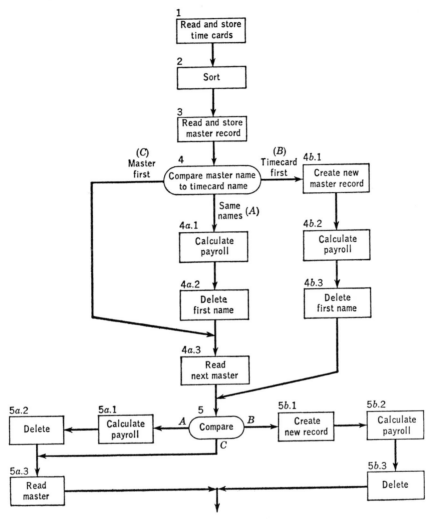

Fig. 2-7. Further consolidation.

set (except possibly the next-to-last set). We were careless not to notice this before, when we were looking for blocks to consolidate. Actually blocks 4 and 5 are identical and are followed by identical sets of blocks. We were looking sideways for consolidation, not up and down!

Therefore, we should like to be able to replace block 4, block 5, and all succeeding blocks by one *general* block, as in Fig. 2-8.

Examine the line marked X carefully; what does it say to the program? "After executing block 4a.3 or 4b.3 repeat block 4." Simple—but powerful! The ability to return to an earlier part of its program and repeat certain steps on different data gives the computer the power to perform long repetitious tasks with relatively short simple sets of instructions. A little reflection on the matter will convince you that this technique is not new to your experience. On the contrary, you use it every day. In a class, for example, the instructor does not say, "Read page 105, then page 106, then page 107, then page 108, then. . . ." He says, "Read from page 105 through page 137." You know that this implies starting on page 105 and reading *each succeeding page* until page 137 has been read. In programming, this technique of repetition is called *looping* because the corresponding lines of the flow diagram form a complete loop.

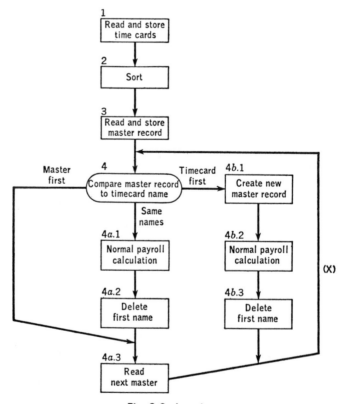

Fig. 2-8. Looping.

Now that we have been introduced to the concept of the loop, we must go back and examine certain aspects of the loop in our problem which we have not treated explicitly. Ordinarily, the loop (or loops) in a program perform the major part of its work. If this were not so, the problem would probably not be worth the programming effort involved, because a block in a program requires a certain effort to write whether it is executed once (blocks 1, 2, and 3) or executed many times (blocks 4, 4a.1, 4a.2, 4a.3, 4b.1, 4b.2, 4b.3). Even in writing a loop, however, a great deal—sometimes the majority—of our programming effort is devoted to the construction of the beginning and the end of the loop. For example, block 3 is necessary only for starting the loop. In fact, it may not be necessary for that purpose; we could proceed from block 2 to block 4a.3, if the first master record were found at the beginning of the tape.

In general, however, loops *will* require special instructions preceding them to get them started. Similarly, a loop will ordinarily require special instructions to terminate it after it has been executed the proper number of times. Otherwise a loop could "go on forever." Frequently, because of an error in the program, such a loop is written. It is called a *closed* loop and can ordinarily be terminated only by operator interruption of the program. Upon examining our flow diagram, you can see that it has no provision for ending the loop. Does our program then form a closed loop? If not, what will terminate the loop?

Actually, our program will stop when there are no more input-data records on the master file. This type of loop—which goes on and on until it uses up all input data—is frequently used. When the program stops, it will indicate to the operator that it needs more data. If there is no more, the problem is finished. This seems quite a simple way to end a loop—and it is, but nothing is *that* simple in programming. We must always be extremely critical of our programs and examine them under every conceivable type of situation which might arise.

In this problem, suppose the last name on the master file is "Wayne." Therefore, after writing Mr. Wayne's check, the program will stop in block 4a.3—when it tries to read another master record. Suppose, however, we have a new employee named Yeats. His time-card will not have been processed, nor will his name have been added to the master file! In other words, of all our new employees to be added to our master file, several may not be processed at all by this program.

There are several ways to remedy this situation, but one is especially simple. We shall simply prevent the addition of new employees after the last name in the master file! But must we refuse to hire a new man just because his name comes late in the alphabet? Not at all. We will tell a lie to the computer! That is, we will doctor our data to fit the problem!

To the master file, we shall add an employee named Mr. Zzzzz. He never works; in fact, he doesn't exist. All he does is have a name such that no other name will come after his in the alphabet. Therefore, we shall never need to add a name after the last name in the file. Therefore, we prevent any encountering of this error in the program. Since Mr. Zzzzz never works, he never gets paid. By adding his name, we correct our error and do not cause other errors. It often happens that the programmer can "fool" the computer like this and thereby simplify his task. After all, the machine is a "perfect fool"; it does everything it is told—right or wrong. It is the programmer's job to tell it right—for all cases.

In addition to setting up the beginning and end of the loop properly, the programmer must also provide instructions which will cause the program to take the data in the proper order. In this problem, we used two techniques to do this. The master file was arranged in order, and each time a record was read the magnetic tape automatically moved to the next record. The timecards had to be sorted in order, and the first one had to be discarded after use—thus making the second the first.

When we use the technique of looping, then, we must provide the program with three things *in addition to* the instructions to perform the basic work of the loop:

1. Starting instructions ("read page 105")
2. Instructions to progress through the data (one page at a time implied)
3. Terminating instructions ("through page 137")

In planning a loop, it will usually be easiest to write the basic instructions first, then 2, then 3, and finally 1. Thus a good rule (which like all good rules should not be applied with unthinking faith) when programming is this: *Start in the middle, and end at the beginning.*

Improvements on the Basic Organization

It is time to return to the topic of the organization of the computer, because now we have a better idea of what the computer must be organized to do. If we look at our flow diagram in Fig. 2-8 in relation to Fig. 2-2, we see that in *every* block of the flow diagram the control unit and the processing unit must be used. The input and output units—and to a certain extent the memory—are used only intermittently. In order to get fuller use out of the same components, computers may have a slightly different organization.

One step to getting a more balanced computer could be to connect the input and output units more or less directly to storage, as in Fig. 2-9. This organization frees the processing unit from the necessity of waiting as data move through it. The control unit, however, is not freed by this step, as it must still *control* the data flow. But the processing unit needs the control unit to guide it at every step; so we have not really freed the processing unit either. To rectify this situation, we could add other control units subsidiary to the main control unit, as shown in Fig. 2-10. These units are capable of executing small programs dealing with the input or output of data—but

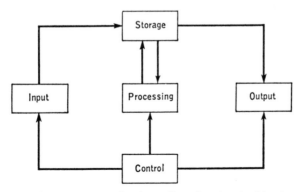

Fig. 2-9. Computer organization—direct input-output to storage.

these programs must be *started* at the direction of the main control unit.

Now all units can be kept operating simultaneously, being forced to wait for one another only when they need simultaneous access to

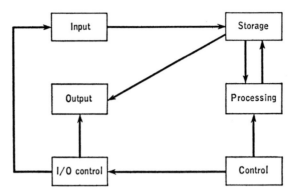

Fig. 2-10. Separate input-output control.

storage. Of course, few programs will tax the capacities of all the different units equally; but to the extent that a program can do this, it makes efficient use of this machine.

Let us turn our attention once again to the control unit. We have seen in our example (Fig. 2-8, block 4) that the control unit must have the power to change the sequence of instructions it gives to the processing unit or to the input-output units. In other words, the control unit should also have the power to control *itself*. We can illustrate this feature by adding line Y, as in Fig. 2-11.

On early computers, the program was inserted into the control unit on a metal-and-plastic board, or control panel. Wires plugged from one set of holes to another on the control panel indicated the sequence of operations to be performed. The programmer, in essence, was

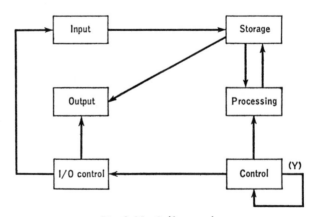

Fig. 2-11. Self-control.

completing the wiring of the machine in such a way as to make it do his problem. Several wires were required for each step in the program, indicating which operation was to be performed on which data. Also, enough holes had to be provided for all reasonable circumstances. Therefore, a large machine with a large memory would require unwieldy control panels, intricately wired.

Most computers of any general nature are used to treat a variety of problems. It would be most desirable, then, to have a method for changing from one program to another rapidly and automatically. Still another desirable feature would be the ability of the computer to modify its instructions, as in successive times through a loop, under the direction of the program, something which might not be possible with a wired set of instructions.

Do you remember the definition of a program? If you examine that definition you will see that a program is no more than the *information* required by the control unit for the processing of certain data in a specific way. But the computer is an information machine. It has the ability to "read" and "remember" information it is processing. Why not also have it read and remember that information which is its *program?* Machines which can do just this are called *stored-program* machines, as opposed to *wired-program* machines. The stored program enables the computer to do large complex problems, to change from one problem to another automatically, and to modify its own instructions (not merely modify the *sequence* of its instructions). All this simply by adding one line (Z) to the organization diagram, as shown in Fig. 2-12.

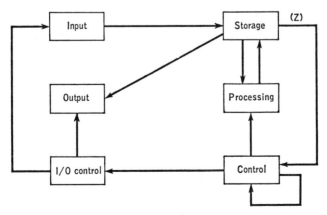

Fig. 2-12. Stored program.

These advantages do not come completely free, however. Storage space used for the program is not available for data, and storage may be the most expensive and limited component of the machine. Also, if an operating program is incorrect—as programs have an annoying tendency to be—it may start modifying itself in such a way as to cause extremely subtle errors. In general, however, the stored program, combined with the logical power of the computer, provides us with many powerful techniques for program checking—if we but use them.

Of course, all computers are not organized just like this. Many of these organizational problems may be approached in other ways, and certainly there is no way of deciding which form will ultimately be best. Probably we shall see many radically different organizations coming into being in the future, each with its peculiar advantages. Presently, however, the large majority of machines are organized in ways differing only in detail from these. It is in the specific means of accomplishing these functions—such as storage, input, and output—not in their interrelationships, that the great differences are found.

Coding

Let us focus our attention on a single block in the flow diagram in Fig. 2-8, block 4a.1. This block is, after all, the "heart" of the entire payroll calculation; and we have treated it rather lightly, keeping our attention on the blocks and lines surrounding it. In the block, we require that the computer perform the "normal payroll calculation." Clearly, we must be more explicit than that. What else, then, must we do to direct the computer?

If we were teaching a new employee how to calculate a payroll, we would try to use clear simple English, so there could be no misunderstanding of any part of the instructions. If we simply said, "Calculate gross pay," a person with no previous experience with payroll computation would not understand. Therefore, we might give him an instruction list like the following:

1. Copy hours H from the timecard.
2. Copy hourly rate R from the employee's master file card.
3. Multiply $H \times R = A$ (regular pay).
4. If H is greater than 40 hours, do steps 5a.1 through 5a.4. Otherwise do step 5b.
5a.1. Calculate $H - 40 = B$ (overtime hours).

5a.2. Calculate $R \times B = C$.

5a.3. Calculate $\frac{1}{2} \times C = D$ (overtime bonus).

5a.4. Calculate $D + A$ = gross pay, or

5b. A = gross pay.

In order to follow these instructions, the new employee must have the ability to copy numbers (1, 2); add and subtract (5a.1, 5a.4); multiply (3, 5a.2, 5a.3); recognize which of two numbers is the larger (4); and save numbers as final or partial results (3, 4, 5a, 5b). All these abilities are possessed by the computer, as we have seen. We have, in fact, come quite close to describing the calculation in the way it must ultimately be described to the computer. The computer, unfortunately, cannot read English—an ability we would normally assume a new employee to have. The computer has its own language, and this language is usually different for each different machine. Consequently, if the computer is to be our employee, we must translate our simple English statements into the machine language. This process of translation is called *coding*.

Whenever we use a computer, we require two basic kinds of information—instructions and data. Data may be simply numbers or some form of alphabetic information. The computer operates on the data, changing, defining, making decisions, producing resultant information. The instructions tell the computer how to operate on the data. In order for our computer to carry out our instructions effectively it makes use of a storage area or memory. The computer, of course, must be able to distinguish the different data retained in this storage area and to manipulate each piece individually. In order to provide all these abilities, the storage area is divided into smaller independent units called *words*. Each word contains information which can be referred to without disturbing any other word's information. The testing of each word is not affected by the information outside that word. On most machines, all words hold the same amount of information. We call the size of the word the *word length*. Typical word lengths might be 5, 10, 12, or 20 digits.

Those computers which refer to such a fixed amount of information with each instruction are called *fixed-word-length* machines. On a fixed-word-length machine, the size of the word determines the maximum amount of information which can be manipulated with a single reference. Those machines which can manipulate other than a fixed amount of information with one reference are called *variable-word-length* machines.

Families of Computers

As discussed in Chap. 1 (Fig. 1-1), computers are classified into general categories. Within each classification there exists a wide range of capability. For example, within our chosen classification, "general-purpose automatic digital," the range of capability to solve a given set of applications can be a hundredfold or more. One computer might take 100 hours to forecast the morning weather. Another might take 50 hours, or 10 hours, or 5 hours, or even 1 hour. Which would we use? We would certainly *like* to use the fastest, but the cost might be prohibitive, so we might settle for 10 hours. Here, however, we have the problem of the computer's operating for a sufficient continuous period of time for the possibility of error to become a vital factor. As we will see, there are procedures to *prepare* for error, but there are *no* procedures that we can take to *prevent* an error forever.

The normal problem encountered by computer users has not been one of seeking performance improvement by a factor of 100, or 50, or even 10. In the majority of cases, an improvement of from 1.5 to as high as 5 has been generally deemed satisfactory. The computer installation that finds itself operating, say, at a load of 60 hours a week could well be satisfied with a 2 or 2.5 times improvement. Justification for this requirement would normally include the removal of the expense and additional control required for a second shift of operating personnel. The rare times when an improvement in performance is required of more than 10 times would be most likely to occur when a new application has to be solved within a given time frame.

Over the years, the majority of computer users have experienced a continuing increase in computer use, so that 1 to 2 years after the initial installation, plans for greater computer performance have to be formulated. Aside from that portion of the available computer time that is wasted due to poor use, the increased load may be attributed to the combination of growth of number of users within the organization, the extension of existing applications, and the addition of new applications. One means for dealing with the growth problem has been the development by the computer manufacturers of a "family of computers." Such a family is composed of two or more computers, where the performance factor may vary from 2 to 3 times between computers and as much as 50 times between the two extremes. The computers in the family have significant identical characteristics, such as: the same word length for fixed-word-length families; identical character representation; identical machine-language format (the construction internally for a given instruction would not vary); the use of some basic group of identical input-output devices (generally the basic set of such devices would be the complete facility for the smallest computer in the family); the use of a basic set of machine-language instructions (again, the smallest computer might have this as its total set). Such a family of computers might achieve improvement in performance—and of course, higher cost—through improved organization of the computer components, primarily through improved input-output devices; larger and faster memories; and expansion of the machine-language instruction set. A larger computer in the family could well have single instructions equivalent to a combination of the smaller computer's set; for example, it could have instructions with capabilities not available at all on the smaller computer.

Such a family would permit a user to change more easily to the next or larger computer in the family. The identical characteristics would permit him to utilize parts of his existing programs without change. We emphasize that this conversion to the new computer is not automatic; for every new computer organization requires its own analysis —and methods of solution that were satisfactory on the smaller machine may not be efficient at all on the larger. Use of previously developed programs can be of temporary assistance while the installation users are making the necessary changes for the new computer. As we will emphasize again and again, the degree of success and ease in making this transition will depend upon the excellence of documentation support of the existing programs.

In our determination of what computer or computers should be used in our discussion, we first had to decide whether we should "invent" such a machine or whether we should use a real computer. Although the "invented" machine might have provided a somewhat easier description since we could control its "perfect" facilities, we chose a real computer, for perfection or purity of this type would only lead to sterility. The use of a real computer has permitted us to provide some feeling for the types of decisions and the types of compromises one must face in a real situation. Furthermore, there is always the possibility that the reader will be able to actually use the real computer or a member of its family.

In determining our choice, we came to the conclusion that the International Business Machines 7090 computer and its associated programming systems offered a good representative example of the many types of hardware and programming features of current machines. A second consideration was that the 7090 is part of a family of computers, and also has what we might call a family of "first cousins." In the 7090's immediate family are the 704, the 709, the 7094, and the 7094II. In the family of first cousins there are the 7040 and the 7044. We say "first cousin" because the 7040 family has many characteristics identical with the 7090 family, including the same word length, the same machine-language format for those equivalent instructions, and the use of many identical input-output devices.

It is not our intention to present or analyze fully the 7090 or its family. We will employ only those facilities we feel necessary to explain some computer or programming feature or some general principle of computing. For additional information on the 7090 or any of the family members, the reader may consult the manufacturer's manuals, some of which we have listed at the back of the book.

Computer Storage Reference

The data are initially placed in storage by instructing the computer to read, say, numbers from some type of input component (such as a magnetic tape) and to put them into the desired words. The means by which such a word selection is made, or more generally, the means by which any reference to a word is made is through a *location number*. Each word is assigned a unique location number, and it is only through the use of this number that an instruction may refer to a particular word. Generally, the first word in storage is given the location number zero; the second word, one; the third word, two; and so forth. Our illustrative computer, the IBM 7090, has 32,768 words of storage. Thus we have location numbers assigned from 00000 to 32767. The term *location* is often used when referring to a specific word or words. We might say, for example, that locations 21316 to 28402 contain our input data, or that location 789 contains the factor x.

One way of representing the contents of the 7090 word is as a 12-digit, signed number—that is, the word may be thought of as having a plus or minus sign associated with its contents. We might say that the number +402 is found in location 1056 (the word having location number 1056) or that the number −1000000 is found in location 20. At times, we may keep two (or more) small numbers in the same word. We could, for example, keep the numbers +13754 and +50632 in location 22 as +137540050632. Ordinarily, when we want to use some datum, we refer to the word containing that datum, through the use of its location number.

Words have the property of retaining a datum no matter how many references are made to that datum. In other words, the removal of a number from a word for further processing does *not* destroy the number in the word. If, for example, the number in location 1056 were added to a sum, the number +402 would still be found in location 1056 after the addition. This ability to retain data removes the necessity of continually reentering numbers, thus saving time and reducing the complexity of programs. Only when we put new information into a word is the old information destroyed. Thus we do not have to make a special operation of eliminating unwanted information; we simply store something else in its place as the need arises.

Thus the storage location is much like a billboard. We put some poster (information) on the billboard (in the word), and then we may read this poster (information) as often as we wish. When we no longer want the old poster (information), we simply cover it with a new one. Of course, the billboard eventually becomes covered with a thick layer of old posters, while the word can be written over indefinitely without "filling up."

The Instruction Layout

The instruction to the computer must be constructed so it can operate with the data in the storage area. An instruction usually consists of two basic parts. The first part, called the *operation* part, specifies to the computer *what it is to do* (multiply, add, read, etc.); the second part, or *address* part, tells the computer *what data are to be used* with the specified operation. Normally this address part is a reference to a location in the storage. Thus the address part must contain a location number. For example, we might desire to add the number +402 to a sum. In this case, we would put into the address part of the instruction the number 1056—the location of the word containing +402. This type of referencing is known as *direct addressing* because the address portion of the instruction refers directly to the location of the data.

The instruction, then, is a simple statement of a single manipulation of data. In a sense, each instruction to the computer is like one of our instructions to a clerk—an imperative sentence. Each sentence has a subject, verb, and object. The subject of a machine instruction is the computer and, like the subject of the imperative sentence, is not stated explicitly. (We do not say, "*You* copy hours," or "*You* multiply H by R.") The operation portion corresponds to the verb, the address portion to the object. For example, step 1 states, "Copy hours H from the timecard." The verb "copy" tells the clerk what to do with the object "hours H from the timecard." Such a sentence has only one object, but some of the other sentences have two or three objects. Our computer, the 7090, will usually be capable of using only a *single* object stated explicitly in each instruction. Other types of computers may use two or three objects in each single instruction. Consequently, we refer to our computer as a *single-address* machine, while the other types are called *two-address* or *three-address* or even *mixed-address*.

If we are coding for a single-address machine, we must reduce a sentence such as step 3 to three separate machine instructions. Because most arithmetic operations involve two factors and get a third as a result, we must use special techniques in order to express such operations with single-address instructions. The address portion then designates one of the factors; the second factor is *understood* to be in a special place—or *register*. The result will also be formed in some register—possibly the same one which contained the second factor at the start of the operation.

Assume, for example, that our machine has two registers which are used in the multiplication operation: register X, which holds the multiplier, and register Y, which contains the product when the multiplication is complete. Step 3 could be broken down as follows:

3.1. Put H in register X.
3.2. Multiply by R.
3.3. Save the contents of register Y (and call the result A).

Steps 3.1 and 3.3 indicate that we shall have to have special operation codes for each register which can place factors in it and remove factors from it. As we learn more about coding, we shall see that we may have four types of operations for using each register, those which:

1. Place information in the register.

2. Remove information from the register to be placed somewhere else.

3. Use the register contents in some arithmetic operation.

4. Test the contents for various qualities.

In fact, learning to code for a computer is basically a matter of learning how to manipulate its various registers in these four ways so as to accomplish the task outlined in our flow diagram. We might point out that each word in storage is, of course, a type of register. As such, it can be used in each of these four ways.

In order for the stored-program computer to execute instructions, it must have them in its storage. The instruction, like data, must be kept within the machine word. If this is the case, the instruction itself must be represented internally by the same type of configurations representing the data. But, if instructions and data look the same, how does the computer differentiate between the two? The *computer* does *not* differentiate. It has no means by which to make any distinction and must be "told" what is an instruction and what is data. It is, of course, the *program* which does the telling. Once the computer is started, it will automatically carry out instruction after instruction in ascending location-number sequence unless otherwise·instructed. If a number, or other data, is misplaced after an instruction, the computer will attempt to interpret the number as an instruction. If, by coincidence, the number happened to have the form of a valid instruction, woe to the poor program—and programmer!

Just what is the exact form an instruction takes? On the 7090, there are several possible forms, but the most common is the following:

The operation code occupies the leftmost four digit positions and the sign position. The address portion consists of the rightmost five digit positions; and for the time being, we shall consider the remaining positions as unused. Thus we may think of the instruction as two numbers, operation part and address part, occupying the same word.

We are now in a position to make another step toward representing our program in the machine language. Let us say that the operation code for multiplication is +0200 and that the factor R is kept in location 4133. Then step 3.2 (multiply by R) would be represented by the numbers +0200, 04133 placed in one word. This instruction literally states "Multiply the number in register X by the number in location 4133 and produce a product in register Y." We may multiply the number in register X by any number in storage simply by putting a different address with the operation code +0200. Thus the instructions +0200, 05367; +0200, 31763; or +0200, 00000 will cause the factor in register X to be multiplied by the number in either location 05367, location 31763, or location 00000, respectively. The product, of course, would always be formed in register Y.

There is no definite limit to the size of our program. It may be 5 instructions long or 30,000 instructions long. We may, in fact, write programs which have more instructions than we have words in storage. In this case, we must split the program into smaller parts, each of which can fit into storage.

There are many other operations besides multiply which the computer can perform. Each operation has its own unique code and usually may be used in combination with any location number. Thus coding resolves itself into the writing down of proper combinations of these compact instructions. Each individual instruction manipulates the data in some register or pair of registers in a prescribed way. The over-all effect of these combinations of simple manipulations is the execution of the task indicated on the flow diagram, just as our simple English instructions directed the more complex calculation of gross pay.

CHAPTER 3

THE LANGUAGE BARRIER

The Representation of Information

Computer storage or memory, as we have defined it, is divided into words. Each word is capable of containing a fixed amount of information. If we are to store our program in these words, this information must certainly be in a form that is recognized by the control unit of the computer when an instruction is sent to it. If we were to define what the information is, we might say that it is a set of *bits* which can be easily translated into some representation or code * that may be recognized by the computer control circuitry.

What do we mean by a bit? A familiar example of a bit-structured code is the Morse code. In this system a sequence of dots and dashes is used to represent information: namely, the alphabet, the numerical digits, and some special characters such as the comma, period, and question mark. We could define the sequence of dots and dashes to be simply a sequence of "off" and "on" switch positions or impulses. We now would say that the dot and dash were the bits upon which our Morse-code structure was built. To make representation of the "off" and "on" bits easier to manage in a digital computer we can let zero represent our "off" condition and one represent our "on" condition. Applying this to our Morse-code representation, the letter V, sent out as a dot-dot-dot-dash, would be written as 0001. If we are developing a new code structure for any particular purpose we have the *complete* freedom of choosing any combination of "off" pulses (0 bits) and "on" pulses (1 bits) to represent the information we desire. We need only be consistent.

* Note the use of the word "code" in two ways: (1) to indicate the series of instructions and (2) to designate a scheme for representing information. The meaning should always be clear from the context.

Some bit-structured systems use more than two representations to define all their information. For example, if we defined a musical score as being our information or a musical bar as being the "sentence" of our score, then the bits of this system would be the representation of the notes. The recognition of a particular note would depend upon its placement on the staff. Thus in some cases, information can be coded by the relative positions of the bits.

All digital computers make use of some type of bit structure to represent the information they process. Depending upon the computer being used, we may have the option of working directly with the bit structure itself. There are many computers, however, where only the discrete bit configurations, such as the entire alphabetical character, may be handled directly by the coder. In utilizing the 7090, the coder has the facilities to work either directly with the bits themselves or with the entire character. These bits, which are represented by the 0 and 1, are combined together at the user's option into various groupings in order to represent the more common alphabetic and numerical information.

The 7090 storage is divided into words capable of holding any combination of 36 bits (0's and 1's). For convenience the word's information is often considered to be composed of some special structure. An example of a special structure is one in which the bits are grouped into 6-bit configurations representing the common alphabetic, numerical, and special character symbols. For example, the letter V represented by a dot-dot-dot-dash (0001) in Morse code happens to have the representation of 110101 in the 7090. The letter A happens to have the representation 010001, the number five the representation 000101, the dollar sign the representation 101011. Notice, as opposed to a Morse-code type of representation in which the character length varies (thus requiring spaces between the characters), this code uses a fixed size of six bits per character. This permits the storing of six of these characters into each 36-bit word. For example, the information, John Jones—4/22/28, represented in this code would occupy three of the 36-bit words, as illustrated in Fig. 3-1.

This 6-bit code has a particular name, binary coded decimal, or more commonly BCD. Figure 3-2 illustrates the use of this code for the 7090 computer. Notice that, although each character is represented by a unique combination of six bits, not all combinations of 6-bit characters are used. This does not mean, however, that we could not assign

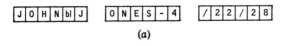

(a)

1000011001100110001001011100001000001001 1001101000010101011100101000000000100

11000100001000001011000100001000010001000

(b)

Fig. 3-1. (a) Literal representation.   (b) Actual computer representation.

additional combinations of 6-bit groups to our table.

It is most important to point out that the coder may either consider and treat his information in the 36-bit word as six BCD characters or as simply six groups of 6-bit combinations. In either case the coder does not have to memorize the meaning of these 6-bit configurations. He only needs to refer to Fig. 3-2 for his information.

Character	BCD	Character	BCD
0	00 0000	—	10 0000
1	00 0001	J	10 0001
2	00 0010	K	10 0010
3	00 0011	L	10 0011
4	00 0100	M	10 0100
5	00 0101	N	10 0101
6	00 0110	O	10 0110
7	00 0111	P	10 0111
8	00 1000	Q	10 1000
9	00 1001	R	10 1001
#	00 1011	$\bar{0}$	10 1010
@	00 1100	$	10 1011
&	01 0000	*	10 1100
A	01 0001	Blank	11 0000
B	01 0010	/	11 0001
C	01 0011	S	11 0010
D	01 0100	T	11 0011
E	01 0101	U	11 0100
F	01 0110	V	11 0101
G	01 0111	W	11 0110
H	01 1000	X	11 0111
I	01 1001	Y	11 1000
$\left.\begin{array}{c}+\\0\end{array}\right\}$	01 1010	Z	11 1001
		‡	11 1010
.	01 1011		11 1011
□	01 1100	,	11 1011
		%	11 1100

Fig. 3-2. BCD representation.

A second method of combining the 36 bits is to consider them as representing only numerical information, as we mentioned previously. We sometimes call a numerical representation of information, rather than the bits themselves, the *machine language*. From a utilization standpoint, we often find that it is easier to manipulate our information in this compressed form than in the bit-structured form. For example, the addition of the numbers in Fig. 3-3 illustrates the ease of manipulation of our *compressed* numerical representation system over the less compact bit-structured system.

It can be seen that working in the bit-structured code system requires a great deal more concentration than working in the compressed

Compressed numerical	*Bit-structured*
1340	001011100000
2215	010010001101
4101	100001000001
7656	111110101110

Fig. 3-3. Two numerical representations.

numerical system. Furthermore, the bit-structured system certainly has a higher possibility of error occurrence.

PROBLEMS

3-1. Show how your name and birth date might be laid out in computer storage.

3-2. Translate the layout of Prob. 3-1 into the actual computer representation, as in Fig. 3-1*b*.

Instructions

One of our important axioms was that the computer does not distinguish between instructions and data. Both the instructions and the data which occupy the words of the computer are simply composed of the 0 and 1 bits. Through the sequence of words entering the control unit, which is directed by the program, the computer has the ability to decide which words are to be treated as instructions and which words are to be regarded as the data. Each different instruction then is just some discrete combination of the 0 and 1 bits. If we were to write down an instruction on a piece of paper, we could construct it using these 0 and 1 bits. For simplicity, however, we shall consider the bits in terms of compressed numerical information, thereby reducing the space required for representation of our instruction (on paper). We know that the instruction is composed of several different parts, or fields, each with a specific independent function. We may consider that each of these fields is numerical. For example, the four-digit signed number +0400 might be used to represent the operation part of an instruction concerned with addition.

If we look at some of the operation portions of instructions we have previously used as illustrations, we can see immediately that these instructions *to* the computer are not in the form that can be utilized *by* the computer. Only the discrete bit code that represents each of these operations can be interpreted and then executed by the control unit of the computer. We have already decided that the utilization of the actual bit structure is not conducive to the writing of information on paper. We shall find that the best way of writing down operations is to write them in an alphabetical format. A format used for writing down these alphabetical instructions is called the *programming language* or *paper language,* to distinguish it from the machine language or from that representation acceptable to the machine circuitry. Because we use this programming language we have a problem in communication between the coder and the computer. We have, essentially, a language barrier; and our problem is overcoming this barrier without paying for more than we gain from having such a programming language.

Proposed Solutions

A partial solution might be for the coder to learn the compact numerical codes of the computer since these codes are easily translated into the *true* machine language. In many cases, such a procedure was followed during the initial phases of computer utilization. But let us take a moment to see some of the difficulties that occur using such a system. For one thing, the coder must memorize the particular configurations for each allowable instruction. This will necessarily result in slower coding. A numerical-type code does not have any of the mnemonic (rememberable) qualities of an alphabetical code. The numerical structure does not provide a format that one may easily scan in order to see the meaning of a group of instructions. A single instruction by itself carries little information to the computer. It is the combination of instructions that makes the computer capable of carrying out complex and sophisticated operations.

For example, let the numerical codes +0400, +0402 represent addition and subtraction. As an illustration of the difficulty involved, scan the following list of instructions.

+0400
+0402
+0402
+0400
+0402
+0400

Despite the fact that we are dealing with only two instructions we still have some difficulty in any sort of rapid look at the list. Certainly the following equivalent alphabetical list is much simpler to scan and understand:

ADD
SUB
SUB
ADD
SUB
ADD

Think of the complexity of coding in numerical form when dealing with computers having 100 different instructions or, in the case of the 7090, over 300 instructions. Indeed, numerical coding is a poor joke under these conditions.

The coder will have more difficulty learning a numerical system than an alphabetical system since there is no necessarily logical way of memorizing numbers to stand for explicit operations. The coder will also make more *errors* using numbers. Normally, dealing with lists of numbers is an error-prone procedure. Adding to the use of numbers the logical problems of coding will certainly create additional error hazards. Imagine trying to construct a program and at the same time trying to remember the relationship between a number and an instruction. Making corrections to the program will be more difficult for the same reasons. Another reader will most likely find the program quite difficult to follow in its numerical form. This in itself is a serious problem. It is difficult enough to try to understand the *logic* of another person's program without having to translate numerical operation codes mentally to their respective instructions. Remember that the reader is confronted with single simple instructions that must be combined to produce the over-all logic. Anything that can be done to ease the communication problem is most desirable. A concentrated study of a numerical code system will surely leave the reader with tired eyes and frayed nerves.

Language Translation

This is no optimistic picture that we have presented of direct utilization of a type of machine language. What else, then, can be done to solve the language-barrier problem? The solution to this problem is not an uncommon one; for, after all, we meet with the same essential problem when trying to read any language other than our native tongue. If you were presented with a book written in a foreign language, how would you set about reading it? Possibly you would obtain a dictionary relating English to the foreign language. One solution to reading the book might be to look up each word of foreign text and replace it by the equivalent English word; but, of course, the problem is more difficult than this. Often there are several English words for each foreign word, not to mention the problem of grammatical construction. This type of translation usually requires at least two steps for proper results. The first step would be the replacement of each foreign word by its equivalent English word (or words, as the case may be). The second step would be to combine all the English words into a logically constructed sentence. This second step would also entail choosing the best English word equivalent for each foreign word.

One solution to the language barrier between the coder and the computer is much simpler. We have no grammatical or logical construction problems. Furthermore, the source language devised for the coder has for each of its codes only *one* object-language equivalent. (Often the more general terms, *source language* and *object language*, are substituted, respectively, for "programming language" and "ma-

Source language	Machine language	Comments
ADD	+0400	Addition
DVH	+0220	Division
MPY	+0200	Multiplication
SUB	+0402	Subtraction

Fig. 3-4. Simple operation code dictionary.

chine language.") Just as in language translation, a type of dictionary is employed in translating from the source language to the object language. This dictionary generally is a simple one, being in reality a table that contains each alphabetical code of the source language together with its equivalent object-language form.

The table-dictionary in Fig. 3-4 illustrates this relationship. The table is normally arranged in alphabetical order. This allows the coder to write his program in the more usable source-language form. Once completed, the coder may now give his program to a clerk who performs the translation. The clerk does not have to be familiar at all with the method of coding. All the clerk would require is the illustrated table-dictionary. With this table, the clerk only has to replace each source code by its equivalent machine code. This is certainly an elementary form of language translation. Suppose the clerk encountered the source-coded program in Fig. 3-5. His translation would result in the required numerical-type machine code. (Try to translate this program yourself using this table.)

Naturally because the program was small it did not require too much time to be translated. However, you see that it still required your effort to search down the table for each alphabetical code, find its equivalent numerical form, and rewrite the instruction. Imagine the problem for a clerk who has to deal with a table of over 300 codes.

(Machine) location	Operation	Address (reference)
0600	ADD	1202
0601	SUB	1203
0602	ADD	1209
0603	DVH	2700
0604	MPY	5678
0605	ADD	0940
0606	DVH	2160
0607	SUB	1202

Fig. 3-5. A source-coded program

Increase the problem by having him translate a program of 1,000 instructions, which by the way is not unreasonably long. Can you imagine the number of painstaking hours the clerk must work in order to accomplish this translation? Can you also visualize how easy it will be for errors to occur in this process? This problem confronted the early programmers. They found themselves in the position of having to hand-translate their elaborate programs. Where could they find a clerk capable of handling their large problems? Inasmuch as they were utilizing a computer to execute their elaborate programs the question arose: If the computer was capable of carrying out these programs, why not use the computer as the "clerk" required to carry out the translation from source language to object language? If this were possible, then the tedious translations could be done by a clerk who easily handled tables and was not prone to errors resulting from repetitious operation.

Assembly Program

As you see, such a utilization of the computer is possible. What is necessary is the development of a program that would direct the computer to carry out the translation. This program is given the name *assembly program*. Every computer today has such a program available, even several different types of assembly programs. Therefore, we define the assembly program as a program capable of translating some other program from the coder-acceptable programming language to the computer-acceptable machine language.

During the translation period, the *instructions* in their source form *are simply the input data* that are being processed by the assembly program. Let us illustrate the over-all assembly program (Fig. 3-6).

In reviewing this diagram, intuitively, it seems that simple operation-code translation, despite the size of the table or of the program, does not merit such an elaborate procedure. The assembly program should have more to do. It does! As we shall see, the assembly program makes the computer into an extremely competent and well-rounded clerk.

In order to understand the other functions of the assembly program, it is necessary that we spend some time considering the construction of the source-language program. There are many approaches to the formulation of such a source language, and therefore we find that there are at least as many different assembly programs as there are different types of computers. This is easily explained by the fact that most assembly programs are developed independently. All assembly programs follow certain basic principles, but the specific instruction format is a matter of a particular user's preferences.

Preparation of the Program on the Programming Form

The instructions are written normally in the programming language. Usually one instruction is written per line.

↓

Preparation of Instructions for, Use by the Computer

This involves putting the instructions on some type of input device acceptable to the computer such as punched cards or magnetic tape.

↓

The Placement of the Assembly Program into Computer Storage

This, of course, enables the assembly program to direct the computer to carry out the translation.

↓

The Starting of the Assembly Program

Once started, the assembly program will automatically process all the incoming coder-acceptable instructions, translating them into the machine-acceptable format.

↓

The Production of the Results

The translated instructions are returned to the operator in a form that may be directly entered into the computer. In addition, a printed listing of the assembled program is also available.

↓

The Reentry and Execution of the Translated Program

In the machine-acceptable form, the program may now be executed by the computer.

Fig. 3-6. The assembly process

How does one go about setting up such a system? What criteria are used? The most important criterion is ease of usage. The code should have a mnemonic quality about it. Certainly the instructions ADD, SUB, MPY have this quality. A great deal of effort should be taken by the developers of the set of mnemonic operations to arrive at the most usable system. If a poorly thought-out set of codes is developed, it only means that subsequent coding in this programming language will be inefficient and, again, more error-prone. As we stated previously, if we cannot develop a programming system that truly helps us, we might as well code in a machine-type language avoiding the use of a complex assembly-programming system. Unfortunately, too often such programming systems are developed. What usually happens is that they are soon discarded and replaced by a more usable programming system. Such occurrences are inexcusably time-wasting and expensive. Perhaps an answer to this problem is the development of a general programming system that may be universally used on many different computers. (Can a universal system be produced? If so, what type of format do you think it might use?)

In order to carry out its translation, the assembly program has a translation table developed for it not unlike the table used in Fig. 3-4. This table contains a list of all allowable source-language operation codes. Furthermore, this table is equipped to have additional mnemonic codes added to it, if so desired, so as to allow the user to enrich his source language. Certain mnemonic codes in use could be replaced later by more desirable codes.

A most important additional function of an assembly program of any merit is that it will also recognize many of the errors made by the coder when writing or by the individual preparing the program for machine utilization. As an illustration, suppose that the code ADS is substituted incorrectly for ADD. The assembly program would recognize this error and alert the coder. An asterisk or some alphabetical or numerical character might be placed adjacent to an incorrectly written instruction on the printed listing developed as part of the assembly output. This "flag" character would be in a position easily recognized by the coder. Several assembly programs include more elaborate methods of signaling the operator or coder upon the detection of an error. One such method is to print out a message explaining what type of error has been made together with the offending instruction.

Symbolic Coding

We are now ready to discuss some additional functions of the assembly program over and above those responsibilities concerned with operation-code translation. These additional assembly-program functions relieve the coder of other monotonous, tedious, and error-prone responsibilities. We know that every word in storage is assigned a location number used as a means of making references. This reference is made through use of the address portion of the instruction. If you carefully analyze this method of coding you may be able to determine several drawbacks. (What are some of the drawbacks of coding in a source-language system that uses the location number as a means of all referencing in the program?)

Coding in the location-number reference system is known more generally as *absolute coding* since we absolutely define the locations of all instructions and data used. Why should absolute coding limit the coder in any way? Since the coder must assign a location number to every instruction and word of data he uses, he must determine the storage allocation in advance of coding. Since he cannot completely or accurately anticipate the extent of storage needed, he will normally have to redesign this allocation after finishing his program. If storage space is limited, this redesign of the storage area could cause serious problems. The program may well have to undergo a major reconstruction resulting in a loss of time and possibly a change in the application itself.

Another problem occurs in absolute coding when we attempt any modification to the program. Such modifications may occur from a normal redefinition of parts of the program or from errors introduced by the coder. These modifications may occur throughout the program's entire development. In fact, it is quite possible—or, rather, quite normal—that modifications may be made after a program has been operating for some time.

In the normal events surrounding the development of a program, what generally occurs is a broadening and smoothing of the logic involved. As one works with one's program, one cannot help but improve upon the original structural design. Some of these improvements may be of a major consequence. Most of the changes, however, are those which affect particular sections. In either case, the chances are that a code has been written for those areas which are being considered for improvement. This means that the coder must either rewrite the entire program or make modifications to the existing one. For programs of any consequence, the choice usually is to modify.

No matter how experienced the coder, he will make errors. Some of these errors will be discovered when rereading and rechecking and may be corrected prior to the initial execution of the program. Additional errors will be discovered during the actual execution. In making these corrections the coder must again modify his written program.

What do such modifications entail? They may consist of insertions, deletions, and rearrangements of instructions. Let us consider a typical modification to a program. It does not matter whether this modification has resulted from a logical improvement or from an error.

Let us first recall that a program is simply a set of instructions interconnected by means of their sequence and by cross referencing.

The Problems of Program Modification

Suppose that a program is to be written consisting of over 1,000 instructions and that associated with this program is a total of over 6,000 words of data. Because this program is to be coded in absolute language, it is necessary to assign to every instruction and every data word a location number in order that references can be made. Therefore, the coder must decide where his program will be placed in storage. The placement of the program into a storage area is quite arbitrary; any section of storage which the coder considers large enough may be used. The first location number of the chosen section is assigned to the first instruction written. For example, the first instruction of the program might be placed in location 0250. The second instruction will now be assigned to location 0251, the third instruction to location 0252, and so forth. The coder sets aside a total storage area of 1,200 words for instructions anticipating changes to the program. This allows him locations 0250 to 1449 for his program. (Normally instructions are assigned ascending location numbers until it is found necessary or desirable to break out of the instruction sequence. At this time some new sequence of instructions is started at a new initiating storage location.)

In addition to his program assignment the coder must also assign storage blocks to his data. Let us suppose that our data are divided into four groups of about 1,500 locations each. The coder sets aside the following areas for the groups anticipating a possible data increase:

Group 1. Locations 22000–23999
Group 2. Locations 24000–25999
Group 3. Locations 26000–27999
Group 4. Locations 28000–29999

If we are dealing with a computer with a large storage area such as the 7090, which has over 32,000 locations, it seems that there are no real storage problems for the coder of the above-described program. This particular program, however, may require the services of several other subprograms in order to work. It is quite possible that the total accumulation of all the programs and all the data necessary to carry out a particular program may well fill up our storage area. Let us look at a layout (Fig. 3-7) of the storage area.

Locations	*Storage layout*
0000–0249	Other programs
0250–1199	Anticipated storage for program
1200–21999	Unused area or other possible programs
22000–23999	Group 1 data, anticipated
24000–25999	Group 2 data, anticipated
26000–27999	Group 3 data, anticipated
28000–29999	Group 4 data, anticipated
30000–32767	Unused area, possible data

Fig. 3-7. An allocation of storage.

Once the assignments have been made, the coder can proceed to the writing of his program. He is now committed to use references within the framework of the storage layout he has anticipated will satisfy his program. Letting XXX stand for any one of the mnemonic operations available to the coder, such as ADD or SUB, a portion of the written program may look as shown in Fig. 3-8. This is, of course, a small sample of the entire program. It is enough, however, to point out the consequences of using absolute-coding systems.

The coder now reviews his program to see if there are any possible logical improvements or if some error has been made. Some of the types of modification are listed below. (Certainly all these causes do not have to occur during the writing of a given program—but they may.)

1. *Change of data configuration.* The coder learns that the group 2 data are to be 2,500 words in size while the group 3 data are to be only 750 words in size.

2. *Change of the instruction sequence.* The coder finds that he can improve his program by inserting seven instructions between the instructions in locations 0250 and 0251. Because of an error in the program, the coder must remove 15 instructions between 0710 and 0725. The chances are that many more additions and deletions of instructions will be necessary. One case of each is enough to describe our coder's problems.

3. *Change of the over-all areas of the program or data.* In our illustration it may turn out that locations 0000 to 0600 are needed for other programs or that locations 28500 to 32767 are needed for other data. If either of these changes is necessary, the programmer must make major changes to his entire program-data layout. Some-

Location	Operation	Address (reference)
0250	XXX	22003
0251	XXX	26112
0252	XXX	26434
.	.	.
.	.	.
.	.	.
0317	XXX	0251
0318	XXX	0821
0319	XXX	0251
0320	XXX	0278
.	.	.
.	.	.
.	.	.
1167	XXX	29875
1168	XXX	0946
1169	XXX	29876

Fig. 3-8. A sample of an absolute code.

times, as we previously stated, the changes are so broad that the application for the computer may have to be qualified.

Incorporating only changes 1 and 2, let us diagram storage as to the necessary modifications it must undergo (see Fig. 3-9). You can see that with just changes 1 and 2 the coder has many problems. Every numerical reference made in the program to a location affected by the modifications must be changed accordingly so that the program is still operative. This means that *all* references made to the group 2 and group 3 data areas *must be examined* and possibly changed. (The way the coder has modified the system, he does not have to change references made to group 1 or 4.) Furthermore, all numerical references made to locations within the program area must be examined to see if the referenced program location is affected by the additions and deletions. Our coder's problem is greater here since every reference must be tested to see whether it is affected by the additions only, by the insertions only, or by a combination. For example, the location 0356 is affected only by the insertions changing this location value to 0363. Location 1090, however, is affected by both the 7 insertions and the 15 deletions, which change its value to 1082. Imagine the problems that arise when there are several insertion and deletion areas. *Every* reference made must be tested to see how many of the different insertion and deletion areas affect it.

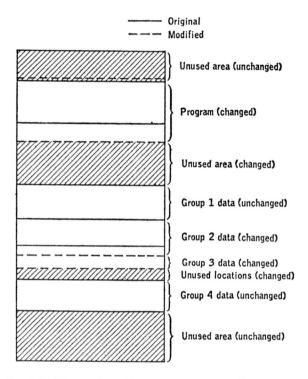

Fig. 3-9. Effects of modifications on storage allocations.

As the program gets longer and the modifications more frequent the programmer finds himself involved in a tedious, long, and highly exasperating task. To make matters worse, the chances are high of overlooking an instruction that requires modification or of incorrectly modifying an instruction. Think of reading through 1,000 instructions for possible modifications. You have probably experienced the much simpler task of checking off a shopping list against the actual items purchased.

Refer to the program example of Fig. 3-8. Modify these instructions using changes 1 and 2. For example, the instruction at location 0252 becomes

Location	Operation	Address
0258	XXX	26862

Even after going through this modification of the program, there is, of course, no guarantee that another reading will not turn up further modifications. In fact, additional readings will be almost certain to turn up further modifications.

Must the coder live with these problems? Certainly not! As long as we are letting the assembly program solve some of our coding problems, why not use it here? We can allow the coder to code in a much more flexible programming language. The assembly program can be extended in its scope to translate this vastly superior language to machine language as easily as it can translate the simpler absolute-coding language.

The Symbolic Language

We call this new language a *symbolic-coding* source-language system. We say "symbolic" because our basic method of referencing is changed. Rather than use an actual location number to indicate every reference made in the program, we give the location a name, a symbol. The symbol has absolutely no numerical significance. Furthermore, it has no direct relationship to any particular storage-assignment scheme. It is strictly a referencing device for the benefit of the coder as he works in his programming language. It is the assembly program's responsibility to define where the program will sit in storage, that is, which location is assigned to each symbol.

What does a symbol look like? For the 7090 assembly program, a symbol is composed of from one to six alphabetical or numerical characters, at least one of which must be alphabetic. Thus we can distinguish numbers from symbols. For example, the following combinations could be symbols: X, A1, START, RETURN, PRESS, BB3. The symbol may or may not have any literal meaning, and the combination of characters the coder uses is strictly up to him.

In Lewis Carroll's *Through the Looking Glass* Humpty Dumpty had this interchange with Alice on the subject of choosing symbols:

"There's glory for you!"

"I don't know what you mean by 'glory,' " Alice said.

Humpty Dumpty smiled contemptuously. "Of course you don't—till I tell you. I mean 'there's a nice knock-down argument for you!' "

"But 'glory' doesn't mean 'a nice knock-down argument,' " Alice objected.

"When I use a word," Humpty Dumpty said, in a rather scornful tone, "it means just what I choose it to mean—neither more nor less."

"The question is," said Alice, "whether you *can* make words mean so many different things."

"The question is," said Humpty Dumpty, "which is to be master—that's all."

As you can see, there is effectively an unlimited number of symbols. Of course, the same symbol cannot be used to reference *different* locations in storage, without confusing the assembly program, as Humpty Dumpty confused Alice. Every reference to a different storage location (instruction or data) must have a unique symbol to make this reference. In order to help the coder, a symbolic-coding form is usually devised for the writing of the program. On this symbolic-coding form, the symbol may appear in the "address" portion of the instruction and in the "location" field of the referenced information, be it instruction or data. Our program, written symbolically, might look like the illustration in Fig. 3-10.

This illustration points out several other important ideas associated with symbolic programming. Let us summarize a few of the pertinent remarks:

1. Every reference symbol is unique. There must be *no* duplication!

2. Every symbol is independent of all other symbols. There is no essential numerical relationship between any two symbols.

3. Once a symbol has been assigned to a particular location, all further references to this location may use the same symbol.

4. The locations of all instructions or data in a program having no reference made to them need not be assigned a symbol of any kind. The location field on the form is simply left blank. (Of course it may be filled in later, if desired.)

5. The locations of data are noted by the symbols in the location field. The other fields on those lines are not filled in because the data will be determined only when the program is executed.

What is the effect of this symbolic system on coding? Let us first consider storage allocation. It is not necessary when using symbolic programming to lay out storage until *after* all coding and modification have been done. Thus we no longer have to make estimates which will invariably be wrong. The coder will therefore be able to design the optimum layout of storage based upon much more reliable information, the completed program ready for assembly. In fact, all the coder has to do is specify where he wants the first location in his program. The assembly program will take it from there, allocating a location for each instruction and each word of data.

How does the presence of an independent symbol reference affect the coding procedure? The key word here is "independent." In the case of numerical referencing or sequencing, this independence of loca-

Location	Operation	Address	Comments
GO	ADD	A1	Instruction
	SUB	A2	area
	ADD	B1	
	DVH	Z	
	MPY	XX2	
	ADD	C3	
	DVH	D2	
	SUB	A1	
		.	
		.	
		.	
A1			Data area
A2			
.			
.			
.			
B1			
.			
.			
.			
C3			
.			
.			
.			
D2			
.			
.			
.			
Z			
.			
.			
.			
XX2			

Fig. 3-10. A sample of a symbolic code.

tions did not exist. If we make the *symbolic* reference ADD A1, it does not matter how many instructions or words for data are found between the *instruction* ADD A1 and the *number* whose symbolic location is A1. Remember that our symbolic reference has no fixed value until the program is assembled. Referring to our symbolic illustration (Fig. 3-10), notice that no matter how many instructions may be inserted, deleted, or rearranged, the instruction ADD A1 need not change. Therefore, we may modify our program as many times as we wish with the knowledge that we need to modify only those instructions and data areas directly influenced by the modification. Contrast this situation with absolute programming, in which a *single change* may affect the *entire* program. Symbolic programming has erased this problem.

Further Assembly-program Mechanics

Once our program is completely written, the assembly program will translate the instructions into an absolute-machine-language program. Because of the presence of the symbol as a means of reference the assembly program must incorporate a new table (in addition to the table of operation codes) which is made up of every symbol in the program together with its assigned numerical value. This table is called the symbol table. The table is ordered alphabetically. For example, using the symbols from Fig. 3-10, the table in Fig. 3-11 might

Symbol	*Absolute assignment*
A1	1202
A2	1203
B1	1209
C3	0940
D2	2160
GO	0225
XX2	5678
Z	2700

Fig. 3-11. Symbol table.

develop. Upon translating all the instructions into their respective machine-language format, the assembly will generally produce two outputs. One is the translated program itself, which is now in a form to be reentered into the computer for execution. The other output is a printed list of the assembled object program showing all the assignments made for the symbols. This listing also represents the layout of storage as determined in the assembly.

A picture of the mechanics of the assembly is shown in Fig. 3-12. It is important to note the following things about the assembly:

1. The assembly program must be in storage before the assembly takes place. Generally the assembly program occupies a substantial amount of storage. It is the assembly program that has complete

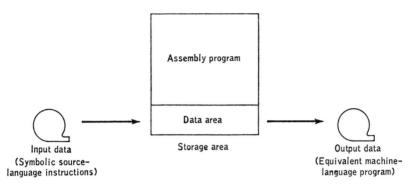

Input data
(Symbolic source-
language instructions)

Storage area

Output data
(Equivalent machine-
language program)

Fig. 3-12. Assembly program—data flow.

control of the computer, directing it through the necessary translation.

2. The symbolic program is treated as *data* during the assembly. An input area is set aside for just this purpose. Any size of program may generally be assembled. This is possible since only a portion of the symbolic program is treated at any one time. During the assembly the input symbolic-program instructions are *not* executed but rather are put into the necessary machine-language form for subsequent execution.

3. The machine-language output of the assembly is again treated simply as data. In order to execute the assembled program it is necessary to reenter this program into the computer. Normally this process is preceded by the removal of the assembly program.

Another most important part of the assembly program is its ability to detect errors. The errors that the assembly program should recognize are those errors resulting from the misuse of the mnemonic operation codes and from failure to follow the symbolic-coding rules. Such errors include:

1. Misspelling of operation codes

2. Using operation codes not recognized by the assembly program

3. Using the same symbol to make reference to two or more locations (called a multidefined symbol)

4. Failing to assign the referenced symbol to any location (called an undefined symbol)

5. Using a symbol not permitted by the assembly program

All these errors would be made known to the coder by means of some kind of flag. Normally the assembly program will attempt to translate as much of the program as possible despite the presence of errors. Often the assembly provides simple means by which the coder may correct these detected errors.

In order really to provide the coder with maximum flexibility, the assembly program should have some means of allowing the coder certain other facilities during assembly. These might include the ability to preserve certain areas, or blocks, in storage; the ability to allow special kinds of data to be assembled; the ability to introduce new symbols or operation codes; the ability to equate symbols; the ability to specify how the total program and associated data will be laid out in storage. All these abilities are found in different combinations in many assembly programs. The 7090 assembly program, which we shall use, embodies all of them.

Higher Level Languages

Although the assembly program removes much of the burden of detail from the programmer, there still remains a vast difference between the symbolic source language and the usual languages people use for communicating with one another. If we wish to simplify the coding task further, we will have to make the source language more familiar. One method would be to try to use English, or some language as similar to English as possible, as the source language. Indeed, a number of source languages have been developed which claim to allow the coder to write programs in English, leaving the translation job to the computer. Such claims, however, must be discounted, no matter how much we should wish them to be true. Consider, for example, the matter of vocabulary. The English language contains over 500,000 words; none of the source languages can recognize even a tiny fraction of that number, so a coder must always learn which words he *cannot* use in a code. Or consider meaning. The ordinary relationship between word and meaning is not the simple one-to-one correspondence we had between source code and machine code in Fig. 3-4. On the contrary, ordinary words have many meanings, so that ordinary sentences are often ambiguous. In instructing the computer, we cannot be ambiguous, so a source language must always assign explicit and often highly specialized meanings to each allowable word. The coder must learn these meanings—a job which can be exceedingly difficult if they are at odds with the ordinary meanings with which he is acquainted. Thus, though a program coded in one of these "English" source languages often appears to be ordinary English, this very appearance may lull the reader into a false sense of understanding.

Then, too, we must be aware of the difference between reading a language and writing in it. A good example of this difference is the so-called "Basic English," which is a simplified version of English with only a 500-word vocabulary. Anyone who can read English can read Basic English, but the difficulties in writing under its restrictions have to be experienced to be appreciated. Even to learn to avoid using forbidden words takes more practice than most people are willing to endure. Whereas a foreigner would not have this difficulty, the resemblance to a familiar, but more flexible and ambiguous, language can be a handicap rather than an asset to the native writer.

Another difficulty we encounter in trying to use English as a source language is the ambiguity in English grammar. In the written description of one of the "English" source languages, we found the following sentence:

"These indicators are not set all the time."

Does this mean that at all times these indicators are not set or that at not all times are these indicators set? Although to a human reader the ambiguity is likely to present no great difficulty, the computer must have an unequivocal method of analyzing such grammatical structures.

Yet in spite of all these difficulties and many others, it is possible to simplify the coding task for many problems through the use of special languages which are likely to be more familiar to the programmer than is the symbolic version of the machine language. In order to create such a language, we first have to give up the idea of a universal language, ideal for all problems. Then we can choose a class of similar problems and try to isolate the common programming difficulties they present. If we are successful at choosing the class of problems, we may be able to create a language which will make it easier to write the kinds of programs needed to solve these problems. We call such a language a "problem-oriented language."

As a general rule, the narrower the class of problems for which a problem-oriented language is designed, the easier it is to gain simplification in the language. For example, one problem-oriented language has been designed for solving problems in simple electrical circuits. To analyze a given circuit, the programmer merely has to list the components in the circuit and state which components are connected to which. He then states a mathematical formula describing the inputs to the circuit, and the computer translates this simple description into a program which will calculate the response of the circuit to the described input. Electrical engineers can learn to use this program for simple problems after a few minutes of instruction, and since there are a great number of important problems involving such simple electrical circuits, the language is extremely useful. On the other hand, this language is of no use whatsoever in solving other types of problems: it certainly cannot help to calculate the payroll, and in fact, it is not even of any use in analyzing more complex circuits—such as those containing transistors. This example serves to illustrate a more general rule, the other side of the coin to the rule that a narrower class of problems leads to a simpler problem-oriented language: namely, the simpler the problem-oriented language, the narrower the class of problems to which it can be efficiently applied—or even applied at all.

Of course, such general rules are applicable only as limitations on what we can expect from different languages developed with a comparable degree of care and understanding. It is certainly possible—indeed, it has been done far too often—to develop a problem-oriented language which is narrow in application *and* difficult to use.

To be justified then, a problem-oriented language must be general enough to pay for the cost of its development by being used a large number of times, yet specific enough to have a chance of being simpler to use than other such languages. Because there is a wide variety of types of problems, many different problem-oriented languages have been developed, though perhaps not all of them have been equally well justified. There are special languages for solving problems in civil engineering, mechanical engineering, electrical engineering, insurance, banking, and so forth. Such languages are probably too specialized for use in a general introductory book, but there are other languages on a slightly more general level which are more suitable. One such language is called COBOL, for "Common Business-oriented Language," and is, as its name suggests, supposed to be suitable for a wide variety of business problems. To cover the general area of "mathematical problems," there are a number of languages, including ALGOL (roughly, "algebraic language") and FORTRAN (for "Formula Translation"). Because of its wide acceptance and use, we have chosen FORTRAN as an example of a problem-oriented language to be presented along with the symbolic machine language of the 7090. Although FORTRAN is not the newest problem-oriented language, it will serve to illustrate the fundamentals of such languages and how they differ from machine languages.

The Compiler

The program which translates a set of symbolic source-language instructions into the equivalent machine-language program is called the "assembly program." The program which does the same kind of translation on a problem-oriented language is usually called a "compiler." Theoretically, the difference between an assembly program and a compiler is that, although the assembly program produces essentially one machine instruction for each symbolic instruction, the compiler may produce many lines of machine coding for each line written in the problem-oriented language. Thus, a 10-line source program in the FORTRAN language might be compiled into a 200- or 300-line machine-language object program. Still, the distinction is not an absolute one, for many assembly programs have facilities which can lead to similar expansion of the source code. Technically, such an assembly program is a compiler, too; and in fact, there exists an almost continuous range of complexity from the simplest assemblers to the most sophisticated compilers.

The compiler, naturally, must solve all the problems that the assembly program solves—symbol translation, storage assignment, and so forth—but it also has a few problems which are not present in the simple assembly program. The basic problem, however, is the reduction of complex statements to a sequence of simple imperative statements such as those found in the machine language. Recall our earlier example of a payroll calculation (page 38). There we saw how the machine-language programmer had to break down the statement

       3. Multiply $H \times R = A$ (regular pay)

into a sequence of three simpler steps characteristic of the particular machine language (page 44), such as,

    3.1. Put H in register X.

    3.2. Multiply by R.

    3.3. Save contents of register Y (and call the result A).

That step in the calculation could have been written in a FORTRAN program as

    3    $A = H * R$

and the FORTRAN compiler would do the job of breaking the statement into the simpler statements. Inasmuch as those simpler statements must be in the machine language of the machine on which the program is to be run, we will have to have a different FORTRAN compiler for each different machine—even though the FORTRAN language may be used to write programs for many different machines. Thus, even though FORTRAN is supposed to be a "machine-independent" language, there is always the possibility that there may be slight differences in the interpretations of a statement made by FORTRAN compilers for different machines. Such differences may or may not be important, but the programmer who attempts to use the same FORTRAN program on different machines should be aware of the possibility of getting different results.

In order to illustrate some of the difficulties which the compiler must solve, let us examine a few examples of what it must do with typical FORTRAN statements. Even though we may not understand the exact meaning of the statements or of the machine-language translation of them, we should be able to see the compiler's problem. For instance, statement 3, above, might be translated into the three machine steps (expressed symbolically):

    LDQ H
    MPY R
    STO A

whereas the very similar statement,

    4   A = H + R

might be translated into the somewhat different instructions,

    CLA H
    ADD R
    STO A

Again, the very similar statement

    5   A = H/R

might be compiled as

    CLA H
    DVH R
    STQ A

and so forth. In a sense, then, the compiler must "know the meaning" of the different symbols for the arithmetic operations, in terms of the particular machine for which it is compiling the object program.

More complex statements lead, of course, to more complex compiling

problems. For instance, it is possible to write in FORTRAN the statement

6   Y = A + B * C

which has one meaning, and the statement

7   Y = (A + B) * C

which has quite a different meaning. On the other hand, the statements

8   Y = B * C + A

and

9   Y = A + (B * C)

and

10   Y = (A + B * C)

as well as many others all have essentially the same meaning as statement 6 and we should not, therefore, like to have them compile into
essentially different programs. There is really no limit to how far
such difficulties can extend. Consider, for example, the two statements

11   Y = (A + B) * (A − B)

and

12   Y = A * A − B * B

Again, we have an essential algebraic equivalence, but few—if any—
FORTRAN compilers would generate the same program in the two
cases. Here, then, is an example showing quite clearly how the similarity of the problem-oriented language, FORTRAN, to the ordinary
familiar language, algebra, may mislead the programmer, even though
it had helped him to learn the new language in the first place.

The reason that a FORTRAN compiler will not produce the same
program from statements 11 and 12 (while it might from statements
6, 8, 9, and 10) has nothing to do with the computer's inability to perform the algebraic manipulation necessary to show the equivalence,
$(a + b)(a − b) = a^2 − b^2$. In fact, the computer, properly programmed, is quite capable of doing such algebraic problems. The
difficulty is one of efficiency, not of ability. In other words, the designers of the compiler felt that too much extra work would have to
be done by the compiler to eliminate such difficulties, work which
would not be of benefit to most of the users on most of their problems.
Thus, they left the analysis of such situations to the programmer
himself—making his job (sometimes) more difficult and the compiler's
job easier.

Such trades between work by the programmer and work by the compiler are quite common in the design of problem-oriented languages, though they are not always explicitly recognized. Another example of such a trade concerns the analysis required to determine the most efficient way to write the machine-language object program. Even if statements 11 and 12 did not lead to different numerical results in any cases of significance, they might well result in programs which were quite different in the amount of time they took to execute. Statement 11, for example, might lead to one multiplication step, one addition step, and one subtraction step in the object program; while statement 12 could well lead to two multiplications and one subtraction. If, as is usually the case, multiplications take much longer to perform than do additions and subtractions, the object program of statement 12 could be much slower than that of statement 11. Again, this type of analysis is usually left to the programmer, being considered too much of a burden to the compiler. Thus, the programmer may have to learn quite a few ways in which the problem-oriented language is not at all saying what it seems to be saying, if he is to avoid incorrect or inefficient results.

Another quandary facing the designer of the compiler is the trade-off between the speed of the compiler itself and the speed of the ultimate object program it produces. If a program is only to be used once or a few times, the time used in compiling it may far exceed the actual time it uses in computation on the problem, especially if it must be compiled several times to make corrections or additions. If most of our programs were to be of this type, we would be willing to have a compiler work more quickly even if it should thereby produce generally slower object programs. On the other hand, if our object programs were to be used over and over, if they used far more time in computation than in being compiled, we should like to have a compiler which made the object programs as efficient as possible, even if the compiling itself were thereby made somewhat slower. Experiments in which the same source program has been compiled on several good compilers indicate that there often is a reciprocal relationship between the speed of compilation and the speed of the compiled object program. To say that one or the other compiler is superior without taking into account the circumstances under which it will be used is a folly of the purest kind; but compiler designers are constantly being put on the rack because of such fallacious comparisons.

PROBLEMS

In a recent experiment on the 7090, three different FORTRAN compilers compiled the same set of sample programs. The average compile times and execution times are given below:

Compiler	A	B	C
Average compile time	20.1	32.7	49.8
Average execution time	80.2	61.5	38.7

3-3. Under what circumstances would you choose compiler A? Compiler B? Compiler C?

3-4. Would it be possible to make use of some combination of these compilers? What difficulties can be anticipated under such an arrangement?

CHAPTER 4

FLOW DIAGRAMMING

We have now seen how the programmer reduces his problem first to a flow diagram; then to a symbolic code; and finally, with the aid of the assembly program or compiler, to a set of machine-comprehensible instructions. While these phases of the programming process are most closely related to the computer, they are by no means the entire process. The other steps taken in the solution of any problem are often found in noncomputer problems and are sometimes not thought of as being part of the programming process. Indeed, the early phases of the process must usually be completed before we can even know we are doing a computer problem. Nevertheless, no computer problem can be successful unless all steps are performed.

One of the greatest services the computer provides might be considered a side effect. In preparing for computer application, we are forced to look at our system in a comprehensive fashion. No longer can we just see the problem from our own particular viewpoint. We become aware of many other aspects. The end result is that we may learn more fully how our organization works and how it might be improved.

The Programming Process

What are the steps—the programming * process—that an organization takes to prepare itself for using the computer? Let us first list the steps as general topic names.

A. Recognition of the problem

B. Definition of problem or application

* Often you will find the terms "programming" and "coding" used interchangeably. More often, however, programming includes the entire process of preparing for the computer. Coding is simply one of the steps in the over-all process.

C. Determination of a method

D. Mechanization of the method—process charting

E. Flow diagramming of the computer portion

F. Coding from the flow diagram

G. Testing

H. Getting the application into production

Quite often several of these steps either tend to merge together or are further broken down. As we are aware, any one of these topics is worthy of a book—and many such books have been written. We want to emphasize, however, that in these topics proper over-all understanding can be achieved only through experience. We only hope to introduce enough detail concerning each of these topics so that we shall be aware of the complete procedure necessary to ensure successful utilization of a computer.

A. Recognition of the Problem. It may seem self-evident, but someone must perceive the fact—or simply suspect—that a problem *exists* before we can actively pursue a solution to the problem. Actually most problems remain unsolved because this step—the first step —is never reached. For example, a large manufacturing company may be spending millions of extra dollars each year, shipping merchandise in an inefficient manner from its warehouses. An engineer may design an automobile with a critical part which will fail after 25,000 miles. A wholesaler may have 50 per cent of his warehouse space tied up with inventory which will never be sold. Every year, thousands of problems are solved which in the previous year were not known to exist.

B. Definition of Problem or Application. Information must then be gathered and examined in order to determine precisely what is the problem. (In this phase, computers are often used to condense and dissect unwieldy quantities of data.) The process of attempting to define the problem often leads directly to the solution. Just as often, it leads to the conclusion that no problem exists, or that obtaining a precise definition of the problem would prove more difficult or expensive than the solution to the problem is worth. We, of course, are interested in the problems which can be defined, are worth solving, and need a computer to help obtain their solution. Unfortunately, problems do not come wrapped in packages stamped GOOD PROBLEM —USE COMPUTER or NOT WORTH THE TROUBLE—CANNOT BE DEFINED ANYWAY. Undoubtedly, the largest amounts of money spent in computing are spent in this phase; yet less is known about how to proceed with defining problems than is known about any of the other processes involved.

C. Determination of a Method. When we feel reasonably certain (sometimes just hopeful) that we have a definition of our problem, we attempt to formulate some method which will expose its solution. We have many tools to use here—statistics, mathematics, logic, and so forth. In fact, this wealth of possible tools often makes the analysis a process of selection, rather than a process of creation. We may be tempted to choose a method too quickly, before considering other methods which will prove more accurate or more economical. On the other hand, we may deliberate for such a long time that we would have been better off just going ahead with any method that worked.

D. Mechanization of the Method—Process Charting. Once we have formulated and tentatively accepted a method, we must lay out a procedure for the complete process required to implement the method. The computer processing will generally be only a part of this *process chart,* which shows the flow of data from origination to final disposition. Each part of the process chart will usually be broken down into more detailed steps until the procedure for each machine or person involved is complete. Breaking down the chart requires much more than a knowledge of machines. Neglecting to take human failings, human abilities, and human emotions into full account can lead to the utter collapse of an otherwise carefully planned process.

E. Flow Diagramming of the Computer Portion. The computer portions of the process chart are subsequently broken down into flow diagrams which provide the necessary transition between problem language and symbolic language. The flow diagram is thus an explicit description of each process used by the computer. All operations and decisions must be indicated on the flow diagram. Consequently, we may use the flow diagram to prove the consistency of our logic.

F. Coding from the Flow Diagram. The combining of instructions together to satisfy the logic of the flow diagram makes up the coding phase of the programming process. During this phase the emphasis is toward the coding of the individual small sections of the flow diagram without necessarily being directly concerned with the over-all program logic. Therefore, the coder must take care at this time to fit his pieces together properly so that the complete program is satisfied.

G. Testing. Program checking is a test of the programmer's patience as well as the program's correctness. The term "debugging" is often applied to the process of removing errors, or "bugs," introduced in the coding phase. Of course, any phase in the programming process may expose logical errors in any earlier phase. For example, attempting to find methods of solution may reveal flaws in our definition, or flow diagramming may indicate that our method is inconsistent. Every effort must be made to complete each phase without error before proceeding to the next. Not only will detection of errors in later phases cause undue repetition of work, but errors in one phase will be far more difficult to detect when mingled with errors from another.

In the more formalized steps, especially flow diagramming and coding, much of this checking is a direct product of following rigid rules. In the assembly process, we found built-in error guards so that certain common coding errors will be forestalled. In addition to the assembly program, other techniques and special programs are available to assist the programmer in debugging the code. Although we are unconsciously checking at every step, we simply cannot afford to wait until coding is completed to subject the process to rigid scrutiny.

H. Getting the Application into Production. Production, of course, is the objective of the entire procedure. We must resist going into production until our testing has demonstrated the infallibility of the process, and yet we often need full production to give the acid test. Consequently, if we are replacing some existing process, one or more parallel processings may be necessary. Before we enter production, a set of operating instructions must be prepared, so that the operating personnel will not have to rely on the originators and producers of the problem. Parallel processing should give a basis for realistic operating instructions.

In summary, the process of programming is not a fixed set of analyzable steps but rather a series of tentative trials, followed by careful testing of the results of those trials. Each step may be repeated several times before its particular problems are all solved. Sometimes it is necessary to attempt the succeeding steps in order to verify a particular step. The most important thing to remember, however, is that, once a step in the programming process is found to be incorrect, all succeeding steps are invariably incorrect. In other words, the definition of the problem is the foundation of the programming process. It occurs far too frequently that a program is completed, only to reveal that the problem it solves is not really the problem of interest. Similarly, if the analysis is incorrect, the answers from any resulting program will not be solutions to the problem.

Beginners have the tendency to rush through the earlier stages of programming too quickly in order to see some results from the computer. Such impatience is always costly. It is said that experience is the process of making mistakes. If so, programming is an easy field in which to gain experience.

Because of the importance of problem definition, it would be useful to devote most of this book to that topic. Problem definition, however, is not a subject which lends itself to generalized treatment. Each problem is a case unto itself, and such a variety of problems have been solved with the aid of computers that one could do no more than present a few of them as studies. It is the intent of this book, however, to give the careful reader an insight into some of those elements without which no problem definition is complete, so that he might at least be able to recognize an incomplete definition.

The field of analysis also employs many techniques. Many fine volumes have been written on the subjects of numerical analysis, statistics, experimental design, and symbolic logic. Since this is an elementary book, we shall confine ourselves to examples which the most rudimentary analytical methods can solve. The reader who wishes to learn more powerful techniques—for more difficult problems—will have no trouble finding sources.

We shall say more about process charting, although there are so many ways of generating information for computers and so many ways of manipulating their output information that we shall be restricted to using a few of the simplest ones in our examples. Usually we shall not even examine the actual source of information but shall assume that it comes to us in some machine-sensible form, such as magnetic tape. In actual practice, however, we must always be mindful of the sources of information when programming; because the quality of our information will depend upon its source. We usually provide check points in a computer program to protect against the types of data errors which are to be expected from any given source. Examples of such check points will be given.

The primary emphasis in the following chapters will be on flow-diagramming and coding techniques. These topics are those most closely related to the computer as a tool in solving problems. That is, flow diagramming and coding are to the over-all process of computing what arithmetic is to mathematics. The programmer must master these fundamental skills, not so much for their own use but in order to keep them from distracting him as he studies the other, more difficult, techniques. A discussion of coding and flow diagramming also requires a thorough presentation of the specialized techniques used in detecting and correcting errors in these phases.

In the end, of course, all these techniques lead to and cannot be separated from production. Therefore, special emphasis will be placed on production problems and how they will affect and be affected by the other processes.

The Importance of Flow Diagramming

In Chap. 2 we had a brief introduction to the flow diagram as a pictorial method of coordinating our ideas on a problem. For most people, the flow diagram is a natural way of expressing the relationships between different parts of a program, relationships which would otherwise require many pages of legalistic language to describe. We saw that the flow diagram helped us to see relationships which we had not previously observed. Indeed, our over-all logical thinking was improved by the flow diagrams.

In the construction of flow diagrams for most problems, the information found *inside* the blocks might be described quite easily by employing some form of ordinary mathematical notation—in fact, the blocks are usually filled with some mathematical representation. However, the only really concise, unambiguous way to express the relationships *between* the blocks themselves is by means of the directed lines. For this reason, we prefer to use the name *flow diagramming* to represent this procedure emphasizing the flow of logic, although the name *block diagramming* is probably equally popular.

In addition to providing a convenient and meaningful notation, flow diagramming provides an excellent check point in our process of translating our problem from English into machine language. By following a consistent and logically complete method, we can construct flow diagrams which will immediately indicate certain common errors in program construction. For example, ambiguous English statements would immediately be picked up. Inconsistent relationships between parts of the whole would not escape detection. There is no better way to find logical flaws in our thinking than to lay bare the over-all logical scheme in the flow-diagram format. The flow diagram gives us our first real chance to see if our logic will get us "on the air." By tracing the various flow paths of the different conditions in our problem we can know, before coding a single instruction, whether or not our plan of attack makes sense. Too often, sloppy coding occurs because no well-thought-out flow diagram exists.

The flow diagram has still another great value. A good flow diagram should be relatively machine-independent. That is, once the problem has been flow-diagrammed, only additions—in the form of side comments—should be needed to adapt the problem to any similar machine. We ought to be able to see what the program is doing simply by looking at the other parts of the diagram, even without knowing the specific machine for which the problem happens to be coded. This machine-independent logical flow is one of our important aims. Such a general logical scheme, however, still lacks common usage. Most often the flow diagram is influenced by the standards and capabilities of a particular computer. What happens in many cases is that coding techniques are mixed with and thus influence flow-diagramming logic. Certainly the capabilities and available techniques of a given computer can make that computer a better machine to use than another for certain applications. We may find, for example, that sorting into a particular order is most easily carried out on one type of machine. However, we must be careful to recognize that the technique of carrying out logical directions must follow and not be a cause for the creation of these directions. We are in no way, however, disagreeing with the practice of preparing technique-oriented subdiagrams as the coding progresses, for this type of flow diagram does have many uses. For one thing, it may provide an important link between the general flow diagram and the specific code.

Unfortunately, many variations of flow-diagramming technique are in use, so that flow diagramming is not nearly so universal a language as mathematics. Fortunately, most of the flow-diagramming schemes are not greatly different from one another. Our problems, therefore, are more like those of a New Englander talking to a Southerner than those of an American talking to a Russian.

The Operation Box

In the *operation box*, we indicate what data transformations are to take place at that point in the program. The operation box is the fruit hanging in the tree formed by the flow lines. As with trees, it sometimes seems incongruous that such an elaborate structure is necessary to nurture and support such tiny fruits. The operation box, because it is so supported, is connected to the rest of the diagram by two lines, one entering and one leaving. When an operation box is encountered, we know that the specified operations must be executed, in the order of statement, before the program proceeds to the outgoing flow line.

It is possible, as we have seen, that separate paths in the program eventually come together and enter the same operation box. We must, however, resist the temptation to have both lines enter directly into the box. All lines coming together should meet outside the various boxes of the diagram. A point where two such lines meet is called a *merge point*. There are several advantages to this convention. First of all, it makes it possible to trace the flow diagram *backward* with ease, because we know where to look for points of separation. Secondly, it reminds us that, after two flow lines merge, it is too late to perform any operations which must be done on one path and not the other. That is, when two or more lines merge into one flow path, it is absolutely necessary that all required operations have already been performed upon each individual flow line so that they are all *generalized*. As we know, generalization means that the operation box following the merge point does not care which individual flow line had been the activated one. Thirdly, in machines which normally execute one instruction after another in sequence, merge points provide a logical check on the consistency of the coding. Since there is only one normal sequence of instructions, all lines except, at most, one coming to a merge point must represent logical sequences that deviate from the normal sequence. If, when coding from the flow diagram, we mark each line which represents such a deviation, we can detect any merge point which violates the stated flow conditions.

It is possible that we have omitted the normal sequencing itself, or we may find that a particular alternative sequence has been merged too early or too late at the given merge point. Thus such a point will indicate a logical inconsistency in either the code or the diagram. In no case may a flow line enter somewhere in the middle of an operation box. If we wish to enter some sequence of operations at several points, the sequence must be broken at those points into several operation boxes. Alternatively, it is usually desirable to write any unbroken string of operations in a single box. Such combining makes the flow diagram simpler and easier to trace both forward and backward.

Operation-box Representation

The operation box is represented by a rectangular block. Its entry point is marked by an arrow; so its two flow lines may be easily distinguished. Inside the block, several kinds of statements may be intermixed. We may have, for example, a combination of arithmetic formulas, together with nonarithmetic statements of the type indicating the movement of data or the alteration of data. It will be well to standardize the notation we use in these boxes, so that the various statement types may be distinguished.

Lower-case letters, such as a, b, c, y, and z, will be reserved for the names of mathematical variables and constants. Capital letters, such as A, B, C, Y, Z, and names in capitals will represent storage locations or special registers in the computer. Using these notations, the statement $x = C(Z)$ means "(the quantity) x equals (or is) the contents of computer storage location Z." $C(Z)$ is a shorthand way of writing "the contents of location Z," and therefore only capital letters will ordinarily appear within the parentheses. Another convenient notation is $L(x)$, meaning "the location of the quantity x." Capital letters never appear within these parentheses. If $C(Z) = x$, then $L(x) = Z$; reading this statement in English may make the notation more lucid. It simply states the obvious fact that, if Z contains x, then Z is the location of x. What is $C[L(x)]$? Reading the shorthand in English answers the question. The contents of the location of x is clearly x itself. Similarly, $L[C(Z)] = Z$. Z is the place where its contents are located. It all seems trivial, but some of the most common programming errors arise from a temporary confusion between the container and the thing contained, between the *name* of the container and the *name* of the thing contained. Lewis Carroll points out the kind of careful thinking which must be done on this matter in a scene from *Through the Looking Glass*. Alice has been talking to the White Knight, who is about to sing her a song, and says:

"The name of the song is called 'Haddocks Eyes.'"
"Oh, that's the name of the song, is it?" Alice said, trying to feel interested.
"No, you don't understand," the Knight said, looking a little vexed. "That's what the name is *called*. The name really *is* 'The Aged Aged Man.'"
"Then I ought to have said 'That's what the *song* is called?'" Alice corrected herself.

"No, you oughtn't: that's quite another thing! The *song* is called 'Ways and Means': but that's only what it's *called,* you know!"

"Well, what *is* the song then?" said Alice, who was by this time completely bewildered.

"I was coming to that," the Knight said. "The song really *is* 'A-sitting On A Gate': and the tune's my own invention."

If you can keep straight in your mind the difference between the *song,* the *name of the song, what the song is called,* and *what the name of the song is called,* you should have no trouble keeping the following distinctions in mind when programming. We use patterns of bits in an instruction as the *name* of a location in memory. Through the assembly program we can *call that name* by any symbol we wish (capital letters on the flow diagram). The *contents* of a location are the bits which occupy it. We *refer to those contents* by some symbol (name) like x or pi. Our difficulties, like Alice's, arise because we do not, in normal speaking, keep these four items logically separated. For example, we may say, "We have the constant pi in location Q." What we really mean is that we have the number 3.1415926536 . . . in the location numbered 1056. We have used the *symbol* Q for the *name* 1056; and the *name* pi for the *number* 3.1415926536 . . . , which is contained in the location.

In normal English usage, many cases can be found of confusion between the name and the thing named and between container and thing contained. If someone says, *"Put* the water on the table," we usually understand that he means the pitcher and does not wish to have the water poured on the table. If he says, *"Pour* the water on the table," his meaning is not ambiguous. The verbs "put" and "pour" force us to place different interpretations on the word "water," which is the object of the sentence. In a similar way, the operations symbolized in the flow diagram and the various machine-operation codes force us to place different interpretations on the symbols used. Some cases are unambiguous, but where there is any doubt, it is preferable to overspecify the case.

In the operation box, two symbols are commonly used to indicate redefinition of quantities, $=$ and $\rightarrow$. We shall use the $=$ to represent an actual manipulation of data. Thus the expression $x = a + b$ implies that the quantities a and b are to be added together and the result is called x. If we wish to indicate that the quantity x is moved to some specific storage location, say Q7, we may state, $x = a + b$ to Q7. Thus the statements

$z = C(Y1) + C(Y2)$
$r = z + C(X)$ to Z
$M = L(a) + 2$

can be read, respectively:

"The contents of Y1 are added to the contents of Y2 and the result is called z."

"Move r, which is z plus the contents of X, to location Z."

"The location number M is set equal to the location number of a plus two." That is, M is the name given to the location which is two words after the word containing a.

Notice that the equals sign ($=$) is not used here in the same sense as in algebra. It is not a sign of passive equivalence but a sign of action to be performed. The expression (or formula) to the right of the equals sign is to be calculated, and the result is to be the new value given to the variable named on the left. In other words, each formula or other line of writing in the operation box calls for the performance of an operation, and as such it may represent any number of machine instructions in the ultimate coding—but always represents at least one.

Substitutions

Often we wish to specify the substitution of one quantity for another. This substitution may or may not correspond to any machine instructions but always corresponds to the assignment of a value to a variable on the flow diagram. Often we are making a control count of an operation. For example, if we write $i + 1 \rightarrow i$, we mean that the variable i has the value one greater from that point on. It is possible that we might be keeping track of i in the program by *subtracting* one from some quantity, or by adding *two*. In fact, we may not be explicitly keeping track of i at all. The latter case arises when we wish to use a convenient notation to denote a process which happens as a consequence of some other part of the program.

For example, reading new information into a block of the computer memory erases the information previously in those locations. Thus we might have a program which read, computed, and wrote out results which had the flow diagram in Fig. 4-1. Block XA represents the initialization procedure. By *initialization* we mean the program steps which prepare the program to carry out its function. In this instance the initialization would probably correspond to rewinding a magnetic tape to its starting point in order to position it for reading in the first set of data. On the flow diagram, however, we have not decided how the initialization will be done but only that we wish the variable i

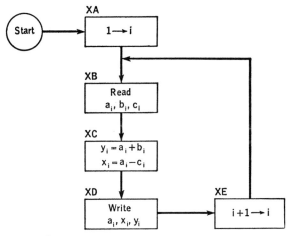

Fig. 4-1. Flow diagram—substitution box.

to start with a value of one, to indicate this *first* set of data. In this diagram, therefore, i will designate the *position* of the data. That is, on the first set of data, $i = 1$; on the second set, $i = 2$; and so forth. We thus have a control count of data sets. The statement in block XE represents the fact that, each time around the loop, we proceed to a new set of data which in reality is a physical movement of the tape. Thus the first time through the loop we read a_1, b_1, c_1. The subscript i on a, b, and c tells us which set of data we are using. Actually, the increasing (stepping up) of the value of i is done automatically by the reading of new data into the locations occupied by the old. The statement $i + 1 \rightarrow i$ only serves to remind us that, *if this stepping up is not effectively done elsewhere, we must code the instructions to do it at this point.* When first drawing the flow diagram, it is not usually desirable to have to think too specifically how each block will be coded. In this way, the flow diagram will provide a description of the problem which is easier to follow than the code itself, because it *explicitly* states certain things which are only implied in the code.

Suppose we make a slight change in this flow diagram as shown in Fig. 4-2. We have changed block XD so that the quantity i is now needed in the output. This seemingly minor change to our flow diagramming changes the effect of i upon the the over-all *specific* coding procedure. In Fig. 4-1 the value of i is merely a control check to us

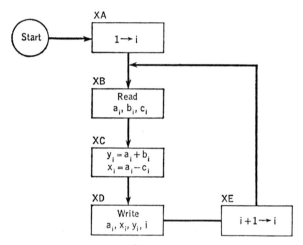

Fig. 4-2. Explicit use of subscript.

on which set of data is being processed. It has neither an equivalent set of actual programming steps nor an equivalent value stored in the computer. However, by requiring the *value* of i to be part of the output, as shown in XD of Fig. 4-2, we find that i now needs to be an actual quantity found in the computer storage. Now we must insert instructions in steps XA and XE to set i to an initial value of one and to increment i by one each time we go through the loop. The important thing to remember at this point is that the changes occurred at the coding level and not the flow-diagramming level. The fact that we use the same letter i in both diagrams is incidental. Even less important is the fact that the specific coding of i is changed. There should be no confusion, because from the flow-diagramming standpoint the i in Fig. 4-1 and Fig. 4-2 serves the same function— that of keeping track of our sets of data.

Thus one of the beauties of preparing general machine-independent and coding-independent flow diagrams is that we do not always have to think of the coding when preparing diagrams. We need only think of satisfying the problem description. We must not, however, lose sight of the fact that the flow diagram is still not complete. It represents only the first step of two stages, namely, the one preceding the actual coding. After coding, as we have stated, we would add notes to the diagram where necessary to indicate in detail how we have accomplished certain steps. We would also show how we have placed certain of our values in storage. At this stage our flow diagram changes its function from the general machine-independent diagram to that of a specific guide to program check-out or modification. In modifying the general flow diagram at this time we have an excellent opportunity to check the logic of our approach.

In Fig. 4-2, for example, we find that there is no indication of how this program will come to an end. It is important that the beginning and end of a program be clearly indicated. For this purpose we use the large circular block, which is easily recognized among the other blocks of the diagram. If there is more than one ending point, each should be labeled so as to indicate the significance of arriving at that point in the program, such as INPUT ERROR, END, or WAIT FOR MORE DATA. Since no end is designated on this program, the flow diagram clearly must be revised before actual coding could even begin.

In order to end this program properly, however, we require the use of another flow-diagramming box, the alternative box, but there are some additional procedures we wish to consider first. Every block in the flow diagram representing the program should be labeled. This label (symbol) should always be attached to the first machine instruction corresponding to that block. This technique facilitates the correlation of flow diagram and code and makes it possible to write large programs without searching through pages of coding for reference symbols. There is no particular way in which these symbols must be assigned, but some ordered, systematic technique is preferable. An ordered method will make referencing to sections of the code or diagram simpler, and a systematic approach will help prevent duplication of symbols in the code. By checking the code symbols against the flow diagram, we can easily see which blocks have not yet been coded.

In the completed flow diagram some of the blocks may not correspond to *any* machine instructions. (See box XE of Fig. 4-1.) In such a case their symbols do not occur in the code. Such boxes are often referred to as *substitution boxes*. A small s may be placed on their upper right corner to indicate that no corresponding instructions will be found in the code.

The Alternative Box

The next basic flow-diagramming box which corresponds to machine instructions in the code is the *alternative box*. (We shall assign this

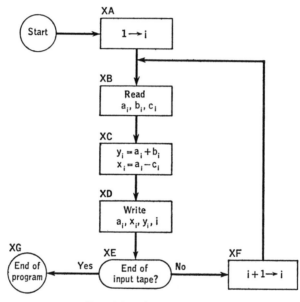

Fig. 4-3. Alternative box.

box an elliptic or oval shape.) The alternative box indicates a place in the program where a test must be made in order to choose one of several courses. The box specifies the test to be made, and the flow lines leading from the box indicate the possible results of the test. A simple type of alternative box contains a question whose answer may be "yes" or "no." For example, suppose we wish to end the loop of Fig. 4-2 when the end of the input tape is reached. Figure 4-3 is a flow diagram of this revised problem. In block XE we ask the question "Have we reached the END OF INPUT TAPE?" If the answer is yes, we want to end the program; so we follow the line leading to block XG. If the answer is no, we simply proceed as we did in Fig. 4-2. (Note that there is nothing sacred about the label XE.

In a systematic labeling system we simply take each symbol in order as we require one.) The alternative box itself never indicates a change in any information in the computer. It indicates *only* a possible change in the course of the program. Consequently, an alternative box or series of alternative boxes is unnecessary if all the exit lines lead to the same place. In other words, never have the computer ask a question when the answer is of no consequence.

Another type of decision often used is based on comparison. In a comparison, the alternative box contains the two quantities to be compared separated by a colon indicating the comparison. Both quantities may be variable or one may be constant. That is, we might write $a:b$ or $a:100$. (Compare a with b; compare a with 100.) A comparison of two constant quantities, e.g., $100:50$, always has the same result. Such a comparison is therefore not a decision at all and does not belong in the alternative box.

Three results are possible from a comparison, namely, the first quantity can be greater than $(>)$, less than $(<)$, or equal to $(=)$ the second quantity. Thus an alternative box containing $a:b$ could have three exit lines labeled "$>$" for $a > b$, "$=$" for $a = b$, and "$<$" for $a < b$. Often we are not interested in separating the three relations as such. In these cases, two of the alternatives are combined, and special symbols are used for the combinations. $>$ and $<$ are combined to form $\neq$ (not equal), $>$ and $=$ form $\geqq$ (greater than or equal to), and $<$ and $=$ form $\leqq$ (less than or equal to). Suppose, for example, we wish to end the program of Fig. 4-2 whenever y_i and x_i are equal. Figure 4-4 illustrates this flow diagram. Note that Fig. 4-4 has the same logical sequence as Fig. 4-3. Each performs the loop one time, then makes a test to see if the end has been reached. Only the content of the alternative box, XE, determines *what* the test will be. By changing the content, we change the terminating condition. Figure 4-5 illustrates the same program terminated when 3,500 sets of data have been processed. The quantity i furnishes a count of the number of sets processed, so that, by comparing i with the constant 3,500, the program can determine when to stop. In this case, it seems that we are interested only in two of the three possible results of the comparison. Since i starts at one (XA) and increases by one each time through the loop (XF), it will reach 3,500 and cause the program to stop without ever getting greater than 3,500. Since the case of $i > 3{,}500$ can never occur, why should it be shown on the diagram? Even if shown, what difference does it make to which exit-ing flow line it corresponds?

What do we mean by "can never occur"? We mean never—*as long as the program is working properly and the machine makes no error.* Of course, these cases are just the two in which we are *most* interested. If they do occur we certainly do not want to continue as if nothing

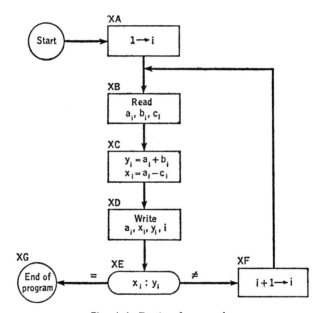

Fig. 4-4. Testing for equals.

had happened. In Fig. 4-5 the program will be stopped if $i > 3{,}500$. This stop would not be immediately distinguishable from a normal end of the program, but an examination of the last set of output data would reveal the difference, since i is present. Usually it will be de-sirable to indicate "impossible" conditions by providing separate pro-gram endings, because such a convenient indication as i will not always be available.

In computing, a common comparison is with the number zero. We often wish to know if some quantity is zero or not zero, or positive or negative (loosely, greater than or less than zero). These cases are often indicated in a different manner from other comparisons: The quantity to be compared with zero is placed in the alternative box, and the decisions are indicated as shown in Fig. 4-6a.

Some programmers prefer the use of this type of zero comparison for tests involving numbers while reserving the colon technique for nonnumerical tests such as the comparison of two names to see which comes first (lowest) alphabetically. Although there may be some advantage to such a formal distinction (it may, for example, correspond to actually different methods of comparison), we shall not attempt to maintain it in the book. Possibly this is one of those bad

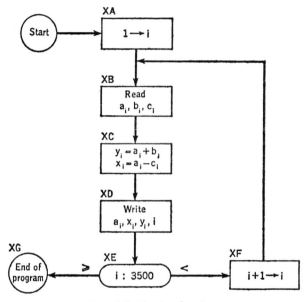

Fig. 4-5. Testing for size.

habits we human beings (especially programmers) fall into, but we should like to think that we have not insisted on this convention because it may make more of a restriction on the thinking process than its small contribution.

Often we wish to test a single bit or several bits in a word. We have pointed out, for example, that the 7090 word is composed of 36 bits. Usually we label these bits from left to right. In the case of the 7090 the leftmost bit position is given the label S or the label zero (0). The next 35 positions of the word are labeled 1 to 35, respectively. For example, we desire to know the value in bit position 7. Such a test is shown in Fig. 4-6b, where the notation $C(Y)_7$ means "contents of the seventh bit in location Y." In Fig. 4-6c this notation is extended to indicate a test on the third through seventeenth bits of location $ZX[C(ZX)_{3-17}]$. These quantities would be better indicated as variables through the use of the memory box, thus removing reference to actual locations from the alternative box. (See the following section.) Sometimes the program must test certain switches which may be set on or off from the operating console of the computer. Such switches can provide a simple means of communication between the

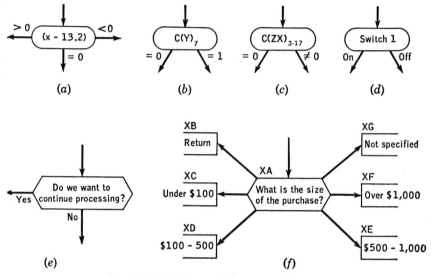

Fig. 4-6. Variations of alternatives boxes.

operator and the program while the program is being executed. The flow diagram need only name the switch to be tested and note the two possible exits as in Fig. 4-6d.

It should be adequately clear by this time that the alternative box must tell two things: (1) what test or comparison is being made, and (2) which exit lines correspond to each of the possible results.

All the tests we have discussed so far have been quite simple. If we are to solve complex problems with the computer, we shall have to cause it to make complex decisions. These complex decisions will always be built upon sets of simple decisions and will be represented by sets of interconnected alternative boxes on the flow diagram. Because we shall be forced to code complex decisions as a series of simple decisions, it would not be wise merely to indicate their over-all nature on the flow diagram By breaking down vague statements of decision criteria into explicit and simple stages, we can trace the ramifications of all possible circumstances before attempting any coding. Still, when we first attempt to represent our problem in the formalized language of the flow diagram, we often find it necessary to make oversimplifications of alternative-box contents. We must do this simply because we are human. We cannot at once conceive of the entire problem laid open in complete detail. But the flow diagram is a tool to help us. Therefore, if we find its formalities hindering our thought processes, we are misinterpreting the rules. By all means state criteria in general terms where necessary—but mark such a block clearly—and return to clean up the job when the over-all flow diagram has been laid out. (The hexagonal block, as shown in Figs. 4-6e and 4-6f, serves to remind us to break this block down later into more detail.) Any indecision on the part of the programmer *must* be resolved before coding is completed, or the computer will resolve it—and not generally in his favor.

One last word on the alternative box. It is apparent that no more than one of the exit lines may represent the normal flow of control in a sequential machine. Since, when coding, we shall be marking all lines which deviate from normal flow, the alternative box also supplies a logical check point, as did the merge point.

PROBLEMS

Draw an alternative box for each of the following tests:

4-1. $r > s$

4-2. $r < s$

4-3. $r = s$

4-4. Are bits 9 through 17 of word ZZ3 all ones?

4-5. Is character c a digit, a letter, a punctuation symbol, or a blank?

Assertion Boxes and Memory Boxes

Many circumstances arise in coding which a given programmer may have difficulty describing within the formal confines of the operation box and the alternative box, although we believe that all circumstances are so describable. Also, we would not wish to be prevented, by our flow-diagramming technique, from making use of those many coding subtleties and "hardware" advantages available on any specific machine.

Once the general machine-independent flow diagram is complete, the particular machine hardware will most certainly influence the further detailed breakdown of portions of the general flow diagram. Here techniques dependent upon circuitry of a specific machine would be brought into use. As a general principle, any programming aids (not just flow diagramming) we use should make our common problems as easy as possible but not make our uncommon problems insoluble. Of course, what are common problems to one user on one machine may be uncommon problems to another; so we must, above all, be sure that our methods do not prevent a simple expression of a given type of process.

The Assertion Box

In order to provide necessary flexibility in our flow diagramming, we use the *assertion box*. The assertion box provides, if you like, a way for the individual programmer to *assert* his individuality in those cases where it may not be clear to others what he is doing. The assertion box *never* corresponds to any machine instructions not implied in other boxes. Consequently, it is placed to the side of the line of flow and connected to the diagram by a broken line.

A common use of the assertion box is to rename a quantity. In an assertion box, the statement $y = y_n$ means that the quantity formerly referred to as y_n may now also be called y. In an operation box, this statement would mean replace y by y_n.

Most often, however, the assertion box is used to note specific details of coding related to a particular machine. As we shall see in later chapters, coding from the flow diagram is usually a much simpler task than creating the flow diagram. By keeping the main body of the flow diagram as machine-independent as possible we may greatly reduce the effort involved in reprogramming a problem for another machine. At times such discipline is extremely difficult. Most often we find that our thinking is influenced by whether a particular logical sequence best fits the computer in question. However, if we try to stay within logical principles independent of the specific computer we may be doing ourselves and our organizations a great service.

Reprogramming is a common problem at a time when advances in computer design and the growth of new applications often force an "application obsolescence" of existing machines. No computer user wishes to be forced into a position of being unable to afford to take advantage of cheaper or faster or more reliable equipment. In the past, however, the cost of reprogramming has often prevented such steps and has forced manufacturers to try to build machines which are "program-compatible" with their predecessors. Assembly programs and higher level languages have been developed to reduce the cost of coding and code check-out. Only infrequently, however, do we find an installation where a standard, consistent, unambiguous flow-diagramming scheme is in use. Despite the known difficulties and necessary logical discipline, in view of the benefits such installations receive, the practice of creating truly machine-independent diagrams should be more widespread.

Possibly another answer lies in the great emphasis which has been placed on the *coding* phase of programming. This emphasis has been so great that there are many programmers who do not use any scheme of flow diagramming and make the transition from problem statement (if they even do that) to code in one blundering, expensive leap. As our problems get more and more complex, the cost of doing business in such a haphazard manner multiplies. As machines get faster and faster, the benefits from mere coding tricks, as opposed to clever system reorganization, diminish. Therefore, we emphasize the straightforward, disciplined approach to coding. We should be especially careful to make the code for each block on the diagram independent of the code for any other block and to make the entire flow diagram independent of special properties of the computer, in so far as seems reasonable.

Therefore, we give the programmer the assertion box so he can do "fancy" coding without losing communication with anyone else who might have an interest in the programming of the problem, now or in the future. How often the assertion box is used, or how detailed its content, should be determined by how the problem is ultimately coded, not by how much time the programmer can spare when coding.

The Memory Box

The *memory box*, like the assertion box, is incidental to the flow of the problem. It is generally added to the flow diagram as the coding is being done and serves to remind the programmer where he has placed the different pieces of information. Each entry in the memory box consists of a variable or con-

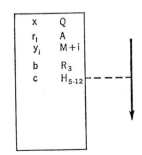

Fig. 4-7. Memory box.

stant and a location symbol associated with that quantity. For example, we may interpret the memory box in Fig. 4-7 as follows:

x is in location Q.

r_1 is in location A.

y_i is in location M $+ i$. That is, y_0 is in location M, y_1 is in location M $+ 1$, y_{15} is in location M $+ 15$, etc.

b is in bit position 3 of location R.

c is in bit positions 5 through 12 of location H.

By using the memory box, we can remove from the operation and alternative boxes all references to specific storage locations or portions of locations. Thus, if we change the assignment of certain locations, we need not change the main body of the flow diagram. The memory box gives us a method for keeping track of all data locations, just as the labels on the operation and alternative boxes do for instruction locations. The memory box helps us avoid duplication of symbols and indicates where a single location can be used for several quantities at different times. (This practice should, however, be avoided unless space in storage is a *primary* consideration.)

Input and Output

Since input and output may be proceeding simultaneously with the internal operations indicated on the flow diagram, we have a problem when we try to represent exactly what is taking place. In general, each input or output operation in the problem will require two indications on the flow diagram: (1) the initiation of the process, and (2) the test to indicate successful completion. Between these two points, the operation may be thought of as taking place, but we can have no idea of just how far it has progressed without indicating an intermediate test.

The completion test is indicated by an alternative box, and the initiation by an operation box. The flow diagram will be more easily understood if each input or output operation is indicated in its own operation box, even if this means writing several operation boxes where one might have been sufficient. The operation box should clearly answer several questions:

1. Is this a reading operation or a writing operation?

2. Which I/O (input-output) unit is to be used? (Is it magnetic tape, a card reader, a printer?)

3. What information is being transmitted?

4. In what order are the items transmitted?

5. In what format is information being transmitted?

Questions 3 and 4 are answered by writing a list (in order) of the information. Question 5 should be answered by a reference to a drawing or layout of the format. The easiest way to indicate formats is simply to draw pictures of them, and such drawings should always accompany the flow diagram but be on separate pages. Thus the operation box in Fig. 4-8a says:

"Write, on unit MT1 (the units may be given symbolic names), a, then b, then x_1, x_2, x_3, and x_{10}. Use the format number 1.2, which is described elsewhere."

Figure 4-8b shows an operation box where the list is implied by the format specified, MASTER RECORD.

(a)

> Write MT1
> a, b, x_1, x_2, x_3, x_{10}
> Format 1.2

We may, of course, have several formats coming from an input device. In this case, deciding which format is being used must be done by the program. The

(b)

> Read IT2
> Master record

Fig. 4-8. Examples of input-output boxes.

operation box then simply states how much information is to be read and how it will be named. After the tests have been made to determine which format was read, an assertion box can be used to indicate renaming the information. Figure 4-9 is a portion of a flow diagram which illustrates this technique. Block XA initiates the reading of a five-word record, and block XB causes the computer to wait for the operation to be completed. The first word h_1 indicates, by being positive or negative, one of two types of record. Block XC tests h_1 and causes a separate path to be taken for each type of record. The assertion box on either path indicates that the quantities h_1 to h_5 are now to be renamed, so that block XD could have said $y = h_1 + h_4$ and block XE, $g = h_1 + h_3$. If the formats had been more complex, the assertion boxes could have referred to drawings, instead of listing the new names.

Other operations could have been performed between blocks XA and XB. These operations operating parallel to the input are restricted in the sense that they could not have referred indiscriminately to the data h_1 to h_5 without possible error. The reason for this restriction

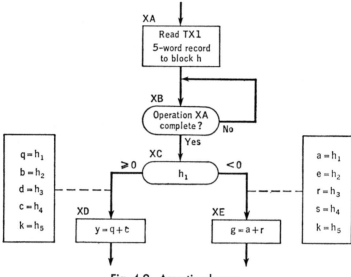

Fig. 4-9. Assertion boxes.

is that, until the program leaves the small loop containing XB, we do not know whether or not these quantities have yet entered storage.

Remote Connectors

Often on a large flow diagram, we are forced to draw flow lines which cross one another or move all the way across the page. If we wish, we can substitute *remote connectors* for such lines, thus making the diagram somewhat less cluttered and tangled. The remote connector provides a way of indicating that two separated lines are joined. In Fig. 4-10, the line leading out of block XG leads to the remote connector β. We consider that the circle containing β is really the same point on the diagram as the other circle containing β (between XA and XB). These two circles take the place of a line joining the exit of block XG (and XJ) to the entry of XB and are called *fixed* connectors because they are always joined. We shall *always* proceed in sequence from one like connector to the other.

On the same diagram, we have an example of the *variable* connector. The circle marked α (after block XD) is connected to either the circle marked α_1 or the one marked α_2 (as indicated by the "1, 2" written under α). Which connection is made at any time depends on which block, XA, XE, or XH, was last entered in the flow of the program.

XA and XH set the connector (or "switch") * to α_1, while XE sets it
to α_2. Let us trace this diagram to see what process it describes.

First, we traverse block XA, which sets the switch to α_1. We then
read a record from tape IT2(XB) and wait for the reading to be completed (XD). Since the switch was set to α_1, we then proceed to block
XE, where we set the switch to α_2, and then write the record on tape
OT1(XF). When the writing is completed, we return to block XB
(by way of the fixed connector β), where we read the next record from
IT2. This time, however, when we reach α, it has been set to α_2 (by
block XE); so we proceed to XH. The switch is set *back* to α_1, and
the record is written on OT2 instead of OT1. If we continued tracing

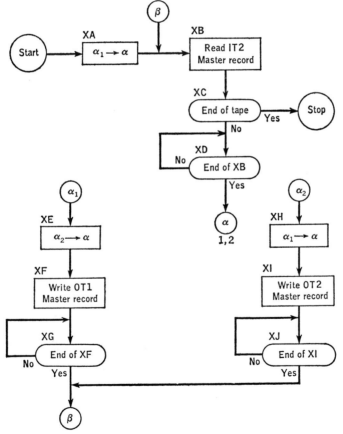

Fig. 4-10. Remote connectors.

* These program "switches" are, of course, not the same as the switches on the
operating console referred to earlier.

the flow, we would see that the alternation of α continues until the process is stopped when block XC detects the end of the input tape. Each time the program travels down one side of the switch it sets the switch back to the other side. Thus this program copies half of tape IT2 onto OT1, half onto OT2.

Such an alternation between parts of a program is quite common, though the use of the switch is not confined to simple alternation. Often the switch may have three, four, or more possible settings. Frequently there are several such switches in a program, and the variable connector gives us a convenient way of representing them. Switches could, of course, be represented by alternative boxes; but especially for more than two settings, variable connectors are simpler to use. Aside from the convenience, there is a logical reason why two notations are used. The alternative box represents a decision, but the variable connector really represents the execution of a decision previously made. In other words, the switch is a way of remembering what course the program took at some earlier time without the necessity of saving the information which caused the program to take that course. The switch helps simplify what could be a difficult or impossible test.

PROBLEMS

4-6. Draw a complete flow diagram of a program which will divide the master tape of Fig. 4-10 into three equal parts.

4-7. Draw a complete flow diagram of a program which will divide the same master tape into three parts, as follows: The first record goes on tape 1, the second on tape 2, the third on tape 1, the fourth on tape 3, the fifth on tape 1, the sixth on tape 2, the seventh on tape 1, and so forth.

4-8. Assume that some of the records on the master tape are blank. Draw a flow diagram for a program which will copy the master tape onto tape 1, except that it will not copy the blank records, and except that it will copy any record following a blank record onto tape 2 instead of tape 1.

4-9. The problem statement in Prob. 4-8 is ambiguous. Determine where the ambiguity lies, and show how the two different interpretations may be diagrammed.

The Development of the Flow Diagram

In a book, it is difficult to present adequately a feeling of how the flow diagram is developed. Each diagram is presented complete and presumably without flaws, whereas in a lecture, the students may watch the process by which the instructor reduces the problem statement to concrete and consistent decisions and operations. From a book, you get the impression that flow diagrams spring forth complete from the mind of the programmer. The first real problem you attempt shakes the foundations of this illusion. You might even get the feeling that something is wrong with you, because it all seemed so simple in the book.

The flow diagram does not spring into being. It grows, first, out from the middle in both directions, then in depth and detail. It stops growing only when the last instruction is coded and checked. Let us take an example and carry it through some of the flow diagramming as the programmer might do. Suppose we wish to write a program which will combine (merge) the records (which might be customers' charge accounts) on two tapes into a single tape. The records on both input tapes are supposed to be in ascending sequence, and there should be no duplicate account numbers. The programmer would, of course, have detailed information on the format of the records, but we shall just use the account number a.

The Initial Attempt

First, we would turn our attention to some stage in the middle of the process. We might plan to set aside two areas of storage, one for a record from each input tape. A comparison of the two account numbers would decide which record was to be written next. This reasoning helps us create the partial diagram of Fig. 4-11. The alternative box tells us to compare account number a_1 with account number a_2, where a_1 and a_2 represent records from tapes 1 and 2. Thus if $a_1 > a_2$ we write a_2 (record 2). If $a_1 < a_2$ we write a_1 (record 1). The "equal" case presents a problem, for there were to be no duplicate

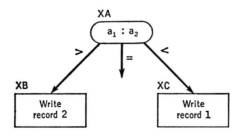

Fig. 4-11. Merge program—deciding which record to write.

account numbers. Since this is a deviation from the basic procedure, at this time we might dismiss it by attaching a box labeled PROCE- DURE FOR DUPLICATES and draw it in detail later, on another page. To indicate that there is more detail about this block elsewhere, we make it a distinctive shape, a hexagon, such as we used when indi- cating complex alternatives. Returning to our main procedure, we see that we must next replenish the storage area from which we have just written a record. We must, to be sure, wait until the writing is completed before reading a new record, lest we destroy the earlier record before it is completely written. We do not, however, wish to be concerned with such matters of detail now; we therefore make blocks XB and XC hexagonal and plan to include the necessary delay when we do them in detail. We seem to be "putting off till tomorrow what we can do today" but remember that first we are concerned with the creation of the over-all logical sequence. Once we have accom- plished the over-all procedure (which is the most difficult part) we can go back and complete all our details.

We have as yet made no provision in this latest diagram for check- ing the sequence of the accounts on each input tape. It is possible that they are not in ascending order by account number. We cannot do this step until the new record has been read. Thus we might put these steps together in the familiar hexagonal box, which could say READ NEW RECORD AND CHECK SEQUENCE. We now have the flow diagram shown in Fig. 4-12, which roughly outlines the basic

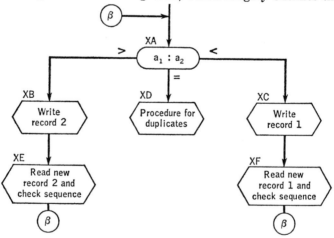

Fig. 4-12. Reading and sequence checking.

procedure. In block XA, the program determines which record is next in sequence (or if there are duplicate records). That record is written next (XB or XC) and replaced in storage by the following record from the proper tape, following which the program returns to block XA (by way of the fixed connector β) to repeat the process.

Beginning and End

At this point the programmer must turn his attention to the exceptional parts of the procedure, the beginning and the end. Clearly, we cannot simply start the program at block XA. In the first place, we have no records in storage yet; so we have no account numbers to compare. In the second place, reading the first record from each tape will require a procedure different from that of reading the others, because there will be no previous record against which to check the sequence. In a sense, the first records cannot be out of sequence since they determine where the sequences start. Consquently we start the program simply by reading one record from each tape without checking sequence (XG in Fig. 4-13). A hexagon is employed here to remind us of any other initial steps the program may have to make.

Before the process is finished, one of the input tapes will be exhausted. At this point, we shall not be able to continue with the same procedure but must simply copy the remaining records from the other tape (while checking sequence) until it too is exhausted. Of course, we cannot know in advance which tape will be used up first, since this will depend on the data. Therefore, even though we know that only one of them will be used, we must provide for two separate ending procedures. The program will be able to determine whether a tape is exhausted when it tries to read a new record and none exists [a special mark, called the end-of-file mark (EOF), will be on the tape instead]. Therefore, blocks XE and XF will have alternative exits, depending on the condition which terminates them.

Further Considerations

We now have the general diagram as shown in Fig. 4-13. The diagram is not quite logically complete because the programmer still must decide what is to be done after block XD, which has no exit. Only END blocks may have no exit line. Therefore, if a block does not end the process, it must lead to some procedure, which in this case would be an error procedure. Another part of the flow diagram must

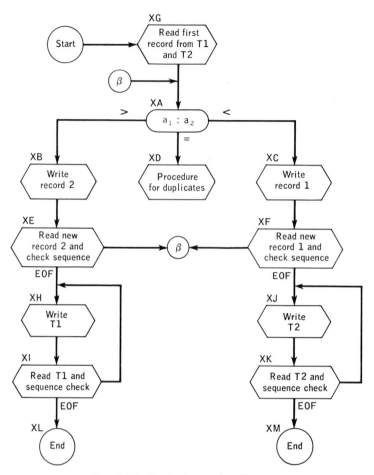

Fig. 4-13. Beginning and ending.

also be considered. What is to be done in the case of a sequence error arising from an incorrect sequence check occurring in blocks XE, XF, XI, and XK? The sequence error is actually another alternative which can arise in these boxes and should be indicated as such on the diagram.

In order to determine where the program should lead in these two cases, it would be necessary to go back to the problem definition. In a simple case, the program might be required to print out some record of the erroneous condition and then stop. Since this is just a problem to demonstrate flow diagramming, we shall choose this simple, though not necessarily realistic, course. Thus our final over-all diagram might look like Fig. 4-14. Note that we have changed the information in block XD to meet with our error procedure. Our first important phase of flow diagramming, the over-all schematic, appears complete. We cannot, however, rest on our laurels.

Filling in the Details

Now that we have such a consistent over-all diagram, we must take each of the hexagonal boxes and break it down into further detail before we can proceed with coding. There is a temptation at this point to skip the detailed flow diagramming and proceed to the actual coding. All we can say is—patience! Coding from the general flow

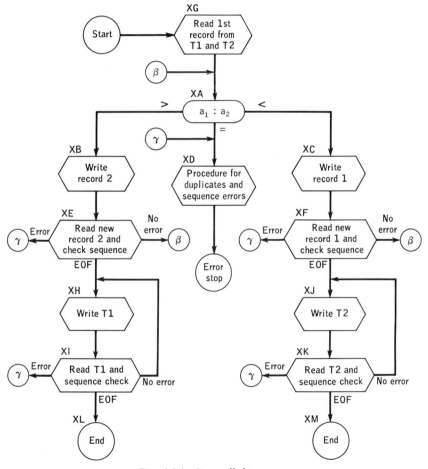

Fig. 4-14. Over-all diagram.

diagram would be like driving across the United States using a map showing only each state outline with no road detail. You will know what state you are in, but any further knowledge will be gained only through brute-force techniques—that is, you go. The chances of coming up with a good route (code sequence) across the entire United States (program) are rather small.

To illustrate the detailing procedure, we shall use block XE, which says, "Read new record 2 and check sequence." In order to check the sequence, we must have the new account number. Therefore, we must first read the new record. Reading the record, however, will destroy the previous account number, which we also need. One way to solve this problem is to arrange to save the old account number before reading the new record, as shown in Fig. 4-15.

The first block (labeled XE, because it represents the beginning of block XE from the over-all diagram) indicates saving the old account number a_2 by setting another variable b_2 equal to it. The second block (labeled XEA to show it is a subblock of the large block XE) indicates the reading of the next record. Notice that block XEA still

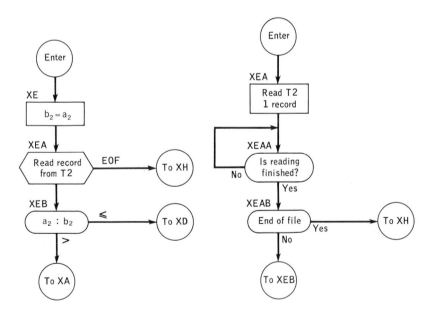

Fig. 4-15. Detail of block XE.   Fig. 4-16. Detail of block XEA.

requires more detail, which will have to be shown elsewhere. Here again we approach our detailed flow chart in steps. There is no reason for us to attempt all detail at one time. By carefully approaching the complete detail we allow ourselves the full facilities for preparing the simplest coded solution.

What representation should we use for the account number of this newly read-in record? Up till now we have let a_2 represent any account number from tape 1. There is no reason to stop now. Therefore, we use a_2 again, carefully noting that the a_2 in XEB and the a_2 in XE are *not* the same quantity but actually represent sequential records. Our test then has full meaning. Block XEB compares a_2 with b_2. Since there should be no duplicates, $a_2 = b_2$ represents an error just as does $a_2 < b_2$. That is, the new account number, a_2, should be greater than the previous account number, b_2, if the records are in sequence. As with the original diagram, each path in the subdiagram must terminate in a circular block. These blocks, however, need only indicate the end of that particular subblock and will not represent stops. They may, as shown, indicate which block is to be used next.

Even when all subblocks of the original diagram have been broken down, we are not finished with the flow diagram. Each hexagonal block occurring in any of the subdiagrams must be reduced until we eventually have only simple blocks which can be coded directly. Often the same hexagonal block will appear several times in a flow diagram, only slightly modified. For example, our procedure for reading a record will be used six times in this program—only changing in a few details. One of these times is illustrated by block XEA, which might be broken down as in Fig. 4-16. The other five similar blocks will utilize the same diagram, with exits labeled differently and possibly using T1 in block XEA instead of T2. When we have such repeated blocks, we often use subroutines to perform the tasks outlined in them. (Subroutines will be treated in detail in later chapters.) In that case, we need only diagram a typical block and use it as a model for the others when coding. Frequently, the subroutine may be so useful that someone else has already written it and checked it for some other program. We then may simply copy that subroutine into our program. In this case we need not break down its hexagonal block in detail, since the coding is a mere transcription and the diagram exists elsewhere.

PROBLEMS

4-10. Suppose that the merge program to be written had to merge three files instead of two. Draw the flow diagram for this program. Can you use switches to minimize the repetition on the diagram?

4-11. Suppose we had four tapes, T1, T2, T3, and T4, which we wanted to merge into a single tape. How could this be done using the program diagrammed in Fig. 4-14? Draw the additional flow diagram necessary to accomplish this four-way merge (on which the diagram in Fig. 4-14 can be represented by a single hexagonal box).

4-12. In Prob. 4-11, what will be the most efficient order in which to merge the tapes if they each have the same number of records? If they have 100, 100, 100, and 100,000 records, respectively?

Summary

We have gone through the development of the flow diagram, in which we tried to emphasize careful, logical planning. It is so easy to overlook some of the so-called minor ramifications occurring in a given program. To prevent real headaches during later check-out and production phases we must take that extra bit of time to examine all the detail.

Starting with a rough conception of the problem, we were able to unfold and record the over-all possibilities, the special conditions for starting and ending, and the details of each process and subprocess. The process of breaking down each block may continue through any number of levels, until we reach basic operation boxes, simple alternatives, and blocks representing prewritten subroutines. At that point, we may proceed with the coding—ordinarily a straightforward, though meticulous, task. Learning to code, then, will be a matter of learning to represent the operations specified in the several types of blocks and to connect those blocks as indicated on the flow diagram.

CHAPTER 5

CONTROL INSTRUCTIONS

Classification of Instructions

The individual instructions which the computer performs may be placed in several functional categories. When faced with the description of a new instruction, we can immediately know many of the things it does *not* do if we can place it in one of these categories. For example, if an instruction is classed as an arithmetic instruction, we can be sure it will have no direct effect on input or output units. To be sure, a number of instructions cross the category boundaries, but in attempting to classify such instructions we shall at least be reminded of their multiple effects and so use them with proper caution. The categories are, of course, only aids to learning and to selecting instructions for certain jobs. There is nothing sacred about the categories, and indeed, after we become thoroughly familiar with a given machine, we usually select instructions without thinking in these terms.

Arithmetic. The arithmetic instructions perform what we think of as the basic work of the machine, for they perform the additions and multiplications as well as less familiar types of transformations on data. Because of their fundamental nature, the arithmetic instructions are usually easiest to learn, in concept, though their details are often tedious. On the other hand, they often constitute a minority of the instructions actually written in a given problem.

Any instruction which is used to change data already in the storage of the computer is classed as an arithmetic instruction. The arithmetic instructions do not necessarily change data—we might add zero or multiply by one, for example—but their normal intent is some change. The computer has special registers in which one or more of the operands (data to be operated on) are placed and in which the result appears. Learning the arithmetic instructions, then, becomes a matter of learning how these arithmetic registers may be used— often a mechanical procedure which becomes second nature with repeated use.

Input and Output. Another important and quite obvious set of instructions is the input-output set. These are the instructions which the computer must execute when it wishes to communicate with the "outside world." To a large extent, input and output operations are simple opposites—when you have learned input techniques, you have mastered all the basic knowledge needed for output.

On some machines, the input-output instructions are all executed by the central, or main, processing unit. As we have seen, however, much of the detail work of input and output may be turned over to separate, subsidiary computers. Because the main and subsidiary computers usually share the same storage area, for both data and instructions, we must be careful to distinguish between two distinct types of input-output instructions. The first type—that executed by the control section of the main computer or *central processing unit*— will be referred to simply as "instructions." In order to make the distinction clear, then, we shall refer to the instructions which the subsidiary computer—the input-output unit—executes as "commands."

Naturally, the basic function of input and output instructions and commands is the transmission of information. As we have seen, however, the computer does not always receive information in the form most convenient for use. Also, the results of a process are not usually in a form which can be directly transmitted out of the machine for human use. The process of editing input and output data is, strictly speaking, an arithmetic process as we have defined arithmetic. Nevertheless, the process of editing and the process of transmission are normally closely associated, and it will help the beginner to try to recognize just where one begins and the other ends. Often, in fact, part of the editing process is built into the circuitry of the input-output devices or furnished as part of an input-output subroutine.

Control. The control instructions are the threads with which the other operations of the computer are bound together. They do not affect data; they do not transmit data; they simply guide the computer through the other instructions in fixed or variable sequences, as indicated by the lines of the flow diagram. It is quite possible to perform useful work in a program which contains no arithmetic instructions, but without control instructions the largest computers would be about as powerful as cash registers. The control instructions reflect the operating logic of a program and must therefore be quite correct before one can even begin to check the actual computation. Consequently, we shall try to build a firm foundation in this area before filling in the arithmetic and input-output gaps.

Indexing. Since the repetitive aspect of problems is so important in computer work, many machines have special circuitry designed to facilitate common operations associated with repetition. The usual problems are keeping track of how often an operation has been done and what data are to be used by that operation on each iteration. In mathematics, indexes, or subscripts, are used to keep track of such processes. As an outgrowth of these terms, the words *indexing* and *index arithmetic* have been given to the type of computer instruction which does this job, although indexing may be thought of as a special type of control which also takes over certain tasks of *counting* from the regular arithmetic instructions.

Mixed Instructions. As we have said, any simple classification scheme will require a certain amount of forcing to cover all cases. Certain instructions, such as those used to move data from one register to another, are commonly used with all types of instructions. Other instructions definitely combine two or more of our categories. Most of the instructions, however, will fit nicely into one class or another; and in any case, the process of learning will probably be furthered by the attempt to classify.

Instructions to the Assembly Program. As we have seen, the programmer does not ordinarily write instructions in the language of the computer itself but in a symbolic language somewhere between English and the machine language. An assembly program is then used to complete the translation. Often the programmer wishes to give the assembly program special instructions about translating his program. He may, for example, wish to have the program assembled for some special area of memory, or he may wish to enter certain constants as part of the program. A multitude of such routine tasks may be left to the assembly program. In a very real sense, then, the assembler is a clerk working for the programmer.

Suppose a human clerk were to reproduce a list of instructions for people in your building to use in case of fire. You might hand the clerk a piece of paper which said:

IN CASE OF FIRE

1. Do not use your telephone except to report the fire. DIAL ???
2. Close all windows.
3. Walk—do not run—to the nearest exit.

KEEP CALM.

Make 100 copies of this memo and have it posted on each bulletin board in the building. Also, look up the fire number and put it in line 1.

It is quite clear that the last two sentences do not tell people what to do in case of fire. Nevertheless, they are instructions. We see that these instructions are used to direct the *clerk* in preparing the set of emergency instructions. Similarly, in writing programs, we have the ability to give instructions to the *assembly program*, telling it how we want our computer program prepared. Instructions of this type are called *pseudo-instructions* (meaning "false" instructions) or *pseudo-operations*, because they *look like* they might be ordinary symbolic machine instructions—but they are not. They are written on the same coding sheets as the symbolic instructions, and the two types may be intermingled. Therefore, we must be careful to remember when we are instructing the computer as part of our program and when we are simply instructing the assembly program or compiler.

We can further break down pseudo-operations into three types: data pseudo-operations, non-data pseudo-operations, and *macro-operations*. The data pseudo-operations tell the assembly program to put some information—other than instructions—into certain words that will be used with our program. Constants such as pi, 0, 2, or −8.197 would be examples of this type of information. The non-data pseudo-operations affect the assembly *process* in some way but do not cause any words of data to be placed with the program. The instruction to locate the program in some particular region of storage would be a non-data pseudo-instruction.

From time to time a particular sequence of machine instructions occurs, with minor variations, in several parts of a program or in several different programs. For convenience, the assembly program can be instructed to recognize this instruction sequence through the use of a single form called a *macro-instruction*. In fact, this macro-instruction will normally have the ability to represent a *basic* sequence of instructions together with a limited number of variations upon this basic sequence. Recognition of the "macro" form causes the *assembly program* to assemble the corresponding sequence of one or more machine instructions. Thus the programmer has increased his computer machine-instruction vocabulary by considering that he has a single large (macro) instruction which does the work of a common combination of machine instructions (or subroutine). An interesting sidenote is that many of the so-called mixed instructions on an advanced computer can be considered macro-instructions to an earlier machine.

In the following chapters, we shall introduce pseudo-instructions of all three types as the need for each arises during the presentation of the machine instructions for the 7090. It is not the intention of this book to present the entire set of available 7090 instructions, nor is it the function of this book to serve as a reference on the 7090. Such reference literature (see appendix) is well taken care of by the International Business Machines Corporation publications. Only that portion of the total set of instructions needed to illustrate principles and techniques will be used.

In describing a particular instruction, we shall write out the name together with the symbolic code that is used with the associated 7090 systems. For example, we have the instruction SUBTRACT (SUB); but we shall not give the actual bit codes involved, for it is, in general, unnecessary for the programmer to know them.

Control Instructions

In a sense, every instruction executed by the machine is a "control" instruction. If this were not so, we would have no sequence. By "normal flow of control" we mean the following: After an instruction is executed, a normal flow of control occurs if the next instruction executed is the next instruction in sequence. That is, normal flow indicates that the sequence of *written* instructions is the sequence that is actually being *executed* by the computer. A certain physical aspect of sequence is implied here. We think of normal flow as the execution of instructions in ascending location-number order, the order we think of as the "natural," or "physical," sequence of the words. For example, the normal flow of reading control for English sentences is from left to right, one adjacent word after another. An American learning German finds that in some German sentences he has to jump from the beginning to the end and then back to the middle in order to put the text into the more familiar English sentence structure. This procedure is analogous to non-normal flow because the words of the sentence are not read in the order in which they were written.

We must be careful to distinguish the concept of *normal flow* from the idea of the *common flow* taken by the program—that is, the path which the program will ordinarily follow when working with data. Thus the program may ordinarily (or even always) perform instruction 500 after instruction 100, but the *normal* flow from instruction 100 would still be to instruction 101. As we have seen, the concept of normal flow, or normal sequencing, will help us in checking the consistency of our programs through the flow diagram.

How is this normal flow accomplished? In the computer control unit is a special register, called the instruction counter (IC) or instruction-location counter (ILC), whose function is to control instruction sequencing. When the control unit completes the execution of an instruction, it asks the IC for the location of the next instruction. As soon as this new instruction is brought to the control unit, the number in the IC is increased by one. Therefore, until an instruction is encountered which changes the value of the IC in some other way, instructions are taken one at a time from successive storage words. We consider this stepping up of the IC as a normal by-product of the execution of an instruction; hence the term "normal flow." Therefore, when an instruction can cause some other action to be taken with the IC, we classify it as a control instruction. We similarly classify those instructions which can cause the computer to stop for an indefinite amount of time. Although such instructions may not affect the direction of flow, they definitely affect the rate of flow and thus also deserve classification as control instructions.

One such instruction is called HALT AND PROCEED (HPR). When the control unit receives this instruction, the IC is increased (stepped) by one, and the computer stops. When the operator presses the START button on the console, the processing continues with the next instruction.

One special instruction, which on first glance may seem unusual, does nothing. That is, NO OPERATION (NOP) tells the machine to do nothing *except* increment the IC. NOP can be inserted anywhere in the program and has no effect on anything except the IC (and the amount of time taken by the problem). Nevertheless, NOP has important uses. For example, we may wish to remove an instruction from our program. Since the machine has its natural sequence, something must be placed in that location even though we wish to do nothing at that point—so we use the NOP to maintain the sequence. The NOP instruction can also serve a useful function in error checking. We can purposely create known errors in a program using the NOP instruction in order to try out error-checking routines.

Starting the program is not so easy as stopping it. Obviously, the starting procedure must be something external to the program itself— otherwise we could not start a program unless it was already running. We say that such an observation is "obvious," but many beginners become confused between the methods for entering and starting a program and the methods used by the program itself. There is an understandable curiosity to learn loading techniques before fully understanding the computer instructions themselves. For the present, however, we must simply assume that our program can be loaded into the computer and started with any instruction we desire.

The Unconditional Transfer

As we saw in our flow diagrams, we do not always desire to continue taking instructions in sequence. In order to change the sequence, we must change the value of the instruction counter. The simplest way to do this is with the TRANSFER (TRA) instruction. Unlike HPR and NOP, which automatically cause the IC to be stepped by one, TRA uses its address part to hold a location number which is placed in the IC. Consequently, this address part specifies where our next instruction is found. For example, if we wish to take our next instruction from location X1, we write TRA X1. The normal sequence of instructions is now resumed—but now starting at X1—and will continue until another transfer-type instruction is executed. The transfer can be made *from* any location *to* any location, including the location of the TRA instruction itself.

Location	Operation	Address	
Z	TRA	Z	?

We may wonder why we should ever wish to do this operation since it will put us in a one-instruction loop. The important point, however, is that, whether we want to do this or not, if we *write it*, the computer will *do it*. The computer does not try to judge the reasonableness of the instructions we give it. In this case, it will proceed, faithfully executing this one instruction over 25 million times a minute (7090 speed), until we release it in some way. Of course, this is not too subtle an example of the complete *lack of judgment* on the part of the machine. The programmer can be confident (or fearful) that the computer will execute his instruction to the letter (or bit). A single wrong instruction destroys the efforts of any number of right instructions, and a great deal of effort must be made to detect and remove erroneous instructions after coding is complete.

Probably (not facetiously) the best technique for simplifying checking is to write the code correctly in the first place, and one of the best ways to avoid mistakes is to write the code in a straightforward way. The most straightforward way is the way which is easiest for each individual programmer. Consequently, there is no such thing as the "best" code for a particular problem. One way might result in a faster program; another might result in a program requiring fewer storage words; still another might be easier to operate. All these factors might be considered, but the usual code will be something of a compromise between various kinds of "best." In the coding problems and examples in this book, we shall try to present codes which represent simple methods of coding. If several methods exist, each of which presents certain peculiar advantages, we may try to mention each, indicating those advantages. **In no case are the examples to be taken as *the* way to code a problem.**

The Accumulator Register

The flow of control is the progress of the program from one set of arithmetic or input-output instructions to another. In order to lend some significance to the control instructions which we are learning, we should like to be able to perform at least one simple data operation. For this purpose, we shall make a slight diversion from our discussion of control instructions and introduce a pair of instructions which may be used to perform the operation of moving a word from one location in storage to another. The 7090 provides instructions for moving data into the special registers *from* storage and for moving data out of these registers *into* storage. Therefore, to move a word from one location to another we must first move it to one of the special registers, then move it from that register to storage. We must, of course, choose a register which is large enough to hold at least a full word of information. The register must also be available at the time we wish to move the word, because we shall destroy its contents in the process. Both these considerations exclude the IC as the register to be used. In general, the IC has only the special function of keeping the sequence of operations and should therefore not be used for other operations.

One register we might use is the *accumulator* register (AC), which has a capacity of 38 bits and is commonly used to hold arithmetic factors and results. Thus it is large enough to hold a full word and will commonly be available (or can be made available) for our movement of data. For reference, the bits in the AC are named S, Q, P, and 1 to 35; but for the present, we shall ignore the Q and P bits and consider S and 1 to 35 as a 36-bit group.

The instruction CLEAR AND ADD (CLA) takes a word from storage and places it in the AC bits S and 1 to 35. Which word is taken depends on the address portion of the CLA instruction. For example, the instruction

$$\text{CLA} \qquad \text{ZX}$$

takes the contents of location $ZX_{S,1\text{-}35}$ and places them in the $AC_{S,1\text{-}35}$ respectively. The information also remains in ZX, as we have previously noted, and may be used repeatedly. Note, however, that whatever information was *previously* in the AC is destroyed by the execution of CLA and cannot be recovered by any means unless we had the foresight to save it in some other register. Of course, we may not want to save this information. In that case, the CLA gives us a convenient way of getting rid of old information remaining in the AC.

When we wish to reverse the process and move the bits from the AC to some storage location, we use the STORE (STO) instruction. The address portion of the STO instruction specifies where the 36 bits from $AC_{S,1\text{-}35}$ are to be sent. Consider the following part of a program:

$$\begin{array}{ll} \text{CLA} & \text{XX} \\ \text{STO} & \text{YZ} \end{array}$$

The first instruction replaces the contents of the AC with the contents of location XX. The second replaces the contents of YZ with the contents of the AC. What was formerly in location XX is now also in *both* the AC and YZ. We have thus effected a transmission of one word from XX to YZ.

PROBLEMS

5-1. Write portions of a code which will:
    (*a*) Transmit a word from R3 to both XQ and ZLH.
    (*b*) Transmit a word from AA1 to XXR and another word from M to AA1.
    (*c*) Exchange the words in XX and YY.

5-2. What is the importance of the sequence of instructions in the examples of Prob. 5-1?

5-3. Could Prob. 5-1*c* be done more simply if we had some additional special register on the machine? What would be the properties of this register?

Conditional Transfers

An ability that the computer must have in order to even be classed as a computer is the ability to make a decision. The computer *must* be able to choose between alternative courses of action (as shown by the alternative box of the flow diagram). The 7090 computer can add over 200,000 numbers a second, but if it could not make a decision, this speed would be worthless.

There are several ways for the computer to make a decision. The choice might be predetermined by some special code in the data or might be determined by the result of some calculation. One way in which the computer makes such decisions is with a class of instructions called *conditional transfers*. A conditional transfer is an instruction which looks to see if a particular condition exists in some register. If that condition does exist in the register, the instruction acts as a TRA; but if the condition does not exist, the instruction acts as a NOP. In other words, the conditional transfer does one of two things, depending on the outcome of some test which it makes. The two possible outcomes are the two paths leading from an alternative box on the flow diagram.

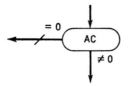

Fig. 5-1. An alternative box representing a TZE.

For example, consider the instruction TRANSFER ON ZERO AC-
CUMULATOR (TZE). The condition for which the TZE is looking
is *all zero bits* in $AC_{Q,P,1-35}$ (it does not examine the S bit). If *all
these bits are zero*, the next instruction is taken from the location
specified by the address portion of the TZE. This single instruction
could be indicated on the flow diagram by the alternative box shown
in Fig. 5-1. (When coding, remember, we put the slash on a flow line

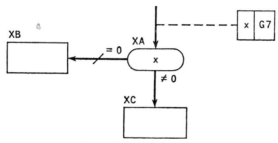

Fig. 5-2. A test for zero.

of the diagram to indicate the deviation from the normal sequential
flow.) In this case the *nonzero* condition causes the TZE to be treated
as an NOP; so the program would proceed in sequence. Suppose we
wished to test some word in storage for all zeros in positions 1 to 35.
If the word we were testing was called x and was in location G7, our
flow diagram could look like Fig. 5-2. Operation boxes XB and XC
would contain the alternative operations we shall perform in the zero
and nonzero cases, respectively. The coding for box XA would be

$$\begin{array}{lll}
\text{XA} & \text{CLA} & \text{G7} \qquad \text{Clears } p \text{ and } q \text{ bits while} \\
& & \qquad\qquad\quad \text{putting } x \text{ in AC} \\
& \text{TZE} & \text{XB} \qquad \text{Tests } x
\end{array}$$

The next instruction would be labeled XC, being the first instruction
in block XC.

Example. If $C(R) = 0$, store $C(X)$ in Z; otherwise store $C(Y)$ in Z.
Figure 5-3 shows the flow diagram, the code for which follows:

```
YA    CLA    R
      TZE    YB
YC    CLA    Y
      STO    Z
      TRA    YD        Transfers around block YB
YB    CLA    X
      STO    Z
YD    HPR
```

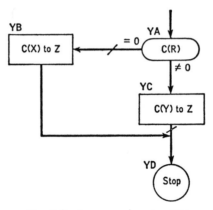

Fig. 5-3. An example using TZE.

Notice that, when the program reaches block YD, the control unit retains no evidence of which path was taken, YB or YC, although the proper substitution has been made in Z. The merge point before

```
YA    CLA    R
      TZE    YD
YB    CLA    S
      TZE    YD
YC    CLA    Y
      STO    Z
      TRA    YE
YD    CLA    X
      STO    Z
YE
```

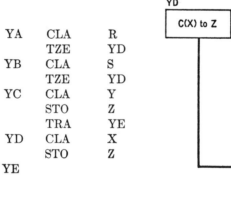
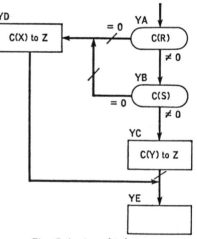

Fig. 5-4. A multiple test.

YD warns us that either YC or YB must terminate with a transfer in order that the two alternate sequences do not run into one another.

We may, of course, use more than one conditional transfer in order to effect more complex decisions in the program. Either one, or both, of the branches following a test may be followed by other tests, as well as by operation boxes.

Example. If *either* $C(R) = 0$ or $C(S) = 0$, replace $C(Z)$ with $C(X)$. If neither is zero, replace $C(Z)$ with $C(Y)$. Figure 5-4 shows our flow diagram, and the coding .

In this example, the *order* of the tests is not important. Only if *neither* R nor S is zero will the program reach block YC.

Example. If *both* $C(R) = 0$ and $C(S) = 0$, replace $C(Z)$ by $C(X)$; otherwise replace $C(Z)$ by $C(Y)$. The flow chart in Fig. 5-5 illustrates the logic, and the coding follows:

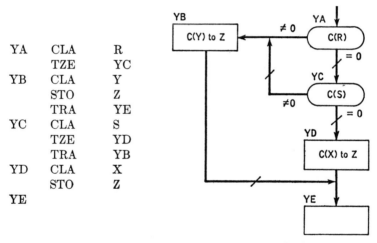

YA	CLA	R
	TZE	YC
YB	CLA	Y
	STO	Z
	TRA	YE
YC	CLA	S
	TZE	YD
	TRA	YB
YD	CLA	X
	STO	Z
YE		

Fig. 5-5. A multiple test.

If $C(R)$ turns out not to be zero, we do not need to test $C(S)$, since they cannot then *both* be zero. Again, the flow diagram helps us check our coding by pointing to places (merge points and alternative boxes) where transfers are necessary.

Example. If $C(R) = 0$ *or* $C(S) = 0$, but not both conditions, replace $C(Z)$ by $C(X)$. If both are zero or if neither is zero, replace $C(Z)$ by $C(Y)$. As the examples become more complex, the importance of the flow diagram becomes more apparent. Figure 5-6 shows the diagram; the coding follows:

YA	CLA	R
	TZE	YD
YB	CLA	S
	TZE	YE
YC	CLA	Y
	STO	Z
	TRA	YF
YD	CLA	S
	TZE	YC
YE	CLA	X
	STO	Z
YF		

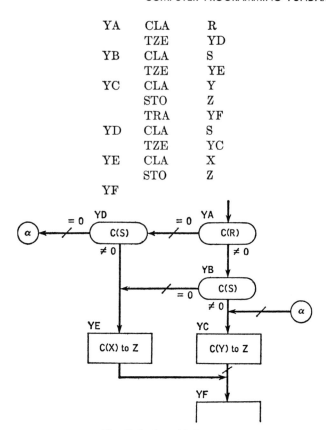

Fig. 5-6. A multiple test.

Unlike the previous examples, we must test C(S) no matter which outcome the test on C(R) had. We must use different blocks (YD and YB) for the testing of C(S) because the result of the test at YB must not be lost before this test. Imagine the problems encountered without the flow diagram as the complexity increases five- and tenfold. With the diagram, it is a simple procedure to check whether step YC is reached on a zero or nonzero R condition. By working backward on the diagram, we easily see that C(R) had been nonzero, because we have the whole picture, not just a part, in one glance.

PROBLEMS

5-4. If C(QZ) ≠ 0, replace C(M) with C(QZ); otherwise proceed without replacing anything.

5-5. If C(Q2) = 0 and C(Q3) ≠ 0, replace C(M) with C(Q3).

5-6. If either $C(Q2)$ or $C(Q3)$ or $C(Q4) = 0$, replace $C(M)$ with $C(Q1)$ unless $C(Q1) = 0$.

5-7. If $C(Q2) = 0$ and either $C(Q3)$ or $C(Q4) \neq 0$, replace $C(M)$ with whichever $[C(Q3)$ or $C(Q4)]$ is not zero.

5-8. If $C(Q2) = 0$ and $C(Q3) \neq 0$ or if $C(Q3) = 0$ and $C(Q4) \neq 0$, replace $C(Z)$ with $C(Y)$. If $C(Q2) \neq 0$ and $C(Q4) \neq 0$, or if $C(Q3) = 0$, replace $C(W)$ with $C(Z)$.

Complementary Instructions

As illustrated in some of the examples and problems, the TZE, although explicitly a zero test, certainly could be used as a test for nonzero. Simply stated, all the bits of the AC are zero or some of them are not zero—no other possibility exists. The fact that we transfer control on the zero condition rather than the nonzero condition is strictly an arbitrary choice. We could conceive of an instruction, say TRANSFER ON NONZERO ACCUMULATOR (TNZ), which performs the same test as TZE but transfers on the opposite, or complementary, condition. What would be the use of such an instruction, since it performs the same logical test as TZE? Consider the third example (Fig. 5-5) in the previous section. How could we have written this code if we also had a TNZ instruction?

YA	CLA	R	
	TZE	YC	
YB	CLA	Y	
	STO	Z	
	TRA	YE	
YC	CLA	S	
	TNZ	YB	Replaces TZE YD; TRA YB
YD	CLA	X	
	STO	Z	
YE			

The complementary instruction has saved the space for one instruction while accomplishing the same job. Under certain conditions, the machine will execute one fewer instruction. (What conditions?) Actually, one of the important reasons for having complementary instructions is the ease which they lend to the coding task. As the programmer moves through his flow diagram, writing the code, his natural mode of thought may tend to carry him down one branch from an alternative box. If he does not have a set of complementary instructions for that decision, however, he will be forced to consider the other alternative first. Pairs of instructions other than control instructions may also be thought of as complementary, though not in the same sense. An instruction to add might be thought of as complementary to a subtraction instruction, if learning the functioning of one was essentially equivalent to learning the other. This complementarity eases the task of learning the instruction set of a computer, not unlike the way certain principles in language enable us to broaden our vocabularies. If we learn the word "wrapped," we know the words "unwrapped" and "rewrapped." If we know transfer on zero, we know transfer on nonzero; and in fact, many other transfer instructions will prove as simple to learn.

Other Conditional Transfers

The 7090 instruction set contains a great variety of conditional transfer instructions. As with TZE and TNZ, most of them test some property of the information in one of the 7090's registers. Others, however, test for the existence of certain conditions of the input-output devices, and this type will be discussed in the chapter on input-output. The instructions which test the various registers will be treated as those registers are introduced.

In order to illustrate further the use of control instructions in combination, let us look at two other operations which test part of the AC. The first, TRANSFER ON MINUS ACCUMULATOR (TMI), tests the S bit of the AC. In many operations, the S bit is treated as an

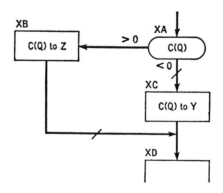

Fig. 5-7. A test for greater or less than zero.

algebraic sign, with zero meaning plus and one meaning minus. TMI will cause a transfer of control if the AC is minus, that is, if the S bit equals one. If we wish to test the S bit (sign) of a word, we can bring that word into the AC and test it with TMI.

Example. If $C(Q)$ are positive $[C(Q) > 0]$, store them in Z; but if $C(Q)$ are negative $[C(Q) < 0]$, store them in Y. See Fig. 5-7.

XA	CLA	Q	
	TMI	XC	Tests S bit
XB	STO	Z	$C(Q)$ remains in AC
	TRA	XD	Transfer around alternate path
XC	STO	Y	$C(Q)$ remains in AC
XD			

It was not specifically stated that the execution of TMI leaves the $C(AC)$ unchanged; but in fact, none of the three control instructions introduced so far—TZE, TNZ, TMI—causes a change to any register (but the IC) as a result of its execution. These three instructions are representative of a group of instructions which test to see if a particular condition exists, without in any way modifying or nullifying the condition in question. With such "nondestructive" tests, provided we do not change it by some other means, we may test the AC repeatedly. In many instances, the ability to repeat testing of a condition or group of conditions (not necessarily in the AC) gives us an excellent means of having the program "remember" previous occurrences.

Since the 7090 has many registers, affected in many different ways by its instructions, it will be simpler to learn which registers *are* changed by each instruction rather than which registers are *not* changed. Therefore, when we are defining the functions of an instruction whose execution does (or may) change a register, that fact will be specifically mentioned.

Now back to our example of Fig. 5-7. Because $C(Q)$ remain in the AC no matter which branch is taken, neither block XB nor XC need bring them in again in preparation for storing. There is, however, a *logical flaw* in the flow diagram (did you see it?). The problem statement told us what to do in the case that $C(Q)$ were plus or minus. We translated that into the cases where $C(Q) > 0$ and $C(Q) < 0$. What about the case where $C(Q) = 0$? Our flow diagram does not provide for this alternative, and we are not quite sure from

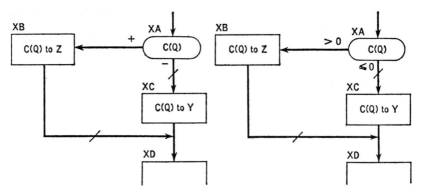

Fig. 5-8. A test for positive and nega-   Fig. 5-9. A test for less than or equal
tive.   to zero.

the problem statement what to do in this case. We can be assured, however, that the *computer* will make some choice when it comes to this point in the code. Even though we did not realize we were coding a decision for the zero case, we were. It matters not a whit what we *thought* we were telling the 7090 to do, but only what we actually told it. Therefore, we should find out what we really said.

We told the 7090 to test the S bit of location Q. If Q contains a number (which is not a necessary presumption but one we shall make), the S bit represents its sign. What is the sign of zero? In algebra, we usually do not consider zero as having a sign, although it is sometimes classed as a positive number. The 7090, however, knows nothing of algebra and affords no special treatment to zeros in this respect. Each word has an S bit and that S bit may be 0 or 1, regardless of the "zeroness" of the other bits. Thus we may have, in the 7090, positive zeros and negative zeros—whether or not such designations are mean-ingful to us. (It is often useful to have the two kinds of zeros, to indicate two different ways in which a zero result was achieved.)

Where do these considerations leave us in our example? Things now seem quite simple: a positive zero will go with the positive num-bers and a negative zero with the negative numbers. If we wish to treat all the zeros as positive numbers, we must make special pro-visions in the code. A correct flow diagram corresponding to this code is shown in **Fig. 5-8**.

Now let us write a code for the diagram in Fig. 4-9, which classes the zeros with the negative numbers.

XA	CLA	Q
	TZE	XC
	TMI	XC
XB	STO	Z
	TRA	XD
XC	STO	Y
XD		

Notice that two conditional transfers are necessary to place the zeros with the negative numbers. (Is the order of the TZE and the TMI important?)

PROBLEMS

(Consider $+0$ as being greater than -0.)

5-9. If $C(Q2) \neq +0$, replace $C(M)$ with $C(Q2)$; otherwise proceed without replacing anything.

5-10. Compare Prob. 5-9 with Prob. 5-4.

5-11. If $C(Q2) \geqq 0$, and $C(Q3) \neq 0$, replace $C(M)$ with $C(Q3)$.

5-12. What would be the complementary instruction to TMI? Do Probs. 5-9 and 5-11 using this instruction rather than the TMI.

Skip-type Instructions

In some cases we should like to test the contents of some word in storage directly. In order to do this we would need an instruction which specifies the test to be made, the storage location to be tested, and the location to which the transfer should be made. It turns out, however, that there is not enough space in a word to hold a single instruction with this much information. The problem is solved by using a *skip-type* control instruction.

An example will best illustrate the technique. Just as we can test the AC for zeroness with a TZE, we can test any storage location for that property with the instruction STORAGE ZERO TEST (ZET) If we wished to test location XX3 (bits 1 to 35) for zero we would write

ZET   XX3

If the zero condition is met, control is automatically transferred to the *second* instruction, rather than the next instruction, after the ZET. In other words, the zero condition causes the location counter to be stepped up by two instead of by one. In effect, the computer *skips* one instruction.

Example. If $C(R) = 0$, store $C(X)$ in Z; otherwise store $C(Y)$ in Z. This is the same problem we did when discussing TZE; therefore, the flow diagram is identical except for the slashes on the flow lines. (See Fig. 5-3.)

YA	ZET	R
	TRA	YC
YB	CLA	X
	STO	Z
	TRA	YD
YC	CLA	Y
	STO	Z
YD		

What is the difference between the two coding sequences? They both require that the same number of instructions be written, but do they require that the same number of instructions be executed? We have now seen several ways to code this same portion of a flow diagram, and other ways could be shown (one instruction can be eliminated, for example).

At times the programmer may wish to write and rewrite a section of a code in order to make it shorter or faster or both. Usually, however, he will simply wish to find one correct way—a way that comes naturally to him. A point is rapidly reached where further streamlining of a code costs more than is saved in operating expense. Many a programmer becomes trapped by his desire to refine his program until it is "absolutely perfect," but such coding is the mark of an amateur— not a mature professional—programmer. If programming were purely a theoretical subject, such time could be justified. From a practical standpoint, however, the greatest value in a program is that it runs correctly at production time.

We should be careful to point out that we are not criticizing the time spent in creating new techniques or refining techniques of general application, for such "theoretical" work must always precede large improvements in the practical methodology of the industry. The warning we issue is against the tendency to confuse such general contributions with the simple overrefinement or sugar-coating of programs already worked out in a satisfactory manner.

The skip-type instruction can be used in another way, without any transfer instruction. If the single skipped instruction can be used to set some kind of indication when it is not skipped, the indication can then be tested at a later point in the program. Thus we have a simple way of "remembering" the outcome of an earlier test or tests.

PROBLEMS

5-13. What would be the complementary instruction to ZET? Do the examples of this section using this instruction instead of ZET.

5-14. Do Probs. 5-9 and 5-11 of the previous set using ZET and its complementary instruction where possible.

The Comparison Skip

One of the most common decisions to be made in computing is based on the relative size of two numbers. TMI and TPL were examples of such a comparison where one of the numbers was always assumed to be zero; but in general, both the numbers may vary. If we compare two numbers a and b, we have three possible conditions: $a = b$, $a > b$, $a < b$. In order to make this general comparison, we need to specify two words to be compared and two locations for transferring under two of the three conditions. Obviously, all this information cannot fit into one instruction. We could place one of the numbers in the AC; and if we extend our notion of the skip-type instruction, only one address need be specified by the comparison instruction.

One of the comparison instructions on the 7090 is COMPARE AC WITH STORAGE (CAS). This instruction causes either no skip, a one-location skip, or a two-location skip, depending on whether $C(AC)$ are greater than, equal to, or less than the contents of the specified location. Schematically, this skipping might be represented like this:

CAS   X

Execute this instruction next if $C(AC) > C(X)$
Execute this instruction next if $C(AC) = C(X)$
Execute this instruction next if $C(AC) < C(X)$

Thus the CAS gives us the possibility of making a three-branched decision. The alternative box in Fig. 5-10 might be coded as

XA   CLA   M
      CAS   N
      TRA   XC
      TRA   XB
XD

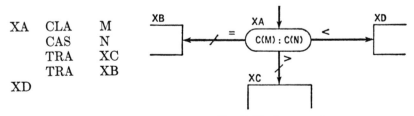

Fig. 5-10. A comparison.

Example. Replace $C(Y)$ by whichever is largest, $C(X1)$ or $C(X2)$. If they are equal, leave $C(Y)$ undisturbed (Fig. 5-11). One way of coding this problem would be

XA	CLA	X1	Prepare C(X1) to be compared with
	CAS	X2	C(X2)
	TRA	XC	X1 > X2
	TRA	XD	X1 = X2
XB	CLA	X2	X1 < X2
	STO	Y	
	TRA	XD	
XC	CLA	X1	
	STO	Y	
XD			

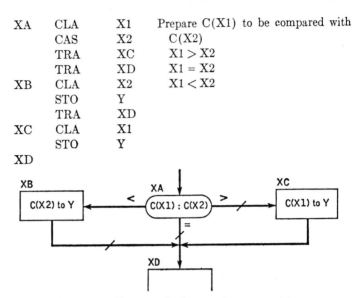

Fig. 5-11. Choosing the larger of two quantities.

When we reach XD, the larger of the two quantities would be stored in Y, unless they were equal. We do not know, however, on reaching that point which one was the largest, and if we wish to preserve that information, we would have to do that before returning to XD.

Example. Replace C(Y) by C(X1) if C(X1) = C(X2). Otherwise, do nothing (Fig. 5-12).

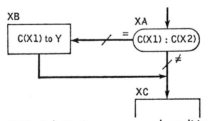

Fig. 5-12. Substitution on an equal condition.

The code might be

XA	CLA	X1	
	CAS	X2	
	TRA	XC	$C(X1) > C(X2)$
	TRA	XB	$C(X1) = C(X2)$
	TRA	XC	$C(X1) < C(X2)$
XB	STO	Y	(X1 remains in AC)
XC			

PROBLEMS

5-15. If $C(X1) \geqq C(X2)$, replace $C(Y)$ with $C(X1)$. If $C(X1) < C(X2)$, replace $C(Y)$ with $C(X2)$.

5-16. If $C(X1) > C(X2)$, replace $C(Y)$ with $C(X1)$. If $C(X1) \leqq C(X2)$, replace $C(Y)$ with $C(X2)$. Are Probs. 5-15 and 5-16 different?

5-17. Place the largest of the three numbers $C(X1)$, $C(X2)$, $C(X3)$ in location Y.

5-18. Place the smallest of the three numbers $C(X1)$, $C(X2)$, $C(X3)$ in location Z.

5-19. Place the middle number of the three $[C(X1), C(X2), C(X3)]$ in location W.

Complex Decisions

Individually, the various tests we are able to code are extremely simple. How then are we able to translate into a code complex decisions such as those indicated in the alternative box of Fig. 4-6*f*? It is easy enough to see how we can make the numerical parts of such a decision, such as determining whether a purchase amount is greater than \$1,000; but how do we determine if a given transaction is a return or if it has no specified amount? We cannot, of course, make such determinations if the input data are not in the digital form or do not contain the necessary information at all, but that information certainly does not have to be in numerical form.

Suppose, for example, that such an alternative box is in a program which is to analyze the sales of some business. We shall assume that one punched card is prepared for each transaction and that one field of six digits in the card is reserved for the amount of the sale. The cards are to be put on tape, read into the computer, and processed one at a time. Sometime during the processing of each card, this test is made in order that the program may analyze how sales are distributed by size—how much income is derived from small transactions, what percentage of the sales are over \$1,000, and so forth. Since we are here concerned with the coding of the alternative box, we shall assume that, by the time we reach this point, the card has been read into storage and the amount has been translated into the internal numerical code in location AMT.

There are many ways in which returns, unspecified amounts, house sales, special orders, and such could be indicated in a card like this— some will tend to simplify the coding of our alternative box; some will tend to make the preparation of the data cards easier; but most frequently a variety of factors will fix the form of designation. Let us assume that, in our problem, the following method is employed:

1. Returns are designated by punching the word RETURN in a special place, or code field, in the card, which is read into location CODE in storage; or else they are designated by a negative sales amount.

2. Unspecified amounts have the code field left blank, or the sales-amount field punched with zeros.

3. Special orders—which are to be treated the same way as unspecified amounts—have the letters SPEC in the code field.

4. House sales—also treated as unspecified—have the letters HS or the word HOUSE in the code field.

Now it is up to us to construct a code which will determine which of these conditions exist, or if none exists, into which range the sales amount falls.

In order not to becloud the current issues, one further simplification is in order; we shall assume that we already have the following alphabetic and numeric constants in storage:

Location	Constant
K100	100
K500	500
K1000	1,000
C1	RETURN
C2	Six blanks
C3	SPEC
C4	HS
C5	HOUSE

The detailed flow diagram of block XA, Fig. 4-6*f*, is shown in Fig. 5-13. One glance at this diagram should reveal the advantages of specifying the alternative in general terms when making an over-all flow diagram. Although Fig. 5-13 is much more specific about *how* the decision is to be made, it really tells us less about *what* we are deciding than the single block in Fig. 4-6*f*. The coding, on the other hand, proceeds directly and easily from Fig. 5-13, while we could not begin to code from the meager information in Fig. 4-6*f*.

Location	Operation	Address	Comments
XA	CLA	CODE	Is CODE
	CAS	C2	Blank?

	TRA	XAC	No
	TRA	XG	Yes
XAC	CAS	C3	SPEC?
	TRA	XAD	No
	TRA	XG	Yes
XAD	CAS	C5	HOUSE?
	TRA	XAE	No
	TRA	XG	Yes

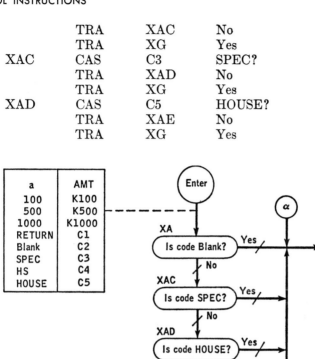

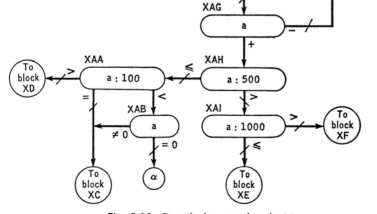

Fig. 5-13. Detail of a complex decision.

XAE	CAS	C4	HS?
	TRA	XAF	No
	TRA	XG	Yes
XAF	CAS	C1	RETURN?
	TRA	XAG	No
	TRA	XB	Yes
XAG	CLA	AMT	Is amount negative?
	TMI	XB	
XAH	CAS	K500	
	TRA	XAI	> 500
	TRA	XAA	$= 500$
XAA	CAS	K100	< 500
	TRA	XD	> 100
	TRA	XC	$= 100$
XAB	TZE	XG	< 100 and zero
	TRA	XC	Nonzero
XAI	CAS	K1000	
	TRA	XF	$> 1,000$
	TRA	XE	$= 1,000$
	TRA	XE	$< 1,000$

Notice how the coding is no more difficult for this large problem than for several small ones because the flow diagram has been broken down into boxes which are individually no more difficult than those in our earlier examples. Once we have the flow diagram worked out, the hard part is over; a problem twice as big is just twice as much coding effort—not four or more times, as it would be without the diagram.

As is always the case, this particular solution is only one of countless ways of doing this problem, some differing only in detail, others being significantly modified. For example, if we could first test something which would tell us whether or not this was an ordinary sale, we could split the problem into two parts immediately—one to determine the range, the other to determine the type of exception. Although the code would be longer, it would probably be faster. On the other hand, we might shorten the code somewhat by making the first four tests into a loop, but this technique would tend to slow the processing. In either case, we have a method which seems to work; so we should not tarry too long over a few locations or a few microseconds until—and unless—we find out that one or the other is a critical consideration in the total problem.

It is interesting to notice that the first five alternative boxes are doing a job which is quite similar to the job an assembly program does when looking up symbols or operation codes—even though each input card in that case represents a symbolic instruction, not a sales record. At the coding level, techniques are common to problems which, at the problem level, have little or no relationship, just as many of the same words or phrases go into a book on algebra as into a book on art history. Still, beginners often seem to have undue difficulty seeing the forms instead of the details—dissociating the technique from the source.

One interesting exercise to help overcome this weakness is to take the flow diagram for one problem, erase the contents of the boxes, and try to invent a new problem which will fill them up without changing the form. Another way is simply to change the names of the input data in such a way as to create another problem which the same routine will solve—a method which has paid off handsomely on occasion when it was possible to move an entire checked-out program from one job to another.

Control Statements in FORTRAN

The concept of flow of control in a higher level language is no different from what is was in machine language. In the higher level language, each statement, or line of coding, takes the place of the individual instruction in the machine-language code, so that in the absence of any special provision, control always passes from one statement to its successor; just as, in the machine code, control passes from one instruction to its successor. As in symbolic coding, the individual lines of coding may be identified with labels, though these labels no longer represent addresses in storage, but merely identify the particular statement. In FORTRAN, for example, any statement may be identified by a number written to the left of the statement, as in the statement

178 $\quad$ A = B

which states that the old value of the variable, A, is to be replaced by the present value of the variable, B. The number 178 identifies this statement, and thus may not be used as a label for any other statement. If, at some point in the program, we wish to have control transferred to statement 178, we merely have to write the statement

GO TO 178

which is, in effect, an unconditional transfer in the FORTRAN language. (Notice that statements do not need to have labels at all, if they are not referred to by other statements. They may, however, have labels even if they are not referred to—for example, for convenience in flow-diagram referencing.)

In the FORTRAN language, there is one basic conditional control statement which can be used in a variety of situations, the IF statement. The IF statement provides a three-way branching based on whether a specified quantity is less than zero, zero, or greater·than zero. For instance, the statement

IF (X) 27,173,16

will transfer control to statement 27 if the current value of the variable, X, is less than zero, to statement 173 if it is zero, and to statement 16 if it is greater than zero. Notice that in FORTRAN, the distinction between positive and negative zeros is not made, which is usually a convenience, but represents a loss of one of the detailed discriminations of the machine language.

A few coding examples should clarify the use of the IF statement and at the same time contrast the FORTRAN language with our previous machine-language examples. First, the flow diagram of Fig. 5-3 could be coded as follows:

```
99      IF (R) 88,502,88
88      Z = Y
        GO TO 15
502     Z = X
15      STOP
```

(The STOP statement terminates the program. The statement number 99 corresponds with block YA in the diagram, 88 with YC, 502 with YB, and 15 with YD.) Notice that there is no normal flow after an IF statement, so that statement 88 must be explicitly referenced and the line between block YA and block YC should have a slash on it. Sometimes this explicit referencing is helpful to the programmer (since it allows him to rearrange the program more conveniently) and sometimes it requires extra effort (since he must always explicitly reference all alternatives).

Example. Code in FORTRAN the diagram of Fig. 5-4.

```
10    IF  (R)20,40,20
20    IF  (S)30,40,30
30    Z = Y
      GO  TO  50
40    Z = X
50    . . .
```

where YA corresponds to 10, YB to 20, etc.

Example. Code in FORTRAN the diagram of Fig. 5-5.

```
10    IF  (R)20,30,20
20    Z = Y
      GO  TO  50
30    IF  (S)20,40,20
40    Z = X
50    . . .
```

Example. Code in FORTRAN the diagram of Fig. 5-6.

```
10    IF  (R)20,40,20
20    IF  (S)30,50,30
30    Z = Y
      GO  TO  60
40    IF  (S)50,30,50
50    Z = X
60    . . .
```

Example. Code in FORTRAN the diagram in Fig. 5-9.

```
10    IF  (Q)30,30,20
20    Z = Q
      GO  TO  40
30    Y = Q
40    . . .
```

Notice that we cannot code the diagram in Fig. 5-8 using the FORTRAN language. (Why?)

The IF statement makes the accomplishment of arithmetic comparisons quite simple, because the expression in the parentheses may be any sort of arithmetic combination. For example, to code the flow diagram of Fig. 5-11, we simply write:

```
10    IF  (X1 − X2)20,40,30
20    Y = X2
      GO  TO  40
30    Y = X1
40    . . .
```

The IF statement performs its test on the numerical difference between the quantities in X1 and X2, as specified by the quite natural expression X1 − X2.

The ability to make tests on complex combinations of numbers can greatly simplify otherwise difficult coding problems, as shown in the following examples:

Example. Replace C(R) by C(S) if C(S) is at least twice as big as C(R). Otherwise, do nothing (Fig. 5-14).

```
98    IF (2. * R − S) 100,100,102
100   R = S
102   . . .
```

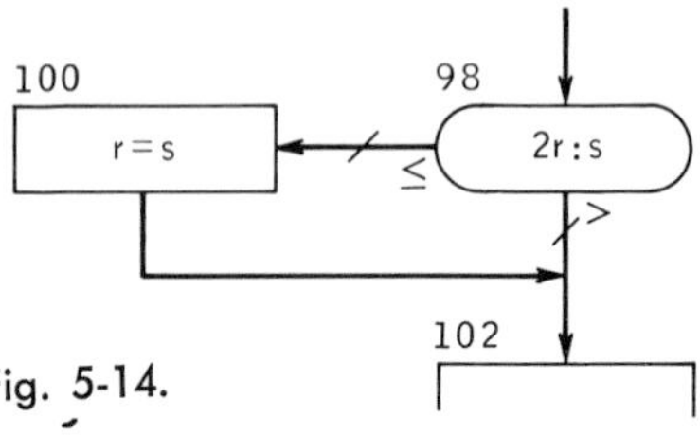

Fig. 5-14.

Notice how the constant quantity, 2., may be introduced directly into the expression, which in a quite natural way expresses the computation of 2 times the quantity in R minus the quantity in S.

Example. Replace C(R) by C(S) if C(S) is at least 7.5 greater than C(R) (Fig. 5-15).

```
75    IF (R − (S − 7.5)) 100,100,125
100   R = S
125   . . .
```

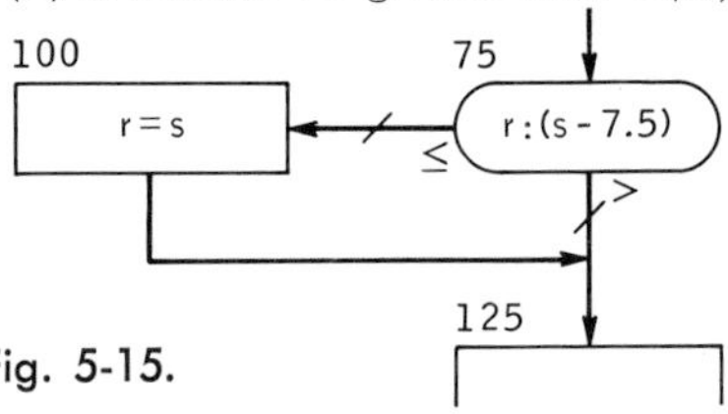

Fig. 5-15.

Notice how parentheses may be used to clarify the meaning of the tested expression, even though it might have been written without parentheses as R − S + 7.5.

It would be appropriate at this point to show how the complex diagram of Fig. 5-13 would be coded in FORTRAN, but we cannot. FORTRAN, being a language oriented to mathematical problems, does not have simple facilities for comparing alphabetical information as is required in blocks XA, XB, and so forth. The specified comparisons could, indeed, be written in the FORTRAN language, but the difficulty of the task precludes its being done in an elementary presentation. Here, then, is an example of the specificity of a problem-oriented language making it more difficult to use than, say, machine language, when the problem is one of a wider range of problems.

PROBLEMS

5-20. Code in FORTRAN the diagram in Fig. 5-12.

5-21. Code Prob. 5-17 in FORTRAN.

5-22. Code Prob. 5-18 in FORTRAN.

5-23. Code Prob. 5-19 in FORTRAN.

5-24. Code the following problem in FORTRAN:

If the difference between C(X) and C(Y) is greater than C(Z), replace C(X) by C(Y). If the difference is less than C(Z), replace C(Y) by C(X). If the difference is equal to C(Z), replace both C(X) and C(Y) by C(Z).

5-25. Flow diagram the following problem and code in both symbolic machine language and FORTRAN:

Four numbers are stored in locations V, W, X, and Y. Place them in those four locations in ascending numerical order.

Trapping

In using the types of control instructions we have seen so far, we had to insert a test instruction every time we wished to examine a particular condition. Even if some exceptional condition happened once in 10 billion cases, we would still have to test every time we reached the place in the program where it might happen. In order to avoid such waste, we should like to have a way of testing certain conditions automatically—with extra time being taken only when they actually occur.

On the 7090, several conditions may be tested in this way.

In certain arithmetic operations it is possible to get a result which is larger than can be held in one word (we call this condition *overflow*). On input-output operations an error might be detected or a certain process may come to an end. In order that we should not have to ask the 7090 whether or not these rare conditions have occurred, we may— at the beginning of a program or of a section of a program—tell the 7090 to *interrupt* the main flow only when they do. This interruption, or *trapping*, is actually an automatic transfer to some special instruction location. In the case of arithmetic overflow, the interruption takes place as soon as the instruction causing the overflow has been executed. In the case of input-output errors, which might happen at any time, the program may be interrupted between *any* two instructions.

In most of the cases where an interruption occurs, we want to perform some "fix-up" function, some job which should be taken care of without delay. After this fix-up occurs—and of course we must have the fix-up program stored somewhere—we should like to resume our original program right where we left off. But how can the fix-up program know where we left off? The instruction counter cannot help, for when the interrupt occurs, the IC contents are destroyed by the transfer which takes place. Just before the interruption, however, the IC is saved in a special fixed location in storage which the fix-up

program may examine to determine where to return control. Some
of the other bits in this special location are used to tell the fix-up
program what condition caused the interruption.

Interrupt—An Example

Possibly an analogy will help to clarify the concept of interrupt.
Suppose you were spending an evening at home, reading and, say,
baking a cake. You put the cake in the oven and then, having nothing
else to do for 45 minutes, you sit down to read. You might depend
on looking up from your reading now and then to see whether it was
time for the cake to come out. If you looked up often enough—at the
end of every page, for example—so that you would not risk burning
the cake, you would seriously disturb the pleasure of your reading;
but on the other hand, if you looked up only at the end of each
chapter, you might find a piece of charcoal in the oven. With an
interval timer on your stove, your problem would be nicely solved.
You set the timer for 45 minutes and then proceed with your reading.
You need not worry about noticing the clock; in fact, even if you
should fall asleep, the alarm will tell you when it is time to get the
cake. When the alarm goes off, you use a bookmark to save your
place and proceed to finish your baking chores. When that activity is
finished, your bookmark tells you where you stopped.

The appropriateness of this analogy is enhanced by the fact that
we may actually have an "interval timer" on our 7090. Our program
can set this clock and then proceed until the clock runs down, causing an interruption. This technique can be especially valuable for
keeping a program from "falling asleep." When checking out a program, we often have errors which cause the computer to be caught in
an "endless" loop (for example, A TRA A). If we make an estimate
of how long our program should run, we can set the timer to interrupt
it after an appropriate time. The fix-up program could, when the
interruption occurs, examine certain locations in memory which would
indicate whether or not the program were making any progress. If it
were not, some indication of the trouble would be sent to the operator
(printed, for example) and the program would be terminated. If
nothing seemed wrong, the fix-up program could start the timer again
and return control to the main part of the program, wherever the
interruption occurred.

Our analogy can be extended to illustrate another indispensable use of the trapping technique. Suppose that, while you were reading, a friend decided to drop in. Now, all sorts of people are likely to come visiting at almost any time, but are you going to peer out the window every minute to see if anyone has arrived? Of course not; you have a doorbell. When someone wants to let you know of his arrival, he rings; you hear; and unless you see through the peephole that it is the bill collector, you let him in.

On the computer, the analogous case occurs when we have input or output devices which communicate more or less directly with the outside world. Suppose, for example, that the computer were controlling the airplane traffic around some airport. As it was performing the job of calculating the positions of each airplane in the vicinity, one airplane might—at any time—send a signal directly to the computer requesting permission to land. This signal must be handled immediately; so we build the computer in such a way that an interruption will occur. Without the interruption device, it would be extremely difficult, if not impossible, to be sure that no airplane would be ignored—and still get any work done.

Once we have several conditions which can cause interruption, our logical problems are compounded. As any housewife knows, just as you start to answer the doorbell, the telephone rings; but before you can answer it, the baby starts crying to have his diaper changed. Halfway through the changing process, the timer goes off and you have to take out the cake. If you are not clever—and maybe even if you are—some disaster is going to happen. At the very best, either you are never going to get back to that book or else you will get so confused that the bookmark will get lost.

The Establishment of Priority

In order to handle such situations effectively, we human beings establish—usually unconsciously—a system of priorities. Such systems—and, analogously, the systems needed to handle multiple computer interruptions—can be extremely complex. You can answer the telephone even if the cake has to come out, but not if it is already 3 minutes since the timer went off. You have to go immediately when the baby starts crying, in case a pin has come open or some other extreme emergency exists, but if he just needs changing, he will have to wait until the cake comes out, the phone is answered, and the visitor is greeted. Once the diaper is off, however, the situation reverses, for then you must not be interrupted by any source until the change is complete.

Just as it is necessary for you to be able to ignore, momentarily, certain interruptions, the computer must have the ability to prevent certain sections of the program from interrupting others—under certain conditions. When a trap is temporarily ignored, we say it has been "disabled." The computer remembers any disabled traps, and when they are finally "enabled" they take place in a "built-in" sequence. Disabling may be done under program control at any time and is also done automatically when certain traps occur; for example, most traps automatically prevent a second occurrence of the same trap until the program enables it.

Figure 5-16 is a whimsical "flow diagram" of a plan for reading a book, baking a cake, tending the baby, entertaining guests, and answering the phone with some kind of priority system. The diamond-shaped boxes represent entries to interrupt routines or returns from them to the interrupted sequence (which may be in some other interrupt routine). The diagram should, by analogy, give some idea of the problems involved in coordinating, say, 30 different interrupt conditions. Even in this "simple" example, careful examination of each individual set of circumstances is needed to determine just what results this procedure will produce. Under what circumstances can we burn the cake? Apparently this event might happen only when the baby has an emergency, and since we value the baby over the cake, it seems unavoidable. How long can the baby go without being changed? If we get enough phone calls and visitors, the baby could wait indefinitely. If we are not satisfied with this result, we shall have to make some change which will effectively raise the priority of changing the baby as time goes on.

In most cases, on the machine, such complex interactions can be handled only in an approximate way at first planning. As operating experience in the actual environment grows, or as various simulated tests reveal weak points, adjustments are made which realign the priority system. This building up of systems which are to operate in real environments—with people, with other machines, with nature— is one of the greatest challenges in programming and machine design.

In this elementary volume, we have made this brief, and—we hope—simple, explanation in order to reveal some of the principles and problems of an extremely difficult situation.

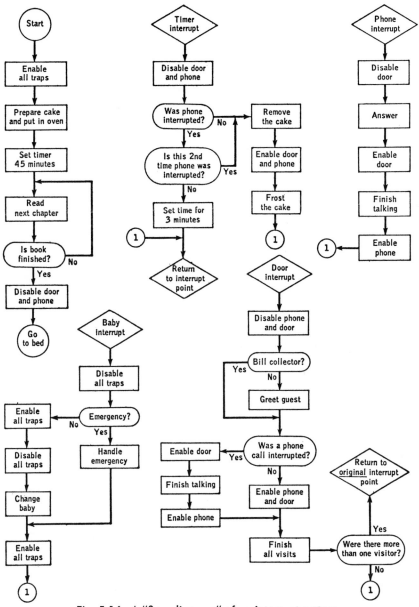

Fig. 5-16. A "flow diagram" of an interrupt system.

Timing

As long as we are discussing clocks and such, perhaps we should examine the question of how to tell, in advance, how long the computer will take to execute a specific program. As we have seen, programs usually consist of loops within other (larger) loops which are in turn within loops themselves. Almost any number of levels of loops might be found in a program, but it seems clear that the instructions in the innermost loops will be executed most often.

Suppose our program consists of the three loops, as shown in Fig. 5-17, and that each of these loops is set to be executed ten times before ending. We perform A (representing some sequence of steps) once, then B; then we do C ten times. We then repeat B, then do C ten more times, and so forth. For every ten executions of C, we do one of B; for every ten of B, we do one of A. Therefore, if we do A ten times, we shall do B one hundred times and C one thousand times. Clearly, then, if A, B, and C are about the same length, C will be most important in determining the total time for the problem; but if B or A is much longer than C, they may appreciably affect the total time involved. To get rather precise timing, we must multiply the time for each loop by the number of times that loop will be executed, and add these times together. For example, if C took 5,000 μsec (millionths of a second), B took 18,000 μsec, and A took 40,000 μsec, the total time would be 1,000 $\times$ 5,000 + 100 $\times$ 18,000 + 10 $\times$ 40,000 μsec, or about 7.2 seconds—of which C alone takes about 5 seconds.

A good rule, then, is that timing the inner loop, or possibly the inner two loops, gives a fair estimate of the total time. If the outer loops are extremely long—if, for example, they contain input

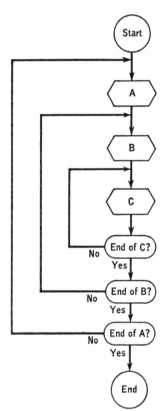

Fig. 5-17. A loop within a loop within a loop.

or output operations—they may then become important, or even domi-nant, factors in timing.

How, then, can we time a set of instructions, ignoring, for the time being, the problem of input-output timing? In a machine of the 7090's type most of the instructions take fixed amounts of time to execute. These times are always multiples of the access time, or cycle time, of the machine—each cycle being 2.18 μsec. Many of the instructions take two cycles, or 4.36 μsec. Of the instructions we have learned so far, all take two cycles except CAS, which takes three cycles, or 6.54 μsec, and TRA, which takes one cycle. Thus, to do

$$\begin{array}{ll} \text{CLA} & \text{A} \\ \text{STO} & \text{B} \end{array}$$

takes four cycles or 8.72 μsec; or, to state it differently, we could move 100 words in less than a millisecond (thousandth of a second).

The problem of timing becomes complicated by the existence of the alternate paths in the program. The seven instructions

(1)	YA	CLA	R
(2)		TZE	YB
(3)	YC	CLA	Y
(4)		STO	Z
(5)		TRA	YD
(6)	YB	CLA	X
(7)		STO	Z
	YD		

take different times to execute depending on whether or not $C(R) = 0$. In the case that $C(R) = 0$, instructions 1, 2, 6, and 7 are executed for a total of eight cycles. If $C(R) \neq 0$, however, nine cycles are taken by executing 1, 2, 3, 4, and 5. Since the data thus determine the timing, we cannot really know in advance how long some sections of the program will take. If we have some idea how often we shall take each particular path, we can make a better estimate; otherwise we can only set upper and lower limits on the execution time. Luckily, we are not usually concerned with estimating the running time of a program to *great* accuracy. After all, if the program runs for 1 min-ute, we would not even notice if it takes a second or two over the estimate. Since 1 second means about 200,000 instructions, we can easily allow a great deal of roughness in the estimating process. On the other hand, if we underestimate the timing of our inner loop by 50 per cent on a 3-hour program, we have made a serious error; so we cannot throw all caution to the winds.

PROBLEMS

5-26. Calculate the maximum and minimum times for Probs. 5-15 through 5-19.

5-27. Assuming each condition in each test is equally likely, what are the average times for Probs. 5-15 through 5-19?

5-28. If the conditions are not equally likely, how can we make a more efficient program?

CHAPTER 6

INTRODUCTION TO INPUT-OUTPUT

The computer may use a variety of media for input and output of information. These media differ in reliability, maximum rate of transmission, sensitivity to environment, and information format. (Figure 6-1 is a table showing some of the characteristics of frequently used input-output media.)

Just as the computer uses a bit-structured code to represent information, so do the input-output media. Punched cards record information as combinations of holes punched in them. Paper tape also uses holes to represent the different characters. Magnetic tape has tiny magnetized spots on its surface which take the place of the holes in cards or paper tape. Because none of these media is intended for direct human use, we need special machines to put "human" information into these forms and special machines to translate from these forms into printed or graphic form.

On the basis of their relationship with the computer, we have two classes of such machines: *off-line*, or *peripheral*, and *on-line*. The off-line equipment, although used to prepare data for and receive data from it, is not under control of the computer. They are, in fact, usually not physically connected to the computer in any way and need not even be in its vicinity. On the other hand, those card and paper-tape readers and punches and those magnetic-tape read-write units which are under direct computer control are referred to as on-line devices. Other on-line equipment might include typewriters, high-speed printing machines, cathode-ray screens (like television screens) for graphic information, and usually some method for entering a small amount of data manually—often through the typewriter. When the computer is a large one, such as the 7090, a smaller computer is often used as an input or output device—either off-line or on-line.

Finally, another class of input-output devices—which, like magnetic tape, may also be thought of as intermediate storage devices—is the so-called "random-access" or "direct-data-access" devices. Specific examples of such devices are magnetic disk and magnetic drum storage units.

Medium	Characteristic				
	Approximate rate of transmission (characters per sec)	Reliability	Sensitivity to environment	Information format
Magnetic tape (input or output)	10,000–100,000	Excellent	Sensitive to heat, humidity, and magnetism; must be kept under carefully controlled conditions	Magnetized spots (usually 7–10 per character)
Paper-tape input	6–600	Fair to good	Somewhat sensitive to extremes of heat and humidity	Punched holes (5–8 per character)
Paper-tape output	6–200	Poor to fair		
Punched-cards input	100–2,000	Fair to good	Somewhat sensitive to extremes of heat and humidity	Punched holes (6–12 per character)
Punched-cards output	100–500	Poor to fair		
Printed-paper output	200–4,000	Fair to good	Rather stable	Ink on paper

Fig. 6-1. Characteristics of some input-output media.

There are a number of reasons why we use peripheral equipment. For one, it permits us to gather—independent of the computer—data from many low-speed intermittent sources which, if tied directly to the machine, could completely limit its processing capacity. Peripheral equipment also permits us to put our data in the best form for computer entry. From the standpoint of quantity and speed, using such equipment, we can translate automatically from a slower and less dense input medium (such as cards or paper tape) directly into a faster and more compact input medium (such as magnetic tape). Thus quantities of data may be presented to the computer in compact batches so it can operate continuously, at high speed, for long periods. Long runs of data usually result in more efficient use of the computer, because if the computer waits between jobs, it waits at human speeds —that is, it waits for human beings to prepare it for the next problem. (Of course, handling extremely large batches of data may create certain other difficulties.)

Peripheral equipment offers similar advantages in output operations. We may, for example, transmit the output information onto magnetic tapes which, as we can see from Fig. 6-1, take information much faster than the attached printers or punches. At our leisure, we may then use peripheral equipment to produce printed or, if we like, punched material. In this way, printed material generated on tape by a single computer may be distributed to several tape-driven printing machines—even if they are in remote locations. Thus the computer can output much more information in a given time than it could through one on-line printer; but the on-line printer might be used if the program has relatively little output, or it might be used to print a part of the total output, the remainder being written on cards or tape.

The several types of on- and off-line equipment give us many different ways of going from basic source information into final output. Figure 6-2 shows, in schematic form, one of the more common processes. Each transformation to a new medium also involves a translation from one code, or format, to another. In some cases this translation is completely built into the equipment; but in the case of the computer, parts of the job may have to be handled by the program. Standard programs, or subroutines, are usually available to relieve the programmer of much of this task; thus the entire process, though containing many stages, is not so difficult as it appears at first glance. It is, on the other hand, not so simple that we do not all dream of the day—far, far in the future—when assorted handwritten documents can be read directly into computers at high speeds, thus eliminating the absolute need for this inconvenient multistep process.

Since our major concern is to learn the principles of input and output, not the details of a variety of input-output devices, we shall, for the remainder of this chapter, discuss only the use of magnetic tape as an input-output media. We shall assume that suitable peripheral equipment is available for preparing or printing the tapes.

Magnetic Tape

Magnetic tape—in one of several forms—is one of the principal input-output media on all the large modern computers. The tape itself is the same kind of tape as used in tape recorders, but of a much higher quality. In the case of the 7090, the tapes are ½ in.

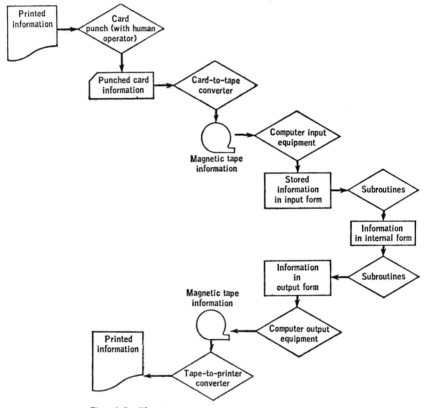

Fig. 6-2. The input-output conversion process.

wide and wound on reels in lengths up to 2,400 ft. The same tape may be used on several different types of tape units on the machine, but we shall discuss only one of the units. On the tape, each character is recorded as some combination of seven magnetized spots across its width. There are, in addition, certain combinations of spots which do not represent the characters 0 to 9, A to Z, and special characters, and which are detected as errors when reading or writing, thus providing one check on the validity of information written on the tape. For example, 556 characters can be recorded on a section of tape 1 in. long. Thus a single 2,400-ft reel of tape could hold over 16 million characters—about enough to hold the complete poetry of Chaucer, Shakespeare, Milton, Donne, Blake, Spenser, Keats, Shelley, Browning, Yeats, and maybe T. S. Eliot thrown in for good measure.

Records

Actually a considerable portion of the space on the tape is not used for recording characters but for separating groups of characters, or *records*, from one another. Any group of characters physically independent from other groups which is to be read (or written) in one operation is generally termed a record—a record might have 5 characters or 5,000 characters. A record might be a logical grouping of information, such as the master payroll record for a single individual; and in this sense, it would correspond quite closely to the same type of information written on a filing card and kept in the files of the payroll department. The tape record is different in several ways, however. For one thing, we would probably not keep a picture of an employee on the tape record. (Pictures can be recorded on magnetic tape—television programs, for example.) Similarly, we would not keep his signature on the tape.

The tape record cannot be read or altered without the use of special equipment, either the computer or peripheral equipment. On the other hand, the tape record is available for high-speed processing of such things as payrolls, tax reporting, payroll analysis, special benefit plans, or mail notices to employees. Figure 6-3 shows an employee record used in a manual payroll system. Figure 6-4 shows the same record as it might be arranged on tape—although, of course, we could not see it on the tape, any more than we can see a symphony recorded on a hi-fi tape.

This record contains 126 characters. Since the tape holds 556 characters per in., all this information is stored on a piece of tape about $\frac{2}{10}$ in. long and $\frac{1}{2}$ in. wide—less than $\frac{1}{10}$ sq in.! The speed of the tape is 112.5 in. per sec, so this record can be read by the computer in about two-thousandths of a second (2 msec). The speed

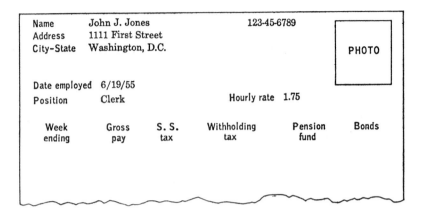

Fig. 6-3. Payroll-record format on filing card.

112.5 in. per sec is over 6 miles of tape per hour. How long would it take to stop an automobile moving 6 mph? The magnetic-tape drive can stop the tape in ⅜ in. and can also bring the tape from a stop to full speed in ⅜ in. In order that the characters may be properly spaced, the tape can be read or written only when moving at full speed. Therefore, since a record is a group of characters which will be read or written in one operation, we must have ⅜ in. of blank tape in front of the record for starting and ⅜ in. behind for stopping. Since records come one after another on the tape, we must have ¾ in. between each pair of records, half for stopping and half for starting the tape. This space is called the end-of-record (EOR) gap.

A tape composed of single employee records (like the one in Fig. 6-4) would be a series of ²⁄₁₀-in. records and ¾-in. EOR gaps. That is, only about 23 per cent of the tape is being used to record information; and consequently the information-transfer rate will be only 23 per cent of the theoretical maximum, since the tape moves over information and EOR gaps at the same speed. Obviously, we should like to reduce the number of EOR gaps so as to eliminate as much "wasted" space as possible, but how can this be done? Think how we could save space in a manual filing system. Just as we might keep two or more employee records on different parts of the same file card, we can keep two or more employee records on one tape record. Notice that the preceding sentence uses the word "record" with two different meanings. The first meaning—in "employee record"—is "a set of information which logically belongs together." The second meaning—in "tape record"—is "a group of characters which will be read or written in one operation."

If we put two employee records into one physical record, we would now be using about 35 per cent of the tape. If we grouped 10 to a record, we would have almost 80 per cent of the tape filled with information, and our records would be 1,260 characters long. At this point, we must ask ourselves just how far we can reasonably carry this process of maximizing the length of our physical records. The size of input and output storage areas and the amount of extra processing needed for grouped records must both be considered before we can choose the optimal size. In any case, it is clear that passing from single records to double records represents a greater saving than passing from 10 to 20—a sort of "law of diminishing returns."

Number of characters

	9	24	1	1	2	3	7	5	6	7	5	6	25	25	

Inter-record gap

Inter-record gap

Information in portion

Number of characters	of tape record of specified length	General category of the information
9	123456789	Social security number
24	JONES	Name
1	J	First initial
1	J	Second initial
2	82	Position code
3	175	Hourly rate
7	XXXXXXX	Gross pay, year to date
5	XXXXX	Social security tax, year to date
6	XXXXXX	Withholding tax, year to date
7	XXXXXXX	Pension fund, year to date
5	XXXXX	Bonds to date
6	061955	Year employed
25	1111 FIRST ST.	Address
25	WASHINGTON, D. C.	City and state

Fig. 6-4. Payroll-record format on tape. All positions not used in a character field are filled with zeros or blanks.

PROBLEMS

6-1. Suppose a school were keeping the complete academic records of its students on magnetic tape.

 a. What information should be in each record?

 b. How much space should be allowed for each item?

 c. Lay out a record format which would hold all the required information, as in Fig. 6-4.

 d. Calculate the physical size of the student record.

 e. What percentage of the tape is used?

 f. How many records could be read in one minute?

 g. If ten students' records were grouped in one physical record, how many records could be read in one minute?

6-2. Suppose each student's record in Prob. 6-1 could be of variable length, depending on how many courses he had taken. If there were equal numbers of students in each of four classes, freshman through senior, how many records —on the average—could be read in 1 minute?

The File

A further division of tape information that has both a logical and physical purpose is the end-of-file mark (EOF), which enables us to combine records into groups of any size up to an entire tape length. We can use the EOF logically to combine records having common characteristics as, for example, in a payroll where each department might be separated by a file mark. Unlike a record, the file mark is found only on the tape and never goes into storage. The EOF is a special bit configuration that originates from the tape-writing device and serves its purpose by being sensed by the reading device which indicates an end-of-file condition. From a processing standpoint, then, the presence of the EOF can be used to indicate the end of a job or the end of a particular phase of a job, without being confused with the actual input data.

A few feet from each end of the tape is a special aluminum marker which the computer can recognize as the physical beginning and ending points of a tape. The beginning-of-tape mark is used for "rewinding" the tape; that is, it shows the point at which the tape must be positioned before the first record can be read or written. The end-of-tape mark is used as a warning device to the computer so that it will not pull the tape off its reel trying to write past the end. If a tape is filled while being written, the program can switch to writing on another tape or can signal the operator to replace the full tape with a new tape. Similar procedures can be followed whenever the computer has read all the information from a tape.

The information on tape, then, is made up of bits *combined* into words (groups of six characters), words *combined* into records, and records *combined* into files. In any problem, we are primarily concerned with the "logical" record—the employee record, for example—and the fields within that logical record. When coding, as we have seen, we have to consider the "physical" record—the information between two gaps. In this way, we may make more efficient use of our tape than by simply making logical records and physical records correspond. In a similar way, we have "logical" files and "physical" files. If the logical file, for example, requires several reels of tape, it would need to be divided into several physical files. We may, of course, have many files (logical or physical) on one reel of tape.

Input-Output Preparation

Ordinarily, the records (and files) are arranged on the tape in the order of use. The same file, however, may be used in several ways; so this arrangement is not always possible. Then the program may have to search the tape for the proper records, or else a preliminary processing must be used to sort the records into the required order and write them onto another tape. Searching will usually prove faster when only a few of the records are needed, but when most of the file is to be processed, a sort will prove advantageous. Programming time spent in organizing input and output operation so as to achieve minimum processing time will frequently be more rewarding than similar efforts made with the internal processing. The internal world of the 7090 measures operations in microseconds, while the external world, the human world, finds seconds or minutes a convenient time scale. Between these two worlds lie the input-output devices whose actions are counted in milliseconds. These devices seem fast to us but are quite slow from the computer's viewpoint—looking out. The programmer, if he wishes to make efficient use of the computer, tries to .avoid situations where the internal processing must wait for some information from its external world—its input devices in general and people in particular. Thus a computer achieves maximum efficiency when its input and output devices can exchange information with the internal program as needed and produced. Naturally a given computer will not be able to produce this kind of efficiency on all jobs: some jobs will overtax the input-output facilities, others the central processing unit. Most computers are designed with this fact in mind—they permit the user to choose from a large variety of input-output configurations and a usually smaller variety of central processor configurations.

The Input-Output Channel

The 7090 has a great deal of this flexibility, but for the purposes of simplicity, we shall confine all our examples to one particular configuration. We shall assume that our machine has four independent "channels" through which data may be transmitted. That is, we may have as many as four separate input-output operations proceeding simultaneously, each under the supervision of one of the channels, which are, of course, the subsidiary input-output control computers of Fig. 2-10. The central processing unit, as we know, has control over these channels.

Once started, however, the channels generally operate independently of the course of the main program. Let us also assume that, to each of these channels (which are designated by the letters A, B, C, and D), five tape units are attached. The tape units attached to each channel are more flexible in assigned designation in that each tape may be given any number 1 through 10 by simply turning a dial on the unit. Just as we assign symbolic names to locations, we shall ordinarily use symbols rather than numbers to designate tape units on any channel. On the other hand, we shall not generally include the channel in the symbolic assignment, because we shall usually want to know the channel of a tape unit so we can tell which other units may be in operation simultaneously. For example, tape 3 on channel A may be reading while tape 6 on channel B is writing or tape 4 on channel C is reading; *but no two tapes on a single channel may be transmitting information simultaneously.*

Since the tape moves 112.5 in. per sec, and 556 characters may be recorded on each inch, one tape can exchange information with the computer at a rate of 62,550 characters per second. Thus, with four such tapes operating simultaneously, over 250,000 characters may be brought into the memory of the computer in 1 second. A large unabridged dictionary could be scanned in about 2 minutes, if recorded on a tape of this speed. The average time, then, for the computer to find any word in such a dictionary would be about 1 minute, a rate possibly a little slower than a person might do. But if people cannot read 250,000 characters per second, why can they look up words faster than the computer can? The answer lies in the concept of *access.*

When looking in a dictionary, you have equal access to any page—one motion opens to the back or front or middle with essentially equal ease. To the computer, however, a dictionary on tape is a long succession of characters. No section is accessible until the preceding section has been read—or at least skipped over. The situation is much like that facing a movie-goer who arrives in the middle of the feature. He must wait until the rest of the film is shown before the part he wants to see comes up; so, whether he watches or not, the same amount of waiting is required. Similarly, the tape can be moved forward only at one speed, whether it is being read or skipped over. As a storage medium, then, the tape is characterized by an *access time*—the time to locate the desired information—which *varies* depending on the data sought.

Information-access Considerations

Before reading a record from the tape, the computer must have the tape in position to read that record—that is, the reading (or writing) mechanism (called "read-write head") must be in the EOR gap before the record. Much time can be saved by minimizing the amount of positioning which must be done. If possible, the program should use the records in the same order in which they occur on the tape; for since each record must move past the read-write head in order to be used, the tape will then always be automatically in position to read the next record. As we saw earlier, such an adventitious circumstance is not always forthcoming; but even when we are forced to search a file, we can often arrange it in such a way as to reduce searching time by large factors. In a great many applications which require file searching, about 80 per cent of the searches are for 20 per cent of the items. By arranging the file so that this active 20 per cent is grouped at the beginning, we can cut our average searching time by about a factor of 5. More generally, whether searching or sorting to obtain the required sequence of information, any special knowledge of the constitution of the file will enable us to process it more efficiently. Usually, however, additional programming effort will be required, and we shall have to balance the cost of programming against the savings in processing time.

It is important to recall at this point that access to words in the primary storage does *not* depend on the location used. One location is as accessible as another, like the pages in a book. We call this type of storage device *random access* as opposed to the *nonrandom* tape. Other computer devices are called *semirandom* because, although all words are not equally accessible, the device never has to be scanned in its entirety for any one word. For example, if we split our dictionary into eight parts and put each on a separate tape, we now have a semirandom-access scheme, with the eight tapes together forming a "device." The program must first decide which tape contains the desired word and then must search only that tape to find it. Thus we never search more than one-eighth of the file for any one word. Again, this procedure requires a more elaborate program than does the simple scanning of a single tape.

We could, of course, combine this "split-file" technique with the technique of placing the commonly used words at the beginning of each tape. At the cost of increased program complexity, this combination could reduce our average searching time to one-fortieth of the average when sequentially scanning the entire dictionary.

Many other techniques are available for speeding up a search. We may note that in the previous method we are not making balanced use of our system; for at any one time, three of our four channels will be idle. Could we utilize this idle equipment to further increase our searching speed? We can if we require a number of searches instead of only one. There is no reason, for example, why four searches cannot be proceeding simultaneously if we have words falling in different parts of the split file. In this case, whether or not we can keep all four channels busy all the time depends on how the data (the words to be looked up) happen to come out. Over a large batch of words, this technique would probably result in two or three times faster searching. We might, then, search 100 times faster than our original method.

Types of Process Limitations

At this point, a word of caution. We have been making our program increasingly complex, but we have continued to assume that the time to move the tape would be the limiting factor in searching. In other words, we have neglected all internal processing time as being negligible because of the substantially faster time scale. As the internal program gets more complex, we may reasonably assume that it will take longer to execute. Eventually, we may pass the point where it takes longer to decide what to do with a record than it does to read that record. When this happens, it will no longer be profitable to search for more complex methods, unless they reduce the total number of records processed. When a program runs in this way, so that the central processing unit is occupied 100 per cent of the time while the channels are idle some of the time, we call the program "process-limited" or "process-bound." Such a program can be improved (timewise) only by speeding up the internal processing or by reducing the number of cases considered.

The opposite case, when the central processing unit must stand idle waiting for more data to flow in or out, is called "input limited," "output limited," or "input-output limited," as the case may be. It would clearly be foolish to spend time trying to speed up internal processing in this case, since the internal program is already waiting for the input-output units. If you catch the first train in the morning by walking to the station, you will not get to work earlier by running. Of course, many programs are neither process-limited nor input-output limited. Some are balanced; others are limited by processing some of the time, by input or output at other times.

Still, the concept of a limiting operation is a useful one when choosing methods. The relationship between the internal processing speed and the rate at which information may flow in and out often determines which method is best for a given computer. If the internal speed is relatively great, we can execute complex programs without getting process-limited; otherwise we are forced to stick with simpler methods. For example, let us return to the simple method of searching an entire file not arranged in any special order. On the 7090, this process would be so input bound that we could actually search for *over ten thousand* words simultaneously—*using four channels at once* —and still pass the tapes at full speed. Thus we might achieve an *average* searching time *forty thousand times* faster than on a machine with the same tape speed but with much slower internal processing (provided, of course, we had ten thousand words to look up). In other words, a *change in the relative speeds* of the various units (including a change of the entire system relative to human speed) may mean a *change in kind*—a change in basic methods. This phenomenon is especially important when moving an application from one computer to another (or considering such a move). It is so easy—and therefore it commonly occurs—to treat a new machine as just a "hopped-up" (or "toned-down") version of its predecessor.

One of the worst areas of improper computer usage occurs in this translation of a computer program from one computer to another. If a superior computer is simply treated as a hopped-up version of its less capable predecessor the chances are excellent that we shall cause the former to operate at the logical level and capacity of the latter. The tendency simply to accept a working programmed system "as is" for a new computer is a strong one, but improvements to the operation of an existing system often hold enough weight to cause the creation of a new system for the new machine. If a transition is to be made from one computer to a lesser computer, the problems arising emphasize quite different difficulties. Now we must carefully decide what parts of the current system are to be extracted for operation in the toned-down computer and then combine these extracts into one unified operating system. In neither case will the transition be hindered by the existence of complete, accurate, and clear documentation of the present system.

If the program has been written in a higher level language, such as FORTRAN, it may be possible to get a working program on a new system simply by recompiling the old program using the new system's FORTRAN compiler. In fact, one of the early arguments for higher level languages was this ability to move programs from one machine to another with a minimum of difficulty. Experience over several generations of machine changes indicates that with FORTRAN, at least, such savings have been realized. This experience has also shown, however, that FORTRAN programs are not always machine-independent, particularly when it comes to the matter of organizing input and output, for this task is left mostly to the programmer and depends on how he organizes his FORTRAN program. The ease of conversion may make it worthwhile to retain old FORTRAN programs without revision—particularly if they are infrequently used—but most installations have found that a rethinking of their most popular programs paid handsome dividends to a new machine.

Positioning the Tape

In general, the central processing unit is responsible for putting a tape in the position required for a particular reading or writing operation. If that positioning does not occur automatically as a result of past operations, it is necessary to issue special positioning—or "non-data"—instructions to the appropriate data channel. As the names imply, no data are transmitted as a direct result of these operations, although they may cause certain conditions to be detected by the tape unit and indicated to the central processing unit. For example, when spacing forward along a tape, we may detect an end of file or an end of tape. These conditions can be tested by the program.

At the start of a program, all tapes used will usually be placed at the beginning-of-tape mark, or *load point*. The load point is always the starting position for the first record of the first file on the tape and thus serves as a convenient reference point. In order to position the tape at the load point, we use the REWIND (REW) instruction. Execution of the REW causes the designated tape to start moving backward. This operation in no way interferes with the program, which proceeds with the execution as the tape is moved backward to the load point. If the tape was at the load point to begin with, nothing happens. If we try to do something else to that tape while it is rewinding, that operation is delayed until the load point is reached. Thus we cannot interfere with the rewinding process.

Example. A program is to use five tapes, as follows:

Channel	Symbolic tape name
A	INTAPE
B	EXTAPE
C	ERRTPE
D	OUTTPE
A	AUXTPE

We wish, in block A1, to put all five tapes in the starting position. The coding would be as follows:

A1	REWA	INTAPE
	REWB	EXTAPE
	REWC	ERRTPE
	REWD	OUTTPE
	REWA	AUXTPE

(Notice that we append the channel letter to the operation code, while the symbolic tape name is written as an address.) Instruction A1 will start INTAPE rewinding on channel A, and the succeeding instructions perform similar functions. In this case, we shall have two tapes— INTAPE and AUXTPE—rewinding on the same channel at the same time. This operation is possible because, since no data are being moved, it does not violate the rule which prevents two tapes on the same channel from *exchanging data* with the central processing unit simultaneously.

Of course, rewinding is not restricted to the beginning of a program; tapes may be rewound at any time. Tapes are often rewound at the end of a program, especially if they are to be removed; for although the operator can manually initiate the rewind of a tape, it will simplify his task if the program does this job for him.

When reading a tape, we may not wish to start with the first file, or we may wish to skip over some file. Also we may wish to move back to the beginning of some file other than the first. In order to move the tape backward, we may use the operation BACKSPACE FILE (BSF), which moves the designated tape back until it moves across an end-of-file mark. In other words, BSF causes the tape to be positioned at the end of the previous file. Executing a BSF when the tape is at the load point will not move the tape. Instead an indication is made that the tape is at its beginning. Obviously, if we wish to move back over several files, we can execute more than one BSF.

If we wish to move *forward* one file, we must use a series of instructions. Consequently we shall defer discussion of this procedure.

Selecting the Tape

When positioning a tape by rewinding or backspacing, it was necessary for the program to designate the channel involved and to tell that channel which of its tapes to use. This process is appropriately referred to as *selection*. Selection, in general, implies movement of the selected tape, the only exception being when the designated movement would have caused the tape to be backed over the load point. The selection instructions fall into two classes: the *non-data* selects, of which BSF and REW were examples, and the *data* selects. The data selects always result in a *forward* movement of tape, but they do *not necessarily* result in any data transmission between the tape and computer storage. That is, the data select must be followed by further instruction to the channel for data transmission to occur; otherwise only a forward movement of tape will result.

Let us examine this concept more thoroughly. The data selects may be further broken down into *read* selects and *write* selects, depending on whether the intention is to bring information into storage or to send it out. If a read select is given, and a certain time goes by without subsequent directions being given to that channel, the tape is simply moved forward one record. In similar circumstances with a write select, a section of tape is "erased"—that is, made blank. When that section is subsequently read, it is considered as part of the EOR gap and is, for most intents and purposes, ignored.

Both these circumstances have their uses, even though they result in no information flow. The read select clearly gives us a way of moving forward along the tape one record at a time. If we wish to skip over 17 records, we can issue 17 read selects. For the purposes of the read select, the EOF mark is considered to be one record, and if we space over an EOF in this way, a special indicator called the EOF indicator is turned on. This indicator can be tested with a special conditional transfer, ignored, or used to cause trapping to a special location for that channel.

Erasing a section of tape can be useful in the case where some blemish on the tape surface occurs. Such imperfections as nicks, creases, dirt, blisters, or bubbles may make a certain small area of the tape unsuitable for recording—a fact which will be discovered when we attempt to write on it. A trap can then take place to a routine which erases that section and allows the program to try writing again in a new spot. This procedure enables the program to be less sensitive to slight tape damage and thus enhances smooth operation.

Besides BSF and REW, there is one other non-data select instruction—which also results in moving the tape backward. This operation, BACKSPACE RECORD (BSR), is analogous to a read select in that it can be used to move the tape over one record. BSR, however, moves *back* one record; and, unlike a read select, it can never be associated with information flow and can never result in a movement of more than a single record.

Information may be transcribed onto the tape in one of two code formats, or *modes*. We already know that the information bits used by the computer may be combined into different configurations for different purposes. In the same manner, tape information can be in either a bit-oriented, or *binary*, mode or a character-oriented, or *decimal*, mode—both, of course, being written on the same physical kind of tape. The decimal tape is used in conjunction with character-oriented peripheral devices such as printers or card-to-tape converters;

while the binary tape, on the other hand, might be used to control a milling machine or a plotting device or may have been generated directly from a radar set or the instruments associated with a wind tunnel. In other words, where one machine is communicating more or less directly with another as an end in itself, a bit-oriented code is usually the most economical. This rule holds true when both the machines involved are the 7090 itself, that is, when the tape is written to store temporarily data which will be read back later.

Distinction between the two modes is made directly by having different data-select instructions for each (non-data-select instructions obviously need not distinguish between the modes). Between the binary select and the corresponding decimal select, only the method of code translation changes, not the method of transmission, so that, when we learn two of the following four instructions, we know them all:

READ TAPE	BINARY	(RTB)
READ TAPE	DECIMAL	(RTD)
WRITE TAPE	BINARY	(WTB)
WRITE TAPE	DECIMAL	(WTD)

Each of these instructions may (with the proper channel designator affixed) refer to any channel. For purposes of skipping records or erasing sections of tape, either the binary or decimal mode instructions may be used, although false error indications may be generated.

It is permissible, and is often desirable, to intermix binary records and decimal records on one tape. (A given record must obviously be of a single mode, because if we give a new select instruction to change the mode, a new record is started.) For example, a common practice is to have the first file of every tape in an installation be one or more decimal-mode identification records. Thus not only can the *computer* check every tape for proper identification, but any unlabeled tape may be put on a peripheral printer in order to identify it to the operator.

If the program attempts to read a binary tape in the decimal mode, or vice versa, an error indication will be given. This indication cannot be distinguished from that caused by reading actual erroneous information. By rereading the record in the other mode, however, the two cases can be separated.

PROBLEMS

Assume that TI, on channel A, has 10 files, each two records long (not, of course, including EOF), written on it.

X1	REWA	TI
	RTBA	TI
	RTBA	TI
	RTBA	TI
X2	BSFA	TI
	RTBA	TI
	RTBA	TI
	RTBA	TI
	RTBA	TI
	BSRA	TI
X3	BSFA	TI
	BSFA	TI
X4	BSRA	TI

In the above program where will TI be positioned:

6-3. After instruction X2?

6-4. After instruction X3?

6-5. After instruction X4?

Write a program which will position TI:

6-6. At the end of the second record in the first file.

6-7. At the beginning of the third file.

6-8. Between the first and second records on the second file.

Data Transmission—Writing

Writing is generally the simpler form of data transmission because, when writing, the program is in complete control of the information it wishes to write. This is not the case with reading when we may wish to do different steps depending on just what, and how much, information we find on the tape. Consequently, we shall first consider the process of writing.

Once we have selected a tape for writing, we must supply the channel with a list specifying the words we wish to write on that tape. This list consists of one or more *commands* each of which specifies *how many* words we are to write (word count), *where* the first of these words is found in storage (address), and in *what manner* the writing is to take place (operation). The *instruction*, RESET AND LOAD CHANNEL (RCH), sends the first of these *commands* to the channel. When the channel finishes with that command, it either terminates the writing (disconnects) or automatically fetches a new command in the list.

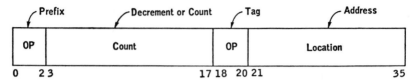

Fig. 6-5. Input-output command format—one word.

Let us start with a simple one-command list. We shall use the command INPUT OR OUTPUT UNDER COUNT CONTROL AND DISCONNECT (IOCD). (The same commands may be used to specify either input or output lists; the previous select instruction determines which type of transmission is used.) If we wish to use this command to cause the writing of an output record of 500 words, from consecutive locations starting with location QRQ, we write it as follows:

C1   IOCD   QRQ, 0, 500

The resultant command occupies one word, which may be referred to as C1. The address portion of that word contains the location number symbolized by QRQ. Bits 3 to 17 of C1 (these 15 bits are often referred to as the *decrement* or *count* portion of a word) contain the number 500. Bits 0, 1, and 2 (often called the *prefix* of the word) and bits 18 to 20 (called the *tag*) specify the operation, IOCD. Figure 6-5 illustrates this word format.

Now, if we have the above command in memory, the following two instructions (be sure you keep in mind the difference between command and instruction) in a program will cause a 500-word record to be written on tape TX2, channel B, in the binary mode:

X1   WTBB   TX2
       RCHB   C1
X2

The instruction at X1, WRITE TAPE BINARY—CHANNEL B— TAPE TX2, selects the tape we have specified, sets up the proper circuits for writing on it in the binary mode, and starts the tape in motion. The instruction at X1 + 1 fetches the word at C1 and sends it, as a command, to the special registers of channel B. There the address, operation, and word count will direct the channel in the actual transmission, and a 500-word record will be written. After the writing of the five-hundredth word the tape unit will be automatically disconnected (unselected). While this writing is taking place, the program proceeds to instruction X2. Thus only five cycles (two for WTBB and three for RCHB) are taken from the CPU (central processing unit) program in order to get the writing under way. Channel B, however, will be busy for a short period of time (several milliseconds); so if the CPU tries to use it again for data transmission within that time, the CPU program will have to wait. Of course, the other channels may be used during this time without interfering with either the CPU program or the operation of channel B. For example, suppose we also wish to write a 375-word record on tape 8RZ, which is on channel C. If the block of words we wish to write starts with location WL, we can set up the following command to direct the operation:

C2   IOCD   WL, 0, 375

Our CPU program could now read

X1	WTBB	TX2
	RCHB	C1
X2	WTBC	8RZ
	RCHC	C2
X3		

When the CPU program reaches X3, three programs will be in simultaneous operation—one in the CPU, one in channel B (writing 500 words), and one in channel C (writing 375 words).

Frequently the data for one record will not be found in a single block of consecutive locations. With the IOCD command *alone*, however, we can write only a single block into a single record. The command INPUT OR OUTPUT UNDER COUNT CONTROL AND PROCEED (IOCP) enables us to bring together several blocks of words into a single record. IOCP differs from IOCD only in that it *does not disconnect* the tape unit when the proper number of words has been counted. Instead the *following* command is automatically fetched from storage and placed in the channel and writing proceeds —*on the same record*. Thus, if we wish to write four blocks—B1 (50 words), B2 (75 words), B3 (28 words), and B4 (81 words)—into one 234-word record on tape A1B, channel D, we could write the following *set* of commands:

$$
\begin{array}{llll}
\text{C3} & \text{IOCP} & \text{B1, 0, 50} \\
& \text{IOCP} & \text{B2, 0, 75} \\
& \text{IOCP} & \text{B3, 0, 28} \\
& \text{IOCD} & \text{B4, 0, 81}
\end{array}
$$

The CPU program can initiate this channel program by executing

$$
\begin{array}{lll}
\text{X3} & \text{WTBD} & \text{A1B} \\
& \text{RCHD} & \text{C3} \\
\text{X4}
\end{array}
$$

As the CPU program proceeds to X4, the channel will execute C3, then (C3 + 1), then (C3 + 2), and finally disconnect after performing the IOCD command at (C3 + 3). Since only the IOCD command can cause a normal termination of the channel program, a channel program can be of any length but can have at most one IOCD.

The ability to write more than one block in memory into a record gives the programmer much output flexibility, especially in combining several logical records into one physical record. We may, however, wish to write one logical record as several physical records; but with only IOCP and IOCD, we would have to reselect the tape each time we wished to start a new record. (Why?) In order that we might eliminate such multiple selection, another command is provided: INPUT OR OUTPUT UNDER *RECORD* CONTROL AND PROCEED (IORP). The IORP acts like an IOCP in that it does not disconnect the tape after writing the specified number of words, but it acts like an IOCD in that it causes an EOR gap to be written. Thus we can both terminate a physical record and continue on with a channel program so as to write the next physical record without reselecting the tape.

Suppose we wish to write the four blocks of the previous problem into *four separate physical records*. We can use the same CPU program—selecting the tape only once—if we change the command program to read

$$
\begin{array}{llll}
\text{C3} & \text{IORP} & \text{B1, 0, 50} \\
& \text{IORP} & \text{B2, 0, 75} \\
& \text{IORP} & \text{B3, 0, 28} \\
& \text{IOCD} & \text{B4, 0, 81}
\end{array}
$$

The first three records are written by IORP's; the last, by an IOCD. (Why is the last record not written with an IORP?)

Sometimes we wish to have *all* physical records, even the last, written with IORP's so that we may rearrange the commands—and thereby rearrange the corresponding output records—with a simple procedure. We can accomplish this task with the following command program:

$$
\begin{array}{lll}
\text{C3} & \text{IORP} & \text{B1, 0, 50} \\
 & \text{IORP} & \text{B2, 0, 75} \\
 & \text{IORP} & \text{B3, 0, 28} \\
 & \text{IORP} & \text{B4, 0, 81} \\
 & \text{IOCD} & \text{0, 0, 0} \\
\end{array}
$$

The IOCD with a word count of zero simply causes the tape to disconnect since no further transmission is specified.

It is clear that each of the records written by the channel program need not be composed of a single block. For example, we might wish to write our four blocks as two consecutive records, one of 125 words and one of 109 words. We could then write

$$
\begin{array}{lll}
\text{C3} & \text{IOCP} & \text{B1, 0, 50} \\
 & \text{IORP} & \text{B2, 0, 75} \\
 & \text{IOCP} & \text{B3, 0, 28} \\
 & \text{IOCD} & \text{B4, 0, 81} \\
\end{array}
$$

PROBLEMS

What would the following command programs write?

$$
\begin{array}{llll}
\text{6-9.} & \text{C3} & \text{IORP} & \text{B1, 0, 50} \\
 & & \text{IOCP} & \text{B2, 0, 75} \\
 & & \text{IORP} & \text{B3, 0, 28} \\
 & & \text{IOCD} & \text{B4, 0, 81} \\
\text{6-10.} & \text{C3} & \text{IOCP} & \text{B1, 0, 50} \\
 & & \text{IORP} & \text{B2, 0, 75} \\
 & & \text{IORP} & \text{B3, 0, 28} \\
 & & \text{IOCD} & \text{B4, 0, 81} \\
\text{6-11.} & \text{C3} & \text{IORP} & \text{B1, 0, 50} \\
 & & \text{IOCP} & \text{B2, 0, 75} \\
 & & \text{IOCP} & \text{B3, 0, 28} \\
 & & \text{IOCD} & \text{B4, 0, 81} \\
\end{array}
$$

Given five blocks of data—H (120 words), I (90 words), J (220 words), K (160 words), and L (98 words)—write them in the order of H, I, J, K, L as:

6-12. One record.

6-13. Five records.

6-14. Two records (H, I, J) and (K, L).

6-15. Three records (H, I), (J), and (K, L).

6-16. Write the blocks H, I, J, K, and L as four records in the order (I), (K, J), (L), (H).

6-17. Why is it useful to be able to rearrange commands when we can rearrange blocks of data instead?

6-18. Can we write part of a block on one record and part on another? Can we write parts of a block and not write others?

Data Transmission—Reading

The pattern, or general scheme, for reading is the same as for writing, but we must suitably reinterpret the input-output commands. Suppose we write the program

```
Y1      RTBA        XYZ
        RCHA        C1
Y2
```

to be used with the command

```
        C1    IOCD        QRQ, 0, 500
```

This example differs from one of our previous examples only in the instruction in Y1, which selects a tape for *reading* rather than for writing. If we are reading one 500-word record, the programs are completely analogous. When writing, such a program would always produce a 500-word record; but when reading, we do not necessarily have a 500-word record forthcoming on the tape. Consequently we must reinterpret the meaning of IOCD. When reading, this IOCD means: Bring in the *next* 500 words from the selected tape and store them in the block starting at QRQ; then disconnect and stop the tape at the *next available place*. In the case of a 500-word record, then, the entire record is read and the tape stops in the following EOR gap. In the case of a record longer than 500 words, only the *first* 500 words will be read, and the tape will stop in the gap at the end of the record, ignoring the remaining record words as input data. Since the tape cannot be stopped in the middle of a record, this EOR gap is the "next available place." Thus an IOCD may cause reading of only part of a record but always causes movement of at least one record.

If the record to be read with this program had fewer than 500 words, the channel would proceed with the following record (or records) until 500 words had been obtained. Thus this one IOCD could read 500 one-word records or 100 five-word records or four 100-word records and the first 100 words of a 350-word record. Just how many records are moved depends on the layout of the records on the tape, but 500 *words are always obtained.* In effect the IOCD command looks at the tape record as being continuous, with no physical record gaps except for the final end of record, which the IOCD seeks after fetching all the necessary words.

The IOCP command again works just like IOCD without the disconnect. With IOCP we can separate the information on one record into blocks of various lengths in storage. When reading, the commands

```
C3      IOCP       B1, 0, 50
        IOCP       B2, 0, 75
        IOCP       B3, 0, 28
        IOCD       B4, 0, 81
```

take the next 234 words—regardless of their division into physical records—and transmit them into four blocks in storage. In other words, an IOCD or IOCP always causes transmission of the number of words specified in the word count.

In many applications, we do not know in advance how many words we wish to read. For example, suppose we were processing a file for personnel statistics, where each record contained information on a particular individual. Since the amount of information available on different individuals might vary greatly, we would waste a great deal of space on tape if we made all records of equal length—the length of the longest record. We would also experience some difficulty if a new longer record were introduced into the file, because *all* records would now have to be expanded to meet the new size. Consequently we might plan to let each record have its own unique size—just long enough to hold the necessary information. Now we have minimized the length of the tape, but we can no longer read the records under count control. The IORP command, however, gives us a way to read one and only one record *no matter what its length.*

When reading, the command

$$\text{IORP} \quad \text{B1, 0, 50}$$

means "Read into a block starting at B1 all the words—up to 50—from the next record. In no case read more than one record or more than 50 words." This command could then be used for reading any record which was 50 words long or less. The word count protects the program from reading a record which was longer than the space allotted in storage, for by making the count equal to the longest record we expect to find, we can safely read all legitimate records. If we do not wish to continue after reading one record, we can follow the IORP with an IOCD having a word count of zero, which simply disconnects the tape.

To summarize: Under *count control,* we always get a *fixed number of words;* under *record control,* we always *move the tape one record* and we *get at most the number of words specified in the count.* The following examples will illustrate these principles:

Suppose we have a tape which has five 50-word records—A, B, C, D, and E. We execute the following commands after selecting a tape for reading:

Case I   IOCD   X1, 0, 250

reads all 250 words into block X1 and stops the tape after record E.

Case II   IORP   X1, 0, 250
            IOCD   0, 0, 0

reads 50 words from record A into block X1 and stops the tape at the end of record A.

Case III   IOCP   X1, 0, 75
             IORP   X2, 0, 50
             IOCD   0, 0, 0

reads the first 75 words (record A and 25 words of record B) into block X1, reads the last 25 words of record B into block X2, and stops the tape after record B.

Case IV   IORP   X1, 0, 25
            IOCD   X2, 0, 75

reads the first 25 words of record A into block X1, reads record B and the first 25 words of record C into block X2, and stops the tape after record C.

Editing

Editing is the process of putting data into a format more conducive to operation. Generally we distinguish the editing process from the translation process that must take place between computer, on-line component, and user, though both these processes are normally found working together. Translation puts our data into a form that can be recognized by certain instructions of the computer, while editing consists in taking these translated data into and out of a format which is easier for the computer user to handle.

Two important editing functions are the extraction of particular portions of a block of information either for computer use or for output, and the rearrangement of a record into different formats. The latter function deserves some additional comment. A common occurrence in the handling of a tape is for the different users to request a printing of its information in different combinations based on different criteria. The information on the tape is found in a format that is best suited for general operation and as such is not going to satisfy the majority of user requests. Hence we shall often edit this information as it is being read into storage. At other times, we shall edit the information just before the printing or just before we place the output data onto a tape for peripheral processing.

A slight modification to our normal commands gives us a most convenient method of selecting out of a tape record only those particular words desired. By simply placing an N after the last letter of a command, we cause it to function exactly as it did without the N except that *no* data will pass from tape to the computer storage. For example, the following command sequence:

$$\text{IOCPN} \quad 0,\ 0,\ 34$$
$$\text{IOCD} \quad \text{X1},\ 0,\ 57$$

will cause the first 34 words encountered to be passed over without entering storage. The second command results in 57 words entering storage starting at location X1 with the tape being disconnected after the fifty-seventh word is read. From this example we see that it does not matter what we place into the address field of a non-data transfer command since the words designated by this command do not enter storage.

Let us consider several other examples using the five 50-word records—A, B, C, D, and E.

$$\text{Case V} \quad \text{IORP} \quad \text{X1},\ 0,\ 50$$

IORPN	XX, 0, 50
IORP	X2, 0, 50
IORPN	XX, 0, 50
IOCD	X3, 0, 10

reads 50 words from record A into block X1, skips record B, reads 50 words from record C into block X2, skips record D, reads 10 words from record E into block X3, and stops the tape after record E.

Case VI	IOCP	X1, 0, 105
	IORPN	XX, 0, 1
	IOCPN	XX, 0, 40
	IOCD	X3, 0, 18

reads 105 words from records A, B, and C into block X1, skips the remaining words from record C (note that any value of the count in the second command would accomplish the same thing), skips the first 40 words from record D, puts the last 10 words of D and the first 8 of E into block X3, and stops after record E.

Now that we have spent some time dealing with both the input-output *instructions* and input-output *commands,* we can see more clearly the distinction between them. The input-output instruction deals with the *physical* operation of the tape itself. Are we rewinding the tape; backspacing the tape; reading the tape; writing the tape? All these instructions tell us how we manipulate the tape. The commands, however, do not refer to the physical tape, but to the *information* on the tape. Do we read in the next 10 words; do we skip the next 40 words; do we ignore end-of-record indications? Our command is indeed the "editor."

PROBLEMS

Using the five 50-word records do the following:

6-19. Bring in every other 10 words.

6-20. Read in only the first five words of record E in inverse order.

6-21. Combine the first five words of each record, the second five words of each record, etc., into 10 new 25-word records.

A Complete Program

Now that we have learned some of the input and output operations, we can combine this knowledge with the control and processing instructions we already know to write our first complete program. Suppose we have a decimal tape composed of a file of 20-word records. We do not know how many records are in the file, but we know that an EOF mark is placed at the end. We wish to select from this tape all those records whose first word is zero and whose last (twentieth) word is negative. These selected records are to be written on another tape—which is our output. Figure 6-6 gives a flow diagram for this problem (Figs. 6-6b and 6-6c give details of blocks X2 and X7).

Block X1 simply puts the tapes in the starting position—the load point. Block X2 reads a record from ITAPE (which the memory box indicates is our input tape), and if the reading is successful, blocks X5 and X6 determine whether or not this record should be selected. If the record is selected, it is written on OTAPE; otherwise control is returned to block X2 for reading the next record. The process continues—some records being written, others being passed by—until an attempt is made to read the EOF mark. Since this mark indicates that there are no further input data, control is passed to block X3, which terminates the output tape with an EOF mark and rewinds the two tapes. Block X4 then ends the program.

It is clear from the flow diagram that we do not yet know quite enough instructions to write a code for this problem. In block X3, for example, we shall have to write an EOF mark on the output tape. This job is done with the WRITE END OF FILE (WEF) instruction.

In blocks X2A and X7A, we shall have to determine whether or not the specified channel has completed its operation. This test can be made with the conditional transfer instruction TRANSFER ON CHANNEL IN OPERATION (TCO). If the channel designated by the instruction is in operation (not disconnected) when this test is made, a transfer of control is executed; otherwise the CPU takes the next instruction in sequence.

In block X2B, we must find out if we have just passed an EOF mark. The recognition of passing over the EOF mark automatically causes the EOF indicator to be turned on for that channel. The conditional transfer instruction TRANSFER ON END OF FILE (TEF) will test that indicator and transfer control if the indicator is found to be on. As a result of the test, the EOF indicator is turned off.

Now that we seem to have an adequate stock of instructions, we must decide on the locations (or symbolic names of locations) for

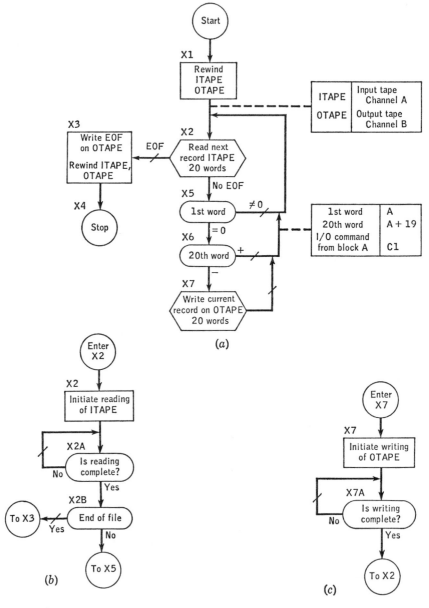

Fig. 6-6. A complete program for selecting certain records from a tape.

our data. In this case, we have 20 words which we shall place in a block starting in location A. It is not enough, however, simply to decide on a name for our block of data; we must *inform the assembly program* of our intentions. We want to tell the assembly program to set aside a block of 20 locations and to name the first location in the block A. How do we give the assembly program directions? We make use of a pseudo-instruction, that is, one that is used simply to relay information to the assembly program. In this case, we shall use the pseudo-instruction BLOCK STARTING SYMBOL (BSS) as follows:

A   BSS   20

This line in the code tells the assembly program that A is the symbol for the first location in a block of 20 locations. The assembly program remembers the name A and reserves the block.

We shall also need an input-output command for controlling transmission of this block. Since all records are fixed at 20 words in length we can write

C1   IOCD   A, 0, 20

Notice (Fig. 6-6) how the memory box may be used to show the location of the I/O command as well as the location of the data.

Now we may begin to code our CPU program. Let us start with the subblocks and work outward. First, block X2:

X2	RTDA	ITAPE	Selects decimal-mode input tape for reading
	RCHA	C1	Sends command to channel A
X2A	TCOA	X2A	Delays until operation is complete
X2B	TEFA	X3	Tests for end of file
	TRA	X5	No EOF—continue

Let us examine the third instruction, X2A TCOA X2A, more carefully. What does this instruction do for us? TCOA, remember, tests to see if channel A is in operation. Now, if channel A is *not* in operation, control simply passes to the next instruction at location X2B; but if channel A is operating, we transfer control to the location specified by the address portion of the instruction. In this use of the instruction, however, we find that control passes back to the instruction itself. In fact, as long as channel A is operating, control will not pass beyond this one instruction, TCOA; so we effectively have a control "road block" until all our required tape data have been read into storage, and this is exactly what we desire (see Fig. 6-6a). The use of TCOA in this form is an important, though crude, means of controlling our central processing unit—preventing the CPU from prematurely interfering with the tape data processing. For example, we certainly do not want to test the contents of the location supposed to contain our twentieth word before that word has entered the computer storage. Next, block X7 is coded:

X7	WTDB	OTAPE	Selects decimal-mode output tape for writing
	RCHB	C1	Sends command to channel
X7A	TCOB	X7A	Delays until operation is complete
	TRA	X2	

Blocks X5 and X6 are simple tests:

X5	CLA	A	Tests first word
	TNZ	X2	
X6	CLA	A + 19	Tests twentieth word
	TPL	X2	
	TRA	X7	

Notice how the address, A + 19, may be used to specify the nineteenth word *after* word A. Since A is the first word in the block, the nineteenth word *after* A is the twentieth, or last, word. This notation —called *relative addressing*—enables us to refer to locations which have no special names by indicating their relative positions to a given symbolically referenced location. Normally such relative addressing is limited to data references in that we gain very little, but may lose a great deal, in employing such a coding system throughout the program. (Why?)

Blocks X1, X3, and X4 are straightforward:

X1	REWA	ITAPE
	REWB	OTAPE
	TRA	X2
X3	WEFB	OTAPE
	REWA	ITAPE
	REWB	OTAPE
X4	HPR	X4

If we put all these parts together, selecting the order of the blocks so as to eliminate certain TRA instructions, we obtain the following code:

```
A     BSS     20
C1    IOCD    A, 0, 20
X1    REWA    ITAPE
      REWB    OTAPE
X2    RTDA    ITAPE
      RCHA    C1
X2A   TCOA    X2A
X2B   TEFA    X3
X5    CLA     A
      TNZ     X2
X6    CLA     A + 19
      TPL     X2
X7    WTDB    OTAPE
      RCHB    C1
X7A   TCOB    X7A
      TRA     X2
X3    WEFB    OTAPE
      REWA    ITAPE
      REWB    OTAPE
X4    HPR     X4
      END     X1
```

The END pseudo-operation tells the assembly program that there are no more parts of the program to be assembled and that the program starts with the instruction in location X1. Notice how each deviation from the normal flow of control is marked on the flow diagram by the slash on the flow line. Can you check the diagram for consistency? Can you check the code to see that all blocks have been coded?

PROBLEMS

Using the same input tape used in the above example, do the following problems.

6-22. Write a program to select all records whose fourth word is positive *or* whose sixteenth word is *not* zero.

6-23. Write a program which will prepare both the output tape of the example and the output tape of Prob. 6-22, while reading the input tape only once.

6-24. Write the code for the flow diagram in Fig. 4-14, replacing block XD with a simple stop. Assume *a* to be the fourth word in a 100-word record.

6-25. Do any of the above programs take advantage of the computer's ability to perform several operations simultaneously?

FORTRAN Input and Output

In a higher level language, a great deal of the input-output structure of a machine may be concealed from the programmer. In FORTRAN, for example, the programmer knows nothing of the channel structure of the 7090, but merely designates by a number the tape used. Also, most of the tape-positioning facilities are not directly available, because FORTRAN is primarily oriented to mathematical problems in which the input and output are of a rather simple nature. There is, for example, no direct way for the FORTRAN programmer to utilize the file structure of 7090 tapes, for the only statements for moving tapes backwards are BACKSPACE and REWIND. Thus, he can only treat his input as a single logical file on each tape, unless he knows exactly how many records there are in the file, or puts a special record on the tape to mark the end of the logical file.

On the other hand, as long as the FORTRAN programmer stays within a certain range of input and output forms, the logic of his program may be vastly simplified over the corresponding machine-language program. For instance, to write a record consisting of three words, A, B, and C, on binary tape, the programmer simply writes the statement

WRITE (2)A,B,C

To read such a three-word record into locations X, Y, and Z (assuming the tape is properly positioned) he merely writes the statement

READ (2)X,Y,Z

In order to read or write longer records without specifying each word in detail, FORTRAN provides a special notation, related to the use of subscripts, to denote lists of variables. Because the ability of the input-output media (cards, tapes, etc.) is limited to representation of single lines of characters, FORTRAN must replace the subscript notation with some notation that can be written all on one line. Thus, a variable such as a_i is represented in FORTRAN by A(I), or c_7 is represented by C(7), and so forth. If more than one subscript is needed, as in x_{jk}, it may be written X(J,K).

Now, in the machine language, when we wish to reserve a space for a particular list or array of words, we used the BSS pseudo-operation. In FORTRAN, the analogous task is performed using the DIMENSION statement which, like the pseudo-operation in the symbolic machine language, is an instruction to the compiler, not to the machine.

Thus, to reserve space for an array of 50 words for the variable z_i, we write the *specification statement*

DIMENSION Z(50)

To reserve space for a variable with more than one subscript, we can write such statements as

DIMENSION R(10,15)

which reserves space for a 10 by 15 array of the variable, r_{ij}, or 150 locations in all.

As long as we are dealing with an entire array as defined by a dimension statement, we can specify reading as follows,

READ (4)Z

which will cause the next 50 words on tape to be read into Z(1) through Z(50). If we wish to write the array R, we can use the statement

WRITE (1)R

which will cause a 150-word record to be written on tape 1 with the words R(1,1), R(1,2), . . . R(10,15). If we wish, we can read or write more than one array with a single statement. In fact, we can mix arrays and single variables in the list of one READ or PRINT statement, as in

READ (4)A,Z,X,Y,Z

which will cause the next 203 words on tape 4 to be read. We notice, of course, that the precise meaning of such a READ statement cannot be determined merely by looking at the statement itself, for the DIMENSION statement also contains relevant information. By changing the DIMENSION statement, the programmer can change the meaning of the READ statement—often a useful programming device.

We now have enough information to be able to code our example of a complete program (Fig. 6-6) in the FORTRAN language. We cannot, however, use the ordinary end-of-file marking as an end-of-file test in FORTRAN, so we must have a special record to mark the end-of-file. Let us assume that the last (and only the last) record in the file has the first word equal to 1.0, so that this feature can be used as a test for the last record in block 2. The code, then, might read as follows:

```
        DIMENSION A(20)
1       REWIND 1
        REWIND 2
```

```
2     READ (1)A
      IF (A(1) − 1.0)5,3,5
3     WRITE (2)A
      REWIND 1
      REWIND 2
4     STOP
5     IF (A(1))2,6,2
6     IF (A(20))7,2,2
7     WRITE (2)A
      GO TO 2
      END
```

Notice that we have had to reinterpret the test in block 6, with "minus" meaning "strictly less than zero" and "plus" meaning "positive or zero." Also notice that the FORTRAN language has an END statement identical in function to the pseudo-operation, END, in the symbolic assembly language.

PROBLEMS

6-26. Write a FORTRAN code for the program in Prob. 6-22.

6-27. Write a FORTRAN code for the program in Prob. 6-23.

6-28. Write a FORTRAN code for the program in Prob. 6-24.

6-29. Write a FORTRAN program which reads a five-word record from an input tape, copies those five words on an output tape, then reads back the output record and checks to see that all five words have been correctly written, copying the entire file in this manner.

6-30. Write a FORTRAN program which reads four-word records from an input tape, and writes those four words, *sorted into numerical order*, onto the output tape, copying the entire file in this manner.

Coordination of Input and Output with the CPU Program

In order to plan input and output operations more effectively, we need some simple scheme for representing the sequence of operation of both the CPU and the channels with respect to time. The flow diagram contains this information, but it also contains a great deal more information which may obscure the purely *timing* relationships of the various units. Furthermore, since this scheme is to be used in planning operations, we shall generally want to prepare this time representation before the flow diagram is completed—although we may certainly use this tool as an aid in analyzing an existing program or flow diagram.

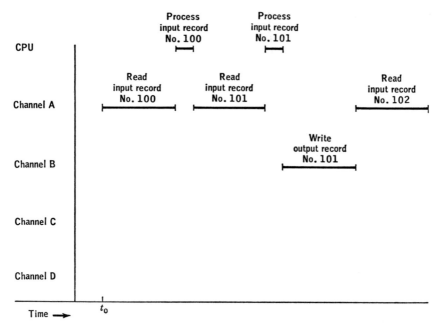

Fig. 6-7. Timing diagram—program of Fig. 6-6.

One scheme for making this representation is a *timing diagram*. A timing diagram for the example of the previous section is shown in Fig. 6-7. Down the left-hand margin are listed the several major units whose activities we wish to portray—the CPU and the data channels, in this case. Along the bottom margin, time is plotted. On the timing diagram, we do not attempt to show the entire course of the program but only certain portions which are representative of the several timing situations which can occur. A solid line to the right of one of the unit designations indicates the duration of operation of that unit. The space above the line may be used to indicate what specific event is occurring on that unit.

The first event which occurs (in a typical sequence of operations once the program is under way) is the reading of an input record which occupies channel A for a certain time. (Sometimes we need to draw the timing diagram to exact scale; but often, as in this case, we want only an indication of the *sequence* of events.) When the channel is no longer in operation (how did the program know this?), the CPU program operates for a short time to process the record just brought in.

In this particular program there are two distinct situations which we should represent on the timing diagram, namely, when a record is selected for writing and when a record is not selected for writing. The timing diagram shown assumes that the first record shown (100) is not selected and that the second record (101) is selected. Since these two cases cover the possibilities, we do not need to extend the diagram past, say, the third record.

What does the diagram tell us? First of all, it is clear that none of the operations on the separate units ever occur simultaneously. Thus we are not taking full advantage of the abilities of the computer. Before we attempt to change our program, we would be wise to determine to what *extent* we are failing to operate efficiently. A good way to go about this determination is to look at the other extreme, where all operations are overlapped to the maximum theoretically possible. We know, for example, that we can never operate more efficiently than indicated by the timing diagram in Fig. 6-8 (assuming we do not attempt to use channel C or D). This diagram was created on the assumptions that (1) processing a record could begin immediately after, but not before, that record has been read; (2) writing (if any) could begin immediately after processing; and (3) the program could coordinate the reading of records in such a way that channel A would be continuously occupied with that task— anticipating the need for each new record. Assumptions 1 and 2 were already used implicitly in Fig. 6-7. Assumption 3 can be quite closely realized in practice. Studying the diagram, you will notice that no two units are ever processing the same record at the same time. This observation also holds true for Fig. 6-7. Our overlapping is achieved by having each unit performing its own function on a record, then releasing that record to the next unit and proceeding to the following record, if available. Consequently, with three units, we may have as many as three records in various stages of the process at any given time. For example, when the CPU is processing record 102, channel A is already beginning to read record 103, and channel B is completing the job of writing record 101.

A Time Study of Dishwashing

We can think of a number of simple yet illuminating analogies for this process. Let us imagine three people working together to clean up after dinner. One person brings the dishes into the kitchen and

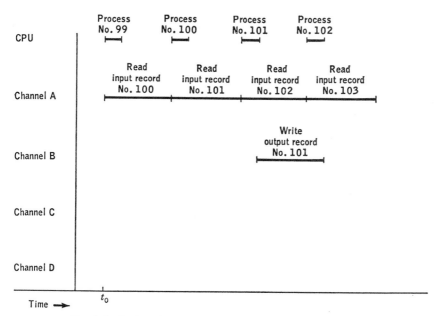

Fig. 6-8. Timing diagram—maximum overlap of operations.

possibly scrapes off the garbage. The second person washes the dishes, while the third dries them and puts them away. We can even see an analogy with our selection process, if we do not dry the glassware but let it drain dry on a rack. Now, at any one time, all three people are working at their separate tasks and any one dish is in only one stage of the operation. Nevertheless, each dish will eventually be put through the entire process.

It is quite clear, to anyone who has ever washed dishes, that, if it takes longer to wash a dish than to perform any of the other tasks, this procedure will be "wash-limited." That is, we can pretty well determine how long it takes to process the dishes if we determine how long it takes to wash them. This observation does not hold true if some dishes take longer to scrape or to dry than they take to wash; in that case we must make some sort of statistical guess at the time or else measure the entire process in detail. We have also not taken into account the amount of time necessary to start and stop the process. The washer cannot start washing until at least one dish has been brought in, and the dryer cannot start drying until at least one dish has been washed. Similarly, when the last dish is brought in, it still must be washed; and after being washed, it may have to be dried. Therefore, at the beginning and at the end of the process, all three people cannot be kept busy simultaneously. If we are washing five or ten dishes, this inefficiency at the ends of the process can be significant to the over-all timing. If, however, we are washing a thousand dishes, we can quite well ignore this starting and stopping time in the over-all estimate of timing.

Assuming that we have a large number of dishes—let us say N dishes—and the process is "wash-limited," we can easily calculate the time T to do the entire job. If T_w is the time to wash one dish (assuming all dishes are washed at the same rate), then $T = N \times T_w$. That is, the time to do all the dishes is the time to *wash* one times the total number of dishes. On the other hand, if we have only one person on the job and he runs each dish through the entire process— scrape, wash, dry—one at a time, the time T' it takes him may be calculated by the formula

$$T' = N \times T_w + N \times T_s + n \times T_d$$

where T_s is the time to scrape one dish, T_d is the time to dry one dish, and n is the number of dishes which must be dried. N will be greater than n if we leave some of the dishes to dry on the rack.

Now, how much more efficient are three people at doing this job than one? We can measure this "efficiency" in several ways, but suppose we say that $E = T'/T$ is the formula for calculating relative efficiency. Thus, if $E = 1$, the two methods are equally efficient and there is no improvement; or if $E = 3$, the overlapping process is three times as efficient. If $E = T'/T$, we may express this formula as

$$E = \frac{T'}{T} = \frac{N \times T_w + N \times T_s + n \times T_d}{N \times T_w} = 1 + \left(\frac{T_s}{T_w} + \frac{n}{N} \times \frac{T_d}{T_w} \right)$$

Thus we see that the overlapping process is always at least as efficient as the other, since $E \geqq 1$. This result is not surprising *in view of our assumptions*, but do not conclude from this that such an overlapping process must always be more efficient.

When can this process be three times as efficient? (Why can it not be more than three times?)

This is not a book on dishwashing; so let us return to the original processes we are trying to study. Since our program is clearly "read-limited" we can calculate the relative efficiency here by a completely analogous formula:

$$E = 1 + \frac{T_p}{T_r} + \frac{n}{N} \times \frac{T_w}{T_r}$$

where T_p is the time to process one record, T_r is the time to read one record, T_w is the time to write one record, N is the total number of records, and n is the number of records written. By examining the conditions of the program itself, we can determine values for T_p, T_r, and T_w. It turns out that T_w and T_r are the same, and they are approximately equal to 7 msec. T_p will vary depending on the results of the two tests, but its maximum value is about 0.02 msec. In other words, the processing time *in this problem* is much less than reading or writing time—about three-tenths of 1 per cent. Therefore, we can drop the term T_p/T_r from the formula for E without losing anything significant. Thus

$$E = 1 + \frac{n}{N} \times \frac{T_w}{T_r}$$

But we have noticed that T_w and T_r are equal; so we may finally reduce the formula to

$$E = 1 + \frac{n}{N}$$

What is the significance of the quantity n/N? Clearly it is the fraction of the input records selected for output. Then our formula simply tells us that the relative efficiency of the methods depends on how the data turn out—something which we could have observed by comparing the timing diagrams for the two methods.

Which method we choose to program, then, depends on the *meaning of the problem* and *cannot be determined solely by studying the timing diagrams and flow diagrams.* For example, if the process is intended to select erroneous records from the file and we really do not expect any (or many) erroneous records, the difference between the efficiencies of the two methods is slight and probably not enough to warrant the difficulties of attempting to overlap operations. On the other hand, if we really *expected* most (or all) of the records to be selected, the overlapping method would be about twice as efficient as the other.

Now, however, is the time for caution. One of the more dangerous

occupational hazards in computing is the habit of working out a set
of diagrams, formulas, and figures until some impressive statement
like "twice as efficient" emerges. We smile and forget our assumptions.
We straighten out all our working papers and throw away the ones
with the *really* important figures. We promise ourselves some special
treat for being so smart and embark on a course whose rationale will
later prove incomprehensible.

Suppose you were going to the store for groceries. Would you drive
halfway across town in order to get *half price?* Yes, if "groceries"
meant a week's food; but no, if it meant a loaf of bread. In other
words, relative efficiency is just that—*relative.* Without considering
how many records we are going to process and how often we shall
repeat the procedure, we cannot begin to make a reasonable decision
about which method to program. Suppose we have a thousand records
to process. A thousand records may sound like a lot, but it means
7 seconds by one method or 14 seconds by the other. Now at least
we can ask a sensible question: How much programming effort are
we willing to expend to save 7 seconds of machine time? If we can
answer this question, we can compare the answer with that of another—
What difference in programming effort is required between the two
methods?—and then make a decision.

The point of this example, if it even needs to be summarized, is
this: Being a smart programmer usually means *thinking of some good
questions to ask.* We do not say "answers," because the programmer
himself usually cannot provide the answers to the "good" questions.
We do not say "right" questions, because only the answers determine
which were the "right" questions. If we knew the "right way" to do
problems, we could program the computer itself to do all the programming and end *this* book, at least, without further comment.

Programming, then, seems to be largely dependent on the building
of conceptual schemes with the materials available and selecting that
scheme which is, over-all, better suited than the others. If the programmer has not mastered his material, he is likely to apply the
answers to his "good" questions to the selection of a poor scheme.
In fact, he may not even be able to get "good" answers to those questions. For example, we do not, at this point, have any idea how
difficult it would be to implement a program which will overlap operations as we desire. From one point of view, this task would be ex-

tremely difficult, that is, if we were to ignore all past thinking and work on the subject. On the other hand, as we shall learn later, programming the "more difficult" approach may actually prove *easier* if we use programming aids available to us. If this truly is the case, we shall have no difficulty choosing between two methods where one is guaranteed (within the assumption) to be at least as efficient as the other.

PROBLEMS

6-30. Review the derivation of "relative efficiency." What characteristic, in general, must a program have to achieve maximum efficiency by overlapping?

6-31. Conversely, what characteristic would indicate that high efficiency is not likely to be achieved?

6-32. Draw a timing diagram of the example problem with the restriction that processing cannot be overlapped with either reading or writing, but reading and writing may be overlapped with one another. How does this restriction affect the efficiency of this method?

6-33. Suppose the CPU processing time on this example were 7 msec instead of 0.02 msec. How would the restriction of Prob. 6-32 affect the efficiency?

6-34. Suppose the processing took 1,800 msec. How would the number of records selected for writing affect the efficiency?

CHAPTER 7

INDEXING

Counting

At an early age, all of us learned the operation of counting. As with many early-acquired skills, we use counting often but rarely, if ever, think about the process. The computer, however, often forces us to think about a heretofore unconscious process in quite clear and specific terms. Therefore, in order to spare ourselves some difficulty later on, let us consider this very simple subject of counting in some detail.

We use many types of counting every day, but by far the most common type is done as follows:

We assign the number "one" to the first object in the group of objects we wish to count. We then assign to a second member of the group the number "two," which is obtained by adding one to the previous number. If we proceed to assign numbers to each and every object in the group, we take the number assigned to the last object and call it the "number of objects in the group." The procedure is so simple and so automatic that we might easily think of it as the only type of counting we do. A little reflection should prove this supposition untrue. Every child, to the chagrin of his playmates at hide-and-seek, knows how to "count by twos," or by "tens." The space age has pushed the "count-*down*" into prominence, but those of us who have never fired rockets use similar counting-backward techniques every day. And nothing is sacred about starting with "one," either, as anyone knows who has measured an automobile trip.

What then may we accurately call "counting"? The process we have described is actually only a special case of counting, more precisely called "enumeration." The aspect of enumeration that all the counting processes share is the *one-for-one correspondence* of the objects being counted with some *orderly sequence of numbers.*

Essentially, when we count objects we consider them in some order; and if you like, we consider the numbers assigned as being an indication of—or "indexes" to—that order. Often the order seems predetermined, as when counting time or, say, counting a line of people. When counting a flock of sheep, or the number of people in a theater, however, we find ourselves superimposing some order so we shall be able to count. We may choose some form of simple geometric pattern, such as a rectangle with 12 people in it, to help us. We might count the rectangles rather than the people.

When counting in the computer, we usually find some order—such as the order of records on tape or the order of words in storage—to which we can attach our counting process. In the case of records on tape, the *direction* of counting is also pretty well determined by the fact that on many machines we cannot read the tape backward. In the case of words in storage, we can count backward or forward with equal ease, but the word arrangement is quite firmly determined by the sequence of the location numbers—up or down.

Now that we have delved further into the aspects of counting, let us redefine the actual steps utilized in the general counting process:

1. Choose a starting value, say n_0.

2. Choose a process whose successful completion will mean the selection of one subgroup of a number of objects i at a time and that no objects in the group will be missed.

3. Each time the process is completed, modify the current value of the count by adding (for forward counting) or subtracting (for backward counting) the increment i (i, of course, is the number of objects in each subgroup).

4. When all the grouped objects have been selected, terminate the process of counting. The count will have some final value, say n_f.

If we wish to determine n, the number of *objects* we have counted, we can use the formula (for forward counting)

$$n = n_f - n_0$$

For example, if we start counting at 0 and count up to 52, we have counted $52 - 0$, or 52, objects, whether we counted by ones or twos or fours. It is important to notice that the *starting value n_0 is not* the value assigned to the first group. The value assigned to the first group is $n_0 + i$. This fact is easily understood if we consider what happens when there are *no objects* in the group we wish to count. We assign a starting value and then never complete the selection process even once. Therefore, $n_f = n_0$ and $n = 0$, which is the result we want in this case.

Suppose we were counting the records in a file on tape. Figure 7-1

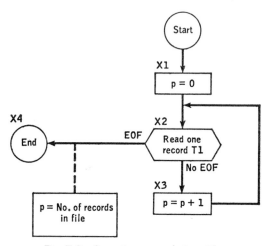

Fig. 7-1. Counting records in a file.

shows a possible flow diagram for this procedure. In block X1, we set up our starting value for p. Every time block X2 successfully reads a record, block X3 denotes the fact by adding one to the previous value of p. When the EOF mark is detected by block X2, the counting process is terminated, and p—as the assertion box states—is then the number of records in the file. We could not make this assertion about p if it were not true in every case, including the one where there are *no records in the file*. As you can see, starting at zero ensures that even in this case the count is correct.

From the diagram in Fig. 7-1 it is a simple matter to pass to a more general counting problem, one of *selective* counting. Perhaps we also wish to count only that number of records in the file whose first word is positive. Figure 7-2 shows how this might be done. Here we are starting two counts in block X1, but we interpose another condition (X4) before the block (X5) which increments our second count. In the case of p, one failure to pass the counting condition (block X2) terminates the counting. q represents the more general case; sometimes it is incremented; sometimes it is not. The alternative box (X4) makes sure that q truly represents the count as indicated in the assertion box. (One must be extremely careful not to make assertions in the assertion box which are not true. This is a trap too often fallen into. Asserting that q is the number of records with positive first

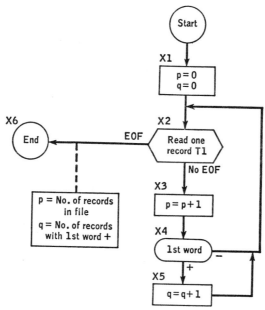

Fig. 7-2. Counting records with positive first word.

words is only a way of helping others understand the diagram—not a substitute for a diagram which *makes* the assertion true.)

Counting as a Control

Often we do not count to determine how much of some object or process we have on hand. Instead we use counting as a control in order to terminate a process after performing it a particular number of times. For example, when paying a bill, we count our money, not to determine how much money we have but rather that we may pay the correct amount. Let us illustrate this approach on the computer. Suppose we wish to take the first 200 records on a tape and write them as one file onto another tape. We do not know how many files it may take to find 200 records—there may be one, fifty, or some other number of files. Figure 7-3 shows how we might create this new tape. Block Y2 ignores any EOF on the input tape by simply proceeding to read the next record. Notice that, in this way, the EOF is *not counted* as a record. Every time a record is written by block Y3, block Y4 counts it, and block Y5 examines the count to see if the process is

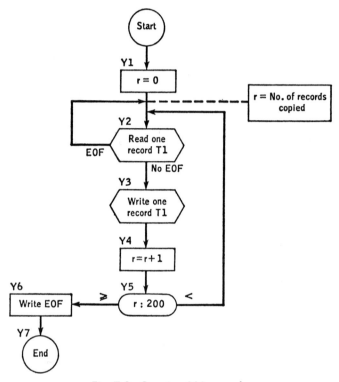

Fig. 7-3. Copying 200 records.

finished. In effect, then, the count *controls* the loop. Consequently such loops are often referred to as *count-controlled* loops.

The count-controlled loop is an example of one of the most important techniques in computing. It enables us to conserve the storage facilities of the computer by permitting the repetition of instructions rather than the rewriting of duplicate sequences of instructions. Although control counting can be done in many ways, we still take into account the universal appeal of simple *enumeration*. Our flow diagrams will be generally easier to follow if we can represent our control logic in enumerative terminology. To do this, we make use of an *index* rather than an actual computed quantity on the flow diagram to show the count. It is possible that the value of this index *could* correspond to the value of a computed quantity. This will be the case, however, only if the process of enumeration is found to be the most convenient way to *implement* the counting logic. In other words, enumeration is shown on the flow diagram because people understand enumeration best, although other types of counting may be used in the machine code because these types of counting may prove "best" for the computer.

The only time when this duality of representation can be misleading is during the transition from flow diagram to a code or vice versa. To avoid confusion several steps may be taken. Firstly, we represent all operations on *indexes* with an arrow rather than an equal sign—as we discussed in the section on flow diagramming. Secondly, we can use assertion boxes to smooth the transition. One simple way is to use the assertion box as a table, showing the index values on one side and the respective computed quantities or conditions on the other. Only a few critical points in the table need be shown. Let us augment this rather theoretical discussion with a concrete example. Instead of using the actual quantity r as shown in Fig. 7-3, we introduce an index j which represents the *number of the record we are processing* rather than the *number of records processed*. Figure 7-4 shows this flow diagram.

Block Z1 says, "Prepare to process record number 1." This inclusive statement informs us that we must prepare everything necessary to process the first record so that we may assign the number 1 to j. Such preparation may vary from a simple assignment of a starting value to a complex initial set of operations. Yet all that is required at this time in the flow diagram is this statement meant to express the logical problem-oriented fact that we must at this point prepare to process the *first* record. We do not, then, have to think in detail how we shall code this block when we wish to concentrate on the planning of the over-all problem. (If we have some idea about how this block might be coded, we can certainly write it down in an assertion box at this time. We are not *prevented* from thinking about coding, only protected from the necessity.)

The reading of the jth record is shown in block Z2, where the jth record is any one of the records being processed. The meaning of the EOF procedure becomes much clearer in this notation because it shows that upon EOF recognition a record j is not read and another attempt is made. Block Z3 states explicitly and simply which record is being written. The power of the index notation should now be more apparent.

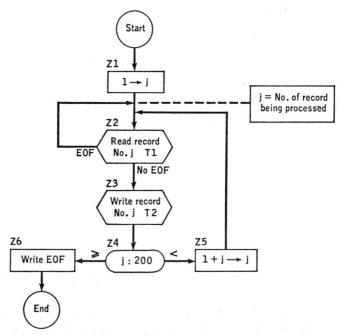

Fig. 7-4. Copying 200 records—index notation.

The test in Z4 asks whether or not the two-hundredth record has been processed. If it has not, Z5 is executed, which steps up the index j. In other words, Z5 says, "We now pass to the next record in the sequence." Notice the difference between this block and block Y4 in Fig. 7-3. That block says, "Add one to the quantity r." The difference is basically the describing of *what* is being done and *how* it is being done. The "how" is probably better expressed in the code and in the assertion boxes—giving us a more general flow diagram.

Suppose, for example, we wish to *implement* the indexing in Fig. 7-4 by counting up by ones starting with a value of 17. We could then construct a table in an assertion box showing the correspondence between the index j and the count. Since the count starts with 17 and moves up by ones, the table would start

j	$Count$
1	17
2	18
3	19
.	.
.	.
.	.

In order that we may properly code the test in block Z4, we shall want to know the value of the count which corresponds to a j of 200. We can easily extend the table to

j	$Count$
1	17
2	18
.	.
.	.
.	.
199	215
200	216

Consequently, if we test the count for 216 we shall effectively be testing j for 200.

Suppose we wish to fix the other end of the count. We might, for example, want to perform the test in Z4 by testing some quantity for zero, since zero is an easy test to make. We know, then, that the final entry in the table is

j	$Count$
200	0

and can extend the table backward until we determine the proper starting value:

j	$Count$
1	-199
2	-198
.	.
.	.
.	.
198	-2
199	-1
200	0

If we start the count at −199, then, when the count reaches zero (when tested at Z4), we end the loop properly.

Suppose the increment is varied. If we count by "sevens," starting at, say, 13, we can construct the following table:

j	Count
1	13
2	20
3	27
.	.
.	.
.	.
199	1,399
200	1,406

which shows that a test for a count of 1,406 would be equivalent to a test for a j of 200.

Even the *direction* of counting may be changed; if we wish to start at zero and count backward by "ones," what test should be made in Z4? The table tells the answer.

j	Count
1	0
2	−1
3	−2
.	.
.	.
.	.
199	−198
200	−199

The test must be made for a count of −199. Notice, however, that, because we are counting backward, as j *increases,* the count *decreases.* Therefore, although a count of −199 corresponds to a j of 200, a count of *less than −199* corresponds to a j of *greater than 200.* In order to be in exact correspondence with the flow diagram, we must test the count for less than or equal to −199 to terminate the loop. In other words, when we are counting in the opposite direction to our indexing, a greater-than test on the index is equivalent to a less-than test on the count. Remember that, while 200 is greater than 199 and 201 is greater than 200, −200 is less than −199, which is in turn less than −198.

Counting backward can play an important role in count-controlled loops. A convenient way to write such loops is to arrange that all loops end with the same test. Then we need to be concerned about *starting* the loops properly. A test for zero, for example, would yield this table:

j	$Count$
1	199
2	198
.	.
.	.
.	.
198	2
199	1
200	0

Possibly a simpler case would be to end with a count of one:

j	$Count$
1	200
2	199
.	.
.	.
.	.
198	3
199	2
200	1

In this case, we can formulate the following rule: If we count *backward* by "ones" and end at one, then we start the count with the *number of times* we wish to repeat the loop.

PROBLEMS

7-1. What must be changed in Fig. 7-4 if we want the first 386 records copied?

7-2. Assume we were counting 386 records. Construct a table of index vs. count for the following cases:

	Starting value	Increment	Final value	Direction
(a)	42	1	?	Up
(b)	?	1	81	Up
(c)	?	2	125	Down
(d)	?	1	1	Down

7-3. Assume we were counting 922 records. Construct the four tables as in Prob. 7-2.

Index Registers

Since counting of all sorts is so common on computers, many computing machines are provided with special registers for such purpose. On the 7090 these registers are called "index registers" (abbreviated XR), thus relating them mnemonically with index notation. There are three such registers—called XR1, XR2, and XR4. They are each 15 bits long, independent, and completely equivalent. Although three is a popular number of such special registers, combinations of from one to a hundred do occur on different computers.

With respect to XR1, XR2, and XR4, all instructions making use of an index register may make reference to any one of the three with equal ease. No change is required of the operation code since a field is provided within the instruction to indicate which index register is taking part in the given operation. This field, occupying 3 bit positions in the word, is called the "tag" field. In the coding structure of the instruction the tag field is placed to the right of the address field and is separated from it by a comma. Thus we have the coding form

LOCATION   OPERATION   ADDRESS, TAG

Because it is a register distinct from the storage words, the index register requires its own set of reference instructions. With such instructions we may make reference to an index register directly, modifying it where necessary without affecting any other index register or word within the computer. Such functions as placing values into these registers, taking numbers out, and testing these values are necessary for normal use. For example, we have several means of placing values into the index register, such as the instruction

LOAD INDEX FROM ADDRESS (LXA)

This instruction refers to the three separate index registers as follows:

LXA   WORD, 1
LXA   WORD, 2
LXA   WORD, 4

depending on whether XR1, XR2, or XR4 is to be loaded. In the first case, the contents of the address portion of location WORD [abbreviated A(WORD) or $C(WORD)_{21-35}$] replace the contents of

XR1. In the second case, A(WORD) is loaded into XR2, and similarly for XR4 in the third case. In other words, LXA provides us with a means of putting a starting value into an index register, provided that we have that value in some location in storage. Since the index register is 15 bits long, we use only 15 bits of the 36 bits in the word, specifically the address portion. LXA is illustrative of an instruction making direct reference to storage in order to carry out its function; so we say that LXA is a "direct-address" type of instruction.

In cases where only 15 bits are to be moved, we have the opportunity to introduce a more restricted, though more direct, type of instruction. The direct-address instruction works, as we know, by using its 15-bit address field for determining the location of the word in storage containing the information to be used. As long as the information in the storage word is itself only a 15-bit quantity, why not place the quantity to be loaded into an index register into the 15 positions of the instruction address itself? That is, we use the 15-bit address field of the *instruction* to contain the actual quantity to be loaded rather than the address reference to the word containing this 15-bit quantity. Such a technique of using the address field to hold the actual data is known as "immediate addressing." To summarize: Direct addressing is the most general reference process enabling any number of bits from 1 to 36 to be referenced. Immediate addressing may be used where the number of bits required is 15 or less.

An example of immediate addressing that performs the same functions as LXA is the instruction ADDRESS TO INDEX-TRUE (AXT). (The term "true" will be explained later.) If we execute the instruction

$$\text{AXT} \quad 25, 2$$

we cause the number 25 to be placed, or loaded, into XR2. If we wish to "clear" XR4, we may write

$$\text{AXT} \quad 0, 4$$

If we want to start XR1 at 2387, we write

$$\text{AXT} \quad 2387, 1$$

Note that the only comma that may be used is the one causing the separation between address and tag; thus we must *not* write

$$\text{AXT} \quad 2,387, 1$$

Incrementing

The next thing we should like to learn is how to increment the index registers. Since incrementing often occurs as the last operation in many loops (note Z5 in Fig. 7-4), the designers of the 7090 decided to make the incrementing instruction a transfer instruction as well. Of course, we can ignore this transfer feature—if we wish only to increment—by transferring to the next location. The instruction TRANS-FER WITH INDEX INCREMENTED (TXI) is this incrementing instruction.

TXI requires three parts or fields besides the operation part in order to function properly. Two of these are familiar: We have the address field to indicate the transfer location, as in a TRA or TMI, for example; and we have the tag portion to indicate which index register is to be incremented. One other field is necessary to keep the increment which will be applied to the index register value. This field is coded adjacent to the tag field, again separated by a comma, giving the coding format

LOCATION   OPERATION   ADDRESS, TAG, DECREMENT

(Although this field contains an increment it is called the "decrement field" because the value found in this field for the majority of index operations is used in a *decrementing*, or reducing, type of function.)

Note that as in the immediate-address instruction the decrement field contains an immediate increment. That is, the actual incrementing value occupies the instruction itself. In fact the decrement value is always of an "immediate" kind. This is not the only use of the decrement field, for as we learned earlier, it is that portion of an I/O command which holds the count. [Y_{3-17}, the decrement portion of location Y, is often written as $D(Y)$.]

Suppose we wish to add one to the contents of XR4 and then transfer to location Z6. We can accomplish this task with the instruction

TXI   Z6, 4, 1

As we stated earlier, the address, tag, and decrement are written in the order as shown, separated by commas. The instruction

TXI   QA, 1, 7

for example, adds seven to C(XR1)—contents of XR1—and proceeds to QA for the next instruction.

Let us apply these techniques to the flow diagram in Fig. 7-1. If we use XR2 as the location of p—$L(p)$—we can code as follows:

X1	AXT	0, 2	
X2	RTBA	T1	Reads one record
	TCOA	*	Waits
	TEFA	X4	Tests for EOF
X3	TXI	X2, 2, 1	
X4			

(The asterisk in the TCOA tells the assembly program that this instruction refers to *itself*.) The diagram in Fig. 7-2 can be reduced to a code with equal ease, using XR1 for counting q:

X1	AXT	0, 2	Sets p to zero
	AXT	0, 1	Sets q to zero
X2	RTBA	T1	Selects tape
	RCHA	C1	Starts channel program
	TCOA	*	Waits
	TEFA	X6	Tests for EOF
X3	TXI	X4, 2, 1	Adds 1 to p
X4	CLA	Z	Tests first word for minus
	TMI	X2	
X5	TXI	X2, 1, 1	Adds 1 to q
Z	BSS	1	Reserves one location
C1	IOCD	Z, 0, 1	I/O command to read first word

Note that the TXI in block X3 simply transfers to the next location, X4.

PROBLEMS

7-4. Write a program which will count the number of records (in one file) whose first word and second word are the same.

7-5. Can we count more than three items at one time? What technique would enable us to do this with only three index registers?

Storing

In our two examples of the previous section, we were forced to leave the results of our counting in an index register. The difficulty is, of course, that we do not know how to use index registers fully. In this case, we have learned only two of the four general techniques for using registers. We should like to know a third, that of storing or saving the contents. A simple way to accomplish this saving is with the instruction STORE INDEX IN ADDRESS (SXA). The instruction

$$\text{SXA} \qquad \text{PR2, 1}$$

stores the contents of XR1 in the address portion of location PR2—
without disturbing the other parts of PR2. We can abbreviate the
description of this movement of 15 bits with the notation "C(XR1) replace A(PR2)."

The sequence of instructions

$$\text{SXA} \quad \text{PR2, 1}$$
$$\text{LXA} \quad \text{PR2, 2}$$

takes C(XR1) and puts them in XR2, using PR2 as an intermediate
storage location. Another way of accomplishing this task is with the
sequence

$$\text{SXA} \quad \text{R10, 1}$$
$$\text{R10} \quad \text{AXT} \quad 0, 2$$

which avoids the use of an extra location for temporary storage. The
SXA stores C(XR1) directly into the *instruction* R10. This modified
instruction then puts its own new address portion into XR2. This is an
excellent example of the manner in which an executing program can
modify its own instructions. Since the address portion of R10 is modified by the program, what we put there originally is irrelevant.

This technique of replacing addresses is commonly employed; so
we use a special notation, the double asterisk, to indicate irrelevant
addresses (or decrements) so no special significance will be attached
to some arbitrary choice of address. Thus, we would write

$$\text{SXA} \quad \text{R10, 1}$$
$$\text{R10} \quad \text{AXT} \quad **, 2$$

and our meaning becomes somewhat more clear.

One of the important uses of the SXA instruction is to expand effectively the number of index registers available for counting. For
example, suppose we are keeping a count in A(X). When we wish
to increase the count, we can write

$$\text{LXA} \quad \text{X, 4}$$
$$\text{TXI} \quad * + 1, 4, 1$$
$$\text{SXA} \quad \text{X, 4}$$

This sequence puts the count in XR4, increases the count by one, and
replaces the count in A(X). XR4 is now free to perform other incrementing functions. Clearly, we can keep any number of counts in
this way with only one index register—three, of course, being an extra
convenience.

PROBLEMS

7-6. Code the example in Fig. 7-2 using only one index register.

7-7. How much difference in time does the program in Prob. 7-6 take because of the restriction to one index register?

Testing

Now that we know how to store the contents of index registers, we automatically have the ability to test them by using the accumulator as a testing place. Since we have gone to the trouble of providing special counting registers, however, we should like to have complete facility to use them without depending on the other registers. Consequently, we have special instructions for testing index registers directly. One such instruction is TRANSFER ON INDEX LESS THAN OR EQUAL (TXL). This conditional transfer compares its own decrement value with the contents of the specified index register. If the index register is less than or equal to that decrement, a transfer is executed; otherwise the computer passes to the next instruction in sequence. Thus,

$$\text{TXL} \qquad \text{H2, 2, 5}$$

will cause the next instruction to be taken from H2 if $C(XR2) \leqq 5$. The instruction

$$\text{TXL} \qquad \text{H5, 4, 0}$$

provides a test for $C(XR4) = 0$, since index registers have no signs and are therefore never negative (less than zero). Let us code the flow diagram in Fig. 7-3, assuming 150 word records.

Y1	AXT	0, 1	Sets $r = 0$
Y2	RTBA	T1	Selects input tape
	RCHA	CMD	Starts channel program
	TCOA	*	Waits
	TEFA	Y2	Tests EOF
Y3	WTBB	T2	Selects output tape
	RCHB	CMD	Starts channel program
	TCOB	*	Waits
Y4	TXI	Y5, 1, 1	Adds 1 to r
Y5	TXL	Y2, 1, 199	Tests r
Y6	WEFB	T2	Writes EOF
	HPR		Stops at end
CMD	IOCD	A, 0, 150	I/O command for 150-word transmission
A	BSS	150	Reserves 150 words
	END	Y1	

The important thing to notice in the above program is how block Y5 is coded. The flow diagram calls for a test to see whether r is less than 200, but our machine instruction TXL tests for less than *or equal to*. We should not be tempted to change our flow diagram because, if r:200 was clear in the first place, it will still be clear. An assertion box may be used if we want to be sure that anyone reading the code notices that testing an index register for less than or equal to 199 is equivalent to testing it for being less than 200.

Now suppose we wish to code the same problem from the diagram in Fig. 7-4. Remembering that our index notation frees us from using any particular counting technique, let us try counting by "sevens," starting with 13. As we worked out earlier, we want to test then for a count of less than 1406 (or less than or equal to 1405). This code looks quite similar to the previous one:

Z1	AXT	13, 1	Starts count
Z2	RTBA	T1	
	RCHA	CMD	
	TCOA	*	
	TEFA	Z2	
Z3	WTBB	T2	
	RCHB	CMD	
	TCOB	*	
Z4	TXL	Z5, 1, 1405	Tests for end of loop
	TRA	Z6	
Z5	TXI	Z2, 1, 7	Adds 7 to count
Z6	WEFB	T2	
	HPR		
CMD	IOCD	A, 0, 150	
A	BSS	150	
	END	Z1	

In fact, only the instructions connected with the counting are changed, and these only slightly. This example should make obvious the fact that the computer can count just as easily in one way as in any other.

PROBLEMS

7-8. Write a program which will skip over 17 records.

7-9. Write a program which will skip over 17 files.

Complement Arithmetic

At this point, we should logically try an example of counting backward—but we cannot with the tools we have on hand. Either we would need an instruction which subtracts from the index register or we would need to be able to put negative values in the decrement field. We would, that is, if we confined our thinking to conventional notions of subtraction. Let us therefore work with what we have and see if we can make use of seemingly limited resources.

A good start would be to inventory those resources:

1. A register in which we can add and which holds only positive numbers (index register)

2. An instruction which adds any positive number we wish to that register (TXI)

Perhaps working backward would provide a clue. How would the counter operate if we *could* subtract? Subtraction is easy enough: If we subtract 5 from 7, we get a plus 2 as a result. If we subtract 7 from 5, we encounter an unusual problem. In ordinary arithmetic, we get *minus* 2, but we cannot represent negative numbers in the index register. If we cannot have minus 2, we should like to get a result which was—in some ways—equivalent to minus 2. For example, if we subtract 7 from 5 and then add 2, the result should be zero, just as it would be if we added 5 and 2 and then subtracted 7. In other words, we should like to have a number which, when added to 2, gave a zero result.

Think for a moment about another register we often use—the odometer on an automobile. When can we go 2 miles and make the odometer go to zero? As almost every child knows, this unusual result occurs when we pass 99,999.9 miles. Why? Because the register has been increased beyond its capacity and thus resets itself to all zeros. The same phenomenon occurs in index registers because of their limited capacity. Assume we have in an index register the largest number it can hold (corresponding to 99,999.9 miles on the odometer). For convenience, we call this number m. If we add one to m, we should get $m + 1$ (which we shall call p), but we get zero. Thus p is equivalent to zero. (On an odometer, we cannot tell the difference between 100,000.0 miles and 00,000.0 miles because the high position 1 in 100,000.0 does not show.) Therefore, m is equivalent to *minus one* because the adding of one to m gives "zero" ($m + 1 = p = 0$).

Let us make use of this ability to "subtract" by addition. To do this we introduce a term to be applied to this unusual kind of arithmetic: "complement" arithmetic. Suppose we *define* the complement of any number a to be equal to a subtracted from p. We designate "comple-ment of a" by the symbol $\bar{a}$. Therefore, $\bar{a} = p - a$. But we previously defined $p = m + 1$, where m is the largest number the (index) register can hold. Thus the register would be able to contain $\bar{a}$ as long as there was room in the register for a. (In the case where a is zero, $\bar{a}$ is also zero since p, which is the sum of a and $\bar{a}$, is itself equivalent to zero.) Now suppose we perform the addition $b + \bar{a}$. By definition, $b + \bar{a} = b + (p - a) = b - a + p$. But p is equivalent to zero. Thus $b + \bar{a} = b - a$.

We therefore have the very useful rule: (a) *Adding the complement of a number is equivalent to subtracting the number itself.* Another rule may be obtained by examining $b - \bar{a}$. $b - \bar{a} = b - (p - a) = b + a - p = b + a$.

Thus (b) *subtracting the complement of a number is equivalent to adding the number itself.* What is the complement of $\bar{a}$ ($\bar{\bar{a}}$)? $\bar{\bar{a}} = \overline{(p - a)} = p - (p - a) = a$.

Thus (c) *the complement of the complement is the number itself.*

If we examine rules (a), (b), and (c), substituting the word "nega-tive" for the word "complement," we see that complements are equiva-lent to negatives—in so far as addition and subtraction are concerned when working with bounded registers. (In fact, some computers use complements exclusively.) Consequently, on the computer, we often represent a complement as a negative for ease of representation and let the assembly program make the proper translation. Thus, if we write the instruction

$$\text{TXI} \quad \text{X1, 4, } -1$$

the complement of one is placed in the decrement by the assembly program. When we execute the instruction, the complement of one is added to C(XR4). By rule (a), this step is equivalent to *subtract-ing* one from C(XR4). If we write

$$\text{AXT} \quad -6, 2$$

the complement of 6 is placed in XR2. The following sequence:

$$\text{AXT} \quad -6, 2$$
$$\text{TXI} \quad \text{X1, 2, 8}$$

then leaves a result of *two* in XR2, as does the sequence

$$\text{AXT} \quad 8, 2$$
$$\text{TXI} \quad \text{X1, 2, } -6$$

So we see that, with the help of the assembly program, we need not even think of complements but may proceed as if we could actually produce negative numbers. We must observe just one cautionary rule:

(d) *For purposes of comparison, complements are not equivalent to negatives.* Therefore, the only time we need to think of complements as such is when we wish to compare two complements (unless we simply wish to see if they are *equal*).

PROBLEMS

7-10. Develop a rule for comparing complements.

7-11. Why are we not concerned with complements in the AC?

7-12. Why are we not concerned with complements in ordinary "pencil-and-paper" arithmetic?

Counting Down

Now we are prepared to do the coding for Fig. 7-4 by counting down. If we start our count with 200 in XR2, the count will terminate when XR2 has been reduced to one. The coding is almost identical to our earlier attempts:

```
Z1      AXT     200, 2          Starts count
Z2      RTBA    T1
        RCHA    CMD
        TCOA    *
        TEFA    Z2
Z3      WTBB    T2
        RCHB    CMD
        TCOB    *
Z4      TXL     Z6, 2, 1        Tests for end of loop
Z5      TXI     Z2, 2, −1       Reduces count by 1
Z6      WEFB    T2
        HPR
CMD     IOCD    A, 0, 150
A       BSS     150
        END     Z1
```

This counting-down technique gives us a chance to apply the simple rule we discovered earlier: When counting backward by ones and testing for one at the end, start the count with the number of times we wish to traverse the loop. This rule, in fact, turns out to be so handy that we have another instruction which makes this special case even simpler to implement.

The instruction TRANSFER ON INDEX (TIX) combines the two operations performed at the end of the loop—testing and counting. The single instruction

$$\text{Z4} \quad \text{TIX} \quad \text{Z2, 2, 1}$$

does the same job as the pair of instructions

$$\text{Z4} \quad \text{TXL} \quad \text{Z6, 2, 1}$$
$$\text{Z5} \quad \text{TXI} \quad \text{Z2, 2, } -1$$

if by Z6 we mean the next location in sequence. In Fig. 7-4, we can thus combine the functions of two blocks Z4 and Z5 into one instruction. As a consequence, we shall have no location Z5 in our code. It may be wise to make a notation on the flow diagram to that effect.

Let us examine the TIX in more detail. Formally, we might describe its operation as follows (assuming XR1 is specified):

If C(XR1) are greater than the decrement value (of the TIX), *reduce* C(XR1) by that decrement value and transfer to the location specified. Otherwise take the next instruction in sequence without changing C(XR1). Thus we can count by decrements other than one as long as we make our test quantity equal to the decrement. For example, TIX   ZA, 1, 3 permits us to count down by threes. Notice by the definition that a TIX can never reduce an index register to zero or to a complement.

With the TIX, then, only two instructions need be added to a program or subprogram in order to put it under count control—an AXT at the beginning and a TIX at the end. To space over one record requires the instruction

$$\text{S2} \quad \text{RTBA} \quad \text{T1}$$

Using these instructions, in order to space over 67 records we require only the following loop:

$$\text{S1} \quad \text{AXT} \quad \text{67, 1}$$
$$\text{S2} \quad \text{RTBA} \quad \text{T1}$$
$$\text{S3} \quad \text{TIX} \quad \text{S2, 1, 1}$$

Indexing and Counting in FORTRAN

In coding problems involving counting and manipulation of arrays, FORTRAN's advantages as a problem-oriented language really come to the fore. Since any variable can be used for counting and for indexing as well, the programmer has, in effect, as many index registers as he needs for his problem. The FORTRAN compiler, however, has the task of allocating the available index registers to the tasks the programmer specifies—in such a way as to achieve maximum efficiency when the program is executed. Poor allocation of indexing facilities can lead to object programs whose inefficiency is exceeded only by the inefficiency of programs with poorly planned input and output. A good FORTRAN compiler, however, can often do a better job of index allocation than can the programmer who is coding in symbolic machine language.

To illustrate the ease of counting in FORTRAN, let us code some of our earlier examples. (We will assume that a zero in the first word of the record indicates the end-of-file, where necessary.) The only new statement we must learn is the simple arithmetic statement for counting, which follows the completely natural form of an algebraic expression. Thus, to add 1 to the value of the variable denoted by N, we simply write

$$N = N + 1$$

and so forth. To code the example of Fig. 7-1, then, we could write

```
1    P = 0
2    READ (3)R
     IF (R)3,4,3
4    STOP
3    P = P + 1
     GO TO 2
```

For the example of Fig. 7-2, the code might read

```
1    Q = 0
     P = 0
2    READ (3)R
     IF (R)3,6,3
6    STOP
3    P = P + 1
4    IF (R)2,8,5
5    Q = Q + 1
     GO TO 2
8    . . .
```

Notice that if the machine should find a zero at statement 4, the condition would represent some sort of error, since R had to be non-

zero in order to pass into block 3 in the first place. An extra statement
—or series of statements—should be provided (statement 8) to catch
this condition if it should ever occur. Under no circumstances should
the condition be ignored by writing either a 2, a 6, or a 5 in the middle
position of the IF statement labelled 4.

We may code count-controlled loops in a similar manner, which we
can illustrate from either Fig. 7-3 or Fig. 7-4. Let us use Fig. 7-4,
yielding the following code in FORTRAN:

```
        DIMENSION A(150)
1       J = 1
2       READ (1)A
3       WRITE (2)A
4       IF (J − 200)5,6,6
5       J = J + 1
        GO TO 2
6       END FILE 2
```

There are two new points to mention about this code. In the first
place, there is no automatic test of the end-of-file condition implied
by the FORTRAN READ statement, as there is in the machine
language. Consequently, there is no need for the EOF test to be
explicitly ignored in block 2, as it was in the machine code. A second
point to notice is that the FORTRAN language does provide a method
for writing an actual end-of-file mark on the output tape, using the
END FILE statement.

We can, of course, also count backwards in FORTRAN, using a
statement such as

$$P = P - 1$$

and using the appropriate test condition at the end of any count-
controlled loop. We can also count by any increment we wish, using
a statement such as

$$Q = Q + 13$$

or

$$R = R - 8$$

again modifying any tests in an appropriate manner.

PROBLEMS

7-13. Write a FORTRAN code for the program in Prob. 7-4.

7-14. Write a FORTRAN code for the program in Prob. 7-8.

7-15. Write a FORTRAN code for Prob. 7-14, counting backwards by sixes.

Effective Addressing

As we make successive passages through a count-controlled loop, some aspect of the loop we are controlling must change. Were this not the case, repeating the loop would accomplish nothing. When reading, the physical movement of the tape makes the necessary change from one record to the next. In some cases, the result of one iteration becomes the starting value for the next time through the loop. In other cases, we may have to provide an additional set of instructions to the loop to make the necessary changes. We may wish to change from word to word, bit to bit, character to character, or group of words to group of words. That is, we want the ability to be able to refer to different data each time we traverse the loop of instructions. This can be done in two ways. One way with which we are already familiar is to change the data in a block of fixed locations after each loop pass. This occurs, as we have noted, during the reading in of tape records wherein each record is treated identically by each loop pass. However, we are not always in a position where we can move our data in and out of a fixed area. It may be necessary to treat data that do not appear at predetermined location blocks. In order to treat this second type of problem we find that we must change the actual instruction *references* to the data locations after each loop pass or passes.

Now what part of the instruction must we change in order to create a new reference? Obviously only the address part of the instruction need be changed since it is the part through which we make our storage references. Since the technique to change our program instructions affects the address field, the term *address modification* is coined to describe the process.

On the 7090, as on many other computers, there are special abilities provided to allow for automatic address modification. That is, we need not go into any form of elaborate arithmetic operation in order to change the value of a given address. Operations concerning references to bits or characters, however, normally require more extensive techniques on the 7090.

The concept of changing or modifying a portion of an instruction so that references may be made to more than one fixed location is one of the most important ones in the programming area. It would just be impossible for a computer to function with any sort of efficiency or scope if it were necessary to repeat instructions or sets of instructions every time a new reference was needed. Imagine the progress of a woodcutter if he had to have a new ax for each swing at a tree; or consider the plight of a seamstress who had to use a new needle for each stitch. Repetitive operation in normal life attempts to make use of the same tools wherever possible. In the same manner a program tries to make use of the same tools, the instructions, wherever possible.

The technique of changing or modifying a portion of an instruction, the address field, for example, will certainly vary with the computer. On the 7090 automatic address modification takes advantage of a quantity already being modified in a count-controlled loop—namely, the index-register contents. We allow this varying quantity to be used in conjunction with a fixed quantity (the address part), or base address, to produce an *effectively* varying reference. That is, as the index value changes, so does the address reference to a location in storage. Such a method is called *effective addressing*. The resulting modification to the instruction which is *not* a physical modification is called *effective address modification*. By not being physically changed we mean that whatever value is in the address field is itself not disturbed. This fixed address value merely acts as the basis, or base, for obtaining other desired location references.

This technique is implemented by placing a *tag* representing an index register on the appropriate instruction: CLA   A1, 2. This combination of address and tag results in a *subtraction* taking place of the index register value from the address fixed value. This subtractive modification takes place only at the time the instruction is being executed. Furthermore this subtraction takes place in such a way that no registers, such as the accumulator or the index registers, and no storage locations or the instruction itself, as we have previously stated, are affected by this operation. Consequently, instructions such as TIX, TXI, AXT, SXA which require tags as a normal part of the operation code cannot make use of this technique of effective addressing.

Consider the following portion of a program:

R1	CLA	X1, 1
R2	STO	Y1, 1
R3	CLA	X1 + 1, 1
R4	STO	Z1 + 10, 1

If, when these instructions are executed, XR1 contains the number two, the program will *effectively* read

R1	CLA	X1 − 2
R2	STO	Y1 − 2
R3	CLA	X1 − 1
R4	STO	Z1 + 8

If XR1 is changed and now contains one, the four instructions automatically become (effectively)

R1	CLA	X1 − 1
R2	STO	Y1 − 1
R3	CLA	X1
R4	STO	Z1 + 9

Notice how the effective addresses all *increase* as the index-register contents *decrease*. This effect is produced because the effective address is obtained by subtraction. Suppose XR1 contained the complement of one. Applying rule (*b*) about complements, we can determine that the effective instructions would be

R1	CLA	X1 + 1
R2	STO	Y1 + 1
R3	CLA	X1 + 2
R4	STO	Z1 + 11

Thus, by putting complements in the index register, we can cause the effective address to be moved forward from the base address.

Handling Blocks of Data

The new techniques introduced in this chapter give us the power to perform many operations with blocks of data. Suppose we wish to determine how many words, out of a block of 1,000 words, are zeros. As the flow diagram in Fig. 7-5 indicates, we examine each word a_i in the list—starting with the first—one at a time. The index i serves to indicate which word is being processed. The number n provides a count of the zeros we find. The a values are located in locations P through P + 999, as shown in the memory box on the diagram. Each block except V2 is familiar to us; so we shall code those parts first.

V1	AXT	1000, 2	Starts count of i
	AXT	0, 1	Sets $n = 0$
	TRA	V2	
V3	TXI	V4, 1, 1	$n = n + 1$
V4	TIX	V2, 2, 1	Tests for end of loop and increments

```
        TRA      V6
P       BSS      1000              Reserves 1,000 words
```

Of course, block V2 is not totally unfamiliar; it will look something like this:

```
V2      CLA      ?
        TNZ      V4
        TRA      V3
```

Our problem is to determine what value should be assigned to the address portion of the CLA that is to serve as the base for the changing location references occurring as we go through the loop. We know

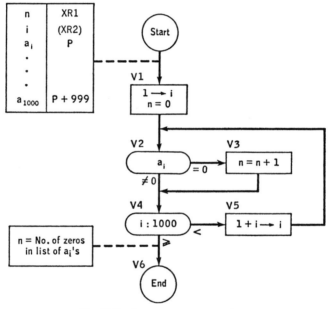

Fig. 7-5. Counting zeros in a list.

that this varying reference can be accomplished using XR2 to obtain the effective addressing.

In order to determine the proper instruction configuration we shall write the desired instruction in the form

$$CLA \quad X, 2$$

where X, used to indicate an address value still to be decided upon, will be effectively modified as the contents of XR2 vary. What method should be used to determine the proper X value? Probably the most general approach is to construct a table as follows:

i	C(XR2)	Effective address	$L(a_i)$
1	1000	X − 1000	P
2	999	X − 999	P + 1
.			.
.			.
.			.
1000	1	X − 1	P + 999

The first two columns may be filled in directly from the flow diagram, the fourth from the memory box, and the third using our knowledge of effective addressing. Since we want the effective address to refer to $L(a_i)$, we can make a simple equation using the last two columns of any line. For example, the first line yields

$$X - 1000 = P$$

from which
$$X = P + 1000$$

We can check this result using any other line. The equations

$$X - 999 = P + 1$$

and
$$X - 1 = P + 999$$

clearly yield the result

$$X = P + 1000$$

as will any equations we form from the table. Thus the instruction

$$V2 \quad CLA \quad P + 1000, 2$$

will refer to each of the a's in turn, as indicated on the diagram.

A reconstruction of the code, eliminating unnecessary TRA's, gives

V1	AXT	1000, 2	Starts count of i
	AXT	0, 1	Sets $n = 0$
V2	CLA	P + 1000, 2	Tests a_i
	TNZ	V4	
V3	TXI	V4, 1, 1	$n = n + 1$
V4	TIX	V2, 2, 1	Tests for end of loop and increments i
	TRA	V6	
P	BSS	1000	Reserves 1,000 words

Another problem will further illustrate this technique. From a block of 3,825 words, we wish to extract the one with the largest value. One way to do this is shown in Fig. 7-6. We start by assuming that the first one is the largest ($c_{max} = c_1$). By comparing c_{max} with the other c's in turn, we test this hypothesis; and if we find it to be false

$(c_{max} < c_j)$, we establish a new hypothesis $(c_{max} = c_j)$. Consequently, c_{max} is always the largest c_j we havé found up to that point. By the time we have tested all the c's, then, c_{max} will be equal to the largest.

Since we start by assuming $c_{max} = c_1$, we do not need to compare c_{max} with c_1 (although such a comparison could not lead to an incor-

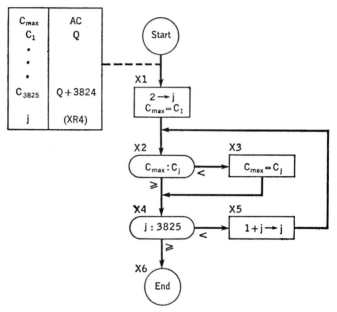

Fig. 7-6. Finding the maximum value in a list.

rect result. Why?). Thus j starts at two, not one. A table should determine the relationship between j, XR4, $L(c_j)$, and the address we must use to get the proper effective address.

j	XR4	Effective address	$L(c_j)$
2	3824	$X - 3824$	$Q + 1$
.	.	.	
.	.	.	
.	.	.	
3825	1	$X - 1$	$Q + 3824$

We start XR4 at 3824 so we can use a TIX, but the choice is arbitrary if we are willing to use a TXL and a TXI. From either $j = 2$ or $j = 3825$, we can determine that $X = Q + 3825$. Thus we can refer to the numbers c_j with an address and tag of $(Q + 3825, 4)$.

Our code could then be as follows:

X1	AXT	3824, 4	Start count of j
	CLA	Q	Starting guess for c_{max}
X2	CAS	Q + 3825, 4	Test latest guess
	TRA	X4	
	TRA	X4	
X3	CLA	Q + 3825, 4	Make new guess
X4	TIX	X2, 4, 1	Test for end and increment j
	TRA	X6	Exit with largest c in AC
Q	BSS	3825	

In the above example, two of the instructions were effectively addressed, a CAS and a CLA. It happened that both had the same

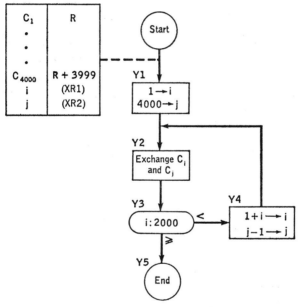

Fig. 7-7. Reversing the order of words in a block.

address and tag. This, of course, is not a necessary restriction. We may use any number of tagged instructions utilizing all the index registers. As long as we follow a systematic plan, we shall have no difficulty manipulating all index registers simultaneously and, if we wish, effectively addressing every other instruction.

A simple problem should build our confidence. Suppose we wish to take 4,000 words and reverse their order in storage. The first word is to be exchanged with the last, the second with the second to the last, and so forth. The flow diagram in Fig. 7-7 illustrates how we can make this reversal using two indexes—one counting up from the beginning of the list (i) and one down from the end (j). Both indexes progress toward the middle of the list, where the process terminates after c_{2000} and c_{2001} are interchanged. Two tables, for i and for j, will show us exactly how to proceed with our index registers and indirect addresses. The first one is familiar:

i	XR1	Effective address	$L(c_i)$	X
1	2000	X − 2000	R	R + 2000
.	.	.	.	
.	.	.	.	
.	.	.	.	
2000	1	X − 1	R + 1999	R + 2000

The second table is somewhat different from our previous examples because j moves backward. Therefore, in order for the effective addressing to proceed in the proper direction, the index register must move forward. Since j will not be tested, any starting value will do. For example, starting with zero:

j	XR2	Effective address	$L(c_j)$	Y
4000	0	Y	R + 3999	R + 3999
.	.	.	.	
.	.	.	.	
.	.	.	.	
2001	1999	Y − 1999	R + 2000	R + 3999

Thus prepared, we can code the problem:

```
R    BSS    4000
T    BSS    1          Temporary storage
Y1   AXT    2000, 1    Start i
     AXT    0, 2       Start j
Y2   CLA    R + 2000, 1    Get cᵢ
     STO    T          Save in temporary location
     CLA    R + 3999, 2    Get cⱼ
     STO    R + 2000, 1    Store in previous L(cᵢ)
     CLA    T          Get cᵢ
     STO    R + 3999, 2    Store in previous L(cⱼ)
Y3   TIX    Y4, 1, 1   Test and increment i
     TRA    Y5
Y4   TXI    Y2, 2, 1   Reduce j
```

With the flow diagram and the tables, we have made straightforward work of what might otherwise seem quite complicated.

PROBLEMS

7-16. Write instructions which will move a block of 1,200 words into another (nonoverlapping) block of 1,200 location.

7-17. Write instructions which will count the number of times a positive word just precedes a negative word in a block of 2,128 words.

7-18. Write instructions which will move all positive words from a block of 5,276 words into another block. The new block will, of course, be shorter —or at least no longer—than the original.

Count-controlled Loops in FORTRAN

Although count-controlled loops may be coded in the FORTRAN language using no more facilities than we already know, the language provides a special facility for coding this frequently encountered situation. This facility, the DO statement, not only simplifies the coding of count-controlled loops, but also simplifies the analysis the FORTRAN compiler must do in order to use the machine's indexing facilities in an optimum manner, since the DO statement makes it easier to analyze the intent of the programmer.

We know that a count-controlled loop has three basic parts, namely:

1. Initializing the count.
2. Testing for the terminating condition.
3. Incrementing the count.

In the FORTRAN language, the DO statement, placed at the beginning of the active instructions of the loop, takes care of all three of these functions for the entire loop. Roughly, the statement

DO 22 I = 1, 50

says that all the statements until statement 22 is reached are to be executed 50 times, with the index, I, starting at 1 and moving up one each time through the loop. To illustrate the use of such a DO statement, let us recode the program shown in Fig. 7-4:

```
      DIMENSION A(150)
1     DO 3 J = 1, 200
2     READ (1)A
3     WRITE (2)A
      END FILE 2
```

When we compare this program with our previous FORTRAN coding of the same problem, we see that the single DO statement takes the place of four statements, 1, 4, 5, and the GO TO following 5. The DO statement also represents three separate boxes on the flow diagram, since it stands for the three different functions they represent.

To understand the operation of the DO statement in the FORTRAN language, we must remember that the DO statement itself is, in effect, executed only once—at the beginning of the loop—and does not belong to the loop as such. The first statement in the loop is the statement *after* the DO statement, in this case, statement 2. The last statement executed in the loop is the statement *mentioned* in the DO statement, in this case, statement 3. It is important to note that statement 3 must be executed each time through the loop, for if statement 3 is not executed, the count will not be incremented. Thus, if there are several flow paths within the loop itself, they must all eventually converge on the last instruction in the loop—the one mentioned in the DO statement—or else the loop will not be executed properly. Of course, if we do not wish to complete the specified number of iterations of the loop, we can have the program exit from it before the count has been completed. The counting variable will, in that case, remain at its final value, showing how many times the loop was executed before it was terminated.

Let us look at a few more examples of the use of DO statements, in order to make these points completely clear. First, let us code the diagram in Fig. 7-5.

```
          DIMENSION A(1000)
   1      N = 0
          DO 4 I = 1, 1000
   2      IF (A(I))4,3,4
   3      N = N + 1
   4      CONTINUE
   6      . . .
```

In this example, we see that the dummy statement, CONTINUE, has to be inserted in the loop so as to bring the two lines of flow to a common termination at the final statement specified in the DO statement. CONTINUE results in no executable instructions in the object program and may be considered equivalent to a NOP in the machine language. Another, more subtle, point to notice is the way we reversed the coding for the two lines in block one, because of the structure of the DO statement. Suppose we had written

```
          DIMENSION A(1000)
```

```
1     DO 4 I = 1, 1000
      N = 0
2     IF  (A(I))4,3,4
3     N = N + 1
4     CONTINUE
```

in the above program. In this case, the statement

$$N = 0$$

would be the first statement *inside* the loop (Why?) and would be executed each time around the loop. Thus, each time through the loop, the count would be erased, defeating the whole purpose of the program. In essence, we would have an elaborate and inefficient program for testing whether the last word in the list were zero. (Why?)

As another example, consider the coding for the flow diagram in Fig. 7-6:

```
      DIMENSION C(3825)
1     CMAX = C(1)
      DO 4 J = 2, 3825
2     IF  (CMAX − C(J))3,4,4
3     CMAX = C(J)
4     CONTINUE
6     . . .
```

This example illustrates how the counting in the DO loop may be started at any desired initial value—2, in this case. It also illustrates how the index value, J, may be used in arithmetic statements as well as IF statements within the loop. Naturally, each time the statement is executed, the index takes on the value dictated by the current count.

The use of the indexes for addressing within the loop is further illustrated by the coding for the example in Fig. 7-7.

```
      DIMENSION  C(4000)
1     J = 4000
      DO 4 I = 1, 2000
2     T = C(I)
      C(I) = C(J)
      C(J) = T
4     J = J − 1
5     . . .
```

Notice that we still use the technique of an intermediate storage location, T, to accomplish the exchange of each pair of words, and that—as in an earlier example—we must put the initialization of J before the DO statement. We should take particular note in this example of the three different types of index or subscript usages—in the tested quantity in an IF statement, on the right-hand side of an arithmetic statement, and on the left-hand side of an arithmetic statement.

The use of indexes in FORTRAN is actually much more flexible than we have yet demonstrated. In particular, we may use arithmetic expressions for indexes, a technique which often simplifies otherwise cumbersome coding. As an example of indexing with expressions, consider the program we just coded. If we refer to our original analysis of the indexing in this program, we may notice that the indexes i and j are in a constant relation, namely, that $i + j = 4001$, or in other words, that $j = 4001 - i$. Since i and j are always in this relation, we need not keep separate track of both of them in the program—either one will do. Suppose we choose to keep track of i; then the program will look as follows:

```
      DIMENSION C(4000)
1     DO 3 I = 1, 2000
2     T = C(I)
      C(I) = C(4001 − I)
3     C(4001 − I) = T
5     . . .
```

Clearly, the coding has been simplified; and it might be even more simplified in a more complex example. We should be aware, on the other hand, that such simplifications may be done at the expense of complication—and consequent loss of efficiency—in the object program. Thus, it may turn out to be less efficient to calculate the index, $4001 - i$, each time through the loop—even if the compiler recognizes that the same quantity is needed twice and avoids a recalculation.

In general, however, the efficiency of a program will not so much be influenced by the characteristics of the compiler as it will by the general method chosen by the programmer. Time invested in analysis is at least 10 times as rewarding as time spent in streamlining coding which already does the job at hand. Of course, the very handiness of certain coding facilities, such as the DO statement, may tempt the unwary programmer down a primrose path of inefficiency, as in the following example:

Example. Suppose we are keeping in memory a table of 10,000 part numbers from a manufacturing operation. Associated with these part numbers is a list of prices, one for each part. At a certain point in one of our programs, we have a part number and need to find the corresponding price. In other words, the program must look up the price in a table of prices, arranged according to part number.

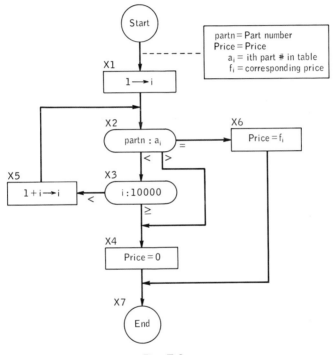

Fig. 7-8.

The flow diagram for one method of performing this table look-up is shown in Fig. 7-8. Here, the program starts at the head of the list of part numbers and compares them one at a time to the desired part number (block 2) until it either finds the number (=) or discovers that it is not in the table (> in block 2 or exceeding the length of the table in block 3), in which case a price of zero is used. The coding of this diagram in FORTRAN is·quite straightforward, particularly because of the DO statement:

```
      DIMENSION  A (10000),F (10000)
 1    DO 3 I = 1, 10000
 2    IF  (PARTN − A(I))3,6,4
 3    CONTINUE
 4    PRICE = 0
      GO TO 7
 6    PRICE = F (I)
 7    . . .
```

In this example, we see a case mentioned earlier, an exit from an unfinished DO loop. We expect that the part number will ordinarily be in the table, so that the program will normally exit from the loop through block 6, not through block 4. In block 6, even though we have left the DO loop, the value of the index, I, has been preserved. Thus, it may be used to find the price corresponding to the last part number examined, a_i, namely, f_i.

Simple as this program is, it is not at all the most efficient way to perform the task at hand. In searching through the part numbers one at a time, we are almost not taking any advantage of the orderly arrangement. On the average, then, we shall find the program going through the loop about 5,000 times to find each price. In the problems of Chap. 1, we considered possible methods of searching through an ordered table. If we answered those questions, we know that there is a better way to find the entry we want in an ordered table. The method is simple; we all use some variation of it when looking in a telephone book or a dictionary. First, we divide the table into two equal parts. Since the table is ordered, we can easily determine which half the desired number is in. We then consider only that half and divide it in half. Again, we can determine which half we want, repeating the process until we have narrowed down to the item we want (or to the place it should be, if it is missing). The entire process is called a *binary search*—because it is based on dividing in half repeatedly—and is often an efficient table-look-up technique in a random-access memory of a computer. (Would it be a good technique for a table on tape?)

Just how efficient is the binary search? To answer this question, we can look at the progress of a binary search on our part number problem. Suppose the part number we were looking up happened to be the 3,726th number in the table. On the first division, we would determine that it was between 1 and 5,000; on the next, between 2,500 and 5,000; then between 2,500 and 3,750; then 3,125 and 3,750; then 3,437 and 3,750; then 3,593 and 3,750; then 3,671 and 3,750; then 3,710 and 3,750; then 3,710 and 3,730; then 3,720 and 3,730; then 3,725 and 3,730; then 3,725 and 3,727; then 3,726 would be found. In other words, about 12 to 14 iterations of the process would be required (fewer if the number happened to be found on an earlier step), essentially independent of the number we are searching for. Since the sequential search requires an average of 5,000 iterations of its loop, we will find a binary search to be more efficient if we can code its basic loop so it will not be more than, say, 40 times slower than the sequential loop. This efficiency is easily accomplished. The flow diagram for the binary search is shown in Fig. 7-9, and though its logic is a bit more complex than the sequential search, it is easily coded in FORTRAN as follows (even though DO cannot be used):

```
        DIMENSIONS  A(10000), F(10000)
   1    L = 1
        N = 10000
   2    I = (L + N)/2
   3    IF  (PARTN − A(I))4,7,6
   4    N = I
   5    IF  (N − L − 1)9,9,2
   6    L = I
        GO TO 5
   7    PRICE = F(I)
  13    . . .
   9    IF  (PARTN − A(N))10,8,10
   8    PRICE = F(N)
        GO TO 13
  11    PRICE = 0
        GO TO 13
  10    IF  (PARTN − A(L))11,12,11
  12    PRICE = F(L)
        GO TO 13
```

First, we should explain the reason for blocks 8, 9, 10, 11, and 12, for they illustrate the kind of care which must be exercised when

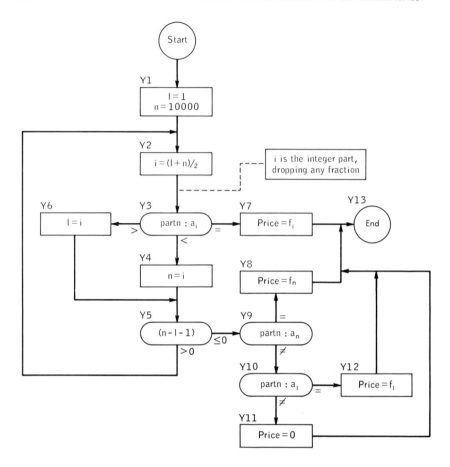

Fig. 7-9. Flow diagram for binary search.

analyzing more complex methods. This special logic is needed merely
to ensure that no part number is overlooked at the end of the search.
Suppose that the actual part number was in the eleventh place in the
table and that the search had narrowed down to L = 10 and N = 11.
When a FORTRAN program calculates an index quantity, such as
$(L + N)/2$, the result is always a whole number (since it would not
make sense to index by a fraction). Thus, at this point the program
would calculate $i = (10 + 11)/2 = 10.5 = 10$, since the fraction is
always dropped. Since a_{10} is not the required part number, and is, in
fact, lower, the program will pass through block 6, which will set

L = 10, thus changing nothing from the last iteration. Our first problem, then, is to be sure we do not get into an endless loop, which we would if block 5 tested the quantity, N − L. We avoid this problem by testing the quantity, N − L − 1, instead. (Why?) When this test eventually ends the loop, we know that the part number we want is either a_L, a_N, or not in the table. (Why?) Thus, we merely test for these conditions and take the appropriate actions in blocks 8, 9, 10, 11, and 12.

This extra logic, though it adds to the difficulty of analysis and to the length of the object program, is not part of the main loop of the binary search. Thus, it does not add significantly to the execution time of the program, which is primarily determined by blocks 3, 4, 5, and 6. Since we are coding in a higher level language, we cannot actually compare the execution time of these statements with the execution time of statements 2 and 3, the central operations of our sequential search program. We can see, however, that it is unlikely that the binary search instructions would take anywhere near 40 times the time of the sequential instructions. Therefore, we can anticipate savings in execution time using the binary search—savings we would not have obtained had we simply taken the quickest, most obvious coding method.

PROBLEMS

7-19. Code Prob. 7-17 using the FORTRAN language.

7-20. Code Prob. 7-18 using the FORTRAN language.

7-21. Suppose that in a certain program you had to sort a block of 5,000 numbers into numerical sequence. Develop at least three different methods for carrying out this sorting. Analyze each one for special starting and ending difficulties, indexing complexity, and efficiency of both time and storage space. Do any of the efficiencies depend on the distribution of numbers in the list? In what way?

7-22. Flow diagram one of the methods you developed in Prob. 7-21, and code the program in FORTRAN.

Indexed Control Instructions

Whenever we are given a new tool in the form of some special computer function, we should spend a little time contemplating other ways in which this tool may be used. Often the designer's original idea becomes one of the secondary uses of a given device. A technique

of utmost importance to one of our programs may not be used again
in the next fifty. In order to keep a large number of techniques fresh
in the mind, we must reduce them to, and associate them with, their
underlying principles. If we have mastered a few of these fundamentals along with the habit of curious exploration, we can rediscover
special techniques as we need them.

One method of discovering new ways of coding is to combine known
techniques in many of the possible combinations no matter how im-
probable, determine how they operate together, and try to think of
circumstances where such a result can be used. Previously we have
first found problems and then sought techniques for solving them.
Now that we have accumulated a small store of techniques, we can
synthesize others and possibly discover unsuspected new problems.

What happens, for example, when we combine effective addressing
with control instructions? How should we interpret

$$\text{TRA} \quad \text{X2, 4?}$$

By applying the rule for effective-address modification, we discover
that this instruction will transfer control to *different* locations depending on $C(XR4)$. If $C(XR4) = 1$, we effectively execute a

$$\text{TRA} \quad \text{X2} - 1$$

If $C(XR4) = -1$ (complement of one), the instruction is interpreted
as

$$\text{TRA} \quad \text{X2} + 1$$

Unlike a conditional transfer which makes a choice between transferring or no-operation, this tagged transfer chooses between a variety
of possible preset transfer points. In other words, this instruction is
a *switch*. In Fig. 4-10, we had a flow diagram using a switch. How
can we implement this switch using a tagged transfer? Suppose the
switching instruction is of the form

$$\text{ALPHA} \quad \text{TRA} \quad \text{X, 1}$$

Sometimes we want to transfer to XE, sometimes to XH; but there
is no necessary relation between the two addresses. How then can
we determine X? In one case,

$$X - C(XR1) = XE$$

while in the other,

$$X - C(XR1) = XH$$

Clearly, the change must be made through changing XR1, and thus the value of X is irrelevant. If we choose $X = 0$, then we have the two cases

$$-C(XR1) = XE$$

and

$$-C(XR1) = XH$$

which can be satisfied only by putting the *complement* of either XE or XH in XR1. Remember that the symbol XE represents only some location *number* to the assembly program and therefore may be complemented. If block XA is coded as

$$\text{XA} \quad \text{AXT} \quad -\text{XE, 1}$$

the complement of location XE is placed in XR1, and the instruction

$$\text{ALPHA} \quad \text{TRA} \quad 0, 1$$

will cause a transfer to

$$0 - \text{comp (XE)} = 0 + \text{XE} = \text{XE}$$

Coding block XE as

$$\text{XE} \quad \text{AXT} \quad -\text{XH, 1}$$

and XH as

$$\text{XH} \quad \text{AXT} \quad -\text{XE, 1}$$

completes the switch.

This technique is easily extended to any number of switching points. If we wish to set the switch for a given location, we set the complement of that location in the index register. The presence of switches in a program gives us a tremendous advantage. Programs of a high degree of complexity include a large group which deal with many variations and many types of data revolving about a basic flow of logic. Such programs are often written as one complete program including all variations rather than as separate subprograms. By presetting switches at the start of the program execution, the entire program logical flow is also "preset" so that the program does not have to continually "remember" what combination of data and variations is required. This allows for common usage of basic portions of the main program, saving considerable space. Say that we have a program built of seven basic sections A, B, C, D, E, F, G. For data X1 and variation V1 we use the sequence

$$A, B, D, F$$

For data X2 and variation V2 we use the sequence

$$B, D, F, G, A, E$$

By presetting our switches, we can achieve these sequences plus any others required.

Switching can occur other than by the combination of an unconditional transfer and index register. The 7090 has actual switching units, for example, which we shall discuss in a later section. We might even apply the transfer index-register-type switch to a conditional transfer. Such usage would be of a much more restricted nature than with the TRA.

Other types of switches may be constructed using effective-address modification. We see in all these types of switches the same indexing feature we saw in manipulating lists of data: a single instruction referring to a number of items.

Our remarks about synthesizing new tools out of combinations of old ones are not as applicable to higher level languages as they are to the machine language. The specialized nature of a problem-oriented language often results in preventing operations that are not explicitly provided for in the language. By limiting the choices the programmer has, the higher level language makes simple problems easier, but may unduly complicate others. The case of indexed control statements in FORTRAN is an example of this inflexibility. Our experience with the machine language would lead us to expect that we could write such statements in FORTRAN as

$$GO\ TO\ K(J + 1)$$

where J is an ordinary variable quantity. Such a statement would be a way of programming a switch in FORTRAN, but unfortunately, it is not permitted in the language. The only expression permitted to the right of a GO TO is a statement number.

In other words, in FORTRAN, statement numbers are distinguished from all other numbers—unlike the machine language, where addresses could be treated in the same way as other numbers. Thus, a special statement must be provided in FORTRAN if switches are to be permitted. One such statement is the *computed* GO TO statement. In it, we may list any number of switch points (statement numbers) and one simple index which is used to select one member from the list. For example, the statement

GO TO (24, 17, 385, 9),M

will cause a transfer of control to statement 24 if $M = 1$, to 17 if $M = 2$, to 385 if $M = 3$, and to 9 if $M = 4$. Although this device has considerably less flexibility than the indexed control instructions in the machine language, it can be embellished by using appropriate calculations for M just preceding the computed GO TO. Thus, if we should write

$$M = I - 3 * (I/3) + 1$$
$$GO\ TO\ (58, 99, 20),M$$

in the middle of a DO loop indexed on I, the GO TO would provide a sort of "rotating" switch, or alternator, which would send the flow of control to statement 99 on the first time through the loop, to 20 the second time, to 58 the third time, to 99 the fourth time, and so forth. (Why?) Of course, we can make a simpler switch merely by setting the index with appropriate arithmetic statements, such as

$$M = 2$$

at the proper places in the program.

Actually, the separation of program variables and statement numbers in the FORTRAN language can have very important consequences to the analysis which can be carried out on the source program by the compiler. Since statement numbers can only be referred to explicitly (and not manufactured in the course of the execution of the program), it is possible to analyze all possible paths by merely looking at the control statements in the source program. Thus, either the programmer (manually) or the compiler (automatically) can easily compare the flow of control of the source program to a flow diagram without concern that some new statement numbers might be created during the computation, thus creating new possible flow paths. Unfortunately, this checking is not done by many of the existing FORTRAN compilers, even though it would be quite a simple matter to have the computer draw a complete flow diagram of the source program as actually coded.

PROBLEMS

.7-23. Show how the switch in Fig. 4-10 could be implemented in a FORTRAN program.

7-24. Try to explain how a program might be able to produce a flow diagram from a FORTRAN source program. (Assume that some sort of graphical output device is available on which the lines and boxes of various shapes could be drawn and labelled.)

Indirect Addressing

Immediate addressing uses the address portion of an instruction as data; direct addressing uses the address to refer to a word containing the data. We can say, therefore, that, in the process of direct addressing, the data are one step removed from the instruction operation; while as the name implies, the data of the immediate address are associated immediately with the operation of the instruction. Let us extend this concept. We can conceive of a further type—many further types—of addressing where the data are two steps—or more —removed from the instruction using them. In the 7090, one further step may be added to most instructions using the direct address, giving us data two steps removed. This technique of operation-data communication is called "indirect addressing." In an indirect-addressing operation the address of the executing instruction refers to a word whose address is no longer that of the data but rather a secondary reference to the desired data location.

Suppose you were having an organization meeting which would be attended by many members from out of town. In order to give them sufficient notice, you might have to mail announcements before arrangements were fully made; or you might wish to determine the number planning to attend before selecting a meeting place. In either case, you could solve the problem by telling the members to come to a certain place from which they would be referred to the meeting location. You would, of course, be using indirect addressing, with some of its attendant advantages. Instead of telling the members where the meeting is, you tell them where to go to *find out* where it is. Clearly, indirect addressing gives us a most desirable degree of latitude.

Analogously, if we write the instruction

$$CLA^* \quad X1$$

(the asterisk after the operation code specifies indirect addressing)
we mean that X1 contains not the data but the *location of* the data.
If X1 contains the instruction

$$CAS \quad Y$$

the address Y is used as the address of the CLA* and the indirectly
addressed instruction becomes, effectively,

$$CLA \quad Y$$

The operation CAS does not affect the CLA instruction in any way;
any operation would do as well—TIX, STO, CLA, or even an invalid
operation. Only the address (and tag) of X1 is used to make the
indirect reference.

Indirect addressing gives us another method of address modification.
We have only to change the contents of one word and all instructions
which refer indirectly to that word are effectively changed. This technique adds a powerful ally to index-register utilization. We can use
any location for an indirect address, as opposed to the availability
of three index registers. We must note, however, that, while tagging
does not affect timing, indirect addressing adds one cycle to each
instruction using it. We can, of course, take advantage of both methods at once—either or both of the addresses involved in an indirectly
addressed instruction may be tagged.

Thus effective indirect addressing becomes a most important tool
for manipulating blocks of data. When sorting, only a single word
need be moved to effect the rearrangement of an entire block. When
using tables or arrays, a single instruction may replace a small routine. Often the input-output command can be used to indirectly
address the block of input or output data which it transmits. As in
our analogous example, indirect addressing gives us the ability to
make efficient use of space without losing flexibility.

To review, then, we have three levels of addressing—immediate,
direct, and indirect—each subject to effective address modification
through the use of the tag. Thus we have effective immediate address-

ing, where the data themselves are modified by the index-register contents; effective (direct) addressing, where the location of the data is modified; and effective indirect addressing, where either the location of the data, the location specifying the location of the data, or both are modified. This array of devices, properly used, gives the programmer a way to multiply the effectiveness of his instructions by mastering a few simple principles.

In FORTRAN, there is no facility for indirect addressing, though it might prove a powerful aid in certain problems. Of course, it is certainly possible to have indirect addressing in a higher level language; and indeed, many languages other than FORTRAN do have this useful facility.

PROBLEMS

7-23. Can we use effective addressing with the immediate address of an AXT instruction? What would it mean?

7-24. Do we lose any power because we cannot use AXT*? Why?

7-25. Cite examples in everyday life analogous to immediate, direct, and indirect addressing.

CHAPTER 8

SUBROUTINES

The subroutine is at once one of the most used and most abused parts of the computer technology. One of the major advantages of subroutine usage is the saving in time. This saving occurs in the calendar time of preparing a program for a computer and in the actual computing time. Yet the many wasted hours resulting from duplicated effort and rapidly constructed, poorly checked-out subroutines tend to offset too large a portion of this saving.

Exactly what is a subroutine? For our initial general discussion, let us choose a general definition, subject to modification as we proceed: *A subroutine is an addition to the basic vocabulary of the programmer.* We know that the computer has a basic vocabulary, encompassing the instruction (or command) definitions. The specific form for writing this working vocabulary may be set up by an assembly program; but the basic computer vocabulary, as we define it, is limited to only those instructions or commands which are available because of the logical circuitry of the computer's control units. This computer vocabulary is certainly the basis of the programmer's vocabulary; in fact, it *is*, as far as we know now, the entire programmer's vocabulary. The programmer is thus capable of communicating with the computer using only the basic set of instructions and commands or even a small portion of them. Therefore, depending on the extent of a particular computer's vocabulary, the programmer may work with a very limited or a very expressive language. We can infer that the basic instruction set of one computer may well contain instructions that would be classed as subroutines on a less comprehensive machine.

The major drawback to the computer's basic language is that, in order to improve it, we must change the circuitry of the machine itself. Usually this is an expensive task. Consequently we do not immediately consider this method of improving a computer; and even when we finally do, we may find such a physical change impossible. We are therefore presented a challenge. We want to increase the basic vocabulary of the programmer without changing the computer's basic language. How do we do this?

Since the subroutine is not a circuit change, it must simply be *one or more basic computer instructions, used together as a unit.*

We have a great deal of freedom in the use of subroutines. Because of such freedom, we also have important obligations. If we produce a new vocabulary word (subroutine) we must not produce something sloppy or something that may be misunderstood or misinterpreted. We want no loosely defined additions to our vocabulary. Furthermore, if a subroutine is needed, we should make certain that the particular function in which we are interested has not been already constructed. When we write a subroutine, we are also obligated to disseminate this information in a proper form so that as many programmers as possible may benefit from our work.

By its nature, a subroutine will be used by many different programs. The programmer must therefore do everything in his power to see that his subroutine is error-free. We can imagine the unfortunate results occurring from the use of a defective subroutine. If used in a production run, expensive losses can occur; if introduced in check-out (which is more reasonable) an already difficult task will be compounded.

General Advantages

Before going into any more specific detail it will be worthwhile to convince ourselves as to the general advantages of the subroutine.

First of all, by being an extension of the vocabulary, the subroutine gives direct assistance to people constructing a program. Most important, it can provide aid to the programmer who is not capable of developing the required routine himself. An economist may require the use of an involved subroutine for solving an equation. He may know what particular equation to use but may have no idea as to the methods of solution for this equation. With the necessary subroutine, he may proceed without any difficulty.

A thoroughly tested subroutine can be regarded as correct. Thus, if subroutines are employed in a newly developed program, their presence helps to home in on errors developing within the main program. Since we consider the subroutines correct, we have, for all practical purposes, a much smaller program to test.

By increasing our vocabulary through the use of subroutines, we provide the programmer with a stimulus to new ideas and techniques. In any language there is an important correlation between the comprehensiveness of the vocabulary and the formation of ideas. With this greater variety comes greater flexibility. Time which might have been spent creating this larger vocabulary can be spent in developing programs *using* the vocabulary.

The above points are important enough to be considered further as to their combined effects. Today we find that in all the many fields employing computers, specialists and experts are applying their knowledge to the creation of outstanding subroutines. A large library of diversified subroutines from all fields has become available and is still growing. Such a wealth of output gives us a tremendous impetus to computer design, for the subroutines of today may well become the foundation for the basic vocabulary of the advanced computers of tomorrow.

What can this library of subroutines do for a new computer user? Today it is possible for a new computer organization to start production quickly, with a minimum of waste and with a minimum staff of professional programmers and machine operators. It is sometimes possible to go into some production without having to create any wholly new programs—basing a system entirely upon available subroutines. Just as the basic instructions are the building blocks of the subroutines—so are the subroutines the building blocks of such programmed systems. In a similar manner we have the ability to *chain* our subroutines. That is, we can have subroutine within subroutine within another subroutine, and so forth. Thus we can increase our programming system in depth as well as in breadth.

Possible Disadvantages

With all these advantages, what are the practical difficulties which could substantially reduce the effectiveness of the subroutine? In broad terms, the pitfalls are misuse, overuse, misdirection, careless-

ness, sloppiness, poor logic, the unanticipated error, uncalled-for duplication (including creation of worn-out discarded methods), and misleading or unavailable descriptions of working subroutines, to name
the "popular" ones. But let us be more specific.

Too often, in an attempt to produce "new" material an installation
or programming group will tend to value quantity over quality. No
matter how impressive their aims may have been, they make no real
contribution. In their rehashing and recoding of some of the functions
and applications that were produced perhaps years earlier by well-
qualified people, they are turning out material that is of small value
to the growth of the computer community. When computers were
first introduced on a mass level, quantity was welcomed because of
the shortage of skilled personnel. Today, however, the production
of quality is becoming much more critical where we now have a firm-
ing foundation of techniques and applications. This is not to say
that new ideas and new techniques are not wanted—this is the only
way the computer industry can grow. What we say is that it is
becoming more difficult today to formulate good ideas and techniques
which are really new. It is becoming too easy to slide down a nicely
prepared smooth path. Quality can be achieved by a new installation
or programming group through proper preparation (becoming as
familiar as possible with what is available), proper discipline (not
allowing the staff of programmers to simply push out material—more
restraint and more time for evaluation are the keys here), and proper
communication (preventing the isolation of the programming group
from other groups with respect to new methods or ideas).

A much more wasteful, though less frequent, occurrence is the production of a major system, such as an assembly system, which incorporates ideas and techniques which have already been proved inadequate. The use of such discarded methods will only result in a
system that first will hinder the user and then will be simply discarded
after he has had a little education. This waste of time, talent, and
capital is something that should be eventually rooted out completely.

Often an excellent subroutine is not used because only a poor
write-up, or perhaps no write-up at all, exists. Many fine pieces of
work are buried by their write-ups; it is amazing how many misconceptions and misdirections can occur in such a description. Fortunately, organizations have arisen (one such group, called SHARE,

includes the users of the 7090) that have attempted, among other things, to establish a set of basic rules to be followed in writing subroutine descriptions. By faithfully following a relatively simple guide, any programmer can turn out a clear, complete, and correct subroutine write-up.

Next to the improper write-up, the most irritating and expensive difficulties are caused by errors in the subroutines themselves. One type of error, the uncalled-for error, will always exist to some degree. Poor use of flow diagrams, poor training, poor supervision, or just a poor attitude will cause these errors. Eventually, sufficient good literature, enough strong computer groups, plus the increasing awareness of management among computer users will tend to drive routines with such errors out of circulation.

The particular error that probably causes the most trouble is the unanticipated error. Especially in complex subroutine systems where we have a great variety of data that must be handled, a particular data combination may occur that is not treated correctly. Such a data combination may not be encountered during months of use. What happens when such an error occurs depends upon how careful (and lucky) the programmer was in setting up error routines within his system. If he was fortunate, such an unanticipated error might be caught within the same error routine as some incorrect data. If no such provision exists, the error may not be noticed until the program has gone through its entire execution. Note how important properly laid-out flow diagrams are at this time. With such a set of diagrams a programmer (not necessarily the originator) has a powerful aid to help him trace down the error in a logical manner. Information about such an error should immediately be distributed to all users of the subroutine or system. Organizations like SHARE have a central distributing agency through which this information can be quickly disseminated.

As in other areas of life, it is possible to try to make too much of a good thing. We may easily get dependent upon existing subroutines to the point that we become lazy. Rather than trying to improve upon our basic vocabulary, we may use whatever is conveniently at hand, even though we may have to reconstruct our logic to fit the existing routines. Such Procrustean techniques may result in a much less desirable solution. Other times there is a tendency to use a subroutine where simple basic programming is much more effective. We find ourselves sacrificing storage and time for convenience. In time of crisis, of course, where we must produce at all costs regardless of the loss, we might use subroutines in favor of a possibly more efficient solution. As usual, the circumstances must determine our approach.

The Subroutine Library

As the production of subroutines increases, it becomes more difficult for the individual programmer to keep up with all the developments. It requires considerable effort to be familiar with so many routines to the point of being able to use them all properly. Actually, it is generally unnecessary for a programmer to be this proficient. How, then, does he decide which subroutines sound interesting enough for him to pursue them further? This responsibility is normally delegated to the librarian. The librarian is usually someone with a fair knowledge of the computer (or computers) being used in the organization, and able to understand technical terminology to the point of properly classifying each subroutine. Is it an input-output type, an arithmetic type, or perhaps a technique for solving a special set of equations? (The computer organizations help in this area by sending out abstracts of the subroutines to all installations.) The librarian normaliy prepares lists of new subroutines together with brief descriptions for distribution within the organization. He answers questions as to the availability of subroutines meeting certain qualifications and is usually responsible for checking out all new subroutines for accuracy. If he does not understand particular techniques or applications, he may assign them to knowledgeable programmers. He is also responsible for keeping current copies of all subroutines for immediate usage.

Where a computer has magnetic tape as one of its inputs (as does the 7090) certain subroutines are kept on this medium. Usually a selection of the most-used subroutines is placed on a special-purpose magnetic tape, which is kept up to date by the librarian. During the assembly-program procedure, when the programmer's language is being translated into its equivalent machine language, the assembly program recognizes a special pseudo-instruction telling it to retrieve the desired subroutine from the magnetic tape. Automatically the subroutine will be combined with the main program that is being assembled.

Let us assume that we require a subroutine for taking average values, whose name is AVGVAL, and that this subroutine is located on a library tape. At a point in the main program sequence where we desire to bring in the subroutine we write

LBR   AVGVAL

This pseudo-instruction, LBR, tells the assembly program to search the library tape for the routine named AVGVAL and to insert it at this point in the program. A number of instructions will then be inserted—how many, of course, will depend on the nature of the particular routine.

We do not put all subroutines on the library tape because too much time would then be consumed in searching the tape. If we are using a less popular subroutine which is not found on the library tape, we can obtain a copy of the routine on punched cards from a file maintained for this purpose. These cards may then be combined with the remainder of our program to produce the same effect as the LBR pseudo-instruction. Cards, however, do not provide the same degree of convenience or speed as the library tape.

The Open Subroutine

The subroutine, as we have seen, consists of a number of instructions used as a unit to perform a given function. One method of using subroutines is to insert this unit at every point in the program where we need to have this function performed. As we make the insertion, we must modify certain instructions in the routine in order to adapt it to its particular use at that point. We might, for example, have to modify some addresses so they would refer to the proper data. In other words, the details of the subroutine must be open to our scrutiny so that we may make it a part of the main program. Because it is thus open to change, this type of program is often called an *open subroutine*.

As we can see, the open subroutine loses its separate identity once it has been inserted into the program. The subroutine simply becomes another set of instructions. Furthermore, it is necessary to recopy such a subroutine every time it is used (outside of a loop, of course).

For this reason open subroutines are often not used where they might provide the most efficient method. Suppose, for example, we desire a routine which clears a block of storage. Using a new instruction STORE ZERO (STZ) which clears the designated storage word, we could construct the following simple routine:

```
AXT    N, 1
STZ    A + N, 1
TIX    * − 1, 1, 1
```

where N is the symbol for the number of words in the block, and A is the symbol for the first location in the block. If we want to clear three blocks of, say, 100, 150, and 75 words starting with locations R, S, and T, we could write

```
AXT    100, 1
STZ    R + 100, 1
TIX    * − 1, 1, 1
AXT    150, 1
STZ    S + 150, 1
TIX    * − 1, 1, 1
AXT    75, 1
STZ    T + 75, 1
TIX    * − 1, 1, 1
```

In other words, where routines are short and simple enough to be used as open subroutines, they are often so simple as not to offer any great advantage over the programmer's own original efforts.

The Macro-instruction

Once again we have a situation where difficulties in using certain computer techniques may be resolved by using the computer itself. Filling in the appropriate modifications to the open subroutine is just the type of tedious repetitive work at which the computer excels. All we need is a way to tell the machine what we want done and when we want it.

One way in which we tell what we want done is by using a form of pseudo-instruction called MACRO. This pseudo-instruction tells the assembly program that we want to *define a macro-instruction*. Now a macro-instruction (meaning "big" instruction) is just a group of words used together as a unit and is often used as a simple means of utilizing open subroutines. Using the MACRO pseudo-instruction we have the facility to define a storage-clearing subroutine as follows:

```
CLEAR    MACRO      A, N
         AXT        N, 1
         STZ        A + N, 1
         TIX        * − 1, 1, 1
         ENDM
```

CLEAR is the *name* of the macro-instruction (called "macro" for short) which we are defining and is an arbitrary choice on our part. The instructions between MACRO and ENDM are called the *skeleton* of the macro. They define the general appearance of the macro we are defining. The ENDM pseudo-operation is used in this case to indicate the end of the skeleton. A and N are called the *parameters* of the macro because they define those parts of the skeleton which normally will be varied with different uses of the macro.

In other words, we have defined a three-word macro, named CLEAR, which has two parameters, the location of a block and the number of words in that block, *in that order*. We now have the means of telling the assembly program concisely what we wish to do. We still must solve the means of having it done—for as yet no words have been inserted into the program. Fortunately there is a simple procedure for accomplishing the insertion. When we wish to have this macro-instruction written into our program at a particular point, we write at that point the following: the name of the macro—which is placed in the operation field—and the values we want for the parameters—which are placed in the variable field *exactly* in the order in which they appeared in the initial MACRO definition. For example, to write our open subroutine three times, as before, we simply write

```
CLEAR    R, 100
CLEAR    S, 150
CLEAR    T, 75
```

The assembly program does the work of inserting the macro three times according to our definition. As a result, we get precisely the same nine words written into our program as listed above—with far less work. Furthermore, the form of the macro makes it much easier to read what the program is doing and enables us to use this type of open subroutine repeatedly, worrying only once about its detailed form.

If a particular open subroutine (or other macro-instruction) is used often, by many different programmers, we may wish to make its availability even more convenient. We can do this by building the definition of the macro into the assembly system, rather than requiring each individual programmer to redefine it. Such a built-in macro is called a *system macro*, as opposed to the *programmer macro* which we just learned. The use of the two types is the same; they differ only in that the programmer need not define the system macro.

The system macro is truly the simplest way of utilizing open subroutines. For example, a sequence of instructions used to skip a file on a tape could be represented by a system macro. Such a macro might look like the following:

SKIPFI   T, N

where SKIPFI is the system macro name located in the operation field, T represents the symbolic name of the tape involved, and N represents the number of files to be skipped.

The programmer macro, as well as providing a simple means for using open subroutines, gives us a way of defining any repetitive sequence of words (not necessarily instructions) which may suit our purposes. Another example of the definition and use of a programmer macro may be helpful.

Suppose we define a macro to find the largest of three numbers—the number to be left in the accumulator after the macro execution. For this example, the macro definition might look as follows:

Location	*Operation*	*Address (variable)*
COMPAR	MACRO	FIRST, SECOND, THIRD
	CLA	FIRST
	CAS	SECOND
	TRA	* + 3
	TRA	* + 2
	CLA	SECOND
	CAS	THIRD
	TRA	* + 3
	TRA	* + 2
	CLA	THIRD
	ENDM	

Now we want to use this macro in finding the largest of nine numbers located in Z through $Z + 8$, the result to be stored in location LARG. The flow diagram for this problem is shown in Fig. 8-1. The coding is simply

H1	COMPAR	$Z, Z + 1, Z + 2$
	STO	LARG
H2	COMPAR	$Z + 3, Z + 4$, LARG
	STO	LARG
H3	COMPAR	$Z + 5, Z + 6$, LARG
	STO	LARG
H4	COMPAR	$Z + 7, Z + 8$, LARG
	STO	LARG

which would result in 40 words being assembled into the program.

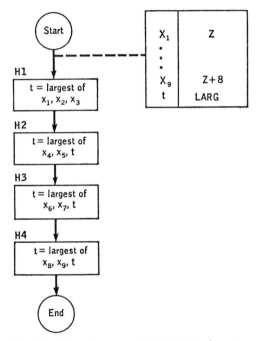

Fig. 8-1. Flow diagram of COMPAR subroutine.

PROBLEMS

8-1. Define a programmer macro which counts the number of zero words in a block.

8-2. Use the above macro in a program to find which of three blocks (differing in length) has the most zeros.

Closing the Subroutine

We see now that, through the macro-instruction technique, we have greatly simplified the use of open subroutines. However, this technique is not the complete answer to subroutine representation. The open subroutine is clearly fast and direct. Where, then, does any restriction or disadvantage lie? When we use the macro form, we tend to obscure the disadvantage; for when writing only one line for each usage, it is easy to overlook just how many words we are actually building into the program. Our COMPAR subroutine was nine words long. Thus, in using it four times, we added 36 words to the size of the program. This effect is magnified if we use the subroutine more often or if the subroutine is longer. It seems somehow intuitively wasteful that we should have to repeat essentially the same instructions many times throughout the code. Is there not some way we can write the instructions just once and then make use of them over and over? If we could find such a way we would be willing to sacrifice something for it, speed, for example. We are already aware that we often have to compromise speed to gain space, and vice versa.

Two major problems must be solved in order to achieve this space saving; two things must be done at the subroutine execution time that —with the open subroutine—are done at assembly time. First, and most obvious, the "closed" subroutine must be able to adjust its own parameters each time it is used. This problem arises since the closed subroutine is now assembled only once and thus is limited to only one initial preset value for each of its parameters. In other words, each time it is used, our closed subroutine must be able to carry out operations modifying itself that are basically equivalent to the operations the assembly program or the programmer performs for the open subroutine. On a machine which we know has the ability to modify its own instructions, such self-adjustment is not conceptually difficult, though it may prove difficult in practice.

The second problem, not so obvious, is that of transfer of control between the main program and the closed subroutine. We put an open subroutine into the flow of control of the main program by physically inserting it at the proper points. Control between main program and subroutine is simply a natural consequence of the normal flow of the program, but with the closed subroutine we intend to insert it only once. No longer is the natural flow of control possible.

Although we can easily send control to a subroutine from several places in the main program by simple transfers, returning control from one point in the subroutine to several main program locations may prove more difficult (see Fig. 8-2). When we have succeeded in making a subroutine self-adjusting and self-controlling, we apply the term we have been using—we have a "closed" subroutine. (Of course, it

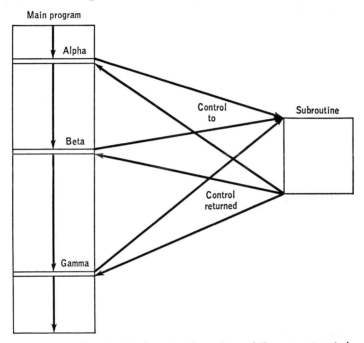

Fig. 8-2. Entering the closed subroutine from three different points (schematic representation).

would be possible to have an open subroutine be self-adjusting, but this combination is seldom seen. There is little advantage to such an arrangement that we have not already gained through use of the macro-instruction.)

The Calling Sequence

In order that the closed subroutine may be able to carry out these two tasks at execution time, the main program must supply certain information—the parameters and the desired return point—each time it sends control to a subroutine. This information is supplied by the *calling sequence*, so named because it is the sequence of words we must write to call the subroutine into use. In other words, the calling sequence must carry all the information contained in the parameters of the open subroutine as well as information necessary to control the return from the subroutine to the main program. Let us first concentrate on the latter aspect, for in some subroutines that is all the calling sequence will contain. We find that the problem of transfer of control is essentially a problem of the main program setting a *switch* in the subroutine. Although there are many ways this setting might be accomplished, there are a number of advantages to having one standard way of linking the subroutine to the main program.

On the 7090, this linkage is accomplished through the use of the instruction TRANSFER AND SET INDEX (TSX). This single instruction provides all the necessary control for proper main program—subroutine communication, requiring the use of only one of the three index registers. (By common agreement through SHARE, index register 4 is used wherever possible.) The following instruction illustrates the TSX execution.

Location	*Operation*	*Address tag*
ALPHA	TSX	SUBR1, 4

After the execution the designated index register XR4 will contain the control-communication information. The location of the TSX instruction—ALPHA in our example—is automatically placed into this specified index register *in complement form* (see Indexed Control Instructions, Chap. 7). Such a procedure will provide an *additive* index-register quantity which is required. Once the index register is thus set up, control is transferred to location SUBR1.

What advantages does such a seemingly unusual procedure give to us? Once the complement (effective minus) value of ALPHA, or any location, is placed into the index register, we can make reference to any nearby location in storage simply based upon its *relative position* from that base value. What, for example, does the instruction

CLA   1, 4

tell the computer to do?

It says put into the accumulator the contents of the storage location designated by the effective address. What is that location? It is $1 - (-\text{ALPHA})$ or $(1 + \text{ALPHA})$ (the address value minus the contents of the respective index register). Thus the contents of

(ALPHA + 1) are placed into the accumulator. This storage location is simply 1 greater than the location value found in the index register.

The following general statement may be made: Whenever an instruction is tagged by an index register containing a quantity resulting from a TSX execution, the number placed in the address portion of this tagged instruction (say n) will always specify a relative position from the location of the TSX instruction. n thus means the location n words away from the location we TSX'ed from. In Fig. 8-2 we see that the returning subroutine instruction could be

$$\text{TRA} \quad 1, 4$$

Obviously the subroutine has no idea as to where it will return control. It knows only that it will return control to a location having a value 1 greater than the location containing the originating TSX instruction—that is, the location from which it was entered.

With this ability to communicate easily between main program and subroutine and, most important, the reduction of linkage to a single instruction, the open subroutine is often effectively replaced by the closed subroutine. Suppose we had a subroutine which looked up numbers in a table. We might, for example, have a part number and wish to know the price of the part. Since the data for the subroutine are one word and the output is one word, we can use the AC for both and avoid the use of any parameters. We could prepare to enter the subroutine by

$$\text{CLA} \quad \text{PARTNO}$$

following which the execution of

$$\text{TSX} \quad \text{PRICE, 4}$$

takes us to the subroutine. The desired price is placed into the AC by the subroutine. Control is then returned to the main program at the next location after the TSX instruction. Thus the sequence of instructions

$$\text{CLA} \quad \text{PARTNO}$$
$$\text{TSX} \quad \text{PRICE, 4}$$
$$\text{STO} \quad \text{PR}$$

stores in PR the price of the part designated in location PARTNO. Only the TSX instruction is actually considered as part of the calling sequence, however, for the subroutine does not care how we (the main program) got the part number into the AC. Neither does it care what we do with the price once it is given to us. Apparently this subroutine makes a return via a

$$\text{TRA} \quad 1, 4$$

Sometimes a subroutine has no parameters in the calling sequence because it has no data whatsoever. We might, for example, have a subroutine which checked the clock to see if some preset time had been used up. Here we want the subroutine to act as a control instruction, to answer a question. We accomplish this control function by having two places to which control may be returned. Thus the calling sequence of this subroutine would be designated in the write-up as

$$\text{TSX} \quad \text{TIME, 4}$$
Time used up return
Time available return

If we wrote in our program

$$\text{TSX} \quad \text{TIME, 4}$$
$$\text{TRA} \quad \text{END}$$
$$\text{TRA} \quad \text{MORE}$$

we would transfer to location END if the time were used up and to location MORE if it were not. This subroutine must have the means of creating two return instructions, one which says

$$\text{TRA} \quad 1, 4$$

and one which says

$$\text{TRA} \quad 2, 4$$

(Which is which?)

Calling-sequence Parameters

Now let us discuss a case where the subroutine requirements are such that parameters must be introduced in the calling sequence. A subroutine is designed to move a block of data from one area in storage to another. The subroutine must know, then, where these areas start, and the number of words in the block. TSX by itself cannot furnish this information. Thus we introduce our parameters.

Figure 8-3 illustrates the flow diagram representing the subroutine. Note that the assertion box may be used to describe the calling-sequence layout. The responsibility for this layout is with the subroutine author since he knows how the subroutine is constructed internally in order to obtain external information. The calling-sequence description must appear in the total subroutine write-up.

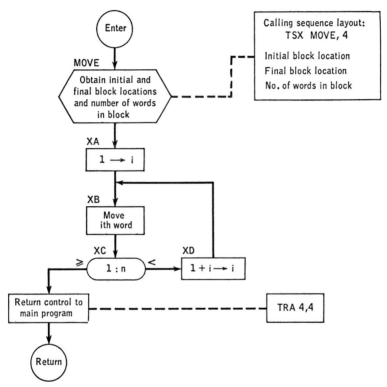

Fig. 8-3. Flow diagram of MOVE subroutine.

A detailed calling-sequence layout to satisfy the requirements of this subroutine, which we shall call MOVE, is shown in Fig. 8-4.

The pseudo-operation PLUS ZERO (PZE) is used here to tell the assembly program to insert some data—usually, as in this case, program parameters—in a word which has an instruction format. The "plus zero" refers to the three bits 000 which are placed in the prefix and which are followed by the specified address, tag, and decrement (blank fields, as usual, give zeros). PZE, then, gives us a simple way of inserting such parameters in calling sequences or elsewhere, with-

Location	*Operation*	*Address, tag*	*Remarks*
ALPHA	TSX	MOVE, 4	Complement of ALPHA placed in XR4
	PZE	FIRST	Parameter specifying initial block location
	PZE	LAST	Parameter specifying final block location
	PZE	N	Parameter specifying number of words in block
		Normal return	

Fig. 8-4. Calling sequence of MOVE subroutine.

out misleading us into thinking that they are parts of real instructions. Whenever this subroutine is required, we would simply insert into the main program sequence a calling sequence of the type shown. We should emphasize that the calling sequence is not a physical part or really even a logical part of its corresponding subroutine; it is simply the connector between two sets of instructions.

The MOVE subroutine knows that the location of the initial block parameter is one greater than the TSX location. Thus it can refer to such information by using an address reference of (1, 4) since XR4 is the conventional linkage index register. In the same manner, a (2, 4) reference obtains the parameter for the location of the new, or final, block location. The number of words in the block then requires a (3, 4). Note that this subroutine's return instruction will not be a (TRA 1, 4) but rather a (TRA 4, 4).

PROBLEMS

8-3. A block of data to be moved by the subroutine starts at location ZZZ, is to be moved to an area starting at location AAA, and is 117 words long. Set up the calling sequence for this case.

8-4. Write a code, using the subroutines described above, which, if more time is available, will move a 320-word block from an area starting at RXY to an area starting at QXZ and which, if no more time is available, moves a 400-word block starting at SXY to the same area (QXZ).

Closing the Subroutine—An Example

It is important to notice that we can use a closed subroutine without knowing anything at all about what goes on inside of it just as we operate mostly on this basis in normal life with cars and appliances, for example. There are many more subroutine users than subroutine writers. Thus we ought to be thoroughly familiar with the *use* of subroutines before we attempt to write them. Nevertheless, it would be instructive to attempt to understand in more detail how the closed subroutine does its job. Those who do not care to know—and it will not make them any less of a subroutine user—may skip this section. Let us begin our efforts by examining how we would write the MOVE subroutine as an open subroutine. The definition of its macro-instruction form could be as follows:

MOVE	MACRO	FIRST, LAST, N
	AXT	N, 1
	CLA	FIRST + N, 1
	STO	LAST + N, 1
	TIX	* − 2, 1, 1
	ENDM	

These four instructions, AXT, CLA, STO, and TIX, corresponding to blocks XA, XB, XC, and XD in Fig. 7-3, do all the basic work of the subroutine. Remember, however, that, if we wish to use the closed subroutine form, the subroutine itself must do the work done by the assembly program for the open subroutine. Thus the subroutine must *generate* the addresses of the AXT, CLA, and STO instructions, using the parameters found in the calling sequence. Only the TIX instruction need not be modified in any way.

Although the actual code could be simpler if we were to introduce some new instructions, we shall try to make do with instructions we already know in order not to obscure the point at hand. Our first task is to get N into the AXT instruction. A little thought, however, will show that, since we must first get N into an index register to do this, we might as well leave it in the index register and use an instruction other than AXT. This observation simply shows that there may be necessary alternatives in the code when closing an open subroutine.

Let us determine how to put N into the index register. Ordinarily, we might use an LXA. LXA requires the tag portion for its execution, however. Since we must refer to the location of the parameter N by using an address of (3, 4), we cannot use LXA. This difficulty can be avoided by first moving N to a fixed location and then loading the index register from that location. Thus we write the three instructions

CLA	3, 4	Moves N to AC
STO	COMMON	Moves N to COMMON
LXA	COMMON, 1	Moves N to XR1

which move N to XR1 through the intermediate use of the AC and a
storage location, COMMON. (COMMON and succeeding locations
may be used, by SHARE convention, for working, or temporary, storage by all subroutines. This reduces the total working storage required by any program using such routines.) We might have used
either XR1 or XR2; the choice was arbitrary. We would not, however, want to use XR4 for this purpose. (Why?)

Our code at this point looks as follows:

```
MOVE      CLA      3, 4
          STO      COMMON
          LXA      COMMON, 1
XB        CLA      **, 1
XBA       STO      **, 1
XC        TIX      XB, 1, 1
```

Notice how blocks XA and XD now have no instructions corresponding directly to them.

The next job is to generate the address FIRST + N and insert it
in the address portion of the instruction in XB. To do this requires
the addition of two numbers. Using only the instructions and techniques we have learned so far, we might obtain addition by placing
one number in an index register and one number in the decrement of
a TXI instruction.

Suppose we set up the instruction

```
MOVEA     TXI        * + 1, 2, **
```

to do our adding and insert N into its decrement with some other instruction. In order to do this, we must break our resolve and introduce
one new—though not unfamiliar—instruction. We already know how
to store an index register's contents in an address (SXA); so it requires no great leap of the imagination to understand the instruction
STORE INDEX IN DECREMENT (SXD), which stores those contents in a decrement—without, of course, disturbing the rest of the
word. Thus, to insert N into D(MOVEA), we write

```
          SXD      MOVEA, 1
```

since N was already in XR1.

We can get the address FIRST into XR2 with the sequence

```
          CLA      1, 4
          STO      COMMON
          LXA      COMMON, 2
```

which is similar to a previous sequence and which may reuse the working location COMMON because N is now safely in XR1.

If we put these instructions together as follows, we get the sum FIRST + N in XR2.

	SXD	MOVEA, 1	Puts N in TXI instruction
	CLA	1, 4	FIRST to AC
	STO	COMMON	FIRST to COMMON
	LXA	COMMON, 2	FIRST to XR2
MOVEA	TXI	* + 1, 2, **	FIRST + N to XR2

We can now insert (FIRST + N) into the address portion of location XB by

$$\text{SXA} \quad \text{XB, 2}$$

By a similar sequence we can insert LAST + N into the address portion of location XBA, thus completing the initializing work required to close the subroutine. We only need the instruction

$$\text{XE} \quad \text{TRA} \quad 4, 4$$

at the end of the code to provide the control linkage back to the main program, and our subroutine is completely closed, as shown in Fig. 7-5. It certainly seems like a lot of stuffing for such a small turkey.

We could, as we have observed, reduce the amount of "stuffing" by the use of some more powerful instructions which we have not yet learned. However, this particular routine offers absolutely no advantage in the closed form. It obviously takes more time to execute, since we have extra things to do. But it does not even offer a saving in space. The calling sequence, which we must write each time we use the closed subroutine, is as long as the *entire* open subroutine. This illustration emphasizes the importance of proper planning, of not going overboard for any particular technique. Let us call the instructions that do the actual work the *execution* instructions. All other instructions whose purpose is to prepare the subroutine to carry out its execution and to ensure proper communication could be called *housekeeping* instructions. The relationship of execution to housekeeping instructions, together with the relative sizes of the calling sequence and execution set of instructions, helps determine whether the open subroutine (macro) or closed subroutine is to be used. The coding in Fig. 8-5 with only 3 of a total 19 instructions used for execution certainly is no example of a useful closed subroutine. A

Location	Operation	*Address, tag, decrement*	Remarks
MOVE	CLA	3, 4	N to ACC
	STO	COMMON	N to COMMON
	LXA	COMMON, 1	N to XR1
	SXD	MOVEA, 1	N to TXI instruction
	CLA	1, 4	FIRST to ACC
	STO	COMMON	FIRST to COMMON
	LXA	COMMON, 2	FIRST to XR2
MOVEA	TXI	* + 1, 2, **	FIRST + N to XR2
	SXA	XB, 2	To CLA instruction
	SXD	MOVEB, 1	N to TXI instruction
	CLA	2, 4	LAST to ACC
	STO	COMMON	LAST to COMMON
	LXA	COMMON, 2	LAST to XR2
MOVEB	TXI	* + 1, 2, **	LAST + N to XR2
	SXA	XBA, 2	To STO instruction
XB	CLA	**, 1	Instructional
XBA	STO	**, 1	Loop to move data
XC	TIX	XB, 1, 1	
XE	TRA	4, 4	Return to main program

Fig. 8-5. The coding of the MOVE subroutine.

case where, say, 80 per cent of the total subroutine code is in execution instructions and where the total length is perhaps 60 instructions should make an excellent closed subroutine.

For our purposes let us assume Fig. 8-5 is a good subroutine, since we have gone so far with it. It will, at least, give us a simple point on which to focus some further remarks.

PROBLEMS

8-5. Define a calling sequence and write a subroutine, called SWAP, which interchanges two blocks of words in storage.

8-6. Define a calling sequence and write a subroutine, called SQUEZ, which removes all zeros from a variable length block of words, moving the non-zero words up into a solid block at the beginning of the block (preserving their order), and also provides a count to the user of the number of non-zero words left in the block.

The Versatile Macro

An interesting and extremely useful application of the macro-instruction may be seen at this point. Suppose we are writing a

program which used the MOVE subroutine many times. Another
programmer has promised to write the MOVE subroutine for us in
both open and closed forms so that we may choose the one which will
be best for our purposes. When we get ready to do our coding, however, we find that he is not finished. How can we write our code so
that, no matter which form we finally choose, only a minimum amount
of work will be required to make the change? If we were just waiting
for him to write an open subroutine, we could of course use a macro-
instruction—waiting until just before assembly to define it. On the
other hand, if we knew it were to be a closed subroutine, we could
establish the calling sequence and enter the subroutine itself at assembly time. But why do we even have to define the calling sequence?
We know that, regardless of the form used—open or closed—the same
parameters must be supplied; so we can simply use the macro-instruction form throughout the code. Just before assembly, we would
define the macro-instruction as either the open subroutine itself or
as the calling sequence to the closed subroutine. In other words, we
can fill our code with such lines as

X1	MOVE	R, S, 280
Y3	MOVE	X, X + 10, 10
Z8	MOVE	S + 40, QL, 20
Z10	MOVE	M − 80, L + 20, 17

to do the work of moving blocks. Then, if we choose the open form,
we assemble the following macro definition with the program:

MOVE	MACRO	FIRST, LAST, N
	AXT	N, 1
	CLA	FIRST + N, 1
	STO	LAST + N, 1
	TIX	* − 2, 1, 1
	ENDM	

If we choose the closed form, we assemble this definition:

MOVE	MACRO	FIRST, LAST, N
	TSX	MOVE, 4
	PZE	FIRST
	PZE	LAST
	PZE	N
	ENDM	

We would also include the pseudo-instruction

MOVE   LBR   MOVE

provided the MOVE subroutine were put on the library tape. (Why do we not make the LBR pseudo-instruction part of the macro-definition of the calling sequence?)

Notice how easy it is, using this technique, to change between open or closed subroutines. In fact we can change from one subroutine to another, even though they may have different calling-sequence formats. For this reason—and because the macro format is easier to read and write than most calling sequences—the use of the macro-instruction to expand the parameters into calling sequences is extremely popular.

PROBLEM

8-7. Write macros which will expand into the calling sequences defined in Probs. 8-5 and 8-6.

Subroutine Obligations

Both the code and flow diagram (Figs. 8-5 and 8-3) for our example are correct as far as the functional part of the subroutine is concerned. We can move a block of words from one area to another. Mechanically the program is working. However, as the subroutine is written now, it has the unfortunate capability of ruining the main program. Index register one is used in the subroutine to control the internal loop. The manner in which this register is used causes the prior value in XR1 to be destroyed without recovery. As a result of the subroutine execution a value of one will always remain in XR1 upon return to the main program. It is possible that at the time of using the subroutine the main program does not require XR1 to remain intact but there is no guarantee that such will always be the case. Index register one could be responsible for controlling a vital section of the main program. The presence of a one in this register in place of the destroyed value could short-circuit the entire remaining execution of the main program. In a similar way, the destruction of XR2 is completely undesirable.

The first important obligation of a subroutine to a main program becomes apparent. The subroutine must do everything in its power to preserve the status of the computer as it is before the entry of the subroutine. If it is impossible or undesirable to preserve some part of the status, such as a register's contents or a switch position, notice must be given to the user. A simple coding addition to the MOVE subroutine of Fig. 8-5 can make the subroutine meet this obligation in so far as XR1 and XR2 are concerned. At the very beginning of the routine, we could write

MOVE	SXA	COMMON + 1, 1
	SXA	COMMON + 2, 2

thus saving the contents of the two registers in the second and third words of the working storage block. The end of the routine would then be revised to read

XE	LXA	COMMON + 1, 1
	LXA	COMMON + 2, 2
	TRA	4, 4

thus restoring the index registers just before returning. As far as the main program is concerned, these registers are not used by the subroutine, for it cannot tell the difference between "not used" and "saved-used-restored."

There is no reason, of course, why this obligation to protect those registers which the main program may be using should be restricted to the closed subroutine. The open form of the MOVE routine destroys XR1 and could be improved by the addition of save and restore instructions. A way to accomplish this feat without using any COMMON storage—a way which may be employed in open subroutines as well—is shown in the macro definition below:

MOVE	MACRO	FIRST, LAST, N
	SXA	* + 5, 1
	AXT	N, 1
	CLA	FIRST + N, 1
	STO	LAST + N, 1
	TIX	* − 2, 1, 1
	AXT	**, 1
	ENDM	

Notice how the first instruction SXA stores the index-register contents directly into the AXT instruction at the end. This instruction, in turn, restores those contents as soon as the loop is finished.

The second obligation of the subroutine is to protect itself from misuse in the sense of incorrect or insufficient data from the main program. In general, however, the subroutine must not allow a stop within its own bounds. The user will generally not be familiar with the inner workings of the subroutine but only with its operation, so such a stop would cause him a great deal of trouble. After all, the manner in which a subroutine works internally is usually of little importance to the user; he knows that, if he puts in a certain set of quantities, he gets out a certain set of results.

Another reason for the subroutine not stopping internally is that, by returning control to the main program instead, it permits the main program to make the decision as to whether or not stopping is desirable. The main program could have the facility to correct the error and return control to the subroutine. Maybe an alternate section of the main program might be the answer to such a subroutine reply. Perhaps it is possible to override the error. All such alternatives must be permitted. Thus stopping is out of the question.

As the calling sequence is now constructed, the subroutine returns control always to the location immediately following the last parameter. In our example, there were three parameters. Thus control was returned, using (TRA 4, 4), to the location following the third parameter.

A calling sequence capable of handling error conditions is readily set up by using the technique of multiple returns to the calling sequence—one for the normal return (error-free return) and one for the error return. There may even be several normal returns and several error returns for a single subroutine. All that is required is that in the subroutine write-up the purpose of each return be duly noted. The error returns generally precede the normal returns. (Why is such a sequence desirable?) Assuming that our subroutine were modified to detect two types of errors—an overlapping of the blocks and an attempt to store data in some restricted area—it might now have the following calling sequence:

```
A     TSX      MOVE, 4
      PZE      FIRST
      PZE      LAST
      PZE      N
      Error return 1—overlapping blocks
      Error return 2—restricted area
      Normal return
```

There are only two types of instructions that would normally be placed into an error-return location of the calling sequence, namely, a transfer or a halt. The transfer instruction allows the main program to send control elsewhere; the halt is self-evident.

Since the main objective of the closed subroutine is space saving, a large number of error returns is undesirable, since it burdens every user with a long calling sequence. Consequently, SHARE has adopted the convention that, where possible, a subroutine should have at most two returns. One of these, the one appearing last, should be "normal." The other should combine all other cases. In order that the main program have the facility to determine which of several returns was made, an identifying number, different for each exceptional case, is left by the subroutine in the decrement portion of its first location (by convention). Thus, to conform to this SHARE standard, our calling sequence might be reconstructed (and suitable changes made in the code) to read as follows:

```
A    TSX      MOVE, 4
     PZE      FIRST
     PZE      LAST
     PZE      N
     Error return: code 1 = overlapping blocks;
           code 2 = restricted area
     Normal return
```

The calling sequence is thereby shortened, although at the price of a slight inconvenience to the user who wishes to separate the two types of error.

PROBLEM

8-8. For the SWAP subroutine defined in Prob. 8-6, redefine the calling sequence and rewrite the subroutine so that there will be an error return in case the blocks overlap or in case either block contains words below location 1500. Be sure that all index registers are preserved by the subroutine.

Main-program Obligations

The obligations of the main program to the subroutine fall into the same two main areas of subroutine obligations to the main program— status protection and error protection. Did you notice that it is impossible for the subroutine to protect the contents of the index register used with the TSX instruction? Thus, if XR4 is being used by the main program at a time that a subroutine is needed, the main program must preserve XR4's contents prior to the TSX execution. Upon receiving control back from the subroutine the main program must restore the index-register value before continuing its execution. If there are any other registers, switches, or other part of the computer status which the subroutine does not handle—and so states in the write-up—then the main program must decide which items are worth saving. If a condition important to the main program cannot be saved by either the subroutine or main program, a change in the execution sequence may be required.

You may also have noticed that the MOVE subroutine, in both forms, destroys the AC contents. Unlike the index registers, the AC is not ordinarily used for any control function. Consequently, it is not considered desirable to burden every subroutine with the task of saving the AC contents. Thus, by convention, a main program which wishes to protect the AC contents upon entry to a subroutine will have to do the job itself unless the subroutine write-up explicitly states otherwise. Similarly, the main program can depend, unless otherwise stated, on the subroutine to preserve those registers which, by convention, it is the responsibility of the subroutine to preserve.

Just as the subroutine must indicate to the main program the presence of an error, so must the main program be prepared to handle each type of error indication. Often that part of the main program given the responsibility of treating error cases is one of the most difficult to create. A properly prepared error routine requires complete understanding of the main-program logic associated with the error in question plus a thorough understanding of the intricacies of the computer operation. An example illustrating the problems involved is the type of error routine known as the *restart*. This routine returns to a previous point in the execution, restoring everything to the status at that point. This is done in order to repeat a portion of the program marred by a possible machine error. During a production run, the main program must do everything in its power to attempt to correct for an error, by either overriding it or compensating for it. The main program must also warn the user (operator) that an error has occurred, if it cannot be really corrected.

FORTRAN Subroutines

When using the FORTRAN language, the programmer has the use of both an extensive library of useful subroutines and several mechanisms for writing his own subroutine-type routines. The use of routines from the FORTRAN library is so simple and convenient that the user is often not conscious of using a subroutine. For example, the FORTRAN library provides a subroutine, AMIN1, which selects the smallest of any number of input quantities. If the programmer wants to use the smallest of the quantities X, Y, and Z in some computation, he need only write, for example,

$$A = AMIN1(X,Y,Z) * C + B$$

which will produce an object program that will choose the smallest number among x, y, and z, multiply this number by c, and add b to the result. Just by mentioning the subroutine AMIN1, the programmer ensures that the subroutine will be compiled into the object program by the FORTRAN compiler from the FORTRAN library. No explicit request—such as the LBR in the symbolic assembly language— is required.

The convenience of FORTRAN subroutines is further enhanced by the ability to use arithmetic expressions in the "calling sequence," that is, within the parentheses containing the list of input quantities. Thus, the programmer might write the statement

$$R = AMIN1(X * Y, X + Y, X/Y, X - Y)$$

which sets the value of R according to which of the quantities, xy, $x + y$, x/y, or $x - y$, is the smaller, thus saving many lines of coding which would be necessary if this ability were not provided.

Although the FORTRAN language provides several special ways of defining and using subroutinelike program sections, the most general of these is provided by the SUBROUTINE statement (used to define the program section) and the CALL statement (used to provide the calling sequence to the section so defined). The definition of the subroutine is quite analogous to the definition of macros in the symbolic assembly language, with the SUBROUTINE statement taking the place of the MACRO pseudo-operation. To illustrate this analogy, let us see how a MOVE subroutine could be prepared for a FORTRAN program. First, we write the statement

SUBROUTINE MOVE(FIRST, LAST, N)

which, like the first line in a macro definition, defines the name of the subroutine, MOVE, and lists the parameters, FIRST, LAST, and N. Following the SUBROUTINE statement, we write the routine itself, essentially in a skeleton form in terms of the parameters in the SUBROUTINE statement. Wherever the routine is supposed to return control to the main program, the RETURN statement is used. Thus, the skeleton might read

```
        DO 5 I = 1, N
   5    LAST(I) = FIRST(I)
        RETURN
```

(Notice that we can use the names of variables in the DO statement. This facility is available in any DO statement, but is particularly useful in defining subroutines which are to work under a variety of conditions.) Finally, we close the definition with an END statement, just as we closed a macro definition with an ENDM pseudo-operation. The entire definition, then, reads as follows:

```
        SUBROUTINE MOVE(FIRST, LAST, N)
        DO 5 I = 1, N
   5    LAST(I) = FIRST(I)
        RETURN
        END
```

To use this subroutine form, we write a CALL statement, naming the subroutine and the variables to which we wish to have it apply. Thus, to move 280 numbers from block R to block S, we write

```
        CALL MOVE (R,S,280)
```

or to move $3n + 2$ numbers from block Z to block QST we write

```
        CALL MOVE (Z,QST,3 * N + 2)
```

and so forth.

Although the definition of subroutines by the SUBROUTINE statement closely resembles macro definition, the subroutines so defined are compiled as *closed* subroutines. Because of the closed nature of the FORTRAN statement numbering, the linkage provided for these closed subroutines by the compiler only allows for a single return point, namely, the statement after the calling CALL statement. Thus, *all* conditions, error or normal, must be signalled by some code and separated by the user after the return. It would be convenient if some parameters in the defining statement could represent statement numbers, so that we could write such statements as

```
        SUBROUTINE MOVE(FIRST,LAST,N,ERROR)
```

where ERROR stood for the statement number to which error returns were to be made. If we could do that, we could write

```
        CALL MOVE (X,Z,85,900)
```

which would mean to move 85 numbers from block X to block Y, and transfer control to statement 900 if there is anything wrong with this operation. Where such operations are not permitted, the restriction is part of the price we pay for having the convenience of the FORTRAN language in other respects.

PROBLEMS

8-9. Write a FORTRAN subroutine for Prob. 8-5.

8-10. Write a FORTRAN subroutine for Prob. 8-6.

8-11. Write a FORTRAN subroutine, SORT, which sorts a variable-length block of numbers into numerical order. (See Prob. 7-21.)

8-12. Write a FORTRAN program which uses the subprograms of Probs. 8-9, 8-10, and 8-11 to accomplish the following task: We have three blocks of 500 numbers each, A, B, and C. We want all the zeros removed from these blocks and the *remaining* numbers sorted into numerical order within each block. Then the blocks are to be rearranged so that the block with the fewest non-zero numbers is left in block A, and of the remaining two, the block with the largest first number is to be placed in block C and the other in block B.

A Redefinition

Now that we have had a broad look at the subroutine—its advantages and disadvantages, its forms and features—we might reconsider our original definition. The way in which we have defined subroutines—as an addition to the basic vocabulary of the programmer— gives the fullest possible indication of the purposes of these sets of instructions. As the definition is now stated, anything that is written which makes a *positive* contribution to the programming field could be considered a subroutine. From a working standpoint, however, we wish to modify our definition. We shall restrict the name subroutine to any set of instructions which, while meeting our general definition, also satisfies the following requirements: Its function must be general enough so that it will be used by a wide variety of programs and, ordinarily, be used many times within the same program. It is important to note that the many different programs employing the same subroutine need not be similar to one another in any way. The most esoteric scientific program and most complex accounting program can make use of some of the same subroutines in the same way they both make use of some of the same instructions. The subroutine thus approaches the general functional use of a basic instruction. Therefore, if we have written a program that satisfies our general definition in that we have extended our language, but this program is restricted in application—that is, even though it may be often used individually on a production basis, it is not used as part of another program or programs—it would not be classified as a subroutine. For this reason, an assembly program is not classified as a subroutine but is rather classified as a "system." A system is normally a multipurpose program—which usually contains many subroutines.

A subroutine by this definition offers general functions that can be used by many programs many times over. By these very functions, the subroutine will be limited in the number of variations it can handle. Once we begin increasing the capabilities of a given routine we find that soon the subroutine label no longer is applicable. Instead we simply develop a program or, if we go far enough, a system. We cannot afford to allow a subroutine to have the flexibility of doing too many things.

Because a subroutine is used largely to save space, we must consider keeping it down to a reasonable size. Why give a routine to a programmer when, say, only 30 per cent of it is useful to him? Why allow for possible error by permitting sections of a subroutine never used by a program to occupy space within it? Every subroutine has to be checked out completely by the user before it is accepted. By virtue of keeping the subroutine as compact as possible, with as few variations as possible, we simplify the task of verification.

A subroutine can be defined now as one that meets with the following requirements:

1. It must make a positive contribution to the existing program library, for our basic programmer's vocabulary is thus increased.

2. It must be general enough such that it will be used by many programs and often used many times within the same program.

3. It must represent a wise choice of the total number of functions it is capable of carrying out, for we cannot allow its very flexibility to make it difficult or inefficient to use in any specific application.

A problem that is still evident in the computing field is the assignment of a subroutine label to a program meeting only requirements 2 and 3. Only through proper education can this mislabeling be stopped. Until this happens a great deal of waste will occur.

With a complete library of true subroutines, a user may only have to write a set of calling sequences in order to create a large complex system. Some installations require that any new system to be developed be broken into smaller sections such that each of these sections may be written in the closed-subroutine *format*. Thus each section would have its appropriate calling sequence. Such sections generally would be classified as subroutine-*type* routines since there is no guarantee that they would satisfy the three specific subroutine criteria.

There is nothing wrong with such use of the subroutine form for routines which do not satisfy our definitions—but only in not recognizing the difference between subroutines and the form of subroutines. One great advantage of preparing the system in this manner is the better control we obtain, for we can develop such a system in less complex parts. The system can also be written faster in that the coding of the system sections can be done simultaneously by groups of programmers who do not even have to be physically near one another. As long as there are good flow diagrams, independent section programming can be accomplished with ease. At debugging time, errors can be isolated more quickly into one of the system's sections. In fact, this method of "subroutinizing" is often the best way of approaching the programming of a large system.

CHAPTER 9

TYPES OF SUBROUTINES

With the concepts and principles of subroutine usage fresh in our minds, we can now examine some representative areas in which we can expect to find help from the subroutine library. Before we embark on this survey, however, we should do well to prepare ourselves by learning some of the methods by which programmers keep others informed of their subroutines.

The Subroutine Write-up

A simple principle applies to the subroutine write-up, namely, that a fine subroutine with a mediocre write-up will usually be classed with the truly mediocre subroutines. No doubt, through plain luck, a fine subroutine may sometimes be extricated from its bad write-up; but this is no way to run a business—and programming is a serious business. We should expect that every subroutine will be described properly, for we really cannot consider a program as a subroutine unless there is an accompanying useful write-up. Certainly any device or tool regardless of expense is truly worthless if we cannot figure out how to operate it. Such a tool can be damaging if improperly used. Nevertheless, every year we see too large a number of subroutines—many of which cost a considerable amount of money to prepare—being discarded because of inadequate write-ups and inadequate up-dating. Often the description accompanying the program is accurate only for an earlier version of this program.

The proper solution to this waste is the establishment of a set of standards. Clearly, the good write-up must impart all the required information to the user in an easily digestible form. Furthermore, it must avoid the inclusion of irrelevant material which will obscure the meaningful. Is it possible to determine a set of rules and regulations which will effectively direct the programmer to create such an adequate write-up? Programming associations, like the SHARE organization, have always considered the question of write-up standards one of their prime reasons for existence. Such organizations can set down rules and refuse to distribute material which does not conform to those rules, although these steps are not necessarily sufficient to solve this problem. The "priceless ingredient," which rules cannot supply, is the programmer's attitude.

To those programmers who consider the write-up as a vehicle for demonstrating the obscurity and subtlety of their thought processes, we offer this assistance: Neglect the rules and guides which have been planned by groups of the most experienced and competent programmers; arrange—if you must include it at all—the critical information in such a way that no part relates to another; embed all pertinent facts in a wallow of irrelevancy; obscure your meanings with esoteric language—a few undefined terms are a great help here; omit a point or two at random, a procedure which will be much simpler if you avoid editing altogether; of course, take a general attitude of disinterest in the whole procedure; and above all, never, never submit the write-up to anyone else for critical review before launching it into the world. We believe that this guide to nowhere can be well used in presenting any write-up of no value.

Helping the serious programmer is not so easy, for we can only offer a form—with a few comments thrown in—which is typical of the standards set down by the various programming associations. On the other hand, we have a feeling that good intentions, and a little work, will provide the missing ingredient to the following prescription:

A. The Name (Title). By name we mean both the written-out descriptive name and the symbolic vocabulary name. Usually in a computer organization like SHARE the symbolic name includes a coded designation of the installation that produced the subroutine. For example, if J. Smythe Company produced a subroutine transferring data internally, the title might look like the following:

SM MOVE
Storage Data Transfer Subroutine

where SM is the code name for J. Smythe and MOVE is the symbolic vocabulary name.

B. The Author(s) and Date. This information is used for purposes of communication as well as credit, for if anyone should know the subroutine well, the author(s) should. The date, of course, chronologically places the subroutine with respect to revisions and other versions of the same routine. For example, we might have

J. Mann
H. Stanley
6/30/58

C. Brief Functional Description. This section provides a potential user with the ability to determine a subroutine's function without having to read the entire write-up. Thus this brief description has the important responsibility to be concise and yet not misleading. Continuing our example, this portion could read

Purpose: To transfer a block of data from one area in computer storage to another

D. Restrictions. As important as what the program can do is what it cannot do. The brief description, which merely indicates what the subroutine can do, leaves a great deal to be answered. When we say that the program will transfer a block of data, do we mean data always in consecutive locations? May the subroutine transfer this data at any time during the execution of a main program? Does this subroutine require any particular computer activity or computer setup to operate properly? (If this were an input-output program, we must know what minimum set of computer components is required for operation. We would also require an indication of the types of format available for the input and/or output data. It is quite possible that a given I/O subroutine may not be used because its format restrictions are either so strict or so cumbersome that too much effort would have to be expended in data preparation.) Does this program destroy any part of the computer status? If it does can it restore this status? Are the contents of the accumulator destroyed? Are there certain combinations of data that the subroutine cannot handle —what are the subroutine's reactions to such data? Perhaps the subroutine in question can handle only the 6-bit configurations shown in Fig. 3-2. If any other configuration is met, what does the subroutine do? Does the subroutine provide any additional error information to assist the main program in carrying out further error handling?

The task of describing restrictions could be quite burdensome, were it not for subroutine standards and machine standards. If we establish as a standard that the subroutine is not responsible for saving the AC contents, we do not need to note such destruction as an explicit restriction. If we establish a "minimum-standard" machine configuration, we need not mention machine-configuration requirements in the write-up of any subroutine which works on that machine. Thus the statement of restrictions may be reduced to a small but pertinent list.

In our example we might have the following restrictions:

1. SM MOVE deals only with blocks of consecutive words.

2. SM MOVE does not recognize references made outside the limits of storage.

3. If the blocks overlap, the receiving area must begin outside the sending area; otherwise data will be lost.

E. The Calling Sequence. This sequence of the operational instructions and parameters certainly must be included in the write-up and must be identical to the format used in actual operation. Every symbol used must be defined precisely even though the symbol's meaning might appear "obvious" to the author. (Most misconceptions appear "obvious" to the author.) A calling sequence like that of Fig. 8-4 might be used in this example.

F. Complete Description. An easily abused section through over- or understatement, the complete description means a thorough analysis of what the subroutine is composed of and what each part of it is to do. References to other subroutines used should be included. As much cross reference as possible to the flow diagram is recommended; for through reference to the symbols designating the different boxes of the flow diagram, any unusual or interesting box can be easily flagged and described. All error procedures should be fully discussed, and suggestions about how the main program might handle certain errors detected by the routine are always welcome.

If sections of the subroutine are capable of independent operation, the author should state this fact with complete details. If possible, additional calling sequences for such sections should be created and inserted into the write-up.

All techniques employed should, of course, be fully discussed. Beyond that, however, references to more complete descriptions of these techniques—especially in the case of mathematical subroutines—can be of great value to the user. In any case, it is preferable to include a description as well, especially since the original papers may not be readily available. Section F for SM MOVE might be the following (which is really a little too trivial an example): SM MOVE will move any number of consecutive words from one area in storage to any other area, provided the restrictions of section D are observed. Words are moved one at a time, through the AC, from beginning to the end of the blocks as specified by the word count and the two starting locations.

G. Physical Description. The size of the subroutine, including all locations used and whether they are instructions, permanent storage areas, or temporary storage areas, is to be recorded here. A physical description of SM MOVE might be

> Instruction area: 19 words
> Temporary storage: 1 word (COMMON)

(although the expanded version described in this write-up could be longer).

H. Subroutine Timing. The operating time of the subroutine is noted in this section. Some subroutines take exactly the same time for every operation, and in this case, the total time is simply shown in the most convenient form. This could be seconds, milliseconds, or microseconds. Most subroutines, however, have an execution time which depends upon the particular use. The total timing in this case is most easily shown by means of a simple formula. All variable factors affecting the time should be shown in the equation, and each such variable must be carefully labeled. Different time measurements such as seconds and microseconds should not generally be mixed. SM MOVE (Fig. 8-5) would require the simple formula

$$\text{Time } T = 67.6 + 13.1 \times N$$

where T is in microseconds and N is the number of words in the block being transferred. (How was this formula derived?) If a block of 100 numbers were to be transferred, the total time T would be 1,377.6 microseconds, or about 1.4 milliseconds.

More complex timing equations will often be necessary, but as long as all variables are defined, all the user must do is substitute the actual values for the variables and perform the necessary arithmetic. If the execution time is variable, formulas for maximum, minimum, and average times should be provided along with an indication of what conditions will cause these times to be realized. When formulas are not derivable, as in the case of certain iterative processes, and even when the formulas exist but are complex, some representative execution times should be supplied to give the user some idea of what he is buying. Nothing is so likely to discourage the use of a subroutine as an uncertainty as to whether its use will cost $10 or $10,000.

I. Check-out Procedures. Since the subroutine will be used by many different people with varying ideas of usage, these people should be given some insight into how well the subroutine is checked out. Therefore, a complete description of the debugging methods that were employed should be included. Examples of the debugging data with corresponding results should always be included as an aid to the user in checking out the subroutine to his own satisfaction. Our example might have under this section

> Blocks of 1, 25, 200, and 3,457 words were used to test out the subroutine, where each block consisted of consecutive integers

Before distributing any write-up of a routine by one of its programmers, an installation should have another individual appointed to read the description for clarity and completeness. (The librarian, of course, would be an excellent choice for this position.) It is interesting to observe how some installations earn a reputation for the quality of their distributed work (good or bad) and how other installations learn to choose subroutines largely according to those reputations.

We should be able now to condense in a few sentences the aim of the subroutine write-up. What we desire is the presentation of the information in such an accurate and complete form that the reader will be able to use the subroutine correctly without hesitation or question. Recalling "Murphy's law"—"If something can go wrong or be misinterpreted, it will"—should be enough stimulus for the goals we desire.

PROBLEMS

9-1. Produce a subroutine write-up for the SWAP subroutine of Prob. 8-5. Derive the appropriate timing formula and describe the data which might have been used to test the subroutine.

9-2. Produce a write-up for the SORT subroutine of Prob. 8-11 and describe the data which might have been used to test the subroutine.

Number Systems

We are departing briefly from our discussion of subroutines to discuss a most important subject, number systems. We are now aware that no computer handles its data in a form exactly identical to the forms of the outside world. In order to make communication possible, then, some form of conversion, whether by computer hardware, by subroutine, or by a combination of the two, must be employed. For example, when we enter the number 1,124 into the computer we want the computer to recognize this number as having a value of 1,124 if this value is used in the processing. Since the computer necessarily handles numbers in a form different than the user, must we be concerned that there may be a change to the number value in undergoing this transition? The following discussion should allay such fears.

In our society, we happen to make use of the *decimal* number system. What do we mean by "decimal"? Simply that the system of counting is based on *ten* distinct characters: 0, 1, 2, 3, 4, 5, 6, 7, 8, 9. When we studied indexing, we examined the counting process in some detail. We learned there what we meant by the number of things (obtained by enumeration) and the number of a thing (which indicated its position in a series). In both cases, we used the decimal numbers to symbolize the result and to help *us* carry out the process. When we employed the computer to carry out the processes, we really did not have to know what number system it used as long as the processes were the same and we did not have to examine the results internally in the computer.

The choice of the decimal, or "10-based," number system probably came from the accident of our having 10 fingers. Such a development does not necessarily make the decimal number system the most logical or even simplest system, and it certainly does not necessarily make it the most suitable for computer use. In fact, the decimal system is not so well suited for the internal computer number system or computer logic. It is usually more costly, more space-consuming, slower for processing, and not so powerful logically as some other systems.

Would the computer be restricted in any way by not using a decimal system internally? It was not restricted in counting—it could, in fact, count in more ways than we could easily do—and there is no reason to believe that it will be restricted in other arithmetic processes. Nevertheless, by our training we find decimal numbers most simple to work with. We do not want to learn some new system just for the convenience of a machine, even if it is an evolutionary accident that we count by tens. Some computers have, indeed, been designed to operate in the decimal system on the basis of such arguments, but as we go to larger machines with the ability to convert from one number system to another economically, the decimal system becomes rather a luxury. Furthermore, as problems get bigger, the relative cost of the process of conversion to that of other types of processing becomes smaller.

The 7090, like many other computers, uses a number system based on *two*, a system which happens to have a particularly fortunate relationship to the bit structure of the internal information. Nevertheless we need not be concerned that, in order to use the 7090, we must become as proficient with this "binary" system as we are with our anthropomorphic decimal system. On the contrary, one of the reasons we use the computer is just so we shall *not* have to do arithmetic. Nevertheless we cannot escape the responsibility of *knowing how* arithmetic is done, for we still must direct the computer in arithmetic processing. Now it so happens that binary arithmetic follows exactly the same rules as decimal arithmetic (using different addition and multiplication tables). Thus many of our anticipated problems are no longer of consequence.

The few difficulties we may encounter with binary numbers will be due to our lack of familiarity with their representation. This problem, too, should be easily overcome, since the principles of binary representation are the same as those of the decimal system—with the details in binary actually simpler.

What do decimal numbers as we generally use them represent? For example, what does eleven, 11, stand for? It is really a shorthand notation representing the sum $10 + 1$. What, then, does 3,406 represent? Again this shorthand notation represents a sum, $3 \times 1,000 + 4 \times 100 + 0 \times 10 + 6 \times 1$. If, however, we were forced to work with numbers in this more explicit long form or refer to them in this form, we would find the system intolerable. A clumsy number format could not last; we need only refer to the Roman numerals to see the results of a cumbersome system. (It is interesting to contemplate that if the Romans had had computers they would probably have had routines to convert Roman numerals to binary, and vice versa, except that, scientifically hampered as they were by their number system, they never would have developed the computers.)

Early in the book, we spoke of a bit code, such as the Morse code, as a means of representing information. At that time we said that *position* could convey significant information. In our shorthand decimal numerical representation position also has a most important significance. Position determines by what power of 10 a numerical digit is to be multiplied. By power of 10 we mean 1, 10, 100, 1,000, and so forth. In order to simplify the determination of the power of 10, we introduce a point to be used as our starting reference. This, of course, is our decimal point. The rule is simple: Starting from the point and moving to the left, the powers of 10 needed to multiply each numerical digit are 1, 10, 100, 1,000, 10,000, and so forth. That is, as we move one place to the left from the decimal point our positional value is increased by multiplying by 10. Similarly, if we move to the right of the decimal point, we again have a power of 10 for each position; except that we *divide* by the power (yielding 1/10, 1/100, 1/1,000, and so forth). This positional representation of numbers gives us the required flexibility of manipulation; for when numbers are added, for example, we only need to ascertain that the respective decimal points are aligned. Thus the numbers 6,457.88 and 61.3459 are added properly together by positioning them like this:

$$6457.88$$
$$61.3459$$
$$\overline{6519.2259}$$

not like this:

$$64\ 57.88$$
$$61.34\ 59$$
$$\overline{125\ 92\ 47(?)}$$

The Computer Number System

The 7090, as we know, does not accept our numbers in decimal form. For example, 1,960 means nothing to the computer; for in order to have meaning, 1,960 must be represented in the "binary" number system of the computer.

How, then, would 1,960 look in binary? To answer this question we need to know the digits making up the binary system. In the decimal number system there are 10 distinct numerical digits (10 itself is not one of these, but a combination of two of the digits). In like manner the binary number system has the same number of distinct digits as represented by its base, 2. Thus the digits 0 and 1 form the complete system.

Arithmetic, as we promised, works the same as always. 1 plus 1 is still 2. What is different in the binary number system is the *representation* of the 2. What, then, is the representation? We can derive it quite readily because positional representation in binary has already been defined for us in the section defining decimal positional representation. By simply replacing all references to "10" and "decimal" by "2" and "binary" we may describe the binary system. (Notice how we find it convenient to talk "in decimal" about binary.) For example, factors in binary are developed by multiplications by 2. Thus the fac-

Position left of binary point	*Power of two (2)*
1	1
2	2
3	4
4	8
5	16
6	32
7	64
8	128
9	256
10	512
11	1024
12	2048
13	4096
14	8192
15	16384
16	32768

Fig. 9-1. Positional numeration in binary.

tors to the left of the point would be 1, 2, 4, 8, 16, and so forth. The point used as reference is called a binary point now since it is used in the binary number system. Because of the fewer combinations we can achieve from the available digits 0 and 1, we get these smaller factors 1, 2, 4, etc. Thus the total number of digit positions required to represent a quantity in binary necessarily will be greater than that required in decimal.

With this information let us construct the binary positional representation of 1,960. To do this conveniently let us introduce a table expressing a list of the binary factors by position (see Fig. 9-1). How is this table used? For example, if a binary number has a 1 in position 8 it would mean that the quantity being represented has a value of at least 1×128, or 128. To represent 1,960 then, we would simply combine enough positional 1's (binary 1's) until the sum of the factors represented by each of these is added up to 1,960. (Of course .a 0 in any position results in no additional value, just as in the decimal system.) With a little manipulation we find that, by placing 1's into positions 4, 6, 8, 9, 10, and 11 and inserting 0's in all other positions, we have the binary representation of 1,960:

$$11110101000$$

On first glance this representation looks strange. One immediate disadvantage from a human standpoint is the length of the binary layout as opposed to decimal. However, the computer is not bothered by this problem, as we shall see. First let us prove that this representation is correct. We must expand our number into a sequence of products which would be

$$1 \times 1,024$$
$$1 \times 512$$
$$1 \times 256$$
$$1 \times 128$$
$$0 \times 64$$
$$1 \times 32$$
$$0 \times 16$$
$$1 \times 8$$
$$0 \times 4$$
$$0 \times 2$$
$$0 \times 1$$

Summing these terms gives us 1,960. (Can you represent 1,961? 1,962? 1,959?)

We said that 1 plus 1 is still 2 in this number system and that only the representation is different. Let us see how different.

Decimal	Binary
1	1
1	1
—	—
2	10

2 in binary requires a combination of the available digits just as 10 in decimal. For 10 in binary is simply $1 \times 2 + 0 \times 1$, or 2. To distinguish between decimal and binary number representation, a subscript is used. Thus $(1100100)_2$ is the binary number while $(100)_{10}$ is the decimal number. In this book, only the binary subscript ordinarily will be used.

The word of storage in the 7090 is composed of 36 bit positions of which the leftmost position can be considered as the algebraic sign, or S position, and the remaining 35 positions as constituting the number. [In the S position, a plus is designated by (0) and a minus by (1).] Now it is easy to see the fortunate relationship between binary numbers and the bit representation of information: each digit position can be represented by a single bit, an arrangement whose economy of space cannot be improved. (As you may have guessed, the word "bit" was originally a contraction of the words "binary digit," although it has since attained more general significance in the representation of any kind of information.) Thus, if we assume that the binary point—which is never explicitly represented in the internal form—follows bit 35, the number 1,960 would appear in storage as follows:

000000000000000000000000011110101000

counting bit positions from the left, S, 1, 2, 3, ..., 32, 33, 34, 35. When the decimal number 1,960 is read in from tape, however, it is not in this form but rather in the form of bit-coded, or "binary-coded," decimal digits, each requiring 6 bits for its representation (see Fig. 3-2). In this BCD format the number 1,960 looks as follows:

110000	110000	000001	001001	000110	000000
Blank	Blank	1	9	6	0
space	space				

If we desired to use the explicit representation of the decimal point, say, in the sixth character position as 1,960., the representation would then be as follows:

110000	000001	001001	000110	000000	011011
Blank	1	9	6	0	
space					

Either case would be treated and converted in the same manner.

A means of converting between decimal and binary representations evidently is a most necessary requirement. Some computers, such as the 7090, have special hardware built into their circuits which aids in making such conversions. In order to simplify the programming task even further, routines—ranging from simple restricted subroutines to large general systems—are found in every library.

It is important to recognize that with a proper set of conversion routines the user does not ordinarily have to think of his data in any representation except the one with which he is familiar. Thus he may consider his numerical data as being in decimal representation and his alphabetical information as being simply alphabetical both in input and in output. When we ask the computer to add two numbers, the knowledge that correct addition is taking place is sufficient. When we had an index register count for us, the knowledge that counting was taking place was sufficient. The fact that we learned to use index registers without knowledge of binary numbers shows how little we need to know about them in order to use a computer.

PROBLEMS

9-3. What decimal number does the binary number 111000111000 represent?

9-4. What does the binary representation of the decimal number 785 look like?

9-5. Convert two numbers, 93 and 57, to binary representation. Add the two binary numbers and convert the result to a decimal representation. Check the result by adding the two decimal numbers.

9-6. What would the number 3.1416 look like in BCD format?

A Conversion Subroutine

At this point, we could use some practice at reading and using a subroutine. We shall introduce, therefore, a rather artificial but quite possible subroutine which combines the edit and conversion functions that occur during the input and output phases of handling data. Let us examine the write-up. (Rather than go into a fairly complex flow chart and accompanying program—which is not necessary at this time for our purposes—we shall limit the write-up to the descriptive part.)

A. Title

Decimal Data Conversion Program   SM-DECCV1

B. Authors

Jeffrey Roberts

J. Smythe Company

Los Angeles, California

April 14, 1959

C. Purpose

To permit the conversion of integer decimal data directly from one area in computer storage into another as binary data

D. Restrictions

1. Input decimal information is acceptable in the form obtained from on-line decimal tape only.

2. Each input number must be integral in value (a "whole number") and a maximum of 10 digits long.

3. All numbers must be separated by commas and may include a leading sign. No blanks may exist between consecutive digits or numbers.

4. The last number making up the input block must be followed by a dollar sign ($) to indicate the end of the block.

5. Data will be stored in consecutive locations in computer storage, in the order found in the input block.

6. Any number entered incorrectly, an unallowable character, or too many digits will cause an error return.

E. Calling Sequence

Location	Operation	Variable field
L	TSX	DECCV1, 4
L + 1	PZE	A
L + 2	PZE	B
L + 3		Error return
L + 4		Normal return

A is the beginning location of the storage block and B is the beginning of the block of converted numbers.

F. General Information

An example of the input data layout is

$$+10034, -234, -98736, +876543089, +2{,}632, -9216\$$$

The method of conversion employed is known as progressive digiting.

(We shall not describe the method here.) All numbers are converted with complete accuracy. Upon encountering an error, the subroutine will immediately return control to the main program. The subroutine will contain in the AC (decrement portion) the number specifying how many numbers had been entered and stored up to the point of finding an error or the end of a block ($).

G. Physical Description

Permanent storage:	DECCV1 to DECCV1 + 141
Temporary storage:	COMMON to COMMON + 17
Total storage:	160 words

H. Subroutine Timing

(An actual figure is not given since the program has not really been written. The timing would be a function of how many numbers were converted.)

I. Debugging Methods

This program has been fully tested for a range of cases by the author. The data shown in paragraph F were used, as well as the numbers 9999999999, −9999999999, 0, and −0.

Example. Using SM DECCV1, convert four blocks of decimal data from storage locations IN1, IN2, IN3, and IN4 into blocks A1, A2, A3, and A4. The solution would be of the following type:

Location	Operation	Address, tag, decrement
START	TSX	DECCV1, 4
	PZE	IN1
	PZE	A1
	TRA	ERROR
	TSX	DECCV1, 4
	PZE	IN2
	PZE	A2
	TRA	ERROR
	TSX	DECCV1, 4
	PZE	IN3
	PZE	A3
	TRA	ERROR
	TSX	DECCV1, 4
	PZE	IN4
	PZE	A4
	TRA	ERROR

In view of the fact that we are transferring to ERROR any time an error is detected, we could define a simple macro for this calling sequence:

```
INPUT    MACRO    X, Y
         TSX      DECCV1, 4
         PZE      X
         PZE      Y
         TRA      ERROR
         ENDM
```

and do our coding in a much simpler and comprehensible form:

```
START    INPUT    IN1, A1
         INPUT    IN2, A2
         INPUT    IN3, A3
         INPUT    IN4, A4
```

PROBLEMS

9-7. Using SM DECCV1, convert six records of input decimal data from blocks B, C1, D1, E1, F1, G1 into consecutive storage areas starting at the location INPUT. The six blocks should be, respectively, 23, 47, 83, 12, 57, and 34 numbers long. Check to see that each block has the proper number of words.

9-8. Compose a write-up for a subroutine which converts binary integers to decimal. Invent a decimal output format.

Operating Subroutines

As we have so far described subroutines, they are subservient to the main program, being given control at its pleasure. There are, however, sets of subroutines that partially control the computer through the trapping mechanisms, returning control to the main program only as their work is completed. Such subroutines are called operating subroutines. The most prominent type of such routines is the input-output set, or "package."

Although such packages usually consist of an elaborate and comprehensive set of subroutines for input, output, editing, and conversion, we shall here discuss a much simpler (imaginary) package whose functions are restricted to the transmission of input and output data. We can then make use of our knowledge of conversion routines to gain some idea of what a complete package will do. Of what value can such a reduced package be to us? Let us recall the discussion we had in Chap. 6 on the overlapping of operations. Although we could see the possibility of such operations, we could also see that they were likely to cause great programming complications. Yet we asserted then that programming such operations could be even simpler than nonoverlapping programming. A means to gain this efficiency as painlessly as possible is through use of the reduced input-output package.

In order to present as realistic a package as possible, the write-up that follows introduces a substantial number of subroutines. This means considerable effort for the reader to comprehend fully the extent of the package. It should be appreciated that any significant piece of work requires the full cooperation of the user. We want excellent write-ups, but we cannot expect such comprehensive write-ups to be of the "spoon-fed" variety. A second most important point to note is the enrichment of the programmer's language that such a system creates. Once we become familiar with the subroutine names and their functions we have all these additional tools at our command.

The write-up of the package SM IOTPKG follows:

A. Name

SM-IOTPKG
Input-Output Transmission Package

B. Author

R. Wolfson
J. Smythe Company
Los Angeles, Calif.
May 30, 1960

C. Purpose

This package provides a set of macro-instructions which enable the programmer to obtain overlapping of input and output operations while relieving him of many of the details of I/O coding, such as EOF testing, error checking, error correction, and notification of uncorrected errors.

D. Restrictions

1. When using the package, *all* I/O instructions must be issued through the use of the package macros.

2. No conversion is performed by any of the routines in the package.

3. Only tape operations are handled by the package.

4. The on-line printer is used for error messages.

5. Input or output records may not be over 200 words long. If they are, an error indication will be printed and the machine will stop. The first 200 words will be used if the START button is pressed.

6. Input tapes must not be composed of mixed binary and decimal records. Output tapes may be mixed.

7. Tape symbols will be defined to include channel designations so the system macros need no channel letter appended.

E. Calling Sequence

The calling sequences to the various routines in IOTPKG are written using the following system macros:

L   DIN T, X, E   (to read decimal tape input)
L   BIN T, X, E   (to read binary tape input)

These routines cause one record from tape T to be read into the block starting at location X. The number of words in the record is placed in $(AC)_{3-17}$ (other positions in AC are set to zero). If an EOF is encountered instead of a record, control passes to location E. Three attempts will be made to correct reading errors by backspacing and rereading. If these all fail, a message to that effect will be printed on-line and a stop will occur. Pressing START will cause the program to continue, treating the data as correct.

L   DOUT T, X, N   (to write decimal tape output)
L   BOUT T, X, N   (to write binary tape output)

These routines cause the writing of one N word record on tape T, from the block starting at location X. (N goes in decrement of L + 2, in case you wish to vary the record length.) One attempt will be made to correct a writing error by backspacing and rewriting. If this fails, a section of tape will be erased and two new attempts will be made. If, after two such erasures, writing still cannot be accomplished, a message will be printed on-line and a stop will result. Pressing START will inaugurate three more tries on new sections of tape. This process may be repeated as often as necessary, and in no case will an erroneous record be knowingly written.

SPACE   T, ± M, E

This routine either skips forward M records (+M) or backs up M records (−M). (M must be less than 16384.) In no case will it move forward more than one file; skipping forward past an EOF ends the operation. Thus, by choosing M large enough, SPACE may be used to forward-space one file. Backing up to the load point causes a transfer to location E + 1, while forward spacing over the EOF causes a transfer to location E.

BACK   T, E

This operation causes backspacing of one file on tape T. Control is passed to E if the beginning of tape is encountered. Thus the sequence

BACK   T, X1
SPACE   T, 1, X1

causes tape T to be moved to the beginning of the current file and control to be transferred to X1, no matter what file tape T is at.

WEOF   T

WEOF causes an end of file to be written on tape T. This instruction should always be used to end writing on a tape to ensure that the last record has been written.

REWIND   T

REWIND causes tape T to be rewound.

REMOVE   T

REMOVE causes the computer to stop and a message to be printed telling the operator to remove tape T (which is rewound). Such a message is automatically given if an end of tape is encountered when writing. When the operator presses START, the program assumes that the tape has been removed and proceeds. If several REMOVE's are given consecutively (as at the end of a job) only the last one causes a stop so that all the removal messages are first printed. If the first record on the tape is a 20-word decimal record, that record is considered to be the tape label (see LABEL) and printed as part of the removal message.

LABEL   T, X

LABEL may be used to write a standard label on the beginning of an output tape. When LABEL   T, X is executed, tape T is rewound and the 20 words starting at X are written as a decimal record at the beginning of the tape followed by an EOF mark.

MOUNT   T, X

MOUNT may be used to tell the operator to mount a tape labeled in the standard way (see LABEL). The following steps occur when MOUNT is executed:

1. The 20-word label starting at X is printed on-line with instructions to mount the corresponding tape on unit T.

2. The program stops (only one stop occurs for a series of MOUNT's).

3. When the operator presses START, all tapes to be mounted are checked for proper labeling and the first information record enters the buffer (see Method).

4. If any tape is improperly labeled, the whole procedure for that tape is repeated until all tapes are properly mounted.

F. Method

IOTPKG uses a simple "buffering" scheme both for input and for output. When the first BIN (or DIN) for a given tape is encountered, a 200-word buffer area is assigned to that tape. The first record is read into the specified block directly. The second record—in anticipation of another BIN (or DIN)—is read into the buffer. When the second BIN (or DIN) is given, the second record is transmitted *from the buffer* to the specified area. The reading of the *third* record into the buffer is started, and control is returned to the main program. Thus, once the process starts, the package will stay ahead of the main program as long as it proceeds in sequence through the records on the tape. [Much backspacing (using SPACE) will, of course, tend to wipe out the advantage of this method.] The programmer, of course, does not have to think of this process occurring. It has no effect on the logic of his coding, only on the timing of the resultant operation. Instead of about 20 milliseconds to read a 200-word record, about 3 milliseconds is taken to transfer a 200-word block from the buffer. (The starting procedure is slightly different when MOUNT is used.)

Output operations are performed in a similar fashion. BOUT (and DOUT) do not cause direct writing on tape but simply transfer the specified block to the buffer, from which it is written as the main program proceeds. Writing, then, stays one record behind the main program. A WEOF should be given to be sure that the last record is written before the main program stops. Since the programmer is not actually writing on, or reading from, the specified tape, any use of ordinary tape instructions, such as WEF, REW, BSR, or BSF, may upset the entire system.

G. Physical Description

Instruction area:	480 words
Common storage:	24 words

Buffer storage: 400 words for each tape used. These
                         must be consecutive locations immedi-
                         ately following the locations of the
                         package

H. Timing

No timing formulas may be given, because timing depends on so
many factors related to the use of the package by the main program.
The only way to determine timing is to run the program. Two cases
were tried by the author to gain a comparison with nonoverlapped
coding.

Case 1. A tape-duplicator program using two channels took 58
per cent of unbuffered time.

Case 2. A tape-merging program using three channels took 40 per
cent of unbuffered time.

I. Check-out Procedures

In addition to the two programs listed under timing, the package
has been used on a variety of programs in our installation for over
a year, including several programs using up to twenty tapes on four
channels. Although it functions correctly in all cases we have tried,
we should appreciate hearing from other users about their experiences.

Operating Subroutines—An Example

Now that we have the greater coding facilities offered by this
package, let us try using IOTPKG to code a previous example and see
what further conclusions we can draw. We can take the complete
program of Chap. 6, using the same flow diagram (Fig. 6-6). Moreover, we do not need the subdiagrams of Figs. 6-6a and 6-6b because
the subroutines of the package handle blocks X2 and X7 of Fig. 6-6.
Thus our new code might read

Location	Operation	Variable field
	LBR	IOTPKG
	BSS	800
COMMON	BSS	24
X1	REWIND	ITAPE
	REWIND	OTAPE
X2	DIN	ITAPE, A, X3
X5	CLA	A
	TNZ	X2

X6	CLA	A + 19
	TPL	X2
X7	DOUT	OTAPE, A, 20
	TRA	X2
X3	WEOF	OTAPE
	REWIND	ITAPE
	REWIND	OTAPE
X4	HPR	X4
A	BSS	20
	END	X1

Do we have any reason, then, for choosing the timing diagram of Fig. 6-7 over that of Fig. 6-8—even without an elaborate analysis?

We might examine how we would take advantage of some of the refinements of IOTPKG—such as MOUNT, LABEL, and REMOVE —and whether or not they cause us any programming difficulty. Before we can work with labels, however, we must know how to assemble alphabetical (binary-coded) information with the program. As usual, a simple pseudo-operation is provided to assist us. The pseudo-operation BINARY CODED INFORMATION (BCI) enables us to enter from 1 to 10 words (6 to 60 characters) of any of the binary-coded information (letters, digits, or special characters) shown in Fig. 3-2. Because a blank is one of the characters we may enter, BCI must use a *count* to tell the number of words to be entered—rather than have a blank end the variable field. For example,

A   BCI 3, SAVE TAPES 1 AND 2

causes the information SAVE TAPES 1 AND 2 to be entered into locations A, A + 1, and A + 2 as shown (uncoded) in Fig. 9-2a. The coded line

B   BCI 5, THE PRICE (C.O.D.) IS $30.26

causes the information shown in Fig. 9-2b to be entered. Notice the different results obtained from

A   BCI 2, SAVE TAPES 1 AND 2 (Fig. 9-2c)

and from

A   BCI 4, SAVE TAPES 1 AND 2 (Fig. 9-2d)

To enter a full 60 characters, we omit the number and simply write BCI and the comma. Thus the line

P   BCI,

enters 60 consecutive blanks (not zeros, remember) into 10 words

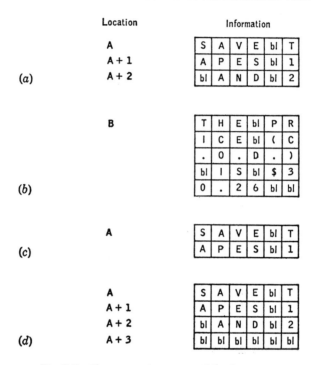

Fig. 9-2. Characters in storage (bl indicates blank).

XT

bl	9	/	2	0	/
5	9	bl	bl	T	A
P	E	bl	3	1	.
7	A	*	bl	bl	bl
2	N	D	bl	O	F
bl	T	H	R	E	E
bl	T	A	P	E	S
bl	bl	bl	bl	bl	bl
bl	bl	bl	bl	bl	bl
bl	bl	bl	bl	bl	bl
S	T	O	C	K	bl
R	E	C	O	R	D
S	/	D	E	P	A
R	T	M	E	N	T
bl	3	/	E	N	C
T	I	O	N	E	S
1	bl	A	N	D	bl
2	bl	bl	bl	bl	bl
bl	bl	bl	bl	bl	bl
bl	bl	bl	bl	bl	bl

Fig. 9-3. A tape label in storage.

starting at P. Thus to enter a 20-word label, at XT, we could write

```
XT BCI, 9/20/59 TAPE 31.7A* 2ND OF THREE TAPES
   BCI, STOCK RECORDS / DEPARTMENT 3 / SECTIONS 1 AND 2
```

which would be distributed in memory as shown in Fig. 9-3.

Now we should be able to recode the main portion of our example. (Blocks X1 and X3 in Fig. 6-6 need slight revisions, which are left to the reader.)

```
L1   BCI, 9/20/59 TAPE 31.7A* 2ND OF THREE TAPES
     BCI, STOCK RECORDS / DEPARTMENT 3 / SECTIONS 1 AND 2
L2   BCI, 10/17/59 TAPE 44.6B 1ST OF ONE TAPE
     BCI 6, SELECTED STOCK RECORDS / DEPARTMENT 3 /
     BCI 4, SECTIONS 1 AND 2
X1   LABEL       OTAPE, L2
     MOUNT       ITAPE, L1
X2   DIN         ITAPE, A, X3
X5   CLA         A
     TNZ         X2
X6   CLA         A + 19
     TPL         X2
X7   DOUT        OTAPE, A, 20
     TRA         X2
X3   WEOF        OTAPE
     REMOVE      OTAPE
     REMOVE      ITAPE
X4   HPR         X4
     END         X1
```

PROBLEM

9-9. Using IOTPKG, code the flow diagram of Fig. 4-14.

FORTRAN Input, Editing, and Conversion

It should be adequately clear by this time that packages of subroutines can make a genuine addition to the programmer's vocabulary. It should also be clear that as we add more and more such facilities to the basic symbolic assembly program, we are essentially moving that language to a higher and higher level. Indeed, the concept of "higher level" is a fuzzy one, especially as useful additions accrue to a language through years of experience. Nevertheless, a language which grows by accretion in this manner may be ultimately limited in its usefulness by some of the early conventions which were adopted for its use; so, from time to time, programmers are tempted to sit down together and try to make a fresh start with a new language which incorporates all they have learned—good and bad—about the old ones. If they do this job well, the new language is likely to have more cohesiveness and consistency than the older, patchwork ones—though it may take a long time in use to smooth out the few unanticipated difficulties which are always found in a language built from scratch.

The FORTRAN language, of course, was originally conceived as a whole unit, though it, too, has had numerous additions throughout its life. Part of the original conception of the FORTRAN system was that it should contain an integrated package of input-output, editing, and conversion routines, oriented toward the type of problem for which FORTRAN was designed. We have already seen a little of the handling of input and output by this system—in those cases where little editing and no conversion were required. Now, let us begin to examine the FORMAT statement, the means for using FORTRAN's extensive editing and conversion system.

If we wish to read a tape created by some external source—where the data have not already been converted to the desired internal form, we must somehow specify the format of the input, which can be different for each program we write. We already know the coding of the input—it is in BCD—so we need only specify the length of the successive fields. We do not, however, know what the internal code will be, for that depends on what sort of processing we want to do with the data. We may wish to use the data in simple counting or control calculations, in which case we wish to have them converted as integers, as we did in our DECCV1 subroutine. On the other hand, we may wish to treat the data as alphabetic information—such as names, addresses, serial numbers, and so forth—which will not be used in calculations. Most often, however, a FORTRAN program will need its data in the general numerical form used by FORTRAN for most of its calculations. Thus, we have at least three internal codings to choose among in a FORMAT statement: integers, specified by I; alphabetic information, specified by A; and general numbers, specified by F.

Let us see, then, how a FORMAT statement can permit us to describe the format of some input data and the conversions we wish to have made on those data. Suppose, for example, that our input format consists of an alphabetic identification code in the first five positions of the input record, followed by four integers, each occupying four positions. A FORMAT statement describing this format and the desired conversion could read as follows:

        22   FORMAT (A5,I4,I4,I4,I4)

and could be used with an input statement such as

READ (3,22) IDENT,N1,N2,N3,N4

in which the 3 identifies the input tape unit, and the 22 specifies our FORMAT statement, which will control the reading and conversion of the five specified input quantities. Notice that the READ statement specifies the number of items to be read and gives them names by which they may be identified for later processing, while the FORMAT statement it specifies gives the details of the layout of the information on the record and the type of data it is to be.

Because of this separation of the reading from the editing and conversion, a number of flexibilities are available. First of all, we can use a single FORMAT statement with as many different READ or WRITE statements as we wish, which is convenient both when the same file may be read or written from different places in the program and when several files have the same format. Second, we can modify a program to different input formats merely by changing the FORMAT statements and recompiling the program. Finally, the separation often enables the programmer to consider problems of program flow and execution independent of problems of formats, records, and files. For example, suppose that instead of wishing to use the four numbers from a single record, as in our previous example, we wanted to perform the same calculations on the first words from each of four different records—ignoring the other numbers in the records. To accomplish this change, we need not change the READ statement at all, since we are here concerned only with the logical structure of the records.

In a FORMAT statement, when we wish to skip over some fields in a record, we may use the X specification, meaning we do not wish these fields read into the computer. When we wish to pass on to the next record, skipping whatever else might be on the current record, we use the / specification. Thus, to solve our revised problem, we could substitute the FORMAT statement,

22   FORMAT (A5,I4/X5,I4/X5,I4/X5,I4)

which specifies the following format:

Read the first five positions of the first record as an alphabetic item (A5), read the next four digits as an integer (I4), skip to the next record (/), skip the first five positions (X5), read the next four digits as an integer (I4), skip to the next record (/), and so forth.

In order to take advantage of the frequent symmetries in input or output formats, and to cut down on repetitious writing within the

FORMAT statement, part of the specification may be put in parentheses and preceded by a number which tells how many times that part of the format is to be repeated. For example, our first FORMAT statement could have been written

22   FORMAT (A5,4(I4))

while the second could have been written as either

22   FORMAT (A5,3(I4/X5),I4)

22   FORMAT (A5,I4,3(/X5,I4))

When reading in ordinary numbers for FORTRAN processing, we have an additional piece of information which we must supply, namely, the number of decimal places. Actually, we could have a decimal point in the input field itself, but since a decimal point takes up a whole position in the record, it is often omitted to save space. Without the decimal point being explicitly punched, the program must know how to interpret a field containing say, the six digits, 123456. Is it .123456? Or is it 12.3456? Or 123.456? In the FORMAT statement, the number of digits which are to be used as decimal places is written in the specification of the number, as follows: If we wanted to specify a six-position field with six decimal places, we would write F6.6; if we wanted to specify the same field with four decimal places, we would write F6.4; with three places, F6.3; and so forth. If, for example, we wished to read the same records as in our previous examples, but with the integers interpreted as decimal numbers with two decimal places, we could write

22   FORMAT (A5,4(F4.2))

or

22   FORMAT (A5,4F4.2)

since parentheses may be omitted when a single field is to be repeated.

As a final example, consider the reading of the tape record shown in Fig. 6-4, the master payroll record. The name, initials, social security number, address, and city and state are to be handled as alphabetical information, while the position code is to be used as an integer in the program. The date employed is to be broken into three 2-digit integer fields, while the rest of the quantities are to be considered as dollars and cents amounts, that is, numbers with two decimal places. The required FORMAT statement could be written as follows:

175   FORMAT   (A9, A26, I2, F3.2, F7.2, F5.2, F6.2, F7.2,
2F5.2, 3I2, 2A25)

and could be read by such a statement as

READ (7,175) SOCSEC,NAME,POS,RATE,GROSS,
2STAX,WTAX,FUND,BONDS,MONTH,DAY,YEAR,
3ADDR,CITY

(When a FORTRAN statement is too long to go on a single line, it may be continued on the following line, preceded by a 2 for the second line, a 3 for the third line, and so forth.)

In our discussions of the FORTRAN language, we have emphasized that no higher level language can be truly machine-independent, as some of its more vociferous proponents may claim.   Many of the difficulties which make a language fall short of machine independence are the result of hard compromises between the desire for generality and the desire for efficiency on a particular machine.   Unfortunately, too many of the inadequacies are often the result of easy compromises—in places where no compromise was necessary or desirable. The actual handling of the A format in the 7090 version of FORTRAN is an example of such an inexcusable compromise.

In the original versions of FORTRAN, there was essentially no provision for handling alphabetic data at all.   As we have seen, even the present version of the language is quite inadequate for problems involving manipulation of alphabetic data.   Nevertheless, the A format was added to the language to meet the quite reasonable demands of the FORTRAN users, and it should have worked as we have described.   In incorporating the A format into the 7090 system, however, the decision was made not to try to hide the word structure of the 7090 from the FORTRAN programmer, but rather to force him— rather than the compiler—to keep track of the placement of alphabetic information among words.   Thus, we cannot actually write, as we did in our last example, specifications such as A9, for if we do, only the first six characters (one 7090 word) will be saved, the rest being simply discarded.   In order to read, say, the social security number in its entirety, we have to allow two words, as with the statement

DIMENSION SOCSEC(2)

and write the A specification as A6, A3, so that no characters will be lost.   Thus, to make our example correct for the 7090 version of FORTRAN, we would have to write the following statements:

DIMENSION SOCSEC(2),NAME(5),ADDR(5),
CITY(5)
175   FORMAT (A6,A3,4A6,A2,I2,F3.2,F7.2,F5.2,F6.2,
2F7.2,F5.2,3I2,2(4A6,A1))

along with the same READ statement. Certainly such a code is quite explicitly *not* machine-independent, and it quite unnecessarily burdens the programmer with the extra task of keeping track of the 7090's word structure. Nevertheless, this example is typical of the sort of nuisance a programmer must accept in using any real machine or language.

PROBLEMS

Using the record format of the first example (five alphabetic positions followed by four 4-digit number fields), write FORMAT and READ statements to perform the following tasks:

9-10. Read in the four numbers on one record as integers into an array defined by the statement

DIMENSION N(4)

9-11. Read in the eight numbers on two consecutive records as numbers with one decimal place into the array specified by the statement

DIMENSION RST(8)

9-12. Into the array specified by

DIMENSION P(4)

read as integers the first number from the first record, the second number from the second record, the third number from the third record, and the fourth number from the fourth record. Also, read the first five positions from the first card as the alphabetic quantity named TAG.

9-13. Read the numbers the same way as in the preceding problem, but obtain the item named TAG from the first field of the fourth card. Why is this problem more difficult?

FORTRAN Output, Editing, and Conversion

In some cases, the same FORMAT statement which has been used for reading a record can be used for writing new records with the same format. In many cases, however, the output format is dictated not by the criterion of compactness but by the criterion of readability, for the output is most often some printed form. Consequently, the interpretations of the various specifications in the FORMAT statement are not completely reversible for input and output. For instance, whereas the F statement on input tells the program where to assume an implied decimal point, the F statement on output tells the program where to put an actual decimal point in the output. Thus, if we were to *print* the number 53.27 under control of the specification F6.3, the number would be printed as

53.270

If we do not allow enough space for the number in our specification, part may be lost in printing (and remember that the decimal point takes a position). Thus, if the same number were printed under the specification F6.1, we would print

53.3

for the output conversion routine would round off the lost decimal place. If we do not allow enough space on the left, the result may be more disastrous, for we may lose significant digits. Thus, if we printed the number under the specification F6.4, we would print

3.2700

losing the most significant digit, the 5. Another type of loss can come when the quantity we are printing is negative, for a separate position is needed to print the minus sign. If we print the number -53.27 under the specification F6.2, we get

-53.27

that is, six characters; but if we print it under the specification F6.3, we get only

53.270

losing the fact that the number was negative.

Further consideration must be given to allowing enough space so that the output is readable, or that it fits on certain preprinted forms, such as checks. Also, we may wish to print various kinds of headings, page numbers, or other indicative information on the output to help the reader identify it. Suppose, for example, that we are preparing a quarterly statement to our employees from the information on the master payroll record. As part of the statement, we wish to print a line which says

YOUR TOTAL EARNINGS TO DATE THIS YEAR ARE $3275.40

with, of course, the appropriate amount filled in for each employee. The only variable information in the line is the amount, which can be printed using the statement

WRITE (4,999)GROSS

while the following FORMAT statement could provide the indicative information:

999   FORMAT (45H YOUR TOTAL EARNINGS TO DATE THIS YEAR ARE $, F8.2)

In such a FORMAT statement, 45 characters of information, following the H (including the blanks) are written on the output tape every time the FORMAT statement is referred to by a WRITE statement.

The same type of specification can be used to put headings on lists of information. Suppose we had a program which looked up the prices of various manufactured parts, multiplied the price by the quantity of each part ordered, and printed out a list of the results for different part numbers. At the beginning of the list, we could print headings with the following statements,

```
   WRITE (2,46)
46 FORMAT (42H PART NUMBER   QUANTITY   PRICE   TOTAL)
```

Then we could print the individual lines under these headings with the statements,

```
   WRITE (2,66) PARTN, QTY, PRICE, TOTAL
66 FORMAT (A6,X8,I4,X8,F6.2,X5,F8.2)
```

with the X specification allowing sufficient blank spaces to align each quantity under its appropriate heading.

The programmer must be particularly careful in counting the number of characters to be placed in such heading information (and specified by the number in front of the H); otherwise the entire FORMAT statement will be misinterpreted. This counting is so tedious and clumsy that some versions of FORTRAN allow the alternative method of merely enclosing the heading information between quotation marks or some other character, not using the H or the count at all. On the other hand, this method has the slight disadvantage of not allowing the marker character to be used within headings. (Why?)

PROBLEMS

9-14. Figure 6-3 shows a filing-card format for the payroll record we have been using as an example. Write the necessary FORMAT and WRITE statements to print a form as close as possible to this filing-card form with the latest payroll information on it.

9-15. In Prob. 6-1, a master record was designed to hold the complete academic information for a student. Design a form in which this information might be printed as a transcript. Write a FORTRAN program which will read the master file and print a transcript for each student.

9-16. Assume we have stored in memory a list of 52 numbers (integers ranging from 0 to 9) representing the level of sales for each week in the year by a salesman whose name is stored (25 positions) in location NAME. Write the statements necessary to print a bar graph of this information in the following form:

```
SALESMAN    JOHN T. SMITH
WEEK        SALES LEVEL
  1         ****
  2         **
  3         *
  4         *******
  5         ********
  6         ****
  .           .
  .           .
  .           .
 51         *****
 52         ***
```

(Can you see how even more complex graphical information can be written by the computer?)

Processing Subroutines

A computer necessarily must have the ability to carry out the basic arithmetic operations of addition, subtraction, multiplication, and division. A detailed description of the associated instructions is given in Chap. 10. Nevertheless, without any detailed knowledge of these instructions, it is possible to carry out a great deal of arithmetic through use of subroutines.

Of basic importance in mathematics is the concept of "function." A function is simply a *rule* for obtaining one set of numbers from another set. As such, the function bears an important relationship to the processing subroutine, which can be considered a "rule" by which one set of computer information is transformed into another set. The result we get entering the PRICE subroutine of Chap. 8 is a function of the part number we place in the AC. Notice that this common use of the word "function" is perfectly consistent with the mathematical use. In fact, when mathematicians use tables, they speak of the "argument" (part number) and the "function" (price).

The importance of processing subroutines is that they enable us to carry out the rule implied by either a mathematical function, like square root or a nonmathematical function like withholding tax. Although we may not have the vaguest notion of what the "Gudermannian" of a number means, if given a subroutine and a calling sequence we can certainly calculate Gudermannians as well as anyone. Thus, the sequence

```
CLA     X
TSX     GUMANN, 4
STO     Y
```

would be all that was necessary to put into Y the "Gudermannian of C(X)," just as the sequence

```
CLA     PARTNO
TSX     PRICE, 4
STO     PR
```

was all that was necessary to put into PR the price of the part whose part number was in PARTNO. In other words, the processes (from the programmer's point of view) of finding Gudermannians, prices, sines or cosines, tax rates, and gamma functions are one and the same. The process of *writing* the necessary subroutines does, of course, require special knowledge in each case; but, then, so does the process of *building* a computer.

Processing subroutines are not restricted to evaluating functions of single arguments nor are they restricted to yielding single results. Suppose, for example, we have given a test, the grades of which must be adjusted to take into account the age of the student. A subroutine to do this task would need as input two numbers, the raw score and the age. At this point we introduce another 7090 register, the MUL-TIPLIER-QUOTIENT (MQ) register. Although the MQ has an important role, as we shall see in both multiplication and division, we introduce it here simply as a convenient place in which to deposit the second argument for use of the subroutine. To use the MQ in this way, we require the instruction LOAD   MQ (LDQ), which puts a 36-bit word from storage into the 36-bit MQ register. Thus the instructions

```
CLA     RAWSCR
LDQ     AGE
TSX     ADJUST, 4
STO     SCORE
```

might be used to store an adjusted score in SCORE, when the raw score was found in RAWSCR and the age was found in AGE. It is of course impossible to continue introducing new registers every time we need a subroutine which uses more words of input data. Commonly, when a subroutine uses more than a two-word argument or produces more than two words as results, parameters in the calling sequence are used to designate the data or result locations. We have already seen this technique in input-output and conversion subroutines. Let us look at another example. Suppose we have a subroutine for calculating averages with the following calling sequence:

TSX   AVGVAL, 4

PZE   A, 0, N

Return

where A is the BSS location of a block of N numbers whose average value is to be placed in the AC on return from the subroutine. Then the sequence

TSX   AVGVAL, 4

PZE   XX, 0, 35

STO   AV

will store in AV the average of the 35 numbers in a block starting at XX.

We therefore have no reason to restrict subroutines in any way to a single block of data or results. Calling sequences, as we see, may specify any number and variety of arrays as well as use the AC or MQ for single words. Again, as in the case of single word entry and exit subroutines, the means of using the subroutine are independent of the particular type of process it is performing.

FORTRAN Processing Subroutines

The FORTRAN language, being especially designed for mathematical calculations, has a particularly nice way of handling subroutines for mathematical functions. We have already seen how this technique worked, though we did not use the "argument-function" terminology in discussing it. Thus, the subroutine, AMIN1, computes the function of a variable number of arguments, "the smallest of the arguments." If we had a library subroutine which calculated the Gudermannian function, called, say, GDMANN, we could write the FORTRAN statement

Y = GDMANN (X)

as the FORTRAN equivalent of our machine-language calling sequence. X is the name of the argument, and Y is the name that will be assigned to the value of the function.

For writing subroutinelike parts of a program, FORTRAN provides a facility much like the MACRO facility in the symbolic assembly language, called the "Arithmetic Statement Function." To use the facility, the programmer first defines the skeleton of the calculation to be used, just as the skeletons of macros had to be defined. Suppose, for example, the program would frequently require that, given three numbers, a, b, and c, the quantity $(b^2 - 4ac)$ be calculated. The programmer in this case could write the defining statement,

DISC(A,B,C) = B * B − 4. * A * C

at the beginning of the program. From then on, whenever he needed this particular calculation, he could use DISC as if it were a subroutine in the library, for example, in the following statements:

IF (DISC(R,H + P,P))10,20,15

Q = AMIN1 (DISC(D,2. * D, AMIN1(D,C)), S + T)

The first statement causes a transfer of control based on the value of the quantity, $((h + p)^2 - 4rp)$, going to statement 10 if less than zero, 20 if zero, and 15 if greater than zero. (What does the second statement do? Flow diagram it.)

As can easily be seen from these examples, the ability to use the macrolike arithmetic statement function can be a powerful tool. It does, however, have one very important limitation. Although such a routine may have any number of inputs (and in the case of library subroutines such as AMIN1, even a variable number of inputs), it may have only one output. As a matter of fact, it must have *exactly* one output. We can see why this limitation must exist, for if we were not assured of always having exactly one output, it would be impossible to know the meaning of such an expression as

A = AMIN1(X,Y,Z) * C + B

In other words, without this limitation, it would be possible to write ambiguous programs in FORTRAN language; and we know that the ambiguity would have to be resolved in the object program—most likely not to our satisfaction. In mathematician's terms, this type of subroutine must represent a *single-valued* function. To represent functions with no values or with more than one value, we must resort to the less convenient, but more powerful, CALL statement.

Another serious limitation of the arithmetic statement function is that the desired function must be expressible as a single FORTRAN arithmetic statement. To overcome this shortcoming, the language provides the programmer with another statement, FUNCTION, which is used in exactly the same way as a SUBROUTINE statement. It is limited, however, to defining single-valued functions, which can then be used in arithmetic statements. Thus, for example, if we wanted to write a subroutinelike function of three arguments which would yield $(b^2 - 4ac)$ if that result were positive and zero if it were negative, we could write the following defining statements:

```
        FUNCTION  DISC  (A,B,C)
        DISC = B * B  −  4. * A * C
        IF  (DISC)  10,20,20
   10   DISC = 0.0
   20   RETURN
        END
```

If we were to substitute this definition of DISC for the previous arithmetic statement function definition, we would be able to write statements using DISC in exactly the same way—but, of course, with the new meaning.

PROBLEMS

9-17. There is a FORTRAN library subroutine called AMAX1 which selects the *largest* among its variable number of arguments. Can you use this subroutine to enable you to define our new DISC function using only an arithmetic statement function definition? Give an example of a function which *cannot* be defined as an arithmetic statement function.

9-18. The *median* of a set of numbers is defined as that number in the set which has exactly as many numbers bigger than itself in the set as it has numbers smaller than itself in the set. Define a function in the FORTRAN language, called MEDIAN, which selects the median out of a list of numbers specified by the arguments. Is the median defined if there is an even number of quantities in the set? Is the median always defined if there may be duplicate quantities in the set? How can we resolve these difficulties?

9-19. The *mode* of a set of numbers is that number which appears most often in the set. Is the mode of single-valued function? Define a FORTRAN function which will find the mode of a set of numbers specified by its arguments. If the mode is not defined for a particular set, have the function return the value zero.

Summarizing Subroutines—An Example

Let us invent a problem which will utilize as many as possible of the subroutine types and other techniques we now know to see how much we can do with them.

Our input consists of two tapes. One (a decimal tape) contains the name of each student along with his age and his scores on 2U tests (Fig. 9-4a). This record has a maximum length of 20 words, although it may not always have a full 20 scores. An EOF occurs after each grade grouping. The other (a binary tape) has one *record* for each grade containing a table to be used for adjusting student scores by age (within that grade). The table is used with the AD-JUST subroutine and is contained in a 200-word record whose format we do not need to know since that is an internal matter to ADJUST.

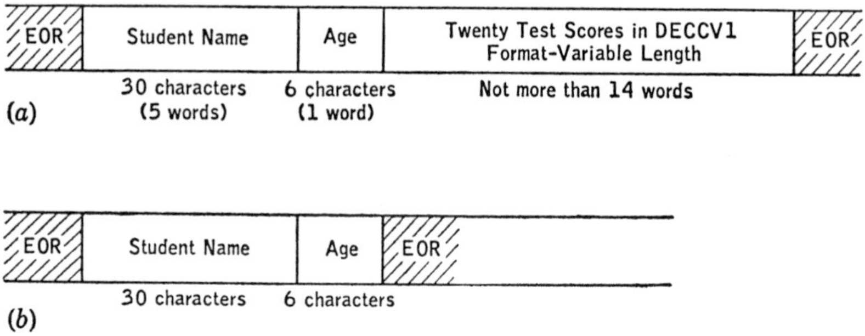

EOR	Student Name	Age	Twenty Test Scores in DECCV1 Format-Variable Length	EOR
	30 characters (5 words)	6 characters (1 word)	Not more than 14 words	

(a)

EOR	Student Name	Age	EOR
	30 characters	6 characters	

(b)

Fig. 9-4. Input-output tape formats.

All these records are in one file, and the EOF thus occurs after the last grade to be processed. Both tapes are labeled in accordance with the IOTPKG label format. The first is labeled STUDENT SCORES TAPE and the second GRADE-SCORE-AGE ADJUSTMENT TAPE.

Our problem, using these two inputs, is to separate passing students from failing students by the following rule: If the "Gudermannian" of the average of the adjusted scores is greater than the first number in the adjustment record, the student passes; otherwise, he fails. Also any student not taking exactly 20 tests fails. Two tapes, one of passing and one of failing students—by grade—are to be prepared with the labels PASSING STUDENTS and FAILING STUDENTS, respectively. The formats for these tapes' records are shown in Fig. 9-4b. These tapes are to be in decimal mode.

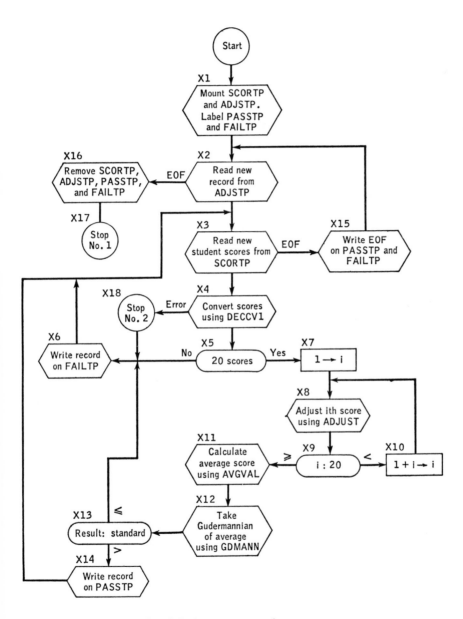

Fig. 9-5. Summarizing subroutines.

Figure 9-5 shows a flow diagram for this example. Study it carefully before examining the coding. In reading the coding use the subroutine descriptions. (The coding assumes that the adjustment table must start in location ADJTBL.)

			Remarks
	LBR	ADJUST	Call subroutines from library tape
	LBR	AVGVAL	
	LBR	DECCV1	
	LBR	GDMANN	
	LBR	IOTPKG	
	BSS	1600	Buffer area
COMMON	BSS	24	
ADJTBL	BSS	200	Reserve area for input
R1	BSS	20	
R2	BSS	20	
L1	BCI, STUDENT SCORES TAPE		
	BCI,		
L2	BCI, GRADE-AGE-SCORED ADJUSTMENT TAPE		
	BCI,		
L3	BCI,	PASSING STUDENTS	
	BCI,		
L4	BCI,	FAILING STUDENTS	
	BCI,		
TWENTY	PZE	0, 0, 20	
X1	MOUNT	SCORTP, L1	Input tapes checked for proper labels
	MOUNT	ADJSTP, L2	
	LABEL	PASSTP, L3	Label output tapes
	LABEL	FAILTP, L4	
X2	BIN	ADJSTP, ADJTBL, X16	Adjustment record to block ADJTBL
X3	DIN	SCORTP, R1, X15	Student record to block R1
X4	TSX	DECCV1, 4	
	PZE	R1 + 6, 0, R2	R1 + 6 is start of scores area
	TRA	X18	Error return
X5	CAS	TWENTY	AC has number of tests taken
	TRA	X6	More than 20 tests
	TRA	X7	Twenty
X6	DOUT	FAILTP, R1, 6	Fewer than 20
	TRA	X3	
X7	AXT	20, 1	
X8	LDQ	R1 + 5	Contains age
	CLA	R2 + 20, 1	Contains ith score
	TSX	ADJUST, 4	
	STO	R2 + 20, 1	Replace raw score by adjusted score
X9	TIX	X8, 1, 1	
X11	TSX	AVGVAL, 4	

Remarks

	PZE	R2, 0, 20	
X12	TSX	GDMANN, 4	Average in AC
X13	CAS	ADJTBL	Gudermannian of average in AC
	TRA	X14	Pass
	TRA	X6	Fail
	TRA	X6	Fail
X14	DOUT	PASSTP, R1, 6	
	TRA	X3	
X15	WEOF	PASSTP	
	WEOF	FAILTP	
	TRA	X2	
X16	REMOVE	SCORTP	
	REMOVE	ADJSTP	
	REMOVE	PASSTP	
	REMOVE	FAILTP	
X17	HPR	1	
X18	HPR	2	
	TRA	X6	
	END	X1	

This example is, of course, a big jump for us; but it contains no new elements. Notice how the liberal use of subroutines allows us to concentrate on the "what" rather than the "how" of our process. Notice also how we can use subroutines whose inner workings are as unknown to us as was the other side of the moon before 1959. It should be even more apparent now why the authors feel so strongly about the production of proper subroutines. If one of the routines in this program failed, our work would be multiplied severalfold. Here is a case where "looking a gift horse in the mouth" seems not only advisable but mandatory.

If it is wise to be skeptical about the condition of subroutines, it is doubly wise—and doubly difficult—to be inquisitive about the meaning of the problem as a whole. Students, of course, have a natural skepticism about how "fair" or "meaningful" is the method by which they are graded, but the programmer commissioned with the implementation of this grading method has an obligation to be inquisitive. He may not, generally, question the "fairness" of the method, for this is the responsibility of the one who presents the problem. He must, however, be sure that the problem description actually describes the problem. Remember that there can be a world of difference between what is *said* and what is *meant*.

Computers often appear magical to the uninitiated; and they do, in fact, have something in common with a certain class of folk tales

about magic—the "three-wish" stories.   For example, there is the
tale of the man and wife, granted three wishes, accidentally using
their first to get a sausage and their second to have the sausage hanging from the wife's nose.   Their third wish must then be used to
restore their original state of affairs, such as they can.   This type of
story is carried to its gruesome extreme in W. W. Jacobs's famous
story "The Monkey's Paw," where the first wish, for money, results
in the hideous death of the son which brings the parents the sought
amount as compensation.   When the mother uses the second wish to
bring the son back to life, they are haunted by his mangled body
pounding at the door in the middle of the night.   Again, their third
wish must be used to bring them back to their original status—minus
their son.   Strange as these stories are, they are reenacted almost
daily where people are making an attempt to mechanize human functions.

The first naïve, oversimplified problem statement, executed explicitly by the programmer, results in a disaster.   The second attempt,
often made in an atmosphere of pressure and chagrin over the first
failure, collapses from the weight of detailed overcompensation.   Finally, the entire project is abandoned and old methods are resumed,
leaving the protagonists poorer but wiser.   The problem, then, is not
what to wish for but how to express that wish to the "genii."

In any case, we should be wary of any problem statement which
strikes the slightest false note; for until we (really) understand what
is (really) wanted, we are not prepared to ask the computer for it.

PROBLEMS

9-20. We introduced a "false note" into the last example in order to illustrate
a point.   What is the point and how might the problem be made more
realistic?

9-21. If a programmer does not even suspect that an applicable subroutine
exists, he is likely to duplicate the work of others.   How might this extra
work be avoided?

9-22. Create a new problem, having nothing to do with students, which
can use some of the same subroutines as our example.

9-23. Create a new problem using some of the FORTRAN subroutines
we have defined.

CHAPTER 10

ARITHMETIC

We can see from our work with index registers that the 7090 computer has the ability to count and to compare numbers. Actually this ability is part of a general ability to perform operations on any information coded in bit form within the words or registers. That is, the 7090 counts by making use of the bits as representations of binary numbers. Comparison of two numbers is in reality, then, the comparison of the bit configurations making up these two numbers. Assuming two positive numbers, for example, the bit configuration 11101 is "larger" than 10111.

Bit manipulation is therefore the basic ability of the 7090. Often, however, we consider this function in more specific terms and tend to think of the bits as numbers. Therefore, we say that the 7090 performs arithmetic, or algebraic (signed) arithmetic, to be more accurate. Nevertheless this more common term "arithmetic" is but one specific form of bit manipulation that takes place within the 7090. In its most general form, the 36 bits of a word are thought of as completely equivalent, with no special meaning, such as "sign" or "high-order" or "low-order." Instructions which treat words as if they were so composed are called "logical arithmetic" instructions (because of their relation to symbolic logic, which does not particularly concern us), and the words themselves are called "logical" words. If we wish to give specific meanings to the bits, we do so by the combinations of instructions which we use to manipulate the words. In other words, the principle that the program defines the *meaning* of the information which it manipulates is carried to the bit level by the logical instructions. Actually the logical arithmetic instructions are so general that, with them, we would not need the more specialized algebraic arithmetic instructions. Operations such as addition and multiplication would become subroutines, but the obvious disadvantages in space and time have prevented anyone from seriously considering a general-purpose machine without some special instructions for algebraic arithmetic. Most applications today rely heavily on this type of arithmetic. However, this may not always be the case.

In discussing the different special cases of general bit manipulation we shall illustrate largely by means of numbers for ease of presentation and in recognition of the widespread application of numerical processing. Nevertheless, a programmer will benefit if he can, when necessary, forget about "numbers" and think in terms of "information."

Algebraic Arithmetic

One of the most fascinating and rewarding areas in programming is the construction of complex programs out of the available simple, direct instructions. As we become more involved in these procedures, we become more fully aware of the subtleties that exist within the creation of our programs. We are aware that the individual instruction, in general, carries little information by itself. Thus there is little direct relationship between the actual application description and any single instruction.

Of all the instructions available on the computer, the algebraic arithmetic group is probably closest to having "human" counterpart. In numerical problems, then, there is a greater chance for direct transition between the actual application and the computer solution. The computer adds, subtracts, multiplies, and divides much as one would do on paper or with a desk calculator. For example, we add and get the sum of two numbers, or we multiply and get the product of two numbers.

In the case of a computer like the 7090, the numbers that we are handling will be in the binary format, but this in no way affects our procedures. Arithmetic operations in number systems with different bases work in exactly the same way. It is the *representation* of the number, not the *value,* that is changed. Thus, when considering arithmetic applications for computer use, we normally treat our numbers as decimal numbers because of their familiarity. Through use of conversion systems or subroutines, our numbers are entered in decimal and retrieved in decimal. We need only know any limits that may be placed upon our quantities, and these limits themselves may be expressed in decimal.

Numbers for Computer Operation

There is a most important distinction between the method of handling numbers when programming and the usual manner of treating numbers in everyday calculation. When we treat numbers on paper, for example, we deal with each individual number's value. We carefully align each number for a given operation. Our only concern with the results is that we have enough paper to write the number down. Usually this is no problem, but if we do run out of space, it is easy enough to make room.

When preparing our data and program for computer use, we do not concern ourselves with individual numbers; for the computer does not usually recognize numbers as such. It can recognize a zero quantity or a non-zero quantity or a negative or positive quantity, or it can compare two numbers; but the recognition of an individual value of a number is beyond the abilities of the computer. Therefore, we treat the *range* of values of the numbers we are treating. What we must know is the range of our input data, the range of our resulting data, and possibly the range of the intermediate results. The program must be capable of handling the largest values that may occur whether they are positive or negative. If this capability is present, then the program will ordinarily be able to handle any smaller value—provided all the numbers are aligned properly. How does one go about aligning perhaps thousands of numbers without ever seeing them? Again the conversion program is used. This time, in addition to translating the number into binary, the number is also properly aligned to fit the required limits.

This technique is more straightforward than it may seem at this time. A payroll is an excellent example for illustrating the technique. If dealing with a weekly payroll, the following limits or ranges might be set for the data. The hourly rate is represented as a 3-digit number with two decimal places: X.XX. We assume, therefore, that no employee in this payroll will earn more than $9.99 per hour. (Note the technique of representing numbers by X's, an extremely convenient method of displaying ranges of numbers.) The hours worked is represented as XX.X, assuming that no employee will work more than 99.9 hours a week. We set XXX.XX as the representation for the weekly wage, again assuming that no employee earns more than $999.99 per week. If the program is built to treat the above ranges it can treat any person whose statistics fall within these limits. Thus a man earning \$2.45 per hour and working 47.3 hours in a week is treated in the same manner as the man who earns \$0.90 per hour and works 31.5 hours a week. When the computer treats these data, they will of course have to be in proper internal format.

It should be easier now to see why the use of numbers in programming differs from our common experience. When we use numbers, we are actually *doing* the arithmetic as well as directing our own operations. When we program the computer, we do only the directing —the planning; the computer does the arithmetic. We can think of the analogy of a printer making up ledgers for bookkeepers. He does not have to know—in fact, he cannot know—exactly what numbers are going to be put on each line of each page, but only the largest number expected in various columns.

Exceptions

A question that logically evolves from this discussion is one dealing with an exception to the standards set up. What does the program do to handle an exception? How does the program recognize an exception? A simple illustration is number of dependents in our payroll. Assume that we set a limit of only one digit, X, for this value. What do we do then with the man having 12 dependents?

The answer depends upon several considerations: the condition of the program, the number of exceptions of a given type, the importance of the exception regardless of its quantity.

A. The condition of the program: If the program is still in its development stage and the exception is serious enough or common enough to deserve consideration, either the range of the data should be extended or an exception routine should be included within the program. In making this decision, the efficiency and logic of the program must be taken into account. For example, the standard input format might be fixed by other considerations, such as the availability of thousands of records already in this format, or by the ease of preparation for the normal case. Under these circumstances some kind of exception routine would be needed—if the computer were to handle this case at all.

On the other hand, an exception routine might be too long and involved to merit choosing it over an extension of the data range, however inconvenient.

B. The number of exceptions of a given type: Suppose our payroll handles 15,000 employees. Three of these employees decide to rent a garage from a private home near our company. The homeowner requests that the company deduct his rent from these three men and send him a check for the total. Imagine the consequences of such a request. Unless these three men are handled specially, it would mean that each of 15,000 employees has to be checked by an additional operation to see if he is one of the three garage users. The time wasted in such an operation does not seem justified. This illustration is over-simplified, but a programmer may trap himself into exceptions just as ridiculous as this which are not so obvious. The way to avoid this situation is by careful analysis of the application together with proper preparation of flow diagrams, a frequent answer to artificially created programming problems.

C. The importance of the exception: An exceptional number which is used as a control figure to change the direction of a program certainly would be included regardless of its frequency. In cases where the removal of a small set of exceptions is costly or impossible (they may be scattered throughout several tape reels of data) the only solution may be to deal with such exceptions within the program, even if only to print them out for manual handling.

It should be noted that this restricted discussion of arithmetic-type exceptions applies to all sorts of exceptions that may occur. Few programs of any magnitude can be expected to have all their cases lie within the general limits that are originally set up. A continuing modification of such limits or ranges may have to take place as the programmer becomes more knowledgeable about his application. Even with all the effort put into a system some exceptions may escape detection. Here it is up to the programmer to develop his logic so that an unanticipated exception is at least detected. Once such an exception is found, he would have the problems of consideration A—the condition of the program. What would be the simplest means or best means of correcting the program would depend upon the size of the program, the degree of logical change, and the size of an exception routine. Possibly the programmer may make no change, feeling that the particular exception was one with little chance of occurring again. In any case, a rapid notification to all users is required specifying the type of exception together with the correction to the program if one is developed.

The Decimal and Binary Points

As we have described the "point," in a system of positional numbers, its purpose is to serve as a reference for determining the value of a number and for aligning of numbers when performing arithmetic. Although we rarely show it, an integer also has a point, e.g., 1342., which appears at the extreme right of the number. Without the point, working with numbers on paper would be almost impossible. For example, suppose we wish to add the following numbers: +1117.843, −43.65, +1.1, and 908. Without the point, we may get into some ridiculous situation like this:

$$
\begin{array}{r}
+1117843 \\
-4365 \\
+11 \\
+908 \\
\hline
1114397
\end{array}
$$

The point, then, helps us remember to do this:

$$
\begin{array}{r}
+1117.843 \\
-\ \ \ 43.65 \\
+\ \ \ \ \ 1.1 \\
+\ 908. \\
\hline
1983.293
\end{array}
$$

The binary representations for the above numbers could be as follows:

(+)	010001011101.110110
(−)	101011.101001101
(+)	1.000110011
(+)	001110001100.

Again it is the point that aligns the numbers. (The true sign representation is not shown.)

How then does the computer recognize a binary point? The answer is that the computer does *not* recognize the binary point. In the case of the 7090 we have a 36-position word wherein each position may hold either a 0 or a 1. The leading position of this word may be used to represent the sign, a 0 being positive, a 1 negative. The remaining 35 bits represent the numerical portion. If no place is

allowed for the point, is it possible for the computer to do any correct
arithmetic? Suppose we look at three addition problems:

37.	3.7	.37
+68.	+6.8	+.68
105.	10.5	1.05

Only the decimal point makes these problems different. Therefore,
if we forget about the decimal point (but do not forget to align the
numbers) we have only one addition instead of three:

$$\begin{array}{r} 37 \\ +68 \\ \hline 105 \end{array}$$

In other words, as long as each number is properly aligned with respect to every other number in a given operation, such as addition, the
absolute size of the numbers does not change the configuration of the
resulting digits (105. vs. 10.5). Therefore, as long as the points are
aligned, we need not be concerned about just where the points are
while we do the arithmetic. We need only remember at the *end* of
the operation where the point is in the result.

The data, lacking points, must be positioned either by a conversion
program which can usually handle the majority of cases or by means
of the main program itself. As in the case of distinguishing between
data and instructions, it is the programmer's responsibility to ensure
that his data are correctly positioned. The computer makes no distinction as to the scale of a number. All it sees is a 35-bit signed
number, a signed integer, we may say. Unlike our paper arithmetic,
all numbers are treated as one size. (This size is slightly larger than
a 10-digit decimal number.) Actually this method of treating all
numbers as being the same size gives us the means by which we are
able to align the numbers properly, for zeros are used to fill in all
unused word positions. These zeros are really "positional zeros" in
that they take the place of the point for purposes of alignment. They
are not "value zeros," however, for the program itself must "remember" the values of the numbers being dealt with; or simply, the program must keep track of the point (binary point in this case). Upon
entry or exit of any number the program would provide the necessary
information as to where the binary point should be to a conversion

program so that a proper translation takes place. The program may also effectively "shift" the binary point in order to align numbers which the conversion programs did not handle. In decimal, positional zeros would look as follows:

$$+0001117843$$
$$-0000043650$$
$$+0000001100$$
$$+0000908000$$

As can be seen these zeros tell us nothing about the true value of the number. Before we, as human beings, could use these numbers we would have to know the decimal-point position. Such a scheme on paper is, of course, impractical.

In binary, the use of positional zeros gives us the following representation of these same numbers:

$$000000000000000010001011101110110000$$
$$100000000000000000000101011101001101$$
$$000000000000000000000000001000110011$$
$$000000000000000001110001100000000000$$

where the leading 0's and 1's are the positive and negative signs, respectively. Again these positional zeros say nothing about the value of the numbers. In the computer, this method is quite practical since the computer arithmetic treats all numbers as being the same size, just as we did in our second example.

The Accumulator Register

Early in the book, we stated that learning to code for a particular machine was largely a matter of learning how the special registers operate. All the algebraic arithmetic operations on the 7090 center around the AC, which we have already used for other purposes. All addition and subtraction using the full-word format (not the 15-bit index-register format) takes place in the AC. Why, then, is the AC 38 bits long when the full word has only 36 bits? There is no direct communication between any word position and the two extra accumulator positions when performing algebraic arithmetic. CLA, for example, will clear all 38 bit positions of the accumulator before it loads the 36 bits of the referenced word into the corresponding 36 positions of the accumulator. The extra two positions, the P and Q positions, remain zero. Yet these two positions do affect the execution of some of the instructions. TZE, for example, will test all 37 positions, excluding the sign position, for a zero case. Thus the presence of a 1 in either P or Q can cause the TZE to make the "wrong" decision even though the normal 35 numerical positions are all zero. If storage cannot communicate with these two positions in normal algebraic arithmetic or data-movement operation and these two positions seem to be a nuisance to a decision-making instruction, what use can they have? Certainly they were not added to the accumulator because some circuitry was left over.

Let us revive our analogy of the printer. Suppose, when using one of his ledgers, we obtained a sum too large for the allotted columns, even though each individual number was small enough. For example, in a 10-column ledger, we might have the following sum to perform to obtain total sales:

25	347	534	76
43	821	906	21
53	893	294	27

The sum 123,062,735.24 is too large to fit on our standard paper; so how do we handle it? We may squeeze one extra digit into the space, although this is not such a neat procedure. We may leave off the leading "1" and circle the number in red, indicating the omission, and we shall be safe enough until total sales get up around 200,000,000.00. A third method is to drop the "cents" columns—which are not too important anyway in a 100,000,000.00 total—by moving the decimal point right two places. The subtotals would still be kept to two decimal places.

All these methods are easily done on paper since we handle each actual number. We have no such facility when programming, so we require a different means of handling this "overflow" case—where by overflow we mean the production of a number larger than the physical limits assigned for arithmetic manipulations. The additional positions of the accumulator are available to help deal with the case of overflow. It is certainly possible for a program built to deal with certain sizes of numbers to encounter a particular pair of numbers which produces an overflow condition. When such a condition occurs, two things happen. The overflow value, which in binary is simply a 1, is held by the P position, thus preventing loss to a bit that would not be recoverable without this facility. In addition, an indicator is set within the 7090 telling that an overflow has taken place. The instruction TRANSFER ON OVERFLOW (TOV) is available to test the overflow indicator and determine its condition. If the indicator is off, no transfer takes place; if it is on, the execution of TOV will cause a transfer to take place and also cause the indicator to be turned off so that subsequent new overflow conditions can be recognized. If the indicator is left on, any additional overflows occurring have no means of being recognized.

Shifting

In order to get at the overflow bits, the computer can use its facility to "shift" the bits in the AC. Shifting simply means moving the bits right or left. When we shift left, zeros are added to the right to fill the emptied space; on a right shift, zeros fill up the spaces on the left. Bits shifted past register boundaries are lost. Since there is no physical binary point within the computer, the effective binary point which the program remembers is shifted along with the number. Thus, if we are rounding a number with 10 fractional bits to 8 places, we physically drop off the last 2 bit positions. The effective binary point is still to the left of the remaining 8 bit positions—a fact which must be given to a conversion routine for subsequent decimal printing.

The instructions dealing with shifting within the accumulator are ACCUMULATOR RIGHT SHIFT (ARS) and ACCUMULATOR LEFT SHIFT (ALS). These instructions are immediate-address in-

Execute CLA A

0 (Sign)
000111000101001111000011100010011010 1
QP1   · · ·   35

Execute ARS 12

0 (Sign)
000000000000000111000101001111000011 1
QP1   · · ·   35

Execute ALS 30

0 (Sign)
000011100000000000000000000000000000 0
QP1   · · ·   35

Fig. 10-1.

structions. Thus we place directly into the address part of the instruction the actual number of bit positions to be shifted. (The sign, which must always occupy the S position, is not shifted.) Figure 10-1 shows how the bits in the AC would look as we execute the following instructions:

$$\text{CLA} \quad \text{A}$$
$$\text{ARS} \quad 12$$
$$\text{ALS} \quad 30$$

The first instruction brings the bits in A into the AC, as shown, clearing Q and P. The second moves the entire pattern right 12 positions, thus dropping certain information which is not recovered when the

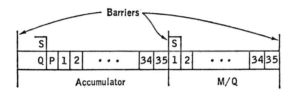

Fig. 10-2. Accumulator and MQ registers.

third instruction moves the remaining pattern left 30 bits. The bits moved left past Q are also lost; and if, as in this case, any 1 bits move into or through P, the overflow indicator is turned on.

In certain operations, we obtain numbers, or strings of information, longer than 37 bits; in others, we find it useful not to lose the bits we are shifting. In these cases, the AC and MQ registers may be shifted together, thus forming a $37 + 35$ bit register (neither sign bit is used). When we combine these two registers we think of them as being side by side with the MQ holding the rightmost positions of the number, as shown in Fig. 10-2. Note that the sign positions are placed above the numerical positions since they are not affected in the same manner as the other positions during an arithmetical shift.

We show three "barriers" or limits to our shifting. The leftmost barrier indicates that the passage of any information beyond this point, the Q position, is permanently lost. The rightmost barrier indicates in like manner that any shifting of information beyond the thirty-fifth position of the MQ results in permanent loss. The middle barrier between the accumulator and MQ works only when shifting is taking place in the accumulator alone. During interregister shifting the barrier is removed and information passes directly from the thirty-fifth AC position into the first position of the MQ and vice versa. As the number is shifted either right or left, zeros automatically fill in the register positions being emptied.

The instructions dealing with intershifting are LONG RIGHT SHIFT (LRS) and LONG LEFT SHIFT (LLS). Again these instructions are immediate-address type. The long-shift instructions perform exactly as the accumulator-shift instructions with one additional function. When long-shifting to the right, the MQ sign takes on the sign of the accumulator. When long-shifting to the left, the AC sign takes on the sign of the MQ. This is only natural, since the part of the number moving into the MQ or AC still must retain the same sign as the original number. Of course, it is possible for the accumulator and MQ to have different signs as they function independently in many cases. Executing the instructions

LRS   12
LLS   30

will cause the AC and MQ to process information as shown in Fig. 10-3.

Accumulator

0 (Sign)
000111000101001111000011100010011 0101

M/Q

1 (Sign)
1100110011001100001110101110101 0101

Execute LRS 12
Accumulator

0 (Sign)
0000000000000001110001010011110000111

M/Q

0 (Sign change)
0001001101011100110011001100001 1101

Execute LLS 30
Accumulator

0 (Sign)
0000111000100110101110011001100110000

M/Q

0 (Sign)
11101000000000000000000000000 00000000

Fig. 10-3.

Uses of Shifting

There are many diversified uses of shifting. So far we have seen that shifting allows us to recover overflow digits (bits). In this same manner shifting permits us to make numbers compatible where required. We simply rearrange the number of leading and trailing positional zeros. We may even perform arithmetic by shifting. For example, every time we shift a number one position to the left within the binary computer, we are actually doubling the number (multiplying it by 2). Remember what happens when a decimal number is shifted one place left, for example,

$$1854.0$$

$$18540.0$$

The shift of one place left is equivalent to a multiplication by 10, in this case.

What is the difference between an ALS 1 in order to shift the binary point one place and an ALS 1 used to multiply by 2? Obviously there is no internal difference; the difference is in the mind of the programmer, who, in the first case, allows his mental binary point to move with the number and, in the second case, fixes the mental point as the number is shifted. We can, in fact, multiply by 2 without any shifting if we allow our mental point to move right one place. Of course, if it moves accidentally, because we did not keep track of it, we shall have introduced an error in our code.

In many cases, we find ourselves dealing with numbers or

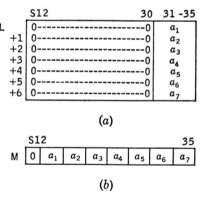

(a)

(b)

Fig. 10-4. (a) Seven unpacked 5-bit quantities; (b) seven 5-bit quantities packed into one word.

other pieces of data which are inherently shorter than 36 bits. If storage space is a requirement, we may find it advantageous to "pack" several quantities into one word for storage and "unpack" them later on for processing. Suppose, for example, we had five-bit quantities in positions 31 to 35 of seven consecutive words starting at L. We want to pack, or squeeze, these 35 bits into one word, at M, as shown in Fig. 10-4. The flow diagram of Fig. 10-5 shows how this task might be accomplished. Notice that we must index backward in order to pack

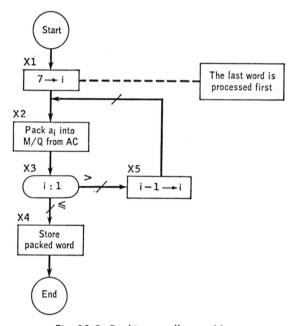

Fig. 10-5. Packing small quantities.

the quantities in the order shown in Fig. 10-4. In the coding shown below, this calls for counting forward in the index register.

X1	AXT	1, 1	
X2	CLA	L + 7, 1	
	LRS	5	Packs next quantity in MQ
X3	TXL	X5, 1, 6	
	TRA	X4	
X5	TXI	X2, 1, 1	
X4	STQ	M	

The last instruction, STQ, STORE MQ, simply stores the MQ contents in the specified word, much as STO stores the AC contents.

If we desire to use these seven quantities at some later time (they may have been stored on tape, for example) in their original form, we can unpack them as shown in the flow diagram of Fig. 10-6. Notice that the words may be unpacked in ascending order because they were packed backward. (Why must the AC be cleared before each new quantity is unpacked?)

Y1	AXT	7, 1	
	LDQ	M	
Y2	CLA	K	(Assume K contains all zeros)
	LLS	5	
	STO	L + 7, 1	
Y3	TIX	Y2, 1, 1	

When we have descended to this level of detail, our flow diagram may, of course, refer to specific machine features such as the AC and MQ.

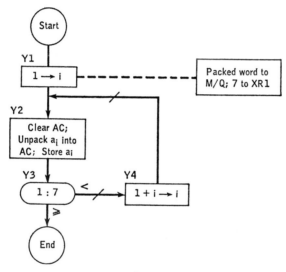

Fig. 10-6. Unpacking small quantities.

Operations such as packing and unpacking are made necessary or desirable by specific machine features; so anyone reading the diagram at this level should understand these features. Packing or unpacking would not ordinarily be specifically mentioned on the over-all diagram, and in fact, they are not usually necessary on variable-word-length machines.

Another use of shifting is in the examination of information at the bit level. Suppose we had a payroll file where one word in each employee's record designated which of 35 possible deductions applied to him. That is, each bit position in that word (excluding the sign) represented a different deduction, a one meaning take that deduction, a zero meaning do not take it. If, then, we wanted to find out how many deductions an employee had, we could count the one bits in his deduction word (DED). The flow diagram is shown in Fig. 10-7. Using the overflow to test for the presence of a one bit moving from AC_1 to AC_p, we can code this diagram in an interesting way. Rather than use an index register to control the process, we can use the data themselves, for when there are no more ones in the AC, we know

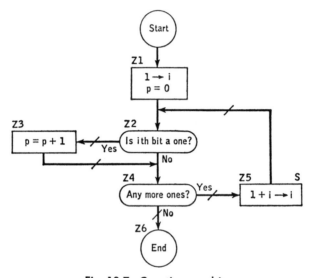

Fig. 10-7. Counting one bits.

we are through counting ones. Thus a TNZ tests for the end of the process. Thus we have an example of the index i corresponding to no number at all in the computer, but rather a position to which a data word has been shifted.

Z1	CLA	DED	$(1 \rightarrow i)$
	AXT	0, 1	$(p = 0)$
Z2	ALS	1	(Also $1 + i \rightarrow i$)
	TOV	Z3	
Z4	TNZ	Z2	Any more ones?
	TRA	Z6	
Z3	TXI	Z4, 1, 1	$p = p + 1$

It is true that this method causes two extra shifts to be made when the thirty-fifth bit is a one (why?), but on the other hand, it may save several shifts when consecutive zeros fill the last few bit positions of

DED (why?). In any case, it presents a variation of a common technique.

It should be quite apparent by this time that we have been treating the sign bit in a special manner in these shifting operations. In many of these cases the sign bit is actually a nuisance bit. What would we do if we wanted to pack 9 four-bit quantities or 6 six-bit quantities or to count the ones in all 36 bit positions. We could, with a great deal of extra manipulation, do these things with our present set of instructions; but that is not necessary. Using the set of logical arithmetic instructions, we would be able to treat 36-bit quantities as easily as we have handled 35-bit signed quantities. That is, the sign position loses its uniqueness to 36 positions of equal value.

PROBLEMS

Write parts of programs which will

10-1. Pack and unpack seven-bit quantities, occurring in bits 21 to 27 of five consecutive words.

10-2. Count the number of *zero* bits in positions 1 to 35 of a word.

10-3. Count the longest string of consecutive ones in positions 1 to 35 of a word.

Addition and Subtraction

The instructions for addition and subtraction are ADD and SUB (subtract). Each causes a number taken from storage to be algebraically applied to the value in the AC, yielding a sum or a difference. For example, the sum of 75 numbers is required. These numbers are in consecutive storage locations from XA, say, to XA + 74. We wish to place the sum into SUM. Figure 9-8 illustrates the flow diagram. Notice that the computer does not add a column of numbers the way most human beings do, one digit at a time. The computer, with its more reliable arithmetic abilities, uses each number once, adding all 35 bits to the AC contents in one operation:

Location	Operation	Address, tag, decrement	Comments
X1	CLA	ZERO	(Zero contains all zeros)
	AXT	75, 2	
X2	ADD	XA + 75, 2	
X3	TIX	X2, 2, 1	Is addition complete?
X4	STO	SUM	Yes. Store sum

This coding works for numbers of any size, as long as all the numbers have their binary points in the same place. Otherwise it is nonsense, as we have seen. On the other hand, the code does lack an important facility, for it does not account in any way for overflow. It certainly is possible for 75 numbers to create a sum or partial sum that will exceed the accumulator. If the maximum range for the 75 numbers had been XXXX.XX, there would be no concern about overflow, for it could not have occurred except through machine error (so we might test for it at the end). Generally we have the facility to prepare the numbers such that programs of this type will not overflow.

If it were felt necessary, a TOV could be placed either between the ADD instruction and TIX instruction to indicate an overflow after every addition, or after the STO instruction to designate that overflow took place at some time during the entire process. In the first case the result of finding an overflow could be a transfer to a special corrective program, called a "scaling" program. That is, the program "scales" down the numbers so that they will not cause overflow. Once scaling has been done to any partial sum, however, this same scaling must be continued for all new numbers being brought in. For example, assume a 10-digit decimal accumulator wherein an overflow occurred into the tenth position.

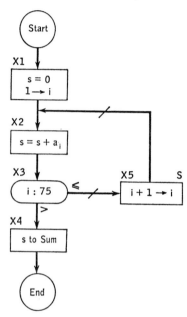

Fig. 10-8. Adding a block of numbers.

$$+1567348.643 \text{ (The decimal point is effectively at the position shown)}$$

A shift of 1 (decimal) to the right gives us $+1567348.64$. The numbers that have been added are three-decimal-position numbers, however. From now on all new incoming numbers to be added (subtracted) must first be "scaled down," shifted one place to the right before being added to the partial sum.

In performing the shift, rounding or half adjusting may be performed. This consists in adding a 5 to the position to the right of the last digit position being saved. For example, rounding the following numbers two decimal places,

+3657.896 results in +3657.90
+3657.894 results in +3657.89

When the final result is ready, this number must be returned to its correct value since every time we shift right one place we effectively divide this number by an amount of 10 (or 2, in the binary machine). Such restoration may occur within the main program or may be taken care of by a conversion subroutine.

We can see now why it is an absolute necessity for the programmer to know to the best of his ability the ranges of the numbers with which he must deal. Wherever possible it is worthwhile to be able to do without a "scaling" program since such a program will often be larger and take more time than the main program. Nevertheless there are cases where no knowledge of number range is available, and so there is no choice but to use a scaling program.

Early in computer history, a need was felt for some type of hardware to combat the scaling problem. The result was a special type of arithmetic that had *automatic* scaling facilities of its own. This arithmetic was given the name "floating-point arithmetic." (You might guess that the arithmetic we have been talking about is called "fixed-point arithmetic.")

Floating-point Representation

The need for a compact system of writing exceptional numbers was felt long before computers came on the scene. For example, astronomers calculate that the mean distance from the earth to the sun is about 14,950,000,000,000 centimeters (a centimeter is about $\frac{2}{5}$ in.), a very small distance astronomically speaking. Physicists, on the other hand, often use numbers such as the "radius of an electron," which is about 0.000000000000281784 centimeter. Clearly, writing such numbers is a great inconvenience—even if paper is essentially an unlimited storage device. Therefore, we make use of the so-called "scientific notation" that enjoys wide application to reduce the work involved in such representations.

The key to the scientific notation is the separation of the *significant digits* of the number from the size, or *scale*, of the number. Thus, instead of having digits and a point, each number has two sets of digits, one telling what the number is and one telling where the point is. For example, the earth-sun distance could be expressed as $0.1495 \times 100,000,000,000,000$ and the electron radius as $0.281784 \times 0.000000000001$. This technique would seem to compound the problem, were it not for the fact that the second part of each of these numbers is what we call a "power of 10," that is, it may be obtained by starting with 10 and multiplying (or dividing) by 10 enough times. Figure 10-9a shows a table of powers of 10. It is easy to formulate a

Power	Written as	Decimal number
11	10^{11}	100000000000
10	10^{10}	10000000000
9	10^9	1000000000
8	10^8	100000000
7	10^7	10000000
6	10^6	1000000
5	10^5	100000
4	10^4	10000
3	10^3	1000
2	10^2	100
1	10^1	10
0	10^0	1.0
-1	10^{-1}	.1
-2	10^{-2}	.01
-3	10^{-3}	.001
-4	10^{-4}	.0001
-5	10^{-5}	.00001
-6	10^{-6}	.000001
-7	10^{-7}	.0000001
-8	10^{-8}	.00000001
-9	10^{-9}	.000000001
-10	10^{-10}	.0000000001
-11	10^{-11}	.00000000001

Fig. 10-9a. Powers of 10.

rule for relating the power and the decimal point: The power is the number of zeros between the one and the point where the one is to the left of the point. The power is one more than the number of zeros between the one and the point where the one is to the right of the point. Thus our two numerical examples may be expressed as $+0.1495 \times 10^{14}$ and $+0.281784 \times 10^{-12}$.

It is only a short step from this scientific notation to a good computer format. If we are always dealing with decimal numbers, we can further abbreviate these numbers by omitting the "$\times 10$" each time, thus yielding $+0.1495 + 14$ and $+0.281784 - 12$. If we adopt the convention that the decimal point is always to the left of the leftmost digit, we can omit writing the point, thus yielding $+1495 + 14$ and $+281784 - 12$. (Note that we have taken out the $\times 10$ and point only because they are identically common in all our numbers.) We could keep these numbers in the computer in this form (using binary numbers and binary powers), but we should like to rearrange them for convenience in testing. Specifically, we should like to be able to use the tests TMI, CAS, and TZE on these numbers as well as on our fixed-point numbers.

Preserving TMI obviously means that the sign of the number (not the sign of the power) must be kept in the S bit, just as it is in a fixed-point number. What about CAS? Any positive number is bigger than any negative number, whatever form is used; so our sign bit takes care of that. In determining the size of the number, however, the power is more important than the "fraction" (we call the significant digits, when expressed in this form, the fraction). If we are to use CAS, then, the power must precede the fraction; so we may write $+(+14)/1495$ and $+(-12)/281784$. The parentheses merely indicate that the second sign belongs to the power. The sign of the power, however, makes this technique incorrect for the CAS. A minus (represented by a 1) would be considered larger than a plus (represented by a 0). Our problem thus becomes one of taking care of the sign of the power. We could solve this problem by restricting ourselves to positive powers; but this is no solution, as we would be prevented from using small numbers. Really what we must solve is two problems simultaneously. We really want to remove the sign of the power but at the same time keep the values of the powers intact. Thus we want $+14$ to remain larger than -12 by the same amount ($+14$ is 26 greater than -12) and yet rid ourselves of their signs. *Making* our powers all positive (not *restricting* them to positive) is our solution. We simply add a large enough positive constant to all our powers such that our smallest negative power added to this constant gives us a sum of zero. For example, we could add the constant 50 to all our powers. This means the smallest allowable negative power would be -50, which expressed as a power of 10 (10^{-50}) means 49 zeros followed by a one to the right of the decimal point. Figure 10-9b shows us the new sum for each power value. Note that we call such a sum a *characteristic* to distinguish it from the true power. Figure

10-9b illustrates our total range (with this characteristic constant) of from 10^{-50} (0 characteristic) to 10^{49} (99 characteristic).

Now we may write our illustrative numbers as $+64/1495$ and $+38/281784$. Note that the larger number is still 26 greater in the exponent (characteristic). Expanding to 10 digits, as $+6414950000$ and $+3828178400$, we would now have a proper comparison using a CAS.

Power	Characteristic
49	99
48	98
47	97
.	.
.	.
.	.
8	58
7	57
6	56
5	55
4	54
3	53
2	52
1	51
0	50
−1	49
−2	48
−3	47
.	.
.	.
.	.
−47	3
−48	2
−49	1
−50	0

Fig. 10-9b. Powers versus characteristics.

In illustrating the 10-digit representation of a floating-point number we were careful to place all positional zeros to the right of our significant numerical digits. From our original definitions of floating point we made it clear that the fractional parts of the floating-point number must all have the decimal point in the same relative place, to the left of the first significant digit of the number. Such a floating-point number whose fraction's first digit is a non-zero is called a *normalized number*. Our illustrative numbers are thus normalized.

Generally we deal only with normalized numbers. Such a format gives us maximum digital representation. In some instances, however, we may encounter floating-point numbers whose fractions have leading zeros—for example, we might have +2301453761. Such numbers are naturally called *unnormalized*. Because of these two methods of representing floating-point numbers we must observe one more caution if CAS is always to work with them. If the fraction is unnormalized, a CAS comparison may be incorrect. (Try, for example, +52/12000000 and +53/01100000, which are 12 and 11, respectively.) Thus we ordinarily restrict our operations to such normalized floating-point numbers, and CAS always works.

What about TZE, our last condition? The last eight digits of a zero will obviously be 00000000, but what is the power (or characteristic) of zero? In order to satisfy TZE, the characteristic must be zero also, so that a floating-point zero looks just like a fixed-point zero. But does this choice fit with the CAS? Since zero is smaller than any positive number and bigger than any negative number, it does. Thus we choose 00/00000000 as our "normalized" (by definition only, since zero obviously cannot be normalized), or "normal," zero.

This decimal format must of course be adapted to our 36-bit binary word on the 7090. The sign, as we saw, must occupy the S bit. Next come 8 bits (1 to 8) for the binary characteristic, which represents powers from 2^{-128} to 2^{+127} (about 10^{-38} to 10^{+38}), and following that the binary normalized fraction, occupying the remaining 27 bits (equivalent to a little more than 8 decimal digits). If our numbers are kept in this format—and only the programmer can keep track of this—the 7090 floating-point instructions will automatically perform correct floating-point arithmetic on them, yielding normalized floating-point numbers as results. We do not have to ask *how* the 7090 does this any more than we have to ask *how* it does fixed-point arithmetic. All we have to do is make sure our input data are translated into floating-point format and that our floating-point output data are translated to our desired output format. Since even our fixed-point data had to undergo translation on input and output, we only need choose different conversion subroutines (or maybe only different calling sequences to the same subroutines) in order to work in floating point.

The most important advantage of this floating-point representation is that the binary point is kept automatically. A second advantage arising from this first one is that the programmer can now deal with problems in which he cannot precisely pin-point the ranges of his numbers. The impact of the floating-point representation has been such that few computers currently being brought on the market lack this system in their circuitry or in an equivalent subroutine system. We must remember, however, that we do not simply discard fixed-point operations. When we have complete knowledge of the numbers we are handling, fixed-point manipulation may actually be the better computer representation. The application must determine the tools used.

Floating-point Addition and Subtraction

The AC and M/Q are used in similar ways in fixed- and floating-point arithmetic. We know that TMI, TZE, and CAS operate equally well on each format, and it is also true that CLA, STO, LDQ, and STQ work the same way. Certain aspects are, of course, different. For one thing, the M/Q is used in all floating-point operations, while in fixed-point, it is involved in only multiplication and division. For ordinary operations, this fact simply means we should not expect the M/Q contents to be preserved in a floating-point operation. More important, we must notice that shifting does not play the same role in the two cases. Whereas shifting a fixed-point number is equivalent to either shifting the point or multiplying (or dividing) by some power of 2, shifting a floating-point number *destroys its format* and thus destroys its meaning. The equivalent of multiplying by shifting is adding to the characteristic, but this is rarely done because of sign problems. Moving the point is never necessary because the machine does that automatically after each floating-point operation.

Most floating-point operations have exact fixed-point counterparts. For example, we have FLOATING ADD (FAD), which goes with ADD, and FLOATING SUBTRACT (FSB), with SUB. If we have floating-point numbers in locations G and H and execute

$$
\begin{array}{ll}
\text{CLA} & \text{G} \\
\text{FAD} & \text{H} \\
\text{STO} & \text{I}
\end{array}
$$

location I will contain, as a floating-point number, their sum. If we execute

$$
\begin{array}{ll}
\text{CLA} & \text{G} \\
\text{FSB} & \text{H} \\
\text{STO} & \text{J}
\end{array}
$$

location J will contain their difference (of course, in floating-point). We need not concern ourselves with the details of the addition; the 7090 does it correctly.

We may now take the example which is flow-diagrammed in Fig. 10-8 and code it as if the numbers in block XA were floating point:

X1	CLA	ZERO
	AXT	75, 2
X2	FAD	XA + 75, 2
X3	TIX	X2, 2, 1
X4	STO	SUM

In this case, overflow need not concern us unless the sum exceeded 10^{38} (approximately). In most cases, this range is sufficiently large to ensure that any floating-point overflow is an error. If overflow does occur, however, we are given an automatic trap which enables us to provide any sort of fix-up routine we want—even a scaling routine for floating-point numbers.

The range of floating-point introduces a new problem not present in fixed-point arithmetic. Whereas in fixed-point operations any small result is either zero or a valid fixed-point number, the difference of two numbers in floating-point may be nonzero but too small (less than 10^{-38}) to be represented as a *normalized* floating-point number. (For example, take the *decimal* floating-point numbers 03/12345678 and 03/12345677, whose difference could be expressed as 03/00000001. The closest the machine could come to normalizing this number is 00/00001000, an unnormalized and therefore improper number.) We call this condition *underflow*, a strange term yet somehow descriptive of the actual condition. Generally it is not so serious as overflow and can usually be remedied by replacing the result with zero. We must exercise caution, however, as sometimes a small difference represents a critical condition which must be treated more delicately. As with overflow, we are given a trap when underflow occurs, so that we may handle the situation as we wish—generally with a standard routine.

Multiplication and Division

In fixed-point, multiplication and division are performed by the instructions MULTIPLY (MPY) and DIVIDE OR PROCEED (DVP). [There is another division operation, DIVIDE OR HALT (DVH), which we shall not discuss.] As with addition and subtraction, we deal with range of numbers and results rather than with individual values. In both these operations the multiplier/quotient register, or M/Q, is required: In the case of multiplication the M/Q will hold the multiplier, while in division the M/Q will contain the resulting quotient. Both arithmetic registers are used in combination to obtain the necessary results. In multiplication, the resulting product occupies both the M/Q and accumulator, with the product developed from right to left, as on paper. In terms of physical position, then, the M/Q has the low-order digits of the product. In division, the dividend, or number being divided, occupies both registers with the AC containing the high-order physical positions. The term *physical positions* is used since there will be many cases where the positions of the accumulator will contain mostly (or all) leading *positional* zeros. The value of the number in both multiplication and division is not derived from these positional zeros, although such zeros may vitally affect the final result. Leading zeros will shift the result to the right, reducing the value of the number by a factor of 2 for each shift right of one. As in all fixed-point arithmetic operations, it is the responsibility of the programmer to know where the significant part of product or quotient will be located after the operation is complete so that the number may be positioned properly to obtain the correct value.

Multiplication

A simple rule applies in multiplication: The number of value digits in a product resulting from the multiplication of two numbers is equal to (a maximum of) the sum of the number of value digits of the two numbers, and may be one less. Thus the numbers XXXXX and XXX would give us a digit product XXXXXXXX or XXXXXXX. For example, 42×57 equals 2394, while 12×57 equals 684. In the computer we always multiply a 10-digit number by a 10-digit number, giving us a product of 20 digits or 70 bits as in the case of the 7090. (Actually 70 bits will contain a larger number than 20 digits. For simplicity, however, we shall assume that 35 bits is equivalent to 10 decimal digits and 70 bits to 20 decimal digits.)

As we have seen, in many cases, a considerable number of these 20 decimal digits (or 70 bits) will be leading and possibly trailing positional zeros. Therefore, the programmer must look at the product as only that portion of it containing the significant part, or value digits. If, for example, we have two 10-decimal-digit arithmetic registers, the product of XXXXX and XXX may be found occupying the last eight decimal positions of the lower register; this will occur if our two numbers in the computer were positioned as 00000XXXXX and 0000000XXX. The product then would look as follows:

AC   MQ
0000000000   00XXXXXXXX

If we had trailing positional zeros, as in 00XXXXX000 and 000XXX0000, the product would appear as

AC   MQ
00000XXXXX/XXX0000000

With just the proper number of trailing positional zeros, as in 00XXXXX000 and XXX0000000, the entire significant part of the product would appear in the low-order part of the AC as

AC   MQ
00XXXXXXXX/0000000000

The positional zeros, then, as their name implies, determine the final position of the product. By expanding our 20 decimal digits to 70 binary digits, we may draw similar conclusions. Even the entry of the decimal point (or binary point) to multiplication does not further complicate matters, for the simple rule is that the number of decimal or fractional places in the product is the sum of the number of decimal places of the two numbers involved. Thus the two numbers XXX.XX and X.XX give us the product XXXX.XXXX.

Division

Fixed-point division makes use of the following rule when dealing with normal algebraic manipulation: The number of digits in the quotient (M/Q) is equal to (or more than) the number of dividend digits minus the number of divisor digits. (It may be this difference plus one.) The computer again considers the dividend a 20-decimal (70-binary)-digit dividend divided by a 10-digit divisor giving automatically a 10-digit quotient. We thus look to significant or actual digit positions. XXXXX divided by XXX gives us XX or possibly XXX. 21000 divided by 300 gives us 70, while 21000 divided by 100 gives us 210.

In setting up for division the combined registers normally contain the total dividend. Upon completion of the division operation, the

M/Q will have the quotient while the accumulator holds the remainder. Often the AC portion of the dividend will simply be composed of positional zeros since the dividend may be less than a 10-digit (35-bit) number. If, for example, the number XXXXXX. was to be divided by XXXX. to two decimal places the numbers would be set up as follows:

Before:

AC	M/Q	
0000000000	00XXXXXX00	Dividend
000000XXXX		Divisor (in storage location Z)

After executing DVP Z, we have

AC	M/Q
000000XXXX	000000XXXX
Remainder	Quotient

where the decimal point is located in front of the last two positions of the quotient. It can be seen that the placing of the decimal point is again a straightforward, though tedious, operation. The number of decimal places in the quotient equals the number of decimal positions of the dividend less the number of decimal positions in the divisor. Note that, if three decimal positions were required, the dividend in the arithmetic registers would have been positioned thus:

AC	M/Q
0000000000	0XXXXXX000

If seven decimal positions were required, the dividend would have been positioned as

AC	M/Q
0000000XXX	XXX0000000

Therefore, by shifting the dividend value to the right or left, the number of significant quotient positions developed together with the number of decimal positions is determined.

Arithmetic Coding—An Example

Let us apply our understanding of the four arithmetic operations to the following example. In order to use the 7090 properly we shall assume our numbers are in a binary form:

Number	Location	Binary layout (from position 35 left, that is,
a	A	XXXXXX.XXX leading zeros are
b	B	XXX.0 0 0 omitted)
c	C	XXXXXX.XXXXXX
d	D	XXXXXXXXXX.XXX

Naturally our X in this case is either a 0 or a 1. We wish to evaluate the following formula to three binary positions:

$$y = \frac{a + b}{d - c} + \frac{cd}{ab}$$

The coding below shows a method by which we may carry out the program, which could be a single line in an operation box:

Location	Operation	Address, tag, decrement	Comments
X1	CLA	D	
	ALS	3	Align d for subtracting c
	SUB	C	
	STO	T	Temporary location to save $d - c$
	CLA	A	
	ADD	B	a and b are already aligned
	LRS	29	Position in AC − MQ for division
	DVP	T	Divide by $d - c$, yielding 3 binary places
	STQ	T	Temporary location to save $(a - b)/(d - c)$
	LDQ	A	Prepare for multiplication
	MPY	B	$a \times b$
	STQ	S	Temporary location for $a \times b$ with 6 binary places
	LDQ	C	
	MPY	D	$c \times d$ in AC − MQ with 9 binary places
	DVP	S	$c \times d/a \times b$ with 3 binary positions
	STQ	S	
	CLA	S	Move quotient to AC for addition
	ADD	T	$y = (a + b)/(d - c) + c \times d/a \times b$
	STO	Y	Store y

This was not a very difficult problem to code, though it was tedious

Basically the problem involved the continual preparation of our numbers for the succeeding arithmetic operations. It was necessary for us *to keep track of the binary point*. Since we knew the maximum ranges of our numbers and made use of the rules of arithmetic, we were able to cope with this particular problem. Nevertheless, if the numbers were in floating point, the coding would be simpler.

All we need to know about FLOATING MULTIPLY (FMP) is that the multiplier goes in the M/Q, the multiplicand is in storage (as specified by FMP), and the product appears (as a floating point number) in the AC. All we need to know about FLOATING DIVIDE OR PROCEED (FDP) is that the dividend goes in the AC, the divisor is in storage, the quotient appears in the MQ, and the remainder in the AC (both as floating point numbers). No rules need be made about significant positions or binary points, since normalizing ensures that the most significant positions will always be kept and that standard floating point format will be retained for results. Thus we may code the previous formula almost (but not quite) willy-nilly if the factors *a*, *b*, *c*, and *d* are in floating point.

```
X1    CLA    D
      FSB    C
      STO    T
      CLA    A
      FAD    B
      FDP    T
      STQ    T
      LDQ    A
      FMP    B
      STO    S      Product always in AC
      LDQ    C
      FMP    D
      FDP    S
      STQ    S
      CLA    S      Move quotient to AC
      FAD    T
      STO    Y
```

A careful comparison of the two codes should illuminate some of the differences between fixed and floating point arithmetic.

PROBLEMS

Code the following formulas using the fixed point numbers defined in the text:

10-4. $y = a^2 + b^2 + c^2$
10-5. $z = a(c + b/d) - b/d$
10-6. $x = b^2/(1 + 2c/d)$
10-7. Code formula 10-4 in floating point.
10-8. Code formula 10-5 in floating point.
10-9. Code formula 10-6 in floating point.

FORTRAN Arithmetic Coding: The Problem of Data Representation

The FORTRAN language, being designed especially to simplify the coding of mathematical programs, makes the coding of arithmetic formulas almost ridiculously easy. In fact, we have already seen how the FORTRAN arithmetic statement is not much more than a transcription of the formula to be calculated. Although we have heretofore coded only simple statements, we can easily see how to pass to more complex formulas, such as the one used as an example in the previous section. The entire coding for this formula in the FORTRAN language would be the single statement
$$Y = (A + B)/(D - C) + (C * D)/(A * B)$$
As a matter of fact, coding arithmetic statements in FORTRAN is so easy that it is hard to think of things to say about it. Still, there is a bit more to the process than meets the eye.

In the last section, we coded this same formula in two different ways—one for fixed point and one for floating point. Now, it happens that the FORTRAN compiler would compile the corresponding arithmetic statement into a floating point program. In fact, this object program would be very similar to the one we coded. But how did the FORTRAN compiler know we wanted a floating point program? After all, we might just as well have wanted a fixed point program. In fact, we might have wanted any one of a number of fixed point programs, depending on the format of our numbers in storage.

One answer to these questions is that FORTRAN cannot be used to do fixed point arithmetic, but this is only a partial answer. Actually, FORTRAN can be used to do several kinds of arithmetic—that is, arithmetic using several types of number formats. One of these formats is floating point, and this is the normal format for calculations, the format specified by the F specification in a FORMAT statement. A second format is the *integer* format, specified by the I in a FORMAT statement. Integers are used for indexing and counting, and are actually 15-bit numbers of the type which can be used directly in index registers of the 7090. How, then, can the FORTRAN compiler know which type of number we are using?

In the original FORTRAN language, this problem was solved by an arbitrary ruling that all quantities whose names began with the letters I, J, K, L, M, and N would be integer quantities and all others would be floating point quantities. As the language was used and expanded, however, two difficulties arose. First, the programmers found it inconvenient to be so restricted in their choice of names; and more important, new types of processing were introduced, that is, additional number formats for special purposes. In order to overcome these difficulties, a set of pseudo-operations—the type statements—was introduced into the language. With the type statements, the programmer can define any deviations from the original FORTRAN formatting convention, so that any name can be used for any type of quantity. Only if an explicit type statement is not given for a particular name will that name be subject to the implicit format choice.

Let us see how this system works. Suppose we write the statement

    A = B + C

If there is no type statement referring to A, B, or C, they will all have been classified as names of floating point numbers, and the compiler will produce machine instructions something like

    CLA B
    FAD C
    STO A

If, however, we have written the type statement

    INTEGER A, B, C

the compiler has A, B, and C classified as names of integers. Thus, when it encounters the arithmetic statement involving only the names of integers, it will know to compile something like

    LXA B, 1
    SXD * + 2,1
    LXA C, 1
    TXI * + 1,1, **
    SXA A, 1

which has not even a single instruction in common with the previous code. Similarly, if the original coding had been

    I2 = IR + J3

the compiler would, in the absence of any type statements, classify I2, IR, and J3 as integers and compile appropriately. If, however, we had written the *type* statement

REAL I2, IR, J3

the statement would compile into floating point operations, for the REAL statement defines the names as names of real numbers (that is, floating point numbers, for FORTRAN).

What happens if we write the statement

A = B + C

along with the two *type* statements

REAL B

INTEGER A,C

What we seem to be asking for is that a floating point number be added to a 15-bit indexing quantity. Nonsense? Indeed, it is nonsense; and the FORTRAN compiler will be able to make no more sense out of it than we can. An error indication will be given, stating that we have written a *mixed expression,* which the compiler cannot interpret. Thus, the programmer must keep track of the formats he is using, even though he is writing in a higher level language.

The original idea, of course, was that the programmer writing codes in FORTRAN should have no such worries, but the compiler writers were not willing to put the complete burden on the compiler. After all, there are situations where we may want to use a mixed expression in a way that is perfectly meaningful to *us,* even if present compilers cannot interpret it. Suppose, for instance, we were writing a program to take the average value of a list of numbers. The average is defined as the sum of the quantities divided by the number of items in the list. We would like to write something like this:

```
       FUNCTION AVERG (X,N)
       SUM = 0.0
       DO 17 I = 1,N
17     SUM = SUM + X(I)
       AVERG = SUM/N
       RETURN
       END
```

but the statement

AVERG = SUM/N

is a mixed expression and not allowed by the compiler. Our trouble arises because we are using the quantity named N as an indexing-type quantity (in the DO statement) and as an ordinary arithmetic quantity (in computing the average).

To make the program acceptable to the compiler, we must first write a statement which will cause the conversion of the number, n, from one format to the other. This can be done by writing

    B = N
    AVERG = SUM/B

since the statement

    B = N

is a permissible mixed statement which will cause the compilation of instructions for converting n to the floating point format, the format specified by B. Such explicit conversion statements are a needless encumbrance to the programmer. There is no logical reason why the compiler cannot recognize the type of a *statement* by the type of the left-hand name and compile the necessary conversions to make that statement meaningful. But it adds to the complexity of the compiler, and compiler designers have not all felt the extra effort to be justified for the convenience it would give to the programmer.

This same inconvenience is shown in the handling of actual numbers included in arithmetic expressions. Here again, the programmer must keep the type of expression in mind, for in an integer expression he must write his numbers in the form 1, 2, 3, 4, while in a floating point expression, he must always include a decimal point, as in

    A = 3 * B + C

as opposed to

    I = 3 * J + K

where he must be sure to leave the decimal point out. Surely, the expression

    A = 3 * B + C

is clear enough; and surely the compiler could have the logical power to supply an integer or floating point 3 as required by the type of the statement in which it occurs. But, unfortunately, most present compilers do not perform this service, and it is left as a pesty nuisance for the coder.

PROBLEMS

10-10. Code formula 10-4 in FORTRAN.

10-11. Code formula 10-5 in FORTRAN.

10-12. Code formula 10-6 in FORTRAN.

10-13. How would you convert the preceding codes to calculations with integers?

Numerical Analysis

In our study of input and output, we have seen how important it can be to analyze the operations to be performed in order to achieve maximum efficiency of the program. Numerical computations, too, can be performed in a variety of ways, ways which often differ radically in their efficiency on a given problem. For example, suppose an important part of our program is evaluating a polynomial, an expression of the form

$$y = ax^5 + bx^4 + cx^3 + dx^2 + ex + f$$

In the FORTRAN language, we could code this computation with the single statement

Y = A * X ** 5 + B * X ** 4 + C * X ** 3 + D * X ** 2 + E * X + F

(In FORTRAN, exponentiation may be written with ** to represent the raising of the exponent above the line of print—and integers may be used as exponents, even though they may not be used as coefficients.) If the compiler does not analyze the expression to obtain the most efficient coding (and current compilers mostly do not), it will require $4 + 3 + 2 + 1 = 10$ multiplications to make this calculation. (We count the multiplications because they take so much longer to execute that they ordinarily determine quite well the efficiency of a particular calculation.)

Now, suppose we had written the same calculation in the form

$$y = f + x(e + x\{d + x[c + x(b + xa)]\})$$

Algebraically, they are equivalent expressions, but if we code the new form into such a statement as

Y = F + X * (E + X * (D + X * (C + X * (B + X * A))))

we have reduced the number of multiplications to five. For higher order polynomials, of course, the second method is even more efficient than the first.

The point of this rather simple example is not to teach a particular technique of evaluating polynomials, but rather to illustrate how analysis can pay off in yet another area of computing. Actually, the analysis of computational techniques is a highly developed and specialized field of applied mathematics, a field known as *numerical analysis.*

Numerical analysts are not only concerned with the efficiency of techniques, they are also concerned with how effective the techniques are at actually computing what they are supposed to compute. As we know, the computation carried out by a program is ordinarily only an approximation to some exact mathematical calculation, because each number in the computer is of limited length. For example, suppose we were to calculate the algebraic expression

$$y = a^2 - b^2 = (a - b)(a + b)$$

by the two methods indicated by the algebraic equivalence of the two right-hand expressions. Suppose that $a = 1$ and $b = .00001$ and that our computer uses floating point arithmetic with eight decimal places in the fraction. Let us compare the two calculations: First,

$$a^2 = 1; \quad b^2 = .0000000001$$

When we subtract b^2 from a^2, b^2 will have to have its fraction shifted 10 places so that the characteristics will be equal. In doing this, however, the 1 will be lost, giving the result,

$$a^2 - b^2 = 1$$

Second,

$$a - b = .99999; \quad a + b = 1.00001$$

When we multiply here, we get .9999999999, but the fraction can only hold eight places, so, depending on whether we just drop two places or round off, we get .99999999 or 1.0000000, neither of which is exactly what we would like to have.

Now, the discrepancy of one unit in the eighth significant digit may not seem important, but when thousands, tens of thousands, or even millions of such tiny differences are compounded one upon the other, the final result may well be meaningless digits. On the other hand, the errors may compensate for one another in certain calculations so that we get much more precision than we might have expected. It is the job of the numerical analyst to determine whether or not a given calculation will give (or has given) meaningful results.

One way to neutralize the results of accumulated truncation (dropping least significant digits) or roundoff error is to carry more significant digits throughout the calculation, thus throwing the errors farther out to the right. In a variable-word-length machine, this can be quite easy to accomplish; but in a fixed-word-length machine like the 7090, we must resort to a more cumbersome method. Since all the registers of the machine are designed to perform the proper calculations with single words, any increase in precision carried by the program will be most convenient in chunks of additional whole words to express each number. If we use two words for each number, we are using *double precision;* three words, *triple precision;* and so forth. In double precision, for example, one of the words would hold the most significant (high order) half of the number while the other would hold the least significant (low order) half. In our numerical example, calculation of $a^2 - b^2$, the double-precision result would be the same in all methods. The high order word would carry .99999999 while the low order word would contain .0000000099 (in floating point, of course, so the leading zeros would not have to be carried).

While no order of precision can guarantee that useful results are obtained, very few problems require more than double precision. Also, of course, the higher the precision, the more time the calculation takes (and it can take more than twice as long to do double precision than it does to do single precision—4 to 6 times is usually a reasonable estimate). Therefore, we cannot simply use additional precision as a substitute for analysis of our procedures and results. Nevertheless, running the same problem (or critical parts of a problem) in double precision is often a fine way to verify or invalidate a single-precision result. Consequently, many fixed-word-length machines have two or more precisions built into their hardware.

Because of the usefulness of double precision, the FORTRAN language was expanded to allow for another type of number, the double-precision number. By redefining the type of the variables through such a statement as

DOUBLE PRECISION A, B, C

the statement

A = B + C

can be given yet another meaning for the compiler. In most cases, an entire single-precision program can be converted to a corresponding double-precision program through such redefining of types and possible minor modifications to FORMAT statements. This facility is one of the outstanding advantages of the FORTRAN language for use in solving numerical problems.

Bit Processing

Up until now, we have concentrated on the *word*-processing abilities of the 7090. Actually, the 7090 is oriented more toward word processing than toward bit processing. Addressing, which applies to whole words only, is the primary example of this orientation. In order to process information on the bit level, then, we must have some convenient way to refer to those bits of interest within a word. One way to do this is by shifting and counting to keep track of the current position. Another way is through the use of "masks." A mask is a word (or part of a word) whose bit configuration is not data but *refers to the positions* of data within another word. The most common form of mask has *ones* in the *pertinent* bit positions and zeros elsewhere.

Although masks are often generated by the program, most often they are entered with the program—that is, assembled with it. In order to simplify the writing of masks, a pseudo-operation OCT, for "octal," is provided in the assembly system. OCT enables us to enter 36-bit words by writing 12-octal digits. The octal code (our "compressed" code of Chap. 2) is shown below:

BITS	OCTAL
000	0
001	1
010	2
011	3
100	4
101	5
110	6
111	7

Let us try a few examples. To enter a word of 36 ones, we write

    MASK1   OCT   777777777777

To enter a word where every other bit is a one (odd-numbered bits), we would write

    MASK2   OCT   252525252525

If we wish to enter a word with ones in bit positions 0, 6, 7, 12, 14, 15, 19, 20, 21, 26, 29, 30, and 34, we can write

    MASK3   OCT   406054341142

Although not restricted to them, most bit operations take place in the AC and another register, 36 bits long, called the SENSE INDICATOR REGISTER (SI). Since, when doing logical arithmetic, we

wish to treat *all* bits alike, we use the designation of 0 for our first
bit rather than S. Thinking this way is not enough, however; we
must have machine instructions which *treat* the 0 bit the same way.
Thus, in logical arithmetic, we replace CLA and STO with CLEAR
AND ADD LOGICAL WORD (CAL) and STORE LOGICAL WORD
(SLW), which make the P *bit* of the AC correspond to the 0 bit of a

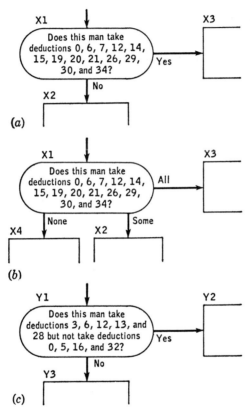

Fig. 10-10. Bit processing.

storage word—essentially ignoring AC_s. The SI, being a 36-bit register, needs only one set of loading and storing instructions, LOAD
INDICATORS (LDI) and STORE INDICATORS (STI).

Now, let us see how we can do bit processing using masks. Earlier
in the chapter, we discussed a payroll file where one word in each
record represented the set of deductions taken by an employee. Suppose we wish to find out whether or not any employee takes *all* the

following deductions: 0, 6, 7, 12, 14, 15, 19, 20, 21, 26, 29, 30, and 34. That is, are each of these bits equal to one in any deduction word? A simple comparison (such as CAS) will not answer this question, because it will involve other bits in which we are not interested. Thus we must use a mask (MASK3, defined above) to indicate that *only* these bits are to enter into the test.

The instruction we shall use is TRANSFER WHEN INDICATORS ON (TIO), which works as follows:

Only those bits in SI corresponding to the mask in the AC are examined. If they are *all ones* (on), a transfer is made; otherwise the next instruction is taken in sequence.

Thus the mask in the AC selects the bits we want to test. Figure 10-10*a* shows the alternative box we should like to code. Using TIO, we can write

X1	CAL	MASK3	Puts mask in AC
	LDI	DED	Deduction word to SI
	TIO	X3	
X2			

Without the mask, shifting and testing for overflow, for example, this test would require a long and tedious code—a code, moreover, which would be quite inflexible. The mask technique is, on the other hand, not only simple to code, but should we decide to change the precise pattern of bits involved in the test, we simply modify the mask.

Another instruction, similar to TIO, is TRANSFER WHEN INDI-CATORS OFF (TIF). Instead of testing for all the specified bits being on, it tests for all being off (0). Thus, if we wish to code the alternative box of Fig. 10-10*b*, we can write

X1	CAL	MASK3	Puts mask in AC
	LDI	DED	Deduction word to SI
	TIO	X3	Takes *all* these deductions
	TIF	X4	Takes *none* of these deductions
X2			Takes *some* of these deductions

(Notice that TIO and TIF are *not* complementary.)

We can, of course, combine such tests while not using the same masks for each test. We can code the alternative box of Fig. 10-10*c* as follows:

Y1	LDI	DED	Deduction word to SI
	CAL	MASK4	First mask to AC
	TIO	Y1A	
	TRA	Y3	Does not take some
Y1A	CAL	MASK5	Second mask to AC
	TIF	Y2	
Y3			

provided we have set up the two masks

MASK4	OCT	044060000200
MASK5	OCT	410002000010

We can, in a book of this purpose, only provide a glimpse of bit-processing techniques. Other instructions on the 7090 enable us to turn bits on, turn bits off, complement bits, combine the bits in several words using all the operations of symbolic logic, and rearrange the bits in any pattern. When we combine these techniques with indirectly and effectively addressed masks, shifting masks, and shifting data, we have more bit-processing ability than many programmers seem able to use. The power of bit processing is evident only when the programmer has the insight to assign powerful *meanings* to the bits. If his vision is restricted to seeing words only as numbers, he will never be able to see the computer as anything but a large calculating machine, tirelessly evaluating formulas. Applications such as design of electrical equipment, control of machine tools, translation of languages, supervision of traffic, simulation of economic situations, and operation of factories and warehouses—to name but a trifling few—will remain impossible mysteries to him.

PROBLEMS

10-14. Create the necessary mask and instructions to test whether or not a man takes all the deductions 8, 9, 10, 15, 16, and 21.

10-15. Create the necessary mask and instructions to test whether a man takes some of the above deductions.

10-16. Create the necessary masks and instructions to test whether or not a man takes deductions 1, 2, 3, and 4 but does not take deductions 10, 11, and 12.

10-17. Suppose we were writing a program which planned shipping routes all around the world. In calculating the approximate distances from place to place by ship, we would have to know where there was land and where there was navigable water, all over the globe. How could such information be stored in the computer? How would a program go about finding a navigable route from one port to another?

Logical Arithmetic in FORTRAN

Because of the usefulness of logical operations such as can be programmed by bit manipulation, users of the FORTRAN language quickly came to desire that such facilities be added to the original specifications. One resulting addition was the *logical* IF statement. In the logical IF statement, an expression is written in parentheses following an IF. The expression, at the time the statement is executed, may take on one of two "values," TRUE or FALSE. If it takes on the value TRUE (or more simply, T), a statement written after the parenthesis is executed. If it takes on the value FALSE (or F), the next statement in the normal flow of control is executed, omitting the statement appended to the IF statement.

To illustrate one use of the logical IF statement, let us see how our previous bit-processing examples could have been coded in FORTRAN. Suppose that the various deduction types are represented by an array, D, defined by *type* statements such as the following:

LOGICAL D0,D1,D2,D3

which defines four of the possible deductions as variables which can take on only the two values, TRUE (meaning, in this case, "takes this deduction") and FALSE ("does not take this deduction"). Then, the alternative box of Fig. 10-10a can be coded with a logical IF as follows:

```
1    IF (D0.AND.D6.AND.D7.AND.D12.AND.D14.AND.
     2D15.AND.D19.AND.D20.AND.D21.AND.D26.AND.
     3D29.AND.D30.AND.D34) GO TO 3
2    . . .
```

Here, if the expression in the parentheses is TRUE (that is, if all the specified deductions are taken by this man) the statement, GO TO 3, will be executed. Otherwise, statement 2, the next statement in sequence, will be executed. (Remember that the 2 at the beginning of the second line simply means a continuation of the same statement, which was too long to write on one line. The same applies to the 3 for the third line.)

To code the alternative box of Fig. 10-10b, we could use the statement already given, followed by the statement

IF (D0.OR.D6.OR.D7.OR.D12.OR.D14.OR.D15.OR.
2D19.OR.D20.OR.D21.OR.D26.OR.D29.OR.D30.OR.
3D34) GO TO 2

4   . . .

The diagram in Fig. 10-10c could be coded as

1   IF (D3.AND.D6.AND.D12.AND.D13.AND.D28.AND..
2NOT.(D0.OR.D5.OR.D16.OR.D32)) GO TO 2

3   . . .

where the .NOT. operation in this case applies to the entire expression within the second parentheses. If we wish to simplify long expressions, we can do the logical computation of TRUE or FALSE in steps, using arithmetic statements. Thus, another way of coding the diagram in Fig. 10-10c would be

1   R = D3.AND.D6.AND.D12.AND.D13.AND.D28
     S = D0.OR.D5.OR.D16.OR.D32
     IF (R.AND..NOT.S) GO TO 2

3   . . .

In this manner of coding, the intermediate logical variable, R, tells whether it is TRUE or FALSE that *all* the deductions, 3, 6, 12, 13, and 28, are taken by this man; while the variable, S, tells by its value whether it is TRUE or FALSE that *any* of the deductions, 0, 5, 16, or 32, are taken.

We see, then, that using the *logical* operators, .AND., .OR., and .NOT., we can make highly complex decisions in a straightforward manner. Unfortunately, the values, T and F, of the logical variables are not stored as single bits in a FORTRAN program, but use an entire word for each. This prodigal usage of storage makes it impractical to use FORTRAN for compiling programs whose main operations involve the testing and manipulating of large bit tables. Nevertheless, the logical IF does simplify the coding of more routine logical decisions.

In addition to the logical operators, the logical IF can use expressions involving various *relational* operators, given by the following list:

Symbol	Meaning of operation
.GT.	Greater than
.GE.	Greater than or equal to

.LT.	Less than
.LE.	Less than or equal to
.EQ.	Equal to
.NE.	Not equal to

These operators may be used to perform tests on variables other than logical variables, yielding the value T or F depending on the result of the test. For example, in the statement

$$H = A.GE.B$$

the variable, H, is given the value T if a is greater than or equal to b, and given the value F otherwise. The same operations could have been coded with the more complex statement

$$H = (A.GT.B).OR.(A.EQ.B)$$

(Can it be coded in other ways?)

Using the relational operators, it is possible to perform all the tests we could perform with the arithmetic IF statement. (Indeed, many users have proposed that the arithmetic IF statement—the original test statement—be dropped from the language as an unnecessary feature.) Thus, the program in Fig. 5-3 could be coded as

```
10      IF (R.EQ.0.0) GO TO 20
30      Z = Y
        GO TO 40
20      Z = X
40      . . .
```

and the program in Fig. 5-4 could be written

```
10      IF ((R.EQ.0.0).OR.(S.EQ.0.0)) GO TO 40
30      Z = Y
        GO TO 50
40      Z = X
50      . . .
```

Sometimes we can make the coding even simpler by using something besides a GO TO as the statement attached to the logical IF. Thus, another method of coding Fig. 5-3 would be this:

```
10      IF (R.EQ.0.0) Z = X
30      IF (R.NE.0.0) Z = Y
40      . . .
```

and an alternative method of coding Fig. 5-4 could be

```
10      Z = Y
        IF ((R.EQ.0.0).OR.(S.EQ.0.0)) Z = X
50      . . .
```

since, if the condition in the second statement is not met, Z will retain C(Y). Notice how this method manages to eliminate all explicit transfers of control.

As a final example of how the logical IF can simplify coding, let us code the diagram in Fig. 5-6, as follows:

```
10    Z = Y
      IF ((R.EQ.0.AND.S.NE.0).OR.(R.NE.0.AND.S.EQ.0)) Z = X
      . . .
```

or we can code it in the form

```
10    Z = Y
      P = R.EQ.0
      Q = S.EQ.0
      IF (P.AND. .NOT.Q) Z = X
      IF (Q.AND. .NOT.P) Z = X
      . . .
```

(Can it be coded in any other forms?)

The logical variable is, of course, in yet another format in which information can be used by a FORTRAN program. Provision is made, by way of the L specification, for reading in and printing out logical variables as T's or F's, using the FORMAT statement in the usual way. Altogether, the inclusion of logical variables in the FORTRAN language is an expansion in the direction of a programming language less specifically oriented to mathematical problems. We can expect to see further changes in the same direction in the future.

PROBLEMS

10-18. Do Prob. 10-14, using the logical IF statement.

10-19. Do Prob. 10-15, using the logical IF statement.

10-20. Do Prob. 10-16, using the logical IF statement.

10-21. Code the diagram in Fig. 5-5, using the logical IF statement.

10-22. Code the diagram in Fig. 5-8, using the logical IF statement.

10-23. Suppose the location SCORE contains a test score from 0 to 100 and we wish to translate these scores into grades according to the following table:

Score	Grade
0–57	0
58–67	1
68–72	2
73–89	3
90–100	4

Write a program, using logical IF statements, to perform the conversion.

CHAPTER 11

PROGRAM TESTING

When we approach the subject of program testing, we might almost conclude the whole subject immediately with the anecdote about the mathematics professor who, when asked to look at a student's problem, replied, "If you haven't made any mistakes, you have the right answer." He was, of course, being only slightly facetious. We have already stressed this philosophy in programming, where the major problem is knowing when a program is "right."

In order to be sure that a program is right, a simple and systematic approach is undoubtedly best. However, no approach can assure correctness without adequate testing for verification. We smile when we read the professor's reply because we know that human beings seldom know immediately when they have made errors—although we know they will at some time make them. The programmer must not have the view that, because he cannot think of any error, there must not be one. On the contrary, extreme skepticism is the only proper attitude. Obviously, if we can recognize an error, it ceases to be an error.

If we had to rely on our own judgment as to the correctness of our programs, we would be in a difficult position. Fortunately the computer usually provides the proof of the pudding. It is such a proper combination of programmer and computer that will ultimately determine the means of judging the program. We hope to provide some insight into the proper mixture of these ingredients. An immediate problem that we must cope with is the somewhat disheartening fact that, even after carefully eliminating clerical errors, experienced programmers will still make an average of approximately one error for every thirty instructions written. These errors range from minor mis-

understandings of instructions to major errors of logic or problem interpretation. Strangely enough, the trivial errors often lead to spectacular
results, while the major errors initially are usually the most difficult
to detect.

Of course, it is possible to write a program without errors, but
this fact does not obviate the need for testing. Whether or not a
program is working is a matter not to be decided by intuition. Quite
often it is obvious when a program is *not* working. However, situations
have occurred where a program which has been apparently successful
for years has been exposed as erroneous in some part of its operation.
Consequently, when we use a program, we want to know how it was
tested in order to give us confidence in—or warning about—its applicability. Woe unto the programmer with "beginner's luck" whose
first program happens to have no errors. If he takes success in the
wrong way, many rude shocks may be needed to jar his unfounded
confidence into the shape of proper skepticism.

Many people are discouraged by what to them seems the inordinate
amount of effort spent on program testing. They rightly indicate that
a human being can often be trained to do a job much more easily
than a computer can be programmed to do it. The rebuttal to this
observation may be one or more of the following statements:

1. All problems are not suitable for computers. (We must never
forget this one.)

2. The computer, once properly programmed, will give a higher
level of performance, if, indeed, the problem is suited to a computer
approach.

3. All the human errors are removed from the system in advance,
instead of distributing them throughout the work like bits of shell
in a nutcake. In such instances, unfortunately, the human errors will
not necessarily repeat in identical manner. Thus, anticipating and
catching such errors may be exceedingly difficult. Often in these
cases the tendency is to overcompensate for such errors, resulting in
expense and time loss.

4. The computer is often doing a different job than the man is doing,
for there is a tendency—usually a good one—to enlarge the scope of
a problem at the same time it is first programmed for a computer.
People are often tempted to "compare apples with houses" in this case.

5. The computer is probably a more steadfast employee, whereas

human beings tend to move on to other responsibilities and must be replaced by other human beings who must, in turn, be trained.

In other words, if a job is worth doing, it is worth doing right. If a job is a computer job, it should be handled as such without hesitation. Of course, we are obligated to include the cost of programming and testing in any justification of a new computer application. Furthermore we must not be tempted to cut costs at the end by skimping on the testing effort. An incorrect program is indeed worth less than no program at all because the false conclusions it may inspire can lead to many expensive errors.

A greater danger than false economy is ennui. Sometimes a programmer, upon finishing the coding phase of a problem, feels that all the interesting work is done. He yearns to move on to the next problem. Thus as soon as the program looks correct—or, rather, does not look incorrect—he convinces himself it is finished and abandons it. Programmers at this time are much more fickle than young lovers.

Such actions are, of course, foolish. In the first place, we cannot so easily abandon our programs and relieve ourselves of further obligation to them. It is very possible under such circumstances that in the middle of a new problem we shall be called upon to finish our previous shoddy work—which will then seem even more dry and dull, as well as being much less familiar. Such unfamiliarity is no small problem. Much grief can occur before the programmer regains the level of thought activity he achieved in originally writing the program. We have emphasized flow diagramming and its most important assistance to understanding a program but no flow diagram guarantees easy reading of a program. The proper flow diagram does guarantee the correct logical guide through the program and a shorter path to correct understanding.

It is amazing how one goes about developing a coding structure. Often the programmer will review his coding with astonishment. He will ask incredulously, "How was it possible for me to construct this coding logic? I never could have developed this logic initially." This statement is well-founded. It is a rare case where the programmer can immediately develop the final logical construction. Normally programming is a series of attempts, of two steps forward and one step backward. As experience is gained in understanding the problem and applying techniques—as the programmer becomes more immersed in the program's intricacies—his logic improves. We could almost relate this logical building to a pyramid. In testing out the problem we must climb the same pyramid as in coding. In this case, however, we must take care to root out all misconstructed blocks, being careful not to lose our footing on the slippery sides. Thus, if we are really bored with a problem, the smartest approach is to finish it as correctly as possible so we shall never see it again.

In the second place, the testing of a program, properly approached, is by far the most intriguing part of programming. Truly the mettle of the programmer is tested along with the program. No puzzle addict could experience the miraculous intricacies and subtleties of the trail left by a program gone wrong. In the past, these interesting aspects of program testing have been dampened by the difficulty in rigorously extracting just the information wanted about the performance of a program. Now, however, sophisticated systems are available to relieve the programmer of much of this burden.

Preliminary Testing

Now that we have successfully (hopefully) eliminated our ego, a false sense of economy, and any fickleness as obstacles to successful program testing, what positive approach can we take? Incongruous as it may seem, we would do well to adopt the attitude of the totalitarian judge toward the accused criminal: guilty until proved innocent —wrong until proved right. We do this since there is no need to worry about the civil rights of programs. Rather we are concerned only about the privileges of the person paying for them. We must make the program demonstrate its ability to perform as specified, and we are under an obligation to show no mercy in demanding this demonstration.

Programs of course have no feelings. It is therefore difficult to understand why some programmers seem loath to embarrass their programs. Certainly these programmers cannot be afraid of embarrassing themselves; for though to err is human, to pretend to perfection is stupidity. It is absolutely necessary to check out our program for every possible variation we can contrive in order to make it slip if we can, rather than eventually slipping ourselves on an undiscovered error.

The first opportunity to perform such checking is the first time we have our program in scrutinizable form—probably when the flow diagram is complete. At this point, as at all other stages of testing, the help of a second person is almost indispensable. As much as we peruse our own work, complete oversights remain complete oversights. The case we forget to account for in writing the program will probably be the same case we fail to think of when testing later. The second person may perceive our oversight in an instant simply because of his fresh viewpoint. Quite often we recognize our own oversights and blunders as we try to explain our work to someone else. However, it is not too good to offer too much interpretation initially other than that furnished in the work itself. Too much detail can distort the program as well as mislead the listener. A properly drawn flow diagram should be its own explanation, good or bad. If obscurities are revealed upon reading, all the better to correct them early.

The following points, at least, should be checked on the flow diagram:

1. A clearly marked beginning and end are present.

2. Each alternative box has at least two alternatives, and each possible result of the test is represented by some flow line.

3. Operation boxes have one and only one exit and all boxes have one and only one direct entry line.

4. No flow lines are unconnected at either end. That is, each flow line must have an origin at some box and must terminate at a box or merge point.

5. All quantities used on the right-hand side of formulas, in alternative boxes, or as output must have been defined in some way earlier in the flow—either as constants entered with the program, as input data, or as quantities on the left-hand side of formulas. All quantities used on the left-hand side of formulas or in input lists must be used at some time later in the program—either on the right-hand side of formulas, in alternative boxes, or as output data. "Input data" include the outputs from subroutines, and "output data" include the quantities supplied to subroutines by the main program.

6. All switches must be set at some point earlier in the flow. Also, each possible position of the switch must be set at least once somewhere on the diagram.

7. Each loop must have the following parts:

   a. Initialization.

   b. A process or body.

   c. At least one test which can terminate it.

   d. A method for passing on to the next case if the end is not reached.

These points are quite mechanical but will nevertheless reveal a large percentage of the bumbles and bobbles. The more subtle errors in logic may have to be rooted out by methods less easily described. Perhaps the method most likely to succeed is tracing mentally all possible paths, especially concentrating on the "unlikely" ones. Another good practice is to put the entire diagram away for a couple of days before rereading. This procedure gives some of the effect of having a second person look at the diagram and may help detach the mind from some persistent rut. Recopying the diagram sometimes helps a great deal, both because it forces close examination and because it may reveal errors concealed by sloppy drawing or erasing.

Each technique differs in value for each individual programmer. The technique of "just sitting back and thinking" about the diagram is somewhat overrated because, when beginners watch experienced programmers working, the systematic approach they unconsciously use may not be apparent. Working without a plan usually leads repeatedly to the same dead ends.

The checking of the flow diagram does not end when coding begins; on the contrary, the coding itself gives us one of the best checks on the diagram. Coding frequently reveals flaws in the small detail of the diagram because we concentrate on one part at a time. For this reason, however, coding seldom reveals larger flaws. In fact, we often get worried about our logic when coding and are tempted to make changes which, on review from a more withdrawn vantage point, prove erroneous. As we code we take several steps to link the flow diagram and the code:

1. All deviations from normal flow (transfers or skips) are marked with slashes on the corresponding flow lines.

2. Locations of data are marked in memory boxes.

3. Coding tricks are described in assertion boxes.

4. The first instruction of each block of coding is labeled to correspond to the label on the flow-diagram block.

When coding is complete, we may make the following simple checks on the now up-dated flow diagram:

1. Are all blocks coded (check the labels)?

2. Does each alternative box have at most one normal flow line (not slashed) coming out?

3. Does each merge point have at most one normal flow line entering?

4. Is there at least one non normal flow line in every possible loop?

These four checks turn up virtually all mechanical errors in the coding of the over-all flow, or program organization, but tell us nothing about whether we have properly implemented the contents of the operation boxes. We shall find, as we discuss testing, that we simplify our job to the extent that we can separate these two aspects of the program, the operations and the organization.

When the coding has been checked on paper—and certainly someone else should examine at least the more difficult blocks—cards will be punched from the coding sheets. (This illustrates a 7090 procedure, as will the remainder of the procedures in this chapter. In other methods paper or magnetic tape might be prepared from the coding sheets, although cards, because of the ease with which changes may be made to them, are by far the most common medium for initially preparing programs in the check-out stage.) Once we have the cards, we may make automatic listings whenever we wish. In this way we save a good deal of copying and erasing. A listing should be made from the cards as soon as they are punched and compared with the handwritten copy to see that all information was punched; that the order is correct; and that no misreadings were made—such as "*i*'s" and ones interchanged, "*o*'s" and zeros, or "*z*'s" and twos. Once this tedious—but absolutely necessary—work is done, all old handwritten copies should be destroyed. If old versions of a program are left lying around, they are sure to confuse matters later on. Putting a date on all work can be a big help, but absolute destruction of previous copies is the best insurance.

An Assembly Output

Now that we have done all that is humanly possible to find the errors in our program, we may proceed to enlist some inhuman aid—that of the computer. The assembly process is the first time the computer gets to look at the program. Therefore, the assembly program has built into it a number of purely mechanical checks for some common errors.

Figure 11-1 shows an example of a program as an output listing from the assembly program. Let us go over this listing in detail. There are four sections to the listing (Fig. 11-1 is actually a composite of four pages): the error list, the undefined and multiply defined symbol list, the text, and the dictionary. The text contains the original symbolic instructions on the right. The first column on the left indicates, in octal, the absolute location in which each instruction is to be located. Following the location number, the octal representation of the instruction itself is shown, broken up into prefix, decrement, tag, and address. Pseudo-operations, such as END and BSS, which generate no words in storage, get certain reference numbers printed in this area instead. Between the octal and symbolic representations is another reference number, which helps to locate various items in the text. An X after this number indicates a probable error in the corresponding coding line. We have a number of such "flags" in this listing; so let us refer to the top of Fig. 11-1 to determine their meanings.

The "compiler error list" indicates two of these errors. An error caused X+ to be punched instead of X5 in line 11, and a + sign is not a permissible character in a symbol. Line 12 is similarly mispunched, this time in the operation field, with TN2 instead of TNZ. The flag in line 12 is not an X, but a /// placed in the operation field. (Notice that the original punching does not show in lines 11 and 12 of the listing, but only in the error indication.)

The list of undefined symbols (there are no multiply defined symbols in this program) shows us the reason for the other flags—three undefined symbols. The symbol AA resulted from a miswriting of the symbol A, while the symbols ITAPE and OTAPE were just plain forgotten. The compiler actually assigns values to these symbols, starting with the location number following the remainder of the program; but they will have to be corrected before the program is run.

The dictionary at the bottom of Fig. 11-1 lists the symbols in alphabetical order along with the number of the page on which each symbol is defined. An asterisk by the page number indicates that that symbol was never referred to by any instruction, and might, if we wished, be removed from the code without error. Since we are using the code to cross-reference with our flow diagram, however, we do not wish to delete these symbols. A glance at the dictionary will tell us just

COMPILER ERROR LIST

11	X+	CLA	AA
			CONNECTOR IN LOCATION,
12		TN2	X2
			ILLEGAL CHAR OP, ILLEGAL OP,

UNDEF SYMBOLS IN TEXT

ITAPE	05737
OTAPE	05740
AA	05741

05714	0	00024
05715	0	77200
05716	0	77200
05717	0	76200
05720	0	54000
05721	0	06000
05722	0	03000
05723	0	50000

PROGRAM TO SELECT CERTAIN INPUT RECORDS

05670	1*			
05670	2*			
	3	A	BSS	20, 0
07137	4	C1	IOCD	A, 0 + 0, 20
10140	5X	X1	REWA	ITAPE
07137	6X		REWB	OTAPE +1
05714	7X	X2	RTDA	ITAPE
05721	8		RCHA	C1
05733	9	X2A	TCOA	X2A +1
05741	10	X2B	TEFA	X3
	11X		CLA	AA +1

Location				Line	Sym	Tag	Op	Operand
05724	0	00000	0	12		+2	///	X2
05725	0	50000	0	13	X6		CLA	A + 19
05726	0	12000	0	14		+1	TPL	X2
05727	0	76600	0	15X	X7		WTDB	OTAPE
05730	−0	54000	0	16		+1	RCHB	C1
05731	0	06100	0	17	X7A		TCOB	X7A
05732	0	02000	0	18		+1	TRA	X2
05733	0	77000	0	19X	X3		WEFB	OTAPE
05734	0	77200	0	20X		+1	REWA	ITAPE
05735	0	77200	0	21X		+2	REWB	OTAPE
05736	0	02000	0	22	X4		TRA	10
				23			END	X1

(Word‑2 / address field)

Line	addr
12	05717
13	05713
14	05717
15X	10140
16	05714
17	05731
18	05717
19X	10140
20X	07137
21X	10140
22	00012
23	05715

Symbol			Symbol		
A	0001	0001	X3	0001	*0001
C1	0001	0001	X4	0001	*0001
X1	0001	*0001	X6	*0001	*0001
X2	0001	0001	X7	0001	*0001
X2A	0001	*0001	X7A	0001	0001
X2B	0001	*0001			

Fig. 11-1. Assembly program output.

where to look for the code corresponding to any part of our flow diagram. This feature may not seem valuable in this listing, but in a large system, where several hundred pages of code may be involved, it is hard to do without.

Undoubtedly any reasonable checking procedure would have turned up the errors in this listing before assembly took place, but in larger programs it is likely that a few such errors will slip by our most meticulous checking. The assembly listing indicates two classes of errors, absolute errors and probable errors. An absolute error is a violation of the rules of the assembly system itself, such as the omission of the END card. The probable errors, on the other hand, may be intentionally placed by the programmer in order to achieve some unusual effect. For example, an illegal operation code might be used to get an operation code of zero into the assembled program. We cannot recommend such techniques, however, since there are usually other, quite adequate, means for accomplishing the same thing. If we avoid the intentional use of illegal operation codes in our programs, we can redefine this type of error as an absolute error. It will then not be necessary to consider every error to see if it was placed there purposely by the programmer. Similar effects may be obtained by avoiding multiply defined symbols; by defining all symbols explicitly; and by filling in all addresses, tags, and decrements where appropriate—even though irrelevant—to the format.

It is, of course, difficult to have the machine check how well the program matches the *intent* of the programmer without giving a great deal of information about that intent. If we had some simple way of presenting that kind of information to the machine for checking, we might just as well have the machine do the coding. Let us not forget that complex logical operations occur through a combination of simple instructions executed by the computer and not by the computer logically deducing or inferring what is desired. We know that programming languages have been developed for specific problem areas in order to make the presentation of such information easier. Of course, such systems are really substitutes for the coding language only; we still have not reached the stage where we can present vague, undefined ideas to the machine and get just the results we did not know we wanted. Such a "utopian system" may never come about. For correct solutions there is still no substitute for hard detailed work.

The Test Cases

By the time we have assembled the program successfully, or at least corrected any errors uncovered in the process, we should have done everything possible to eliminate mechanical errors from the coding. We may, of course, still have such errors; but to the extent that they are eliminated, our further task will be lightened. From this point on, we must prove our program correct by forcing it to pass the most difficult and comprehensive tests we can construct.

Because there are many types of programs, we cannot present any detailed scheme for preparing test cases. We can, however, present a general approach which can be adapted to the details of individual programs.

We base this approach on the principle, previously expounded, of separating the organization of the program from its content. The first tests we prepare are directed toward proving the organization; for until we know that the basic organization is correct, it is frivolous, as well as difficult, to check out the content.

Usually a case may be constructed which follows the "typical" flow of the program and does not severely tax the processing sections. Such a case provides a good beginning, because we are first searching for gross errors and do not wish to be concerned with the program's subtleties. If gross errors are present, we may find it difficult to determine anything at all about the behavior of the program. At the rate of approximately 15,000,000 operations per minute, a program can become hopelessly entangled in its errors in far less than the blink of an eye. When we code certain sections of the program, we are forced to assume that other sections will perform certain tasks. Thus a section which is itself perfectly coded can perform all sorts of weird tricks because of errors in other sections. Our check-out job is therefore simplified if we can keep our sections from being too tightly interconnected—if we avoid the "house-of-cards" approach.

Earlier we recommended the subroutine-type approach to program development. The advantages of such an approach in moderation should be more apparent at this time.

Illustrative of the type of errors that occur is the case of the program handling alternate logical paths in which these paths pass through common areas of code. Let us say that alternate A is tested out correctly. Alternate B is next checked. As a result of correcting alternate B, however, alternate A no longer works because of changes in the common blocks. The same type of disabling may occur to B or even to A and B by subsequent checking out of other alternate paths. Testing out a program is seldom a straightforward step-by-step procedure. We normally must circle around, repeating ourselves, encompassing more of the total program each time we make a pass through it.

Once we have passed this first type of test on organization successfully, we have a fixed point on which we can anchor our further testing. Any time we make additional corrections to the program, we must revert to this first test to assure ourselves that we have not damaged a previously correct portion as we have just illustrated. As we proceed to progressively more difficult tests, we try to obtain a precise picture of the program structure which should, if correct, correspond in detail to the structure of the flow diagram. To this end, we construct cases which will test each alternative and, if possible, all combinations. Often it is impossible, from sheer number of possibilities, to test all combinations of alternatives. In that case, we must certainly test all those combinations which are in any way unusual— which seem to present a different aspect as combinations than as individual alternatives.

As the structure becomes more and more positively confirmed, we start subjecting the processing sections to more searching tests. Whereas in the beginning we tried to keep our tests focused on a few of the larger aspects of the program, we now try to make each test do as much work as possible. What is foolishness with a completely raw program becomes simple economy with a program tested in all but fine detail.

How do we go about testing a processing section? A specific answer again depends on the specific type of processing, but we can set down the following principles which apply to almost any processing function:

1. Test the normal cases
2. Test the extremes
3. Test the exceptions

Usually the normal familiarity with the input data gives some feeling for its extremes and exceptions, while the intermediate results and the final output tend to conceal traps for the unwary programmer. Although we may have some vague feelings about the nature of such traps, no amount of experience seems to furnish absolute protection against surprise. Nevertheless, an example at this point is needed, for it seems contradictory to try to explain about extremes and exceptions in general terms. An actual case, suitably simplified, might furnish the necessary object lesson.

PROBLEMS

11-1. Assume you are preparing to test the program flow-diagrammed in Fig. 4-14.
- a. Perform the seven checks on the flow diagram listed under Preliminary Testing and record your results.
- b. If you have coded this diagram (Prob. 4-11), perform the four steps linking the flow diagram and the code, perform the four checks, and record your results.
- c. Construct a test case which will check the normal flow of the program. (Notice how the two halves of the program can be tested with the same data by interchanging input tapes.)
- d. Make a list of at least four exceptional types of situations which the program might encounter. Prepare a test case for each of these situations.
- e. Construct any other tests you would like to have performed. Explain why you want each of these tests.

11-2. Assume you are preparing to test the program flow-diagrammed in Fig. 9-5 and coded in the text. Perform steps a through e as listed in Prob. 11-1.

11-3. Assume you are preparing to test the program flow-diagrammed in Fig. 6-6 and coded in the text. Perform steps a through e as listed in Prob. 11-1.

A Case of Errors

A program was written to calculate interest on savings accounts. The input consisted of records of all deposits and withdrawals for each account along with information about the type of account and the opening balance. The output, calculated quarterly, consisted of a check for the interest on one type of account or, for the other type, a new balance card with the interest added to the closing balance. The programmer, who had modest experience, neatly illustrated the need for each type of test in the unfortunate history of checking this program.

After subjecting the program to numerous cases of deposits intermingled with withdrawals, he pronounced it ready. As happens so often, the initial production run proved to be just an expensive continuation of the check-out procedure. Twenty thousand or so accounts had been processed before someone noticed that no checks were being produced. Rule number one had been violated; the perfectly normal case of the second account type had been neglected in the testing. The correction proved to be trivial; not so the cost of recalculating twenty thousand accounts.

Somehow the amount of money wasted in checking out a program this way usually seems to increase the programmer's confidence that *now* everything is all right. In this case, the second production attempt had gone a good deal further than the first when someone noticed that the check made out to the institution's best account had just been produced. Everybody was good-naturedly curious about how much interest this large account had yielded, but their curiosity grew more intense when they noticed how small the amount actually was. The programmer, it seems, had used a fixed-point calculation and had never tested a case large enough to give an overflow, thus violating rule number two. Fortunately, only about twenty accounts were affected; and they were easily corrected by hand, although the program, in this case, proved more difficult to repair. These twenty accounts, of course, were the twenty largest, and the institution was somewhat shaken by the thought of the repercussions that might have occurred.

By now, however, the programmer's faith was virtually unshakable. As a matter of fact, it took 6 months to give him, and the company, another shaking. It happened that a customer had withdrawn a large sum one morning, then changed his mind and redeposited the money that afternoon. The institution's rules were quite clear on this point; the customer was to lose the interest that would have accrued. The program was also quite clear, although not in agreement with the rules of the institution. The discrepancy resulting from this travesty on the third rule was large enough—and the situation unusual enough—that it came to notice. The program was corrected by the now rather sheepish programmer. Further investigation revealed that this exceptional case was not quite so exceptional as everyone had supposed. The company, however, with consummate wisdom, made no attempt to get the several overpayments returned.

Things went well for the program from that time on—so well, in fact, that someone decided that a change ought to be made. The programmer, who was not—despite appearances—completely ignorant, had written the program in such a way that the modification was easily made. It seems that some unnamed person in the firm, in a fit of unusually clear vision, had decided that a substantial saving would result if they dropped the practice of rounding out the interest amounts. In other words, instead of rounding to the nearest cent, fractions of a penny were simply dropped. No single customer would notice this penny difference, but on thirty thousand accounts, about $150 would be saved each quarter—a good return for changing a "round" instruction to a "no operation."

Alas, the poor programmer. We would think he might have learned caution by this time. When the last of the checks had been put into envelopes for mailing, one of the clerks remarked how it was strange that so many people were getting checks for $99.99, $9.99, or $.99. A quick check revealed the awful news. About half the accounts were in nice round-number amounts, such as $10,000, $1,000, and $100. Since the current interest rate was 4 per cent, the interest for one quarter was simply 1 per cent of any amount left undisturbed throughout that quarter. The program, however, computed interest on a monthly basis in order to handle the more general case of deposits and withdrawals and could, of course, use any interest rate with equal ease. Four per cent per year is 0.3333333333 per cent on a monthly basis. Therefore, the interest for 1 month on $10,000 was $33.333 and for 3 months $99.999. With rounding, this figure came to a nice even $100.00, exactly the same as any retired old lady with a savings account would calculate. Without rounding, however, the penny-pinching tactic became rudely exposed to the view of all the retired old ladies. No doubt they would have been puzzled, if not displeased, had not one of the company officials put an end to the foolishness by declaring that the company policy was not to pinch pennies from retired old ladies (especially if they might notice). The accounts were recomputed, the checks were placed in new envelopes, and the customers remained blissfully ignorant. The programmer had learned—at least, until next time—that no change, no matter how "trivial," can be made to a program without adequate testing. As Ben Franklin said, "Experience keeps a dear school, but fools will learn in no other."

Anyone who has had experience with computers can relate a dozen similar stories, and yet on and on they go. Because we are human, we will tend to believe what we want to believe, not what the evidence justifies. When we have been working on a program for a long time and someone is pressing us for completion, we put aside our good intentions and let our judgment be swayed. So often, then, the results must provide the impartial judgment we cannot bring ourselves to pronounce.

One of the lessons to be learned from such experiences is that the sheer number of tests performed is of little significance in itself. Too often a series of tests simply proves how good the computer is at doing the same things with different numbers. As in many instances, we are probably misled here by our experiences with people, whose inherent reliability on repetitive work is at best variable. With a computer program, however, the greater problem is to prove adaptability—something which is not trivial in human functions, either. Consequently, we must be sure that each test really does some work not done by previous tests. To do this we must struggle to develop a suspicious nature as well as a lively imagination.

Our story illustrates another case of being misled by human experiences. In those instances where people were formerly doing work now being done by a computer, there is a tendency on the part of those experienced with the work to forget that the computer is not a person. Even when every attempt has been made to duplicate former methods, a change in the program does not necessarily correspond to a change in the manual (or semimanual) method. This lack of correspondence works both ways. In our story, a simple change in the manual method could not be easily duplicated in this program, but just as often a computer approach furnishes valuable "extras" with only the slightest modification. As eager as people are to accept such extra benefits, they do not seem able to comprehend that some "simple" request may not be simple to implement. Undoubtedly the reason for inflexibility often lies in the disorganized way the program was originally written. Still we cannot expect that programs can be written so that any conceivable change may be made with ease. It may sometimes be better to write a new program rather than attempt to incorporate certain changes, but any time the change must be made to a poorly written or undocumented program, it will be better to rewrite. A revealing slogan is often found posted where programmers work: "Why do we never have time to do a thing right but always have time to do it over?"

PROBLEMS

11-4. In the section Arithmetic Coding—An Example, we presented an example of the coding of a single operation box, with four inputs, a, b, c, and d (pages 340–341).

a. Prepare a set of normal cases for testing.

b. Prepare a set of extreme cases for testing.

c. Prepare a set of exceptional cases for testing.

11-5. Figure 5-13 shows a flow diagram of a complex decision. Suppose you were testing a program which contained this diagram. What tests would you perform and in what sequence? There are two inputs to this test, CODE and AMT. If we are to test all possible combinations of these two inputs which yield different possible results, how many cases would we have? If each of the different types of sales codes had to be analyzed into ranges of sales, how many different cases would there be?

11-6. Assume that the two alternative boxes in Figs. 10-10b and 10-10c occur in the same program. Construct a series of tests to test their logic adequately. As there are 19 different codes involved in the tests, there are 2^{19} (about half a million) distinct combinations. Is it necessary to test each of these combinations? Why?

The Philosophy of Segmentation

The difficulty of locating errors certainly multiplies as the number of errors increases. It is generally more than twice as difficult to find two errors as one, for the errors may interact in such a way as to obscure clues to their identity. This interaction gets more pronounced as the number of errors increases beyond two, as in a mystery novel where four guilty parties are planting false clues throughout the house to confuse the detective. Sometimes a programmer gets to feel that nobody could intentionally do a better job of hiding errors, and this feeling contains some truth. Who could be less suited to finding oversights than the original programmer himself? Still, the realities of human nature dictate that each programmer will probably do the major part of his own checking (like a defendant being his own judge and jury). The best we can do is to give some advice on how to work under these circumstances and hope it will also be used under more favorable conditions.

If we are clever, we can largely eliminate difficulties caused by multiple errors. We do this by breaking the program into sections. The smaller the section, the less chance of its containing more than one error, even though some programmers have been known to make three errors in a single instruction (like the freshman who flunked

English because he did not get a single letter right when he spelled "coffee" "kaughy"). If the multiplicity of errors were our only difficulty, we would obviously want to break the program into as many sections as possible. Segmenting, however, is not an unmixed blessing. We are always concerned with the over-all performance of the program. Therefore, when we check out by sections, we must also concern ourselves with the interaction between sections. Thus every time we break off a part from the whole for testing, we must consider just how this part is supposed to function with respect to the other parts. If we determine its role incorrectly, we may check out a number of parts, put them together, and find that the program does not work. Generally the running of the entire program—the dress rehearsal— after testing it by parts will not run error-free. As in the case of building circuits, the complete system may have too much resistance in spots. We therefore want to minimize these errors.

In order to minimize the difficulty involved in properly defining the function of a segment and thus cutting down on the total errors, we break our checking job down along functional lines rather than simply choosing some fixed size of block. At times five or six instructions may be worthy of our undivided attention, at other times forty or fifty.

We can make several types of functional breakdown. For example, we may separate the input, output, and processing sections of a program if they can be uniquely identified. One of these sections itself may break into several phases. A payroll computation, for example, might divide neatly into the calculation of gross pay, the determination of taxes, the application of deductions, and the compilation of payroll statistics. We have already seen the hierarchical division of a program into subroutines. Such a division is especially useful when testing because, as we proceed from the deepest level to the highest, each checked-out subroutine can be considered as the logical equivalent of a machine instruction capable of producing that subroutine's function.

Some programmers will put all sections of their program in the closed-subroutine form so as to reduce interaction between functionally different sections as much as possible in order to further simplify testing. The closed subroutine certainly has the advantage of localizing the points of interaction between parts into the calling sequences, but the universal application of this form may sometimes prove too costly in time or space. Nevertheless the lesson of considering testing when coding should not be forgotten. Probably no single testing technique is of more value than foresight.

Aids to Testing

With most machines, systems have been developed to give the programmer the assistance of the computer when testing. In relatively few cases, however, are these systems intimately connected with the systems which help him assemble his program. Consequently, the programmer must learn two separate systems—two separate languages —in order to do one job. Some of the more sophisticated "automatic-programming" systems still only approach the requirements for dealing with the realities of program testing. Errors are an integral part of the programming process; automatic assistance in error detection *and corrective action* should therefore be an integral part of any programming system.

The assembly process may, as we know, help our checking by indicating certain clerical errors and rule violations. In fact, the error-detection portions often form a major part of the "automatic-programming" schemes. Nevertheless the time must come in the life of each program when it must pass the test of an actual run, and at this point we must start to gather information on what the program *does*. It is at this point that many of the available programming systems part company from the programmer. Even though this situation is common, it is so unsatisfactory that we do not wish to prolong its existence by presenting such an incomplete system in this chapter. Instead, we shall deal with the testing aids which are an integral part of the SHARE Operating System (SOS) for the 7090. These aids are collectively called the DEBUGGING portion (DB) of the system. We do not wish to give the impression that such aids are available in most systems but only to indicate why they should be. Many of the principles illustrated will be applicable to other systems, but the convenience and logical completeness—both of which mean so much in actual operations—may be lacking. This lack is especially evident among the smaller machines, where programming systems of such sophistication would create an unbearable work load. Consequently the users of such machines may find it necessary to live with something less for a considerable time. However, this does not mean that they should achieve satisfaction through ignorance and should not continually request that truly advanced systems be developed. Otherwise, as more and more powerful machines become available at lower cost—as they certainly will continue to do—programming cost will become an increasingly large part of each job.

Since the 7090 operates at a speed which is thousands of times faster than human perception—not to speak of comprehension—we cannot expect to get a very good idea of what a program is doing while it is doing it. It would be wasteful, however, to require the computer to slow down to our own speed for checking purposes. Consequently, we have the computer prepare—at machine speed—a record of what happens for us to study—at human speed. The simplest form of such a record is the "dump," and the simplest form of dump is the "post-mortem." A "dump" is a print-out of some of the information in the machine; and a "post-mortem" is a dump taken after the program has terminated its execution.

The Dumping Method

A common testing method is to run a test problem until the program stops or gets caught in a loop, then dump the entire memory. If the program goes some distance before stopping, a good deal of information may be obtained in this manner; but if it goes too far, information about the earlier sections may be lost. This method, unchecked, will generate a great deal of useless information which tends to obscure the critical items. In the early stages of testing, however, when a program is behaving wildly, a post-mortem may be the only way to ensure that we do not overlook some unsuspected influencing factor. Similarly, if the program behaves unexpectedly later in the testing— if, for example, it gets caught in a loop or stops at some undesignated stopping point—a post-mortem should be taken. We can, with SOS, take post-mortems automatically when something unusual happens, such as the program running overtime or producing too much output.

A much more general technique is that of dumping at selected points in the program. SOS provides a macro-instruction, CORE, which enables us to cause dumps every time a given point in the program is reached during execution. CORE may be inserted at any point in the program (where input-output timing will not be affected) and as many times as necessary. Thus the code

```
X1    AXT        10, 1
      CORE
X2    CLA        A, 1
      TSX        SUB1, 4
      CORE
      TSX        SUB2, 4
      TIX        X2, 1, 1
      CORE
X3
```

would cause 12 dumps to be made every time the program passed from X1 to X3: one before entering the loop, ten during the loop, and one after the loop was completed. We certainly would have a complete picture of what was happening in this section.

Actually the picture would be so complete that we probably would have a hard time finding the few parts of it which were significant. Consider for a moment what twelve dumps consists of. Each dump is 32,768 words. Depending on content, this might yield about 8,000 lines of printing. A page is approximately 40 lines, so one dump means 200 pages of single-spaced printing. Twelve dumps means 2,400 pages—a stack of paper over a foot high. Obviously, this is not the picture we want. We must have some way of separating the wheat from the chaff. One way to do this is to limit the dump to a certain region of storage by specifying a beginning and an end location in the CORE macro. The macro

$$\text{CORE} \quad \text{R, R} + 9$$

would cause the dump to be restricted to the 10 words starting at location R. In addition to any storage locations dumped, CORE dumps the contents of all the special registers and records the status of the various indicators, keys, and switches which are collectively called the *panel*. Thus the sequence

```
CORE    A, Z
CORE    B, B + 2
CORE    M, N
CORE    ALPHA, OMEGA
CORE    X1, X10
```

will cause five selected areas to be dumped as well as the special registers, indicators, keys, and switches.

Figure 11-2 shows the result of the actual execution of the macro

$$\text{CORE} \quad \text{Y}, \text{Y} + 2$$

in a program where Y, Y + 1, and Y + 2 each contained a floating-point number. First, the "panel" is dumped. The first line of the panel dump shows the AC in octal and floating-point decimal (the 01 indicates the contents of AC_q and AC_p, in binary); the MQ in octal and floating-point decimal; the SI in octal; and the status of three special indicators, "overflow," "divide check" (which results from attempted division by zero), and "input-output check" (which results from certain errors in attempting to select input-output units). The second line shows the contents of the three index registers in octal and decimal (notice that they are here designated as IR1, IR2, and IR4, instead of XR1, XR2, and XR4—a common practice); the "sense lights" in binary; the "sense switches" in binary; and the "entry

PANEL

AC	01 + 300000 005670	+.41231686+15	MQ − 002200 000000
IR1	77773 32763	IR2 77400 32512	IR4 76626 32150

	CORE	Y, Y+2	
F	05676	Y	+.12300000+01	+.67889999+02

Fig. 11-2. Selected

keys" in octal (the last three items are devices on the console used for communication between machine and operator).

Following the panel dump is the actual "core" dump. The F indicates floating-point, 05676 is the octal location of Y, and the three numbers are shown across the page. In this form, the exponent (to the base 10) follows the number; thus the first number is +1.23, or 0.123×10^1.

We should emphasize that a sequence of debugging macros may be inserted anywhere in the program *without disturbing its operation*. The program will give exactly the same results with or without the CORE's, but with them, a picture of what is happening while those results are being produced is furnished. Thus, when a CORE has served its purpose in checking, it may be removed without loss. CORE's—like other macros or instructions—may be inserted or removed, without reassembling the program, using the original programming language. This flexibility—not present in most systems— enables us to make pin-point examinations, determine the cause of any errors detected, correct the errors, and remove the examining tool with great ease.

Although a CORE may be inserted at any point in the program and may specify any limited region, we still may find it difficult to keep down the amount of information dumped. Suppose, for example, we had the following program section:

X1	AXT	1000, 1
X2	CLA	A, 1
	TSX	SUB1, 4
	CORE	Y, Y $+$ 2
	TIX	X2, 1, 1
X3		

Even though each CORE gives five lines of printing, we shall produce about 5,000 lines in total. We probably do not need this much information to answer our questions about the program, but we do want

$-.29387359-38$ SI 000000 000000 OVFL OFF DC OFF IOC OFF
              SL 0000   SW 000001   EK $+$000000 00000

$+.32101000+02$

dumping.

some information about what happens in the loop. SOS solves this dilemma by providing a set of "conditional macros" which may precede a CORE (or series of CORE's) and place a qualification, or condition, on its execution.

PROBLEMS

11-7. Suppose the test cases in Prob. 11-5 were not all yielding the correct answers. What information would you like to have dumped? Where would you like the CORE macros to be inserted in the code? Write out the different CORE macros you would like to use.

11-8. Suppose that in testing the program of Fig. 9-5 (see Prob. 11-2) you found that the flow of the program seemed quite correct but that sometimes the wrong records were being selected for PASSTP, for no apparent reason. Write the CORE macros you would like to have inserted at various points in the program with each of your test cases.

Conditional Debugging Macros

A simple conditional macro is EVERY. The macro

EVERY   10

means that the following CORE is to be used only every tenth time this point is reached, starting with the first—that is, the first, eleventh, twenty-first, thirty-first, and so forth. If we rewrite our previous example as

```
X1      AXT        1000, 1
X2      CLA        A, 1
        TSX        SUB1, 4
        EVERY      333
        CORE       Y, Y + 2
        TIX        X2, 1, 1
X3
```

we shall get dumps only on the first, 334th, 667th, and 1,000th time through the loop. This view of the first and last times, along with two intermediate traversals, may give us as much good information as a full 1,000 dumps. If this undiluted view should prove inadequate, we could relax the qualification and try again.

Often we wish to dump only at a certain point when some special condition arises, such as two numbers being equal, an index register exceeding a certain value, or some quantity being negative. To make such a qualification, we may use the conditional macro WHEN. The macro

$$\text{WHEN} \quad \text{A, E, B}$$

means "when C(A) *equal* C(B)." The macro

$$\text{WHEN} \quad \text{2, G, H}$$

means "when C(XR2) are *greater than* A(H)," and likewise the macro

$$\text{WHEN} \quad \text{S, L, 0}$$

means "when C(S) are *less than* zero (the number 0 is a special case, and does not refer to location zero)." Thus, if we wrote

```
X1      AXT        1000, 1
X2      CLA        A, 1
        TSX        SUB1, 4
        WHEN       B, E, SIGMA
        CORE       B, B + 3
        TIX        X2, 1, 1
X3
```

the dump would occur only when C(B) = C(SIGMA). Of course,

this condition might never occur or might occur on every pass; so we cannot tell in advance, as with EVERY, how much output we shall get. In any case, we shall not get any more output than in the unqualified case, and we might get none at all. The absence of output could, in this case, be useful information, since we would know that the condition was never satisfied.

Frequently we wish to use more than one condition for qualification. We may then follow the WHEN macro with one or more AND or OR macros. Thus, if we wrote

X1	AXT	1000, 1
X2	CLA	A, 1
	TSX	SUB1, 4
	WHEN	B, E, SIGMA
	OR	B + 1, L, 0
	CORE	B, B + 3
	TIX	X2, 1, 1

the dump would occur whenever $C(B) = C(SIGMA)$, whenever $C(B + 1) < 0$, or when both conditions were satisfied.

We may combine WHEN and EVERY and so further reduce the amount of redundant output. Other macros are available in the system which enable us to dump *unless* certain conditions are met. We may also restrict dumping until a condition has been met a given number of times or prevent further dumping after so many dumps have been made. In addition to the CORE macro, we have macros which enable us to examine the status of the data channels or to dump the contents of any desired record or records from any tape.

PROBLEMS

11-9. Suppose that your testing in Prob. 11-8 seems to indicate that not all the scores are being adjusted correctly. You suspect that perhaps the first or last of the twenty scores is causing the trouble. Write the conditional debugging macros you might use to get a detailed look at these cases.

11-10. Suppose that the tests of Prob. 11-9 do not locate the difficulties, but that you now suspect that perhaps scores of less than 20 are not being adjusted properly. What conditional macros might you use to test this hypothesis?

11-11. Suppose that the tests of Prob. 11-9 do show that sometimes negative scores are not converted correctly. You think that this may only be happening when the age of the student is over 21 or under 16. What sets of debugging macros might you use to prove this conjecture?

Tracing

By combining the various information macros with the conditional macros, we may decide in advance precisely the information we want from any portion of the program. Still, in the earlier stages of testing, this facility may be of limited usefulness. If we are having difficulty proving the structure of the program, we may not know where to place the macros necessary to give the needed information. In order to solve this problem, the debugging system provides the facility for *tracing* the program or portions of the program. "Tracing," as the word implies, means following the course of the program as it is executed. "Detail tracing," the recording of exactly what happens at each instruction in the code, is generally regarded as too dangerous a tool to put into a system on a large machine. We can, of course, accomplish detail tracing by placing a suitable CORE macro after each instruction in a section. This technique may be necessary as a last resort when a section has been detected as an offender, but no amount of study seems to reveal just why it is not working. The difficulty of using this technique protects it from being misused.

An example of such misuse which is by no means uncommon is the case of a programmer using another programming system where such tracing was the rule rather than the exception. He wished to trace an entire program which he had estimated would require "only two and one-half seconds to run." What he had failed to consider was that over one-half million instructions would be executed in "only two and one-half seconds." Since the trace gave two lines of printing for each instruction, he would have generated a million lines of printing. Fortunately, when he found that one reel of output tape had been filled and the trace was not finished, he decided to seek assistance.

While we should like our system to protect itself from misuse, we should not wish to have such protection prevent maximum or unusual use of the system. A programming system may be thought of as ideal in so far as it makes common things simple, simple-minded things impossible, and uncommon things possible. The debugging system (DB), for example, may be thought of as far from ideal in the way it makes dumping the entire memory (or an entire file on tape) so simple. A programmer should be required to stop at least for a moment and reflect on the desirability of causing so much output. DB is to be commended, on the other hand, making it difficult (though possible) to do detailed tracing and still giving us a means of easily using another, more useful, method of tracing, called "transfer trapping."

When the program does not execute a transfer instruction, we know that the flow of control passes to the next instruction, or at most two instructions away in the case of a skip. Consequently we need not look at such cases when we are simply trying to ascertain the structure of the program. Transfer trapping, which is aided by a special "transfer trapping mode" built into the 7090, enables us to execute a program at normal speed and slow down only to dump some information when a transfer is executed. Thus, when a nontransfer instruction—or a conditional transfer for which the condition is not satisfied —is executed, we get no debugging output (unless a macro is inserted at that point). Reading the output, then, gives us a trace of the path actually taken along the flow diagram.

S	05723	+0 06000 0 05723	X2A		TCOA	X2A
			X7A			
S	05734	+0 02000 0 05721		+1	TRA	X2
S	05723	+0 06000 0 05723	X2A		TCOA	X2A
			X5			
S	05726	−0 10000 0 05721		+1	TNZ	X2
S	05723	+0 06000 0 05723	X2A		TCOA	X2A
			X6			
S	05730	+0 12000 0 05721		+1	TPL	X2
S	05723	+0 06000 0 05723	X2A		TCOA	X2A
			X5			
S	05726	−0 10000 0 05721		+1	TNZ	X2
S	05723	+0 06000 0 05723	X2A		TCOA	X2A
			X6			
S	05730	+0 12000 0 05721		+1	TPL	X2
S	05723	+0 06000 0 05723	X2A		TCOA	X2A
			X5			
S	05726	−0 10000 0 05721		+1	TNZ	X2
S	05723	+0 06000 0 05723	X2A		TCOA	X2A
			X6			
S	05730	+0 12000 0 05721		+1	TPL	X2
S	05723	+0 06000 0 05723	X2A		TCOA	X2A
			X5			
S	05726	−0 10000 0 05721		+1	TNZ	X2
S	05723	+0 06000 0 05723	X2A		TCOA	X2A
S	05724	+0 03000 0 05735	X2B		TEFA	X3

Fig. 11-3. Table of trapped instructions and their locations.

We can cause such tracing to take place by inserting a TRAP macro at any point in the program. Once that point is reached, transfer trapping will take place until an UNTRAP macro is encountered. Thus we can trace any or all sections of the program. The TRAP macro may be followed by a series of conditional and information macros which will apply to the dump taken when a transfc is trapped. Thus the sequence

TRAP
WHEN   A, L, 0
CORE   A, Z

will cause a trace of all subsequent transfers and a dump of A through Z whenever a transfer is executed and $C(A) < 0$. It is easy to see what a powerful tool transfer trapping can be in the hands of an imaginative programmer. Figure 11-3 shows the type of output which is obtained by use of TRAP (without CORES).

PROBLEMS

11-12. Suppose that the tests of Prob. 11-11 had shown that the ADJUST subroutine was not working properly for students over 21 who had scores under 20. You examine the subroutine but cannot determine what is wrong with its logic, so you decide to trace it. What macros would you use to get this trace without tracing unnecessary areas or cases?

11-13. From the trace in Fig. 11-3, how much of the flow diagram of the program can you reconstruct? Actually, this was a trace of the program in Fig. 6-6. How much can you tell about the test case being used when this trace was made?

Program Testing in FORTRAN

There is very little difference in strategy between testing in an assembly language and testing in a problem-oriented language. Naturally, there are differences in details, but these are not sufficiently great to make the transition from one system to the other burdensome to the programmer. Nevertheless, there still are people who feel that some essential difference must exist, an attitude that goes back to the earliest efforts to design and implement higher level languages.

In the early design efforts on FORTRAN, objectives were established for the performance of the compiler—in addition to the obvious objectives for the language itself. These objectives included the following: that the compiler create machine-language codes that were accurate in meeting the *intent* of each FORTRAN statement, both within itself and in relation to other statements; that the compiler produce as efficient a machine-language code as possible—"equivalent to code produced by an experienced programmer"; and that the compiler recognize, label, and attempt to explain errors made by the coder in his *use* of the FORTRAN language—recognizing and signaling violations of FORTRAN conventions within and between statements. It was often assumed that the first and last of these objectives would essentially eliminate the need for the programmer to make tests, once the compiler-recognized errors were corrected.

Let us examine the sort of error detection the FORTRAN compiler did and might have done, to see whether this approach could, indeed, eliminate debugging. Naturally, simple clerical items are checked, just as in the assembly language. If the number of right and left parentheses in an arithmetic expression does not match, for example, the compiler flags the expression as an error. If a symbol appears as a statement number, or in a GO TO, it is flagged as illegal. If a GO TO or an IF refers to statement numbers which are not in the program, this, too, is flagged. In fact, because of the closed nature of the flow of control in a FORTRAN program, the compiler could—but generally does not—perform all the seven tests outlined under Preliminary Testing, for each code must have a unique flow diagram which the compiler can analyze.

The implementation of these seven checks would indeed make the compiler a useful companion in the debugging effort, for in addition to the direct errors found, a number of more subtle things would be turned up in such a complete analysis. For example, one of the classical bugs in the history of FORTRAN arose when a programmer attempted to write the following statement:

DO 3 I = 1, 25

When the cards were punched, however, the comma was punched as a period, yielding the statement

DO 3 I = 1. 25

Because this statement was embedded in a large program—and partly because the programmer had come to depend on the compiler to reveal keypunching errors—this error was not noticed before the program was compiled. Since the FORTRAN compiler ignores blanks—even though the programmer may not be able to do so—the statement was compiled as if it had been written

DO3I = 1.25

a perfectly legitimate arithmetic statement setting the value of the variable, DO3I. As it happened, a previous DO loop had used the variable I, so that the error did not even interfere with the execution (faulty though it was) of the program; it was only after an inordinate amount of testing that the bug was exterminated. Now, if check number 5 had been implemented in the compiler, the bug would have been found immediately, since DO3I would never appear again in the program. Thus, even though check number 5 is intended as a logical check on the flow diagram, it becomes a check on the punching of the program as well, when executed on the actual code.

Since a considerable number of FORTRAN compilers do not implement even the seven checks we have listed, their error analyses obviously cannot meet any claim of essentially eliminating debugging. Suppose, however, that all these checks actually were implemented—as they no doubt will be someday—along with all the other checks we could think of. Would we then have eliminated the need for testing? We can easily see that the answer is "no," for a number of reasons. For instance, if the programmer in our example had just happened to use the variable DO3I as a legitimate variable in the program, even check 5 might not have turned up the error. Furthermore, no conceivable checking could turn up an error such as writing

IF (A − B)5,6,6

instead of

IF (A − B)5,5,6

unless the compiler has some independent way of knowing the intention of the programmer. And as we have seen, if the compiler already knew what the programmer wanted, what would be the use of writing down the program in the first place?

Now, even though the FORTRAN language is essentially closed with respect to vocabulary, syntax, and structure, there are always programmers who will make every effort to find "different" ways of using a language, over and above the stated capability. Indeed, with any real compiler, they probably would find some combinations of statements to operate outside the "legal" bounds; for, once a compiler is constructed, there is an upper limit to the number of logical analyses it can make. There will always be some logical path or combination that remains undetected, even though it is expressly forbidden by the rules of the language. In FORTRAN, for example, the user is warned against transferring into a DO loop from outside the range of that DO, for if the DO itself is not executed, the loop may not be set up in a meaningful way. Nevertheless, the compiler will compile programs which contain such violations; and in some cases, a useful code can be produced by such a trick. However, it is most probable that FORTRAN programs using such tricks will not work when compiled by another FORTRAN compiler—or even by the same FORTRAN compiler in 6 months or a year, due to changes in the compiler itself. Since the language forbids such actions, the people maintaining the compiler are under no obligation to preserve the way in which they are compiled. Thus, a change could easily break down a logical path that was not supposed to work in the first place. All the same, there is one advantage to programmers' trying out unusual statement combinations: they can point out deficiencies in the language to the implementors, eventually forcing the inclusion of new logical paths within the accepted structure of the language.

The many compilers that have been written, as we might imagine, are not consistent in meeting the objectives we have listed. Some FORTRAN compilers have omitted a significant part of one or more of the objectives, while others have changed objectives, added new objectives, and placed different orders of priority on the old objectives. There has been almost endless debate on the importance of error analysis as opposed to compiler speed, on the relative merits of high compiler speed versus high speed of execution of the object-language code, on the size of the object code versus expanded language facility versus speed, and so on. The design of a higher level language is a slow process involving the interaction of the users, the language designers, and the compiler writers. Nevertheless, the early arbitrary decisions of the designers can have an almost paralyzing effect on the future development of a language and its compilers.

PROBLEM

11-14. Compose a list of objectives that should be considered in the design of both a language and a compiler. Try to arrange this list in order of priority, first as different users might order it, then as the language designer might do it, and finally according to the point of view of the compiler writer.

The FORTRAN Debugging System

In the early FORTRAN compiler developments, an independent debugging facility was conspicuously absent, perhaps because the

designers felt that debugging would be so easy. FORTRAN programmers without machine-language experience found themselves dependent
on the FORTRAN language itself to devise methods for checking out
their programs. Furthermore, the statements created solely for testing
purposes had to be compiled as part of the program itself, without
any clear, separate identification. Often, when difficult problems arose,
users required assistance from more experienced programmers who
utilized the created machine-language code for debugging purposes.
In other words, at worst the programmer had to learn a second
language in order to test his programs; and at best it was unnecessarily
cumbersome and time-consuming to arrive at an operating FORTRAN
program.

Efforts to resolve these problems have yielded solutions not too
different from those developed for simpler symbolic languages: A
debugging language has been developed in the FORTRAN format,
designed so that it refers to specific statements within a FORTRAN
program without becoming an intrinsic part of that program. The
programmer can compose sets of instructions in this language—much
as he constructs sets of debugging macros in the symbolic assembly
language—and add them to the object program before executing a test.
Thus, the debugging statements can be removed easily once they
have served their purpose and the FORTRAN program is operating
correctly.

Actually, the FORTRAN debugging system includes many of the
statements of the FORTRAN language itself, including the GO TO,
CALL, RETURN, and STOP statements. Thus, for example, we can
create useful sets of debugging statements in the form of a subroutine.
Of special note is the use of the logical IF statement, rather than the
arithmetic IF, since the relational facilities of the logical IF apply more
easily to the type of conditional situations we would want to set up in
debugging a program. For example, corresponding to the DB system
conditional macro

     WHEN   B,E,SIGMA

would be the FORTRAN debugging statement

     IF (B.EQ.SIGMA)

and corresponding to the statements

     WHEN B,E,SIGMA
     OR   B + 1,L,0

would be the FORTRAN debugging statement

IF (B(1) EQ.SIGMA.OR.B(2).LT.0.0).

As we know, the logical IF statement gives us an extremely flexible tool with which to construct logical decisions.

Included in the debugging language are several new statements to facilitate getting the simpler types of outputs usually required in testing. One such statement has a name which well defines its use, the DUMP statement, which has the same function as the CORE macro in the DB system. DUMP is much like a FORTRAN input or output statement in that it specifies a list of the information we desire to print out, though the list may either be within the statement itself or in another statement which is referred to by the DUMP. For example, we may have the statement

DUMP (R,A,X,B)

or the equivalent pair of statements

DUMP 11
11   LIST (R,A,X,B)

The LIST statement thus offers a means for referencing the same debugging information by more than one DUMP statement without tedious repetition of the list.

Unlike the ordinary FORTRAN input or output statement, the DUMP statement has no reference to a FORMAT statement, for the debugging system automatically interprets and prints each listed quantity according to the format specified for it in the FORTRAN program. In this way, the programmer is saved the trouble of composing fancy formats (and testing them) when he has no particular need for them. In fact, both the DUMP statement in FORTRAN and the CORE statement in DB provide such a convenient means of getting information out of the machine, when format is of no particular concern, that they are often used by programmers instead of the normal, more cumbersome, output methods.

Another convenient facility in the DUMP list is the ability to provide a message along with the other debugging information. The message is recognized by the presence of quotation marks, as in

11   LIST ('ERROR IN STATEMENT 33 CAUSED
            2DUMP,' R,A,X,B)

which will cause the message to be printed, followed by the specified quantities. We can also write the special statement

11   LIST CONSOLE

which essentially specifies the same information as PANEL in the

DB system. Where it is absolutely necessary to obtain all information possible, the format

     11   LIST PROGRAM

.will result in the entire FORTRAN program's being dumped. As we have discussed, this facility is one that should not be made available to the FORTRAN programmer when there is the tendency to dump as much as possible in the hope that mere quantity of information will solve debugging problems.

One way of limiting the amount of output from debugging runs in the FORTRAN system is to use the ON statement, which has somewhat the same function as the EVERY statement in the DB system. For instance, the statement

     ON 1,15 DUMP (X,Y,Z)

would cause the quantities specified by X, Y, and Z to be dumped on the first through the fifteenth times the statement is executed. After the fifteenth time, no more information will be dumped. If we wanted, say, only every fourth request to be honored, we could write

     ON 1,15,4 DUMP (X,Y,Z)

and the specified quantities would be dumped on the first, fifth, ninth, and thirteenth times the statement was executed.

One of the excellent features of the FORTRAN debugging system is that it almost forces the programmer to set explicit limits on his debugging output each time he uses the system. A single card *must* be placed in front of any debugging request, or any group of debugging requests, in the following format:

     $IBDBL   TRAP MAX = 300, LINE MAX = 1000

$IBDBL is a code word which indicates that a number of debugging statements are to follow on successive cards. TRAP MAX = 300 provides an over-all control on all debugging requests specified, stating that no more than 300 individual requests will be honored, regardless of the type of request. LINE MAX = 1000 also provides an upper-bound control, by stipulating the maximum total number of lines to be printed on any debugging run. In this request, after 1,000 lines had been printed, all further information would be lost. Unfortunately, either or both TRAP MAX and LINE MAX can be left off the $IBDBL card, in which case no upper bound is set for that function. Used properly, however (which is not too likely, since misuse is made so simple), this control can place excellent discipline on the

FORTRAN user. Imagine the way a programmer feels when his debugging job is returned with fewer than half the debugging requests honored and less than a third of the output available. Next time he requests debugging service, he will be careful to make his request more precise.

Because the FORTRAN system enables the programmer to execute a program composed of many parts which have been compiled separately (in the closed subroutine form, for example), it is necessary not only to specify which statements are to be monitored in debugging, but also which subprogram those statements are in. Each program, when it is compiled, is given a name, so that it may be referenced even when it is used with other programs. A statement within a program may then be uniquely referenced by a name and a number, as in the statement

        *DEBUG DECK1 12

which says that the following request is to be inserted just prior to statement 12 in DECK1. A control statement such as

        *DEBUG DECK2 14,27,38

permits the same debugging request to be inserted before more than one statement in a given deck. *DEBUG, of course, is a code word which tells that a debugging request will follow. It is interesting to note that *DEBUG is in a fixed format. That is, the statement number is always a fixed number of positions (card columns) from the name of the subprogram.

In order to clarify the use of the FORTRAN debugging system, let us see what a typical debugging request might look like. Suppose we have put together two programs, named DECKD and SQRZ7, and that the key debugging points are statements 17, 32, and 44 in the first, and 32 and 66 in the second. Our debugging packet might look as follows:

```
$IBDBL          TRAP MAX = 750, LINE MAX = 575
*DEBUG    DECKD        17
                ON1,5 IF (B.EQ.SIGMA) DUMP 5,7
5               LIST CONSOLE
7               LIST (A,B,PART)
*DEBUG    DECKD        32,44
                IF (C + D * E.NE.Y - 3.0 * F) RETURN
                DUMP RSLT1, RSLT2
```

```
*DEBUG   SQRZ7        32,66
         IF (PART.EQ.FINAL) RETURN
         DUMP 'PART NOT EQUAL TO FINAL'
         DUMP 5
*DEND
```

The *DEND card, naturally, is a signal that there are no more debugging requests in this packet. Our first request is for the console and the quantities specified by A, B, and PART to be dumped if, on any of the first five times we reach statement 17 in DECKD, C(B) = C(SIGMA). We have also requested that when we are about to execute statement 32 or 44 in DECKD, we will return to the FORTRAN program without a dump if (C + D * E) is not equal to (Y − 3.0 * F). Otherwise, we will dump RSLT1 and RSLT2. Finally, we have requested that, prior to executing either statement 32 or statement 66 in SQRZ7, we would print the message, PART NOT EQUAL TO FINAL, if, indeed, PART were not equal to FINAL, and dump the console. LIST is not restricted to a given *DEBUG. Notice how the specification of the program name enables us to distinguish between two different statements numbered 32 and two different quantities named PART. The $IBDBL card, of course, ensures that we will attempt no more than 750 debugging requests and print no more than 575 lines.

PROBLEMS

11-15. Suppose that you were testing a FORTRAN version of the program of Fig. 9-5. (See Probs. 11-2 and 11-8.) Write the FORTRAN debugging packet that you would use to get the same outputs you wanted in Prob. 11-8.

11-16. Do Prob. 11-9 as if you were debugging a FORTRAN version of the program.

11-17. Do Prob. 11-10 as if you were debugging a FORTRAN version of the program.

11-18. Do Prob. 11-11 as if you were debugging a FORTRAN version of the program.

11-19. Can you do Prob. 11-12 as if you were debugging a FORTRAN program?

11-20. Write a FORTRAN debugging packet which will perform simultaneously all the tests of Probs. 11-16, 11-17, and 11-18. How is this packet related to the individual packets?

11-21. Can Prob. 11-7 be done as if it were a FORTRAN program being tested? Why?

11-22. Can Prob. 11-4 be done as if it were a FORTRAN program being tested? Why? Can exactly the same set of cases be used? Why?

11-23. Can Prob. 11-6 be done as if it were a FORTRAN program being tested? Why? Can exactly the same set of cases be used? Why?

Summary

We have taken a quick look at some of the philosophies of program testing and some of the mechanical aids available. If we wanted to boil everything down to four major principles of testing, they would probably be the following:

1. Write the program correctly in the first place.
2. Think about check-out when coding.
3. Know the debugging tools which are available.
4. Make the program *prove* that it works.

If we want to express these principles more concisely, we might say, "Be a meticulous, thoughtful, well-informed skeptic." That is as close as you can come to a "magic wand" for program testing—and it is not too close.

CHAPTER 12

PRODUCTION

Probably no area of programming deserves more thought—and receives less—than production. Like testing, production is not to be considered as separate from all other phases of the programming process. Production is, after all, the end of the process and, as such, should be kept as the focus of all the other phases.

Efficient production cannot occur without an efficiently run installation. The fact that an installation is producing well-written routines does not necessarily mean that the same installation is geared for well-organized production. With so much emphasis placed on the preparation of programs we may easily overlook the fact that an installation must prepare itself for production just as its programmers must prepare themselves for the development of the most efficient programs. We cannot just assume that with "experience" any given installation will automatically become efficient. In an effort to bring a computer into an organization we find that on occasion too much time is spent in trying to determine which department will control the computer rather than how the computer will be properly put to work. The result is a hit-and-miss operation that will rarely find its way clear without many disasters.

The result of such a disaster could end any truly good applications on the computer for considerable time. In this case, if the organization decides to retain the computer, it will normally limp along with applications that simply justify their existence by filling up computer time. The productivity level of such a computer would usually cost its human equivalent his job.

In preparing for a computer one of the first considerations is that of keeping the "computer room" in proper perspective with the rest of the organization. When computers were first introduced on a mass basis, management people often made the mistake of thinking of them as of no help in management problems. In fact, the people in the computing group were often thought of as being of some special breed. These computing people indeed were and are of no more distinctive a breed than any other professional group. Yet such was the aura often existing around their operations—an aura which initially created a very limited use of the computer.

One of the most important tasks facing any organization obtaining the use of a computer is to make all its management and operating personnel as familiar with computing operations as possible in order to widen the scope of applications.

Today the computer is on the executive's desk. He must consider the computer (or at least its output) in making his decisions. The production of the computer is vital to its organization. Thus we must have a computer room politically pure; no one group should be allowed to make hay with this tool. A general, impartial group representing all company interests established to monitor and select applications from all areas is one approach by which we might obtain the desired production. Further progress can be made by the establishment of management-orientation programs whose purpose is to discuss the computer in its impact and versatility as a tool. We find that what the manager wants is not a detailed course in programming but an understanding of how the computer can help solve problems in his area of the business.

The physical location of a computer is itself an important factor in over-all efficient production. The computer should neither be put into a "back room" nor be the center of attraction. It should be placed so as to be as convenient to the majority of users as possible.

An understanding by management of what computer applications are gives the original impetus to the installation. Now we should see what the installation must do in order specifically to improve upon its efficiency. Production improvement involves the establishment of procedures, the use of programming systems, the orientation of programs to production, and the proper mix of applications. The goals we are aiming for include a minimization of time loss and of error occurrences, the establishment of proper communication between computer and operator and between operator and programmer, the establishment of procedures to protect our programs and data from errors that might arise, the establishment of procedures to allow us to recover from errors that will occur, and the establishment of ground rules to permit the computer to handle with equal ease all types and variations of production.

We have seen some of the problems involved in developing a program. We have emphasized the use of the flow diagram to enable us to produce a program which is logically correct. We have looked at methods to remove errors from our programs. Yet we not only need a logically correct program, we also require one that will operate as efficiently as possible, as simply and directly as possible. Within the structure of the program every reasonable attempt should be made to improve upon computer-operator communication, upon program-operating flexibility. We insert the word *reasonable* since the most efficient operating procedure and the simplest operating procedure are rarely identical. Furthermore, as we have seen, a change to an existing program to produce what is believed to be an improvement upon the efficiency-simplicity combination can have startling, if not adverse, effects if not carefully scrutinized. However, there are some important considerations and basic improvements that we can apply to any program development. One such consideration is the total cost of preparing a program. Such cost includes analysis, coding, and production. We can establish a representative ground rule for making decisions on a cost basis by dividing all programs into two classes:

1. Repetitive programs: those programs where total anticipated production costs exceed total anticipated programming costs

2. Nonrepetitive: those programs whose major cost is in programming

Of course, such a classification is only a convenience for discussing production problems, for we cannot always decide in advance into which class a program will fall. Nevertheless most cases fall far enough on one side or the other to justify the breakdown. How much time, effort, and money can we spend in producing more efficient operation? From our definitions, it is clear that only for repetitive programs can we justify *any* large percentage increase in programming costs in order to realize a small increase in production efficiency.

That is, program improvement cannot just be considered from a production aspect or programming aspect. The actual operating procedure should, and often does, represent a compromise between programming cost and ease of operation. We cannot know the future, but we must try to make some assessment of the value of any operating convenience (or inconvenience) which we consider for inclusion in a program. If this inclusion causes a violation of the limits of the programming cost—and such costs are often high—we probably shall find it best to forego the convenience, even though our aesthetic sensibility may thus be offended.

Preparatory Procedures

The secret of a successful operation lies in preparation. It would be indeed comical—were it not so expensive—to watch a perplexed programmer in front of a computer alternately scurrying about with a look of fierce determination and then standing quite still, one finger to his forehead, in absolute contemplation. Ideally, the computer should not have to wait for such human decisions or actions, for under such circumstances the same rate of cost is being applied to the human processing as to the machine processing. We do not mean that the machine is intrinsically more valuable than a human being; to make such comparisons is absurd. What we do mean is that very few people are worth over three hundred dollars an hour to their *employers*, although people cost approximately that much while they are keeping a 7090 or similar machine idle. It is, of course, easy to say at such periods that "certain delays" on the computer are "unavoidable."

When we hear this argument that certain delays are unavoidable because "unexpected things" do happen, we should examine what is classified as "unexpected." Surely we expect that the program will need its input data or will need a blank tape, or tapes, for its output. If we put a stop in the program, we certainly are not caught unawares when that stop occurs. If we are attempting to run a program which is not checked out, we should not be surprised if it stops or gets in an unending loop. Even if the program is considered to be checked out, we are not really surprised when an undetected program error causes a stop or loop or, as will occur occasionally, a machine error does likewise. All these things can, and should, be prepared for. Excuses can easily be found for delays—what we must have is results. In the worst cases, where the program is not working correctly, the operator should simply obtain a post-mortem dump—a procedure which takes about 20 seconds—and proceed to the next job. The condition which caused the error may then be examined at leisure. If it happens to be a machine error, the next program may not work either (in fact, the dump may not work), but the engineers will at least have some evidence to work with.   Although it is a common tendency to blame the computer, a machine error is *many* times less likely to occur than a program error.   Thus it is a bad gamble to guess on that being the cause.

Of the various types of error occurrences, *errors in input data* fall into a class by themselves.   In some problems, weeding out erroneous input data may be much more difficult than checking out the program.   In such cases, we cannot use the procedure of letting the program run until erroneous data are found, correcting the data, and starting over.   The combination of error input and check-out of a program is impossible.   It cannot be tolerated.   If the data are in the form of punched cards, we can often develop a procedure for using punched-card tabulating equipment for preprocessing the data.   In applications where such input errors are to be expected, it may be desirable to put the data in punched-card form just for the purpose of such a pre-edit, because cards are easy to correct or replace.   On the other hand, cards are easy to mishandle—a careless operator may lose or rearrange them—and the handling difficulties tend to increase as the number of cards increases.   It is just too much to expect that one hundred thousand cards will always be in exact order and contain no punching errors with any reasonable preprocessing procedure.   They may be free from error, but we should not risk too much processing time on the chance.

The Pre-edit Program

One way to avoid input difficulties is to prepare the program in such a way that one long continuous run through the data is not needed to obtain correct results.   Problems where each input card, record, or small group of cards or records is processed independently and yields its own independent output lend themselves to this kind of programming.   However, we often have data which cannot be handled in this way.   In these cases, where a successful production run is dependent upon a continuous processing, it may be profitable to prepare a *pre-edit program*.   A pre-edit program is a separate, complete program with the function of scanning the input data for errors, notifying the operators when errors are found, and incorporating corrections in a new edited version of the input.   Normally the pre-edit program will require two separate runs, one to detect the errors, and one to incorporate the corrections supplied by the operators. The second run, however, should also check for errors, for people have been known to make new errors while trying to correct old ones. In fact, the correction run may often have to be repeated several times until a completely error-free input tape is developed.

Such a pre-edit system is not insignificant in preparation time or cost. Before deciding on one we must fully evaluate the loss to the main production program that subsequent input errors will produce. The major advantage of the pre-edit program is of course in production savings. In pre-edit we are only testing the data. In production we are processing the data. Therefore, the testing-processing timing relationships are most important to determining the practicability of such pre-editing.

For example, in programs where normal processing is input-limited —that is, our program timing is totally dependent upon the input data time—the savings obtained in a pre-edit run could most likely be realized by incorporating the editing within the main program. It is quite possible that by separating the pre-edit phase in this case we would be simply duplicating a tape run. However, let us not forget that a separation of editing and processing can result in a most desirable simplification of the programming phase. Again any decision on a production program must be based upon both programming and production considerations.

With the advent of smaller, less expensive computers, a growing philosophy is one in which the smaller computer works as backup to the large computer. Thus the pre-edit phase becomes adapted to the smaller machine allowing for full production to be assigned to the large machine. Under these conditions we attempt to correct errors on less expensive equipment. We would probably pay a price for such an operation in terms of flexibility; yet on an application-dollar basis the over-all cost per production run would be far lower than that achieved in the use of the large computer for the weeding out of errors of the input-data variety.

Other Edit Programs

Without the small computer, how then can we cut down on cost and time? One method where we can use our main computer for all work is to enlarge the scope of the pre-editor by making it into a full general-purpose data handler. Production-run programs need not concern themselves with this production phase, thus relieving the programmers of this much programming obligation and programming cost. One exceptional means of creating a more efficient production run is to give the pre-editor the facility to convert the input-data format into one that is more easily workable and/or more compact. We therefore could obtain more usable computer storage, a simpler main program, or better data control. What we attempt to do is to make our pre-edit run a maximum productive effort. There is no problem in different data formats since we already know that we have the flexibility to deal with all kinds of configurations. Similarly a *post*-editor would permit the easing of restrictions on the main program, allowing again for a simpler programming effort. A general post-editor is most valuable in that it will give us the facility to present our output data in different formats from the same source. Requests for different arrangements, for different correlations of information of the same output data, are very common. If not handled properly, if all possible information is not extracted at the time of the production run, we can find ourselves forced to rework tapes of input data in order to satisfy one request for a data configuration we had not anticipated. Production without a great deal of preparation cannot ever be truly effective.

Problems of Installation Control

In terms of time loss in computer productivity, it is not only the programming and running of individual systems that must be carefully controlled; we also lose time because of the actual mechanics of running an installation. Let us investigate some of these causes.

One primary cause of time loss is the improper allocation of production time to a given system. A careful account of the number of minutes or hours lost over a week of operation simply because of computer inactivity has raised the eyebrows of many a manager. The time lost between the completion of one program and the initiation of the next can be truly amazing. The unexpected end to a run with no other production run ready will cause a great deal of lost time. Certainly the amount of data to be handled by a system for a particular run can usually be predetermined. Major production runs should be scheduled well in advance. Alternate system runs should be readied in case of any emergency. Small inactive time periods can be filled with check-out periods of both new programs and new subroutines available to the installation. As we shall see, proper instructions to the computer operators play a most important role in keeping the computer active.

Our mention of that poor programmer running around the computer is not an isolated illustration. The tendency of too many programmers is to stay at the computer entirely too long. Such occurrences come primarily at check-out time, but check-out time is an intrinsic part of the daily production schedule. It is too easy for a 10-minute computer period to extend into 25 minutes. Such weakening of control can cut a schedule to ribbons. A production run requiring, say, 5 hours may suddenly find itself with only $3\frac{1}{2}$ hours. A programmer at the computer, or even an operator, not employing proper discipline will attempt manual corrections, will use slow output devices such as the attached printer for large output, or will attempt to change tapes to try out some unscheduled procedure. A rule that should be followed is this: Keep thinking to a minimum when operating the computer. The console is not the place to develop suddenly bright new techniques which must be tried immediately. All planning, all courses of action must be predetermined. Action at the console should be automatic. There is ample time to think in the quiet of an office. It is not unusual during testing time to have a 5-second run on the computer, to spend 5 hours in study, to take another 5 seconds of computer time, and so forth until the happy conclusion of a checked-out routine.

In production running, as we have suggested, any clerical-type operation should be done independently, away from the main computer processing section wherever possible. Thus tape output is to be preferred over on-line printer output; tape input is desired over large-volume card input. Having all programmers keep time checks on their computer runs will quickly pick out those individuals who should be given further training in proper computer use.

Fortunately, as installations have matured, there has been an accompanying graceful and grateful exit of that poor programmer who used to run around the computer. In his place is a staff of professional operators. These operators are concerned with the efficient operation of the computer, rather than with the coding, debugging, and running of a given program. This lack of concern with a given program, lack of personal identification with some code, is a great advantage; for the operator can be much more objective when the program does something "unexpected." Like a surgeon, he is willing to trade "scars" on a program to achieve a healthy working system. However, with the removal of the programmer from the computer, greater installation control is required to ensure that the operator will fulfill his responsibilities. Since the operator is not familiar with the contents or purposes of a program, he must be given clear and concise instructions—in terms of the computer environment—for handling the program. As we will see, these instructions, operating instructions, play a significant role in the achievement of efficient installation operation.

Restart Procedures

Dividing the work of a program into several phases, as we do when we add pre-edit or post-edit procedures to a single computer of course can add extra time to the processing and can add to the total number of instructions written—though we would gain from the usual reduction in the difficulty of programming. Even when programming difficulty is increased, however, we may still wish to divide the program for two main reasons:

1. We reduce the lost time in case the program is interrupted.

2. Fitting several small jobs into a busy machine schedule may be easier than fitting one large one.

These advantages may cause us to consider breaking up a large program even where no "natural" line of division exists.

Machine errors, power failures, human blunders, or high-priority work may prevent the normal completion of a program. Programs which run for more than an hour or two must consider machine errors, for example, as a natural, though not frequent, part of their operating conditions. Computer engineers and programmers often speak of the "mean-free-error time" of a computer, which is roughly the average time the computer will run before making an error. Typical mean-free-error times are more than a few hours and less than a day, but since these are only averages, we can expect that sometimes the machine may run for only a few seconds, and sometimes as long as weeks, between errors. As a result, programs which *must* make uninterrupted runs of several hours are a bad gamble; if they are run often enough, they will certainly cause an appreciable loss of machine time. A wiser course would be to break such programs at certain points so that they may be restarted at some advanced stage of the computation. Of course, with a nonrepetitive program, the gamble may be worth taking against the cost of additional programming.

In a problem which is basically an internal computation—that is, where data are read in initially and then only internal processing and output take place—provision for restarting is not too difficult. The interval-timing clock, if available, may be used to interrupt the program, say, every 15 or 20 minutes. At this time the entire contents of storage, as well as the status of the special registers and indicators, may be written on a tape, following which control is returned to the basic program. If the program is disturbed, the last record of the machine status can be loaded and processing resumed at the break point with a maximum loss of 15 or 20 minutes, as the case may be. This procedure adds a burden of about 15 seconds every time a dump is made—a 1 or 2 per cent increase. A restart may result in a duplication of some of the output, but this usually presents no difficulty.

When the program relies on a continuous supply of input data, preparing for a restart is more difficult. Along with the internal information, the position of each input tape must be preserved. Unless the records are labeled uniquely, the main program must keep track of these positions as it uses each tape. Thus we must be thinking of the restart at all times when programming. Even if the records are uniquely labeled, the program which reloads the main program must have the ability to reposition each tape. In other words, restarting under these circumstances generally means more difficult programming and additional processing time. In both cases, we are better off if we can break the job at places where "natural" separations occur. It is easy to see how rapidly the intricacies of programming develop. After reading the first few chapters we might have assumed that the programmer was concerned primarily with presenting a logically correct program. Although the achievement of a logically correct program does not diminish in its importance, we now see equally important responsibilities in ascertaining the most efficient operation of the program. Knowledge of only the instructions on a computer will permit one to code; but to be a programmer of any professional standing, computer operation must be understood.

Handling Exceptions

One manufacturing firm trying to automate its payroll on the computer had what is an all too common experience. Of the two pay plans in effect, the first was completely programmed in two months. The change-over in methods was delayed two more months, however, in order to complete the programming for the second—more difficult—plan. What made this schedule ridiculous is that two thousand employees used the first plan and nine the second. The amount of effort spent on programming plan two would have been sufficient to calculate those nine paychecks manually for at least fifty years.

The frequency of such errors in judgment probably results from what we might call "the urge to automate." Once swept away by the glamour of automatic data processing, many people cannot be convinced that some things are better done in other ways. Every aspect of every function must be handled by the computer or other automatic machines before a system is allowed to function at all. As a result, the savings otherwise accruing from a system are delayed; and a less efficient system may be produced because the normal functions are burdened with processing related only to the exceptions.

In some cases, the delays are so long and the obstacles so frustrating that the entire system is abandoned; and the irresistible enthusiast is converted into the immovable opponent of all forms of data processing.

In other words, we should always consider handling certain exceptions as exceptions outside the machine. The programming cost for a given procedure is independent of the number of times that procedure is used. Therefore, if an exception is truly exceptional, it bears a disproportionately high programming burden. The program cannot, of course, simply ignore exceptions; it must at least be provided with a mechanism for recognizing them and calling them to the operator's attention. In some cases, we can avoid even this much work if we have some way of screening out exceptional cases before they reach the computer.

No matter how we decide to handle the exceptions, we must avoid having them bring the machine processing to a halt. Quite often the on-line printer is used to list information about exceptions, especially if they are not really expected to occur at all. In many cases, the line between such exceptions and errors is somewhat hazy, and the ability to monitor the program in process may prevent oversights or machine errors from running up too large a bill of wasted machine time. In fact, because there are so many ways a procedure can go awry, it is most important to be able to distinguish *any* exceptional case from the normal ones. Some operators will note such cases by watching the "pattern" a program makes. This pattern is a combination of the sequence and rhythm of the input-output units and the flickering of certain lights on the operating console. In some installations, the operators can tell just which one of 20 or 30 jobs is on the machine simply by observing this pattern for a moment. Although this technique has the advantage of requiring no additional programming, it is certainly not wholly reliable as a measure of the proper functioning of the program. Besides, it depends heavily on the experience of the operator and is of no help the first few times the program is run— just the point at which the most assurance is needed. Even the programming savings are minimized because the more the program is used—that is, the better the operators get to know its pattern—the less extra programming costs would have counted. Nevertheless, as long as computers are designed with visible input-output units and complexly lighted consoles, operators will use these patterns—at least as extra assurance. (Some computers emit audible vibrations when operating, and each program on them may have a characteristic "melody" which is a sufficient pattern for the operators.)

A much more dependable method for reassuring the operator is to print an "all's-well" message at certain crucial points in the processing. The operating notes may give the expected sequence of messages as well as some indication of the expected time intervals. Psychologically, an interval of about 2 to 5 minutes seems quite reassuring: longer periods rouse acute anxieties; shorter ones tend only to confuse. Some of these messages may arise out of the normal operating functions. If, for example, the operator sees the message REMOVE OUTPUT TAPE FROM A3, he knows that a certain point has been reached as surely as if he had seen the message END OF FIRST PHASE. Many programs, of course, do not require changing of tapes during processing—if possible, we plan that they should not. In that case, we may insert messages at restart break points or simply at arbitrary points for reassurance only.

The value of such messages of course depends upon their usage. Certainly the proper sequence of messages, properly timed, cannot always mean that no erroneous processing has occurred. In fact, poorly chosen check points may give false assurance about the nonexistence of certain common errors. Actual operating experience on a particular job is the final judge. It seems that, when a job is written without adequate provision for check points, subsequent conflicts between the operating room and the programmer somehow force the necessary steps to be taken. Watch any job which has been in production numerous times, and you will see a rather consistent pattern of check points (of one type or another)—3, 5, at most 10, minutes apart. We can deduce from this that considerable value exists and is worth pursuing without the prod of expensive personal experience.

If we plan for check points, we can often include them in the original coding and thus gain their help in debugging. This technique is especially helpful when we are checking out a *process* as well as a code. That is, we may have an untried process which—even if coded properly—may not do the job we wish. Suppose we were trying to get the computer to forecast economic conditions. Such a program is called an economic model. In such a program we attempt to reproduce a real situation through use of mathematical formulas, rules of logic, and correlations. In such a model we are often only making "educated guesses" and thus have no precise foreknowledge of results for all cases. In such forecasting, the results of one trial may indicate adjustments to be made to the model itself, rather than to the code. The computer, in this case, is helping to develop the model. It is often possible to detect the need for adjustments without having to make a full run through the program. Check points can trace the development of critical quantities up to the point at which we decide to terminate that particular run, possibly at great savings over a full processing. We cannot emphasize too strongly that this trial-and-error procedure will be economical only for *process* checking; code checking is better done using automatic methods. The objective is to start with a checked-out code of enough generality to incorporate adjustments without disturbing its checked-out character. In other words, such a code should be a framework into which changes can be placed by simple means—changing a number or, at most, replacing one subroutine by another, equally well checked, one. Of course, to some extent every program is subject to a series of adjustments as operating experience accumulates; and as long as we realize when we are process checking and not merely debugging, we can apply such trial-and-error operating techniques with profit.

Machine-Man Communication—At the Machine Console

We have established the need, in certain situations, for an exchange of information during the operation of a program. Perhaps we can gain a better understanding of these situations if we examine some of the specific methods available. We have already mentioned the use of the on-line printer, but we do not propose to examine the details of the printer since its similarity to tapes from a coding point of view will prevent us from adding much to our knowledge of principles. Normally a subroutine is used to operate the printer, since the programmer does not want to be concerned with such details as conversion, spacing of pages, or checking for errors. For example, as part of the input-output package (IOTPKG) introduced in Chap. 9, we might have had a macro described as follows:

PRINT   X

Execution of this routine causes the 20 words starting at location X to be printed on-line as a 120-character message.

How could we put such a printing routine to use? Let us look at several of the programs we have already done. In the student-grading program (Fig. 9-5), block X18 caused a stop whenever the conversion program had some problem with an input record. As we now know, stopping at this point is not a particularly good way of handling this exception—especially since the operator must note where the stop occurred before he allows the program to proceed. On the other hand, if we print the offending record on-line, we shall have a complete record of the information necessary to make adjustments without the need for stopping. Thus we might code block X18 as

X18	PRINT	R1	Print student record on-line
	TRA	X6	

As another example, consider the flow diagram in Fig. 4-14, which we coded as a problem in Chap. 9. We could now take that big block (XD) called "procedure for duplicates and sequence errors" and treat it more intelligently—though not perfectly, by any means. By printing the two records involved, we could allow the operator to make a choice as to which would be eliminated. We would, of course, want to keep the different types of errors separated so that we could print the appropriate records and resume at the appropriate place. (Notice that this problem is of the type where the processing of each individual record is not independent of the processing of the others. Actually, printing only two records will not be sufficient to determine the source and extent of all types of errors.)

When it is the operator who communicates with the program, it is often some quite simple information he wishes to convey. Suppose, for example, that the printed messages indicate that an error has probably occurred in a production program. In order to be certain, before attempting a restart, the operator might like to see a detailed printing of a short section of the program's output. If the output section has been properly programmed, the operator can cause this printing by using a "sense switch."

The Sense Switch

Each of the six sense switches, which are something like large light switches mounted in the 7090 operating console, may be set "on" or "off" by the operator at any time. Each switch may be tested, or "sensed," by the program to determine its current position; and a switch which is not tested—either because the test was not programmed or because it was not reached in the program execution—cannot influence the processing. Therefore, the function assigned to each sense switch is completely the programmer's choice. For example, if we want to assign sense switch 5 the function of causing on-line printing (in addition to tape writing) when depressed, we can preface our output routine with a SENSE SWITCH TEST (SWT) on sense switch

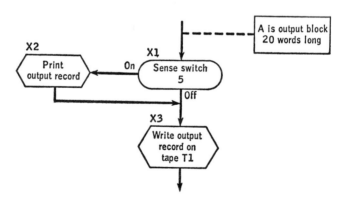

Fig. 12-1. Use of sense switch.

5. This function is illustrated in Fig. 12-1 and might be coded with the skip-type instruction SWT as follows:

X1	SWT	5	
	TRA	X3	Skipped if sense switch 5 is down (on)
X2	PRINT	A	
X3	DOUT	T1, A, 20	

Notice how the familiar skipping function is used to translate the depression of the sense switch into an order to the computer to print on-line. Notice, however, that, although this "order" may not be disobeyed, it might be ignored in the case where no output is called for. On-line printing of all output may be stopped by putting sense switch 5 into the "off" position, and it may be started again at any time by switching back to "on." Perhaps we should qualify the phrase "at any time." The sense switch is a mechanical device and, as such, cannot be used to exercise detailed control over the program, that is, control at the microsecond—or individual-instruction—level. Actually, the limitation is not so much in the sense switch as in the human operator, who cannot begin to perceive the minute details of program execution, let alone move his legs, arms, or even fingers, at the required speed. Consequently, we must give up any thought of detailed control by the operator unless we are willing to stop the computer every time he might want to make a decision. Thus, in our example, if we want the operator to decide *exactly* which output records he wants printed on-line, we would have to code something like this:

X1	HPR		
	SWT	5	
	TRA	X3	
X2	PRINT	A	
X3	DOUT	T1, A, 20	

When the program stops at X1, the operator may set the switch to the desired position, taking—or wasting, if you like—as much time as he wishes before allowing the program to resume. Thus, he has gained individual control over each output record, but he has lost more time than printing each record would have cost.

This technique of stopping before testing a sense switch is not, however, useless. At points in the program which are reached only rarely, such as the transition from a pre-edit phase to a processing phase, this sense-switch technique might be used to make a major operating decision without undue waste. Also, if the sense switch is being used to signal the completion of an operator function, such as tape changing, which must be completed before further processing can take place, the stop furnishes some protection. Actually, in this latter case, the stop is not so good a protective device as we would like. Operators, being human, have a tendency to react to a program stop by pushing the "start" button, thinking, "I already took care of that—whatever it is."

In such cases, we like to make the operator think twice, that is, we force him to make *two* wrong moves in order to make a mistake. We can provide such a double check by making sure he has actually *changed* the sense-switch setting.

Examples of Sense-switch Control

Suppose, for example, we let sense switch 6 provide an indication of the operator's completing a task—any task will do. The operator is instructed to change the position of sense switch 6 when he com-

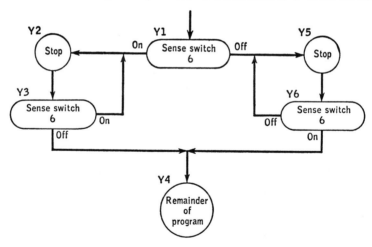

Fig. 12-2. Sense-switch control.

pletes the operation—before pressing "start." The flow diagram in Fig. 12-2, with the following code, will make him think twice:

```
Y1     SWT        6
       TRA        Y5
Y2     HPR
```

```
Y3      SWT         6
        TRA         Y4
        TRA         Y2
Y5      HPR
        SWT         6
        TRA         Y5
Y4
```

If he presses "start" without changing the sense-switch setting the program will simply stop again—and again, until he makes the change. The second stop would, we hope, remind him to do his task or, if he has actually done it, to move the sense switch to tell the program so. In this way, the program automatically makes it hard to make a mistake (though not impossible, for some people do not seem afraid of hard work).

Using the sense switches in combination can increase their effectiveness but can also result in confusing the operator's job. Therefore, proper caution must be exercised Suppose we wished to use sense switch 1 to cause a restart in the program of Fig. 12-1 if the operator decides that the situation is intolerable. Figures 12-3a and 12-3b show two possible ways to set up this function. Method b has the advantage of requiring on-line printing before restart—just for the record, if *only* one record is printed—so that the operator cannot quite so easily make a hasty decision. By being suitably clever, we could force the operator to look at two or three lines of printing before the restart switch becomes effective. In general, a clever program can exercise a great deal of control over the operator, but in the final analysis, *any* operator can ruin *any* program—if he tries. Since the operators are not usually trying, however, the program must generally share the blame for operating mistakes.

A more common use of sense switches is in making the choice between a number of possible operating alternatives—before the program really starts. The various switches may be used to choose between on- and off-line input or output, between several alternative processes, between input or output formats, and so forth. In spite of the frequency with which this technique appears, the use of a "control card," which contains the necessary information to set the desired alternatives, read on-line just before processing starts, has a number

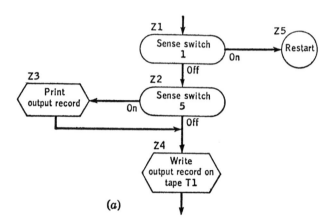

(a)

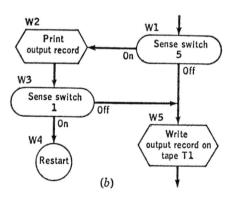

(b)

Fig. 12-3. Restart by sense-switch control.

of advantages over multiple-sense-switch usage. First of all, the control card is not limited to six switches nor is it limited in the ways these different decisions may be designated—single holes, characters, or digits, or even pseudo-operations, may be used in any combination. Secondly, the card furnishes a permanent record of what was done; and since it is prepared in advance, it speeds up operation and lessens the likelihood of error.

Sense Lights

One other device for machine-man communication seems worthy of mention—the sense lights. These four lights, mounted on the console, are completely under the program's control—they may be turned on or off or tested—but

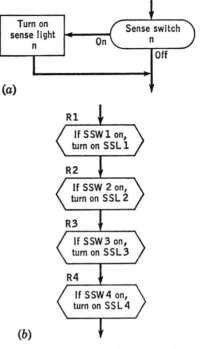

Fig. 12-4. Sense-switch = sense-light operation.

their action may be observed by the operator. Thus, although they may be used as purely internal switches—to be set and tested at will—the sense lights are more important for the indications they may give of the computer's internal state to the outside world. One precautionary remark must be made about sense lights: Although for testing (internal) purposes they operate instantaneously (microseconds), sense lights must be "on" for about a tenth of a second before they can be noticed by the operator. In other words, sense lights are useful as communication devices only if they indicate slowly changing functions (hundreds of thousands of instruction executions).

The instruction SENSE LIGHT ON (SLN) turns on the designated sense light, while SENSE LIGHT TEST (SLT) is a skip-type instruction for testing a specified sense light as well as turning it off. SENSE LIGHTS OFF (SLF) turns off all four sense lights and may be used to give a fresh start to sense-light operations. To illustrate the use of these instructions, suppose we write a set of instructions which, if sense *switch* 1 is on, turns on sense *light* 1; if sense switch 2 is on, turns on sense light 2; and so forth. The flow diagram shown in Fig. 12-4a shows how one sense light is operated; and by defining, from it, the macro-instruction

FLIP	MACRO	N	
	SWT	N	
	TRA	* + 2	Sense switch off
	SLN	N	Sense switch on—turn on sense light
	END		

we can easily code the complete diagram in Fig. 12-4b.

R1	FLIP	1
R2	FLIP	2
R3	FLIP	3
R4	FLIP	4

Machine-Man Communication: Within the User Organization

The growth in the use of computers can only be described as startling. What once was limited to exploratory research, and was perhaps even a curiosity, has become a vital element in meeting production needs, schedules, payrolls, reports, current design requirements and long-term research, to name only some application areas. Along with the diversity of use has come an equally astounding growth in the number and types of computer users. The user today is as diversified in his background as there are different computer applications. Illustrative of this phenomenon is the increasing difficulty of applying the term "programmer" to the many different users. It has become necessary to add qualifiers to "programmer" in order to differentiate the kinds of work performed. Thus we have systems programmers and application programmers; we have programmer-analysts, mathematical programmers, engineering programmers, business programmers, scientific programmers, and data-processing programmers. Sometimes we even have the name or number of the computer tacked on, such as "7090 programmer."

Just what is a 7090 programmer? Is he one who thoroughly understands the machine language of the 7090? Is he one who understands specific application programs prepared for the 7090? Is he one who is expert in using FORTRAN for the 7090? Is he one who is skilled at debugging programs coded for the 7090? Is he one who serves as interpreter between the 7090 and other users? Is he one who is responsible for maintaining and improving major programming systems such as compilers, or assemblers, or sorts? Is he one who is responsible for making the machine room more efficient?

Within an organization the responsibilities of a user may vary from carrying out all functions—designing an application, maintaining programming systems, carrying out all coding—to familiarity with the FORTRAN language only, without any additional knowledge of the makeup of the computer (and without the desire to know its makeup). One of the most difficult responsibilities of a user organization is fitting the computer installation into the user environment so that it best meets the needs of this mix of users and the kinds of applications they are solving. An extremely efficient computer installation within its own boundaries can fail within the organization if it cannot communicate properly with the other organizational components. A computer set up to handle its jobs in the most efficient manner can be significantly affected in its service by poor operational procedures for handling jobs to and from the computer room.

It is possible that a job that has a total computer time of 30 minutes may take 24 hours to be returned to its developer. Even if the computer is improved 10 times so that the job in computer time is now 3 minutes long, it may still take at least 24 hours to return the job to its origin. Just how significant is this 10 times improvement? The answer is not obvious. A case in which jobs taking 3 minutes on the computer represent only 20 per cent of the work load, with 2 to 3 hour jobs representing the remaining work load is much different from a case in which 85 per cent of the work load is represented by the 3 minute jobs.

However, no matter what kind of job is being performed by the computer, a user who has prepared a job for computer use will judge the computer installation's effectiveness by its ability to respond to *his* requests. Often this response is called "turnaround" time. The number of runs a user can obtain on the computer during his workday will clearly affect his productivity. As the number of users increases, and the types of jobs they prepare for the computer become more varied, the problem of turnaround becomes that much more severe.

The problem of computer service becomes a problem of a combination of overlapping time scales. One who works on a major application such as customer billing—and who, for example, requires his input data by the twenty-seventh of each month—considers computer service in the same way as does a FORTRAN user—who is attempting, for example, to debug a FORTRAN job to meet a design specification review in six days. They both feel they are entitled to all the computer time necessary for them to meet their commitments. Very likely, the managers of the two departments will be interested in the amount of computer time expended in completing these programming jobs. In many cases the manager is only concerned with the computer costs charged to his department. Still, he can use the amount of computer time expended to determine the effectiveness of his people in preparing their jobs. Although many managers will not agree with their personnel on the amounts of computer time required, they, as well as their people, will expect their department's work to be given that service necessary for them to carry out the departmental functions.

Perhaps the easiest thing to forget, for people who work with computers as a profession, is that their function is to provide a service, not to a machine, but to people. One of the more common fallacies current in computer circles is that a computer installation is to be evaluated by the amount of time the computer is running, the so-called "utilization." In the name of this *kind* of utilization, bad practices are often encouraged because they use up machine time each time the job must be done over. And yet, surprisingly, as bad as the emphasis on utilization time can be, its equally bad converse is often found in the same installation—the preoccupation with efficiency. This preoccupation often leads to situations where jobs never get into production because their programmer is continually finding a new way to save 10 μsec or three storage words. But whether it results from filling the machine with useless work to run up the "utilization" figures or from the endless procrastination of the "perfectionist" programmer, the result is always the same—reduced service to the ultimate customer. It is on the improvement of this service that our efforts should be expended, and to this end we must examine the elements that go into making that service, with particular attention to the element of time.

What are the different time scales involved in user organization servicing—in machine-man communication? The most intense time scale is that applied to the computer itself. The computer service time for each job (often called "throughput") is dependent upon such things as the internal machine speed, the interaction with input-output, and so forth. As this capability increases, the operator interaction with the computer becomes potentially more damaging. We have seen that it is possible that a computer improved to handle a job threefold faster may provide an improvement of only 50 per cent or less due to operator interference. Giving more responsibility to the computer in controlling the jobs it ingests, together with the refinement of operator and machine communication, has probably resulted in the most analysis and corrective action regarding this time scale.

Let us assume that with improved hardware and better operator procedures, the computer permits handling twice as many jobs within the same time frame. How is the computer installation affected? It certainly should have been prepared for the higher volume of jobs passing in and out of the installation, for without appropriate planning, the computer could find itself with serious idle time simply because the jobs could not be readied for computer service any faster than before. Assuming improved input peripheral facilities to keep up with the computer's new capability, what if the output preparation were not also improved? With twice as many jobs requiring output servicing in the same time frame, the preparation of the output job information could well require an entire extra shift or more. Jobs which had a noon distribution schedule could slip until the next morning for dissemination. What may be a more efficient operation in handling more *different* jobs becomes a poorer operation in the handling of the *same* job. Turnaround time to the user is lengthened, resulting in reduction of his access to the computer for runs. His ability to solve a given problem is thus adversely affected. Despite computer throughput improvement, the user will assume that computer time necessary for him to fulfill his commitments is no longer adequate. From his standpoint, the computer is not as powerful as it was previously. For machine-man communication to be effective, then, the time scales of computer and computer installation must be carefully and completely analyzed as regards their interrelation and impact. Entirely new procedures may be required in the machine room to permit full utilization of an improved computer throughput.

The third time scale further emphasizes the relationship of computer room to other user components. This scale consists of the time used in transporting the job from the user's desk to the computer installation, and back again. This time period can dwarf the other two timing considerations. A computer run of 3 minutes, with computer installation handling time of 2 hours, can be buried by a "station wagon" run taking a full day. Let us assume a 3 minute job throughput time and an improved installation room operation giving internal computer room turnaround time of 2 hours. It is now possible for the user with this job to obtain at least three shots at the computer in the same working day. Our user, however, is at a location remote from the computing center. He is serviced by some form of transportation which theoretically gives him two chances at the computer. The chances of his obtaining two shots is—like his location—remote. User organizations have spent considerable effort in attempts to resolve this problem. Some installations purposely run computer shifts at night with an "early bird" delivery to help remote users obtain an additional machine run.

Computer users with remote sites are investigating methods for eliminating the "station wagon." At remote locations, facilities are being installed to permit transfer of jobs and their data from these sites directly to the computing center. The point of acceptance within the computing installation may be either some peripheral hardware or even the computer itself through special attached input-output components. The remote-site facilities may vary from some kind of terminal device such as teletype or card punch to a magnetic tape transport or even a cathode-ray tube.

But in the last analysis it is still the kind of service the user receives that is the pivotal objective. The computer and its installation which may have started as a bump in the user organization should end as a completely integrated component. In the relationship of user to computer, there are today the following diverse methods of communication: the user personally communicating with the computer—operating the computer himself; the user not being allowed any direct contact with the computer—with trained operators handling computer operation; the user permitted to communicate with the computer by terminal in the remote sense—where he is not operating the computer, but, rather, is acting as an input to the computer. Variations and modifications of these methods also exist. The study and evaluation of each of these variations really would take a book or two. The kind of computer hardware required, the kind of programming support needed, the kind of computer room environment that should be established, the relationship of the computer center to the user organizational structure—these are no longer isolated functions requiring isolated decisions. Still, there do remain fundamental principles of good operation which hold for all types of installations.

The Operating Instructions

The inadequacy of a programming job can often be determined by reading the operating instructions. These instructions must tell the operator only two things: what he is to do and what he should expect the computer to do. Furthermore, he must be told in a language which he will comprehend even though he may know nothing of the theory behind the process—or even about programming. Avoid directions such as "When the partial derivatives vanish, . . ." or "Remove the actuarial statistics tape." Such statements should be translated into machine terms, such as "When sense light 3 comes on, . . ." or "Remove tape C7."

The operating notes, because of the conditions under which they must be used, are no place for flowery language. If a direction cannot be simply stated, the procedure is too difficult—a condition to be rectified in the program code, not the instructions. Of course, it is tempting to leave certain difficult tasks to the operator, and sometimes it is even economical; but we must be fully aware of the costs and probabilities of an operator error. Any step which is left up to the operator has a high possibility of sometimes being done wrong. The same step done under unusual pressure can quickly lead to persistent operator error.

Clearly, the operations should be considered as the flow diagram unfolds. If the operating procedure seems so difficult as to encourage costly errors, the program should be reorganized. If reorganization is difficult, checks must be built into the program to ensure that the operator has not slipped. For example, if the operator is supposed to mount an input tape, the identification on that tape should be checked internally. In cases where positive checking is not possible, the program should be designed so as to make casual errors unlikely. For example, if the operator is supposed to remove a tape, he should be required to do more than merely press START to indicate that the tape has been removed. He might, for instance, have to depress a certain sense switch, press START, and then replace the sense switch to "up"—a procedure he would be unlikely to follow precisely if he were reading the wrong instruction or misinterpreting a direction.

All these cautions might seem to indicate that computer operators are somewhat incompetent. On the contrary, they are less so than most of us; but, being human, they *will* make errors. The conscientious operator of such an expensive device is charged with great responsibilities and operates under a certain tension because of them. A poor programmer tends to be the first person to blame the operators for not running his "pride and joy" correctly. A large amount of operating skill is needed to make up for an awkward program, and no amount can make up for misleading or incorrect operating instructions.

Usually an installation will have a preprinted form on which the operating instructions are usually given. A typical form is shown in Fig. 12-5a. The form is designed so that the programmer can, with a minimum of effort, describe precisely what he wishes to have done on almost any assembly, test run, or nonrepetitive production. Repetitive jobs, when they are finally tested, have a more detailed operating write-up supplied by the programmer. This write-up would describe, for example, how to exercise the various options available to the user. Running the program thus becomes a matter between the user and the operating staff, and the programmer's job would be finished were it not for the numerous changes which ultimately must be made to any large program. Even when such changes are anticipated immediately, the programmer should supply a complete, though pristine, version of the program materials to the operating staff. He will be relieved of the burden of overseeing normal operations, while, at the same time, the operators will gain experience and begin to discover those rough edges which he will ultimately wish to remove.

The form in Fig. 12-5a furnishes several clues to the type of installation using it. For one thing, several coding systems are in use, as evidenced by the three methods of assembly (or compilation) available. This situation is usually brought about by the inability to take clear decisive steps while carrying the weight of past programs and programmers. A second clue is furnished by the box labeled "programmer to be present," which indicates that the stage in this installation has not quite been reached when the programmers are completely forbidden to enter the actual machine room. Until this stage, at least, is reached, there is no hope for achieving any high efficiency in machine utilization. Fortunately much has been done to correct this situation.

The reverse side of the card shown in Fig. 12-5a is a form for communicating to the programmer the results of the run. This form is shown in Fig. 12-5b. (When a misbehaving program destroys the emergency dump routine kept in storage, the panel contents must be copied manually, because reading the dump back into memory may destroy some of the panel conditions.) With the information on this card and a well-chosen set of debugging output, the programmer will be able to learn everything he might have gained from being present at the actual run—and usually a good deal more. If, on the other hand, he *is* present, he generally only confuses the whole operation with last-minute uncertainties and attempted—and unsuccessful— changes.

Supervisory Programs

What an effort it is to prepare a production program! Edits, restarts, check points, write-ups—all this trouble seems to be irrelevant to the job at hand. It is easy to see that we could spend the major part of our time dressing the program up for production. Since certain functions must be performed in the operation of any program, nonrepetitive jobs carry an even heavier penalty of extra programming. As a result, usually only the barest minimum is done to make non-repetitive jobs operable, and their operating efficiency shows it.

In addition to the programming burden, there is a certain minimum operating burden which is roughly independent of the size of the job and the size of the machine. This burden is determined by the (human) time necessary to ready the inputs before the job starts and to clean up all details at the end. A double team of operators can cut this wasted time almost in half by overlapping the setup procedures on one job with the cleanup procedures on the previous one. Nevertheless, 1 or 2 minutes seem to disappear each time a new job is started. Because this is a fixed human time, it gets more and more expensive as the machine gets larger or the programs get shorter. In an installation where any appreciable amount of check-out work or other small jobs are done, several hours a day may be thus wasted.

NAME _____ DATE _____ TIME _____ CHARGE TO _____ PRIORITY _____

ASSEMBLE USING 9AP ☐   SOS ☐

EXECUTE USING SNAP ☐ SOS ☐ RUN DECK AS IS ☐ PROGRAMMER TO BE PRESENT ☐

ESTIMATED RUNNING TIME _____ ON LINE PRINTER USED ☐ PUNCH ☐ FORTRAN ☐

TAPES	LOGICAL	1	2	3	4	5	6	7	8	9	10
	CH. A										
	CH. B										

TO USE SPECIAL TAPE, WRITE NUMBER IN BOX
TO SAVE TAPE, CIRCLE THE UNIT NUMBER
PRINT OUTPUT TAPE NUMBER ____

SENSE SWITCHES	NUMBER	1	2	3	4	5	6
	UP						
	DOWN						

TYPE OF STOP	AT	WHAT TO DO	(TYPE: PROGRAM, DIVIDE CHECK, LOOP, ETC.)

ATTACH PRINT REQUEST SLIP   OTHER INSTRUCTIONS:

ALL DECKS MUST BE COMPLETELY SET–UP.

(a)

424

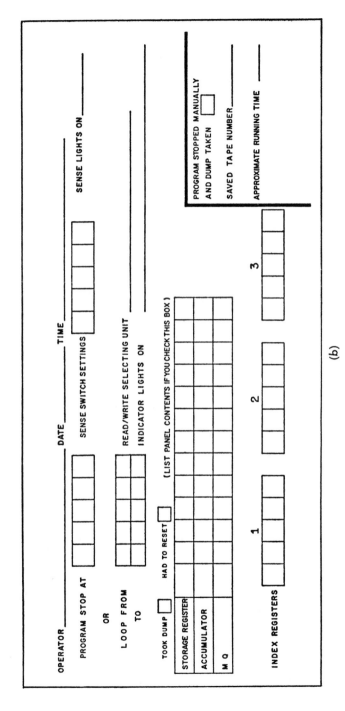

Fig. 12-5. (a) Operating instructions form—to operator; (b) operating instructions form—to programmer.

(b)

425

One of the most common "small" jobs is the assembling or compiling of programs. Many times a day, different programmers will require the machine for such assemblies or compilations; so it quite naturally evolved that assembly programs and compilers were modified to accept one job after another, without restarting. Thus, instead of, say, 25 minutes to assemble 10 programs, only 5 minutes would be used if they were "batched" (assembled independently but during the same machine run). Such spectacular savings seem to indicate a direction to take for further improvement, but subsequent steps are not so simple.

In order to save minutes of setup time by batching, it is necessary that all jobs being batched use the same machine setup. This standardization is automatic when all the jobs use the same program, as in the case of assemblies; but how is it to be achieved in a more general case? All jobs do not use the same tapes or even the same number of tapes, nor do all programs have their stops and restart procedures in common. Perhaps if we cannot standardize the stops or tape units used, we can standardize the *method* of using them. Perhaps we can supply all programs—that is, all programs willing to accept a certain degree of standardization—with the operating conveniences of a large program. Perhaps we can supply even more.

Preparing for Supervision

In order to achieve these benefits, we put the computer in charge of its own operation, just as we have given it so many other responsibilities. The computer thus establishes its own network for handling a continuous flow of diverse jobs. The program we use to take charge of the operation is often called the "supervisory program," or "supervisor," for obvious reasons. Probably the simplest way to understand what a supervisor does is to watch one in action. Suppose we take several jobs which might be batched together and see just what the supervisor would do with them.

In order to prepare for the supervisor run, we set up a deck of input cards consisting of the several jobs to be processed. (These cards would probably be entered from tape.) The cards for each job may be divided into three parts:

a. Job cards, which describe to the supervisor what is to be done

Job cards --- Job No. 1

Program to be assembled

b. The program, if any

c. Data, if the supervisor's input facilities are to be used

Let us consider the following simple set of jobs:

1. An assembly
2. A production job
3. A debugging job
4. Another assembly

(see Fig. 12-6). The following sequence of major events takes place:

1. The supervisor is loaded into storage, reads the job cards for job 1, and determines that this is to be an assembly. (The contents of the job cards may be printed on line to keep the operator informed.)

2. It then finds the assembly program on the system tape, loads it into storage, and transfers control to it.

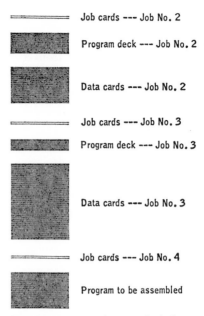

Job cards --- Job No. 2

Program deck --- Job No. 2

Data cards --- Job No. 2

Job cards --- Job No. 3

Program deck --- Job No. 3

Data cards --- Job No. 3

Job cards --- Job No. 4

Program to be assembled

Fig. 12-6. A production deck for a supervisory controlled run.

3. The assembly program reads the program cards, assembles them, punches an assembled deck, and writes a listing on the system output tape. Control is then passed back to the supervisor.

4. The time used by job 1 is computed and a record of the completion of the job is printed for the operator. Tapes used by the assembly program (other than the system's input tape, if the cards were put on tape, and the system's output tape) are rewound.

5. The supervisor reads the job cards for job 2 and determines that this is to be a production job. The program is loaded and control is given to it.

6. The program is executed. Whenever it wishes to read some data, it uses a special routine, supplied by the supervisor, for reading the system input tape. If the data required are large in quantity, a separate data tape might be used. In this case other instructions would be given to the supervisor. Whenever it wishes to write some output for printing, it uses special routines in the supervisor for writing on the system output tape. When the execution is completed, control is returned to the supervisor.

7. If the program comes to a successful completion, the time used is computed and a completion record printed on-line. If the job is not successfully completed, this fact is also noted on-line. Such a completion may result from a determination of difficulty by the program itself or by the supervisor's noticing that the time or output estimates (punched by the programmer into the job cards) have been exceeded. In some cases the operator may be given the option of proceeding to the next job, with or without a dump; restarting; or continuing, in the case where the supervisor has terminated the job. At other times, these decisions may be made automatically by the supervisor.

8. The supervisor reads job cards for job 3 and determines that this is a debugging job.

9. The debugging system, say, is found on the system tape and loaded into storage along with the program deck. Control is passed to the program.

10. The program is executed as was job 2 except that any debugging output is written on one of the system's intermediate storage tapes. When the job is completed, control is returned to the supervisor.

11. The debugging output, if any, is transferred by the supervisor from the intermediate storage tape to the system output tape and edited for proper printing in the process. Then the same terminating procedure used after job 2 is followed.

12. The job cards for job 4 are read and the same procedure used for job 1 is followed.

13. At the completion of job 4, the supervisor attempts to .read more job cards and, finding none, proceeds to rewind all tapes, print a message to the operator instructing him to remove the output tape, and stop.

The supervisor has enabled us to run through these four jobs without interruption (probably), and we have produced a single output tape which, when printed off-line, will be found to contain:

a. Listing of program 1
b. Output from program 2
c. Output from program 3
d. Debugging output from program 3
e. Listing of program 4

Most of the normal functions of the operator have been performed automatically at machine speeds. On a machine like the 7090, these steps are carried out faster than we can even read about them. Economically, the supervisor approach becomes more and more feasible—more and more necessary—as the machine gets larger and faster. Since the supervisory functions to be performed are to a certain extent independent of the machine capacity, the cost of having the machine do them gets smaller (because of the lower cost per unit of processing) while the cost of having the operator do them gets larger (because of the higher cost per hour). Consequently, the growth in sophistication of supervisory programs has paralleled the growth of machine capacity.

Supervisory programs have also been applied to smaller machines with resultant increase in efficiency. With smaller machines, however, we must be extremely careful about what functions should be placed in the supervisory program. Going overboard in "capability" can lead to considerable storage being taken away from the user together with additional time required for execution (the supervisor with more function will most likely require more time to make decisions) without any compensating benefit to the user. The attempt to limit function is a difficult one, particularly where the supervisory program is to service diverse usage. However, it is a responsibility that must be accepted. One procedure to help minimize extraneous function is to design the supervisory system such that functions can be segmented. This approach, which is not different from methods of solving application programs, would permit the removal of unneeded functions from the supervisory program in a relatively easy fashion.

The Sophisticated Supervisor—An Analogy

As the supervisory programs grow more sophisticated—the one we have outlined is a rather basic one—features are being added to new machines to make the task of truly automatic operation simpler: interval timing devices; accounting clocks; memory-protection schemes so the programmer's program cannot accidentally, or intentionally, harm the supervisor; elaborate interruption systems to help track down real or probable errors automatically. With all such extra gadgetry plus all these complex programs, it seems as if the job of programming is getting beyond the range of the average individual. On the contrary, although the supervisory program itself is more difficult, the average programmer only *uses* it—he does not have to understand its intimate operation. A simple analogy is the modern automobile. An automatic transmission, though more complex than a standard gearshift, is, or should be, easier to operate.

This analogy actually carries a bit further. Many people prefer standard shifts because they cost less to maintain or because they give more efficient use of fuel. Similarly, many machine users object to supervisory programs because they cause extremely painful difficulties if they contain errors or because they make some programs less efficient by forcing them into certain restrictive standard patterns. To a large extent, such complaints are complaints against bad supervisors, rather than complaints about supervisors in general. Although we expect that a mechanical device, like a transmission, will wear out, a supervisory program, once correct, will not deteriorate. We may have difficulties, great difficulties, getting the supervisor checked out in the first place; but then, as with any good program, the benefits should begin to repay us for our trouble.

The second objection is just as easy to answer. Because the supervisor is taking over human functions, we shall, without doubt, have more machine processing; but it will save enough machine idle time and programming time to more than pay the cost. Certainly there will be some large production programs where a true loss of efficiency would be the result of operating under a general supervisor. However, we did not develop the supervisor for such jobs, and there is no reason why all jobs must run under the same type of supervision. The important goal is an installation that uses an efficient combination of supervisor-controlled programs and independent programs. What we want is to cut down on unnecessary waste.

Perhaps we should list more explicitly some of the advantages which the programmer should receive by working within the framework of a supervisory system:

1. Operating efficiency between jobs.

2. Elimination of special restart or exception programming.

3. Great simplification of input and output programming for both editing and transmission.

4. Automatic input-output buffering, resulting in increased operating efficiency during execution.

5. More runs on the machine, especially when debugging, in a given

number of days provided the other time frames we have discussed interact properly.

7. Easier treatment of priority jobs.

8. Easier establishment of "remote-control" computer utilization where the user does not have to be physically near the computer at any time.

In other words, the programmer can write fewer instructions, get a more efficient program, and check it out more efficiently. No wonder people have been willing to surmount the difficulties of getting a programming group started using a supervisor.

Multiprogramming

One other great source of operating inefficiency exists; and it too is coming under the assault of a type of supervisory program, a type much more sophisticated than we have yet discussed. Spectacular increases in machine efficiency may result from the elimination of this particular type of waste.

In order to recognize the source of this waste, it is necessary to use the timing-diagram technique which we learned earlier. Suppose we have two jobs A and B whose timing diagrams are shown in Fig. 12-7. Job A is clearly process-bound and job B is just as clearly input-bound. Although we have, in both jobs, completely overlapped all

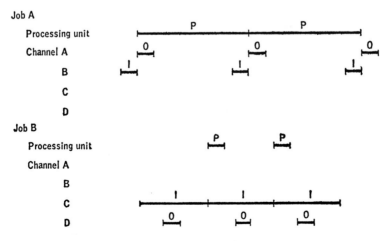

Fig. 12-7. Two timing diagrams.

possible functions, we are not, in either one, making very efficient use of all the units of the computer. In job A, the input-output channels are idle most of the time, while in job B, the processing unit bears only a small load. If only there were some way of getting these two programs to share the facilities, we should be as fortunate as Jack Sprat and his wife.

If the two programs are small enough, they can occupy the storage simultaneously; and since our machine is equipped with an interrupt device for input and output, we can see that clever programming ought to be able to produce the timing diagram shown in Fig. 12-8. By combining A and B, as shown, we do job B at just the cost of its processing time plus whatever time is needed for supervision (not shown) to keep things straight between the two jobs. The time for supervision, of course, will be relatively less the more powerful the machine; and thus we may conclude that a more powerful machine is capable—though we may not be using the capability—of operating itself more efficiently than a less powerful one.

Further examination of Fig. 12-8 reveals the possibility of an even greater gain in efficiency. Most of the channels are still idle most of the time; and we could, in fact, add several more jobs similar to job B to recover some of this lost time. Here we have one of the real limiting factors in "multiprogramming," as this technique of intermingling jobs is called. The efficiency of our operation is limited as much by the *mixture* of jobs that we have as by any other factor. If all our jobs were like job A, no benefit would be obtained from

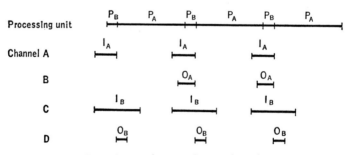

Fig. 12-8. Jobs A and B combined.

multiprogramming, although if all our jobs were like job B, much could be gained. Whether a job is like job A or job B depends on the relative speeds of the various computer units—the processing unit and the input-output devices. Thus, with multiprogramming, the selection of a computer or even the configuration of a computer for a given work load becomes a complex task of high order. In any case, one would be foolish to select a machine which had no flexibility of configuration, for the composition of the work load could be subject to large changes.

This situation is not very different from the situation in a large machine shop. There fifty or more jobs may be in process at one time, with the materials moving from one machine type to another for different stages of the processing. As time goes on, the foreman may notice that one machine, or machine type, is always busy, while others are often idle. In order to increase the efficiency of the shop, as long as the mixture of work remains the same, he can either obtain another of the loaded-type machines or get rid of some of the other types. As any good machine-shop foreman knows, it is not possible to have all the machines operating all the time. Clever planning can increase the efficiency, but attempting to achieve 100 per cent utilization will result in a breakdown of the system.

In a similar way, the efficiency of a multiprogramming scheme can be increased by proper scheduling of work, for the order in which jobs are done will obviously affect utilization. A good multisupervisor should have the ability to look ahead and schedule its work over, say, several hours. More important, however, it must be able to do the multiprogramming job without making the programmer's job more difficult—it could even make it easier. The programmer, for example, might write his program in a completely straightforward manner.

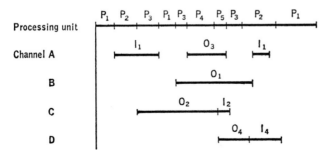

Fig. 12-9. Five jobs multiprogrammed.

He would make no attempt to overlap operations and would leave the selection of specific input-output channels completely up to the multisupervisor. The multisupervisor, for its part, would survey a batch of work and determine the assignment of input-output units and the priority of processing likely to produce the most efficient run.

Figure 12-9 shows a timing diagram which might result from such a multiprogram operation where all the jobs are not even regular. The jobs are given priority, 1 through 5, on the use of the processing unit. That is, job 1 uses the processing unit until it has to wait for some input or output operation to be completed; then it relinquishes the processing unit to job 2, and so forth. Clearly it is not an easy task to determine just what is the most efficient priority to assign, especially since the times to do various parts of the different programs will vary. In fact, the whole multisupervisory task is one of extreme complexity. Nevertheless it is just another example of the way in which, as machines grow more powerful and as programming knowledge grows, the computer is called on to solve the increasingly difficult problems that it itself creates.

The Sophisticated Supervisor—The Operating System

The growth in the use of the supervisor has resulted in a more formalized construction in the programming support necessary to effect the supervisory functions. More and more there is less and less distinction between the computer hardware and its programming control. The operator within this environment most often is communicating with the programming control—as an extension of hardware control. Thus more complex and equally compact communication can be exchanged between operator and computer with the programming control serving as interpreter. This more formalized programming structure is known in its entirety as the "Operating System."

The Operating System is a structure of program hierarchy. Its central network embodies the supervisory or monitor or control programs, which, like the control instructions in the computer, provide the threads of logic for permitting continuous operation of a diverse group of other programs and itself. There may be several levels of control programs with many variations and functions within each level. The control program, with appropriate direction, can: determine the computer configuration for a given job; seek out an input-output unit for functional assignment; call for any number of working programs in many combinations; identify and handle combinations of jobs entering the computer from different input sources such as magnetic tapes, attached card readers, and remote terminals; determine the procedure for handling a job in trouble; and notify an operator when remiss—among other duties.

Normally within the Operating System the control program turns control to some working program. Examples of working programs include compilers, assemblers, application programs, sorting programs, input-output programs, and error-handling programs. Under an operating system, programs prepared in different programming languages may be compiled and/or assembled together, and subsequently executed with previously compiled (assembled) programs in one continuous operation. But whatever the working program or combination may be, once it has completed its tasks it will normally return control to the control program network. Further, any working program finding itself in trouble will also normally seek assistance from some part of the control program complex.

One of the most important facilities of the Operating System is its ability to allocate function. Without having to consult the attending operator, the operating system control can make such decisions in the handling of a given job. These decisions, which will usually involve a multiple set of simple comparisons and branchings, are of course predetermined by the operating system designer. The range of such decisions employed in a particular computer environment is normally predetermined by the using organization.

Why is the facility for allocating function so important? For the operating system to have this capability means that we can *identify* these functions. As we have said several times, one of the most difficult steps in using computers is determination of whether a problem should be solved on the computer. Next we must determine how the problem should be solved. Having an identifiable set of tools within our controlling computer programs gives us that much more opportunity to effect a better solution. It is such identification that enables the multiprogramming solutions, where applicable, to be applied. As more is learned about the interrelations of the many components of the computer—about the function and its relation to these computer components—about the programming allocation of function and computer—about such function and its relationship to the user—we may truly realize the total contribution that these machines potentially have to service our needs.

Multiprocessing

We have explored the area of simultaneous solution of several jobs by one computer—or better, one computer Central Processing Unit, or CPU. This technique of multiprogramming has as its goal more efficient use of the computer. Another method of finding more computer potential has also received considerable emphasis. In multiprogramming, our single-computer hardware control, working with the control programs, allocates function to handle several jobs simultaneously. Why then can we not handle a single job by allocating function such that two Central Processing Units work in conjunction with one another to solve this job simultaneously. Each computer could have its own separate memory or share a common memory. Each computer may have some separate input-output components. More likely the two computers would share common input-output facilities. Each computer would have its own mix of control program functions. At times both computers may have identical operating system control. (Can you think of instances where such function allocation may be useful?) At other times one of the computers may have the prime control and would allocate to the second computer the work it should carry out. Computer organizations of this type are called *multiprocessing* configurations. Having the ability to identify function within the single computer thus permits us to allocate this function to two computers.

What can we gain with this organization? An obvious gain is that we can now divide the solution of any job over two CPU's thus cutting down on solution time. Of course this obvious advantage is only as good as the manner in which functions are allocated. If the job is broken down into parallel solution but each computer must wait sequentially for the other to carry out the parallel parts, we may find very little gain. If, however, we can clearly isolate function to permit parallel effort, then the two-computer combination may reach a clear advantage in performance. The advantage may never be demonstrated in a single job. Rather it shows up in the handling of a continual sequence of jobs. That is, as one job is using one of the computers for its computational solution (usually the faster computer of the two) the second computer can be setting up the next job and/or completing any administrative details on a previously executed job. By identifying one of the computers with the major administrative responsibility, greater control and greater flexibility can be achieved in the scheduling of the jobs. The administrative functions of the operating system that would normally be shared with the computational function of a single computer, resulting in "overhead" interference, can be significantly reduced. With multiprocessing configurations the administrative computer will often be given a considerable amount of peripheral responsibility. As we discussed, the problems of servicing an organization involve more than just the main computer's being fast. By permitting more peripheral function in a centralized organization, over-all operator control of jobs within the computer installation can be simplified, resulting in reducing the turn-around time within the machine room. (Can you list some peripheral operations that could be improved by a multiprocessing organization?)

Clearly, many possible multiprocessing arrangements exist. The most trivial of these arrangements is already widely used—two or more complete and identical processing units operating independently. Because this arrangement is multiprocessing in a trivial form, it is often ignored in discussions of the benefits of various multiprocessing configurations. Ignoring it, however, is a serious mistake; for it provides a standard of operation against which other schemes should be measured. For example, two independent machines may give essentially all the protection against breakdown that can be obtained from any complex interaction of them. A complex interaction of machines may, however, provide better downgraded performance.

For an example of a multiprocessing configuration, we can turn to the 7090. We have already seen, for instance, how the input-output channel of the 7090 can be thought of as a separate processing unit—one which shares the memory unit with the Central Processing Unit and which has a special set of instructions, the commands, tailored to input and output problems. The 7090 with its channels is not ordinarily thought of as a multiprocessing arrangement, but this classification is more a matter of historical accident than anything else.

Another multiprocessing organization being used is formed by connecting a 7040 to the 7090. In this organization the 7040 basically takes on the administrative job scheduling, setup, and completion (peripheral) functions, and the 7090 carries out the computational functions. Communication between the two CPU's is primarily by a few control signals. In the very general sense the 7090 does not really know the 7040 is there. For all it cares, the 7040 looks no different to it functionally than a magnetic tape connected to one of its channels.

Logical design or program design may determine whether one computer controls the other absolutely—in a master-slave relationship—or there is some sharing of control between them, depending on circumstances. In fact, as with all master-slave relationships, it is sometimes difficult to tell who is the master and who is the slave, even in the simplest arrangements.

The necessity for programming in two or more different languages in a multiprocessing system can be either a blessing or a curse. If the machines are radically different and the work load is properly shared between them, the programming may be simplified by having a machine language appropriate to each task. Countering this advantage is the necessity for learning two or more languages and maintaining all the associated systems for the two machines. Here, of course, a suitable problem-oriented language may be of great assistance; but if the division of labor among the machines was originally done to take advantage of different types of work and different machine capabilities, the advantage may be lost by channeling all the programs through the same generalized language.

Oftentimes the problems of multiprocessing seem great and the advantages sometimes tenuous and uncertain though great in potential. Not so many years ago, however, the same things could have been said about general-purpose digital computers. In similar manner the coming years can see the same flowering of applications and the concomitant growth of understanding with multiple-computer systems that we have seen with what are now thought of as "conventional" digital computers.

PROBLEMS

12-1. Can you design a multiprocessing system with more than two Central Processing Units (CPU's)? What kinds of problems can you anticipate?

12-2. List several multiprocessing configurations in terms of the interrelationships between the CPU's.

12-3. Can you describe a multiprocessing configuration in which multiprogramming techniques are employed? Would this be a useful combination? Why?

New Input-Output Components

One of the major hardware development areas as a result of Operating Systems, multiprocessing, and multiprogramming has been in the input/output area. The development of devices with random-access capabilities as opposed to magnetic tape, which is sequential in nature, has resulted in magnetic files (sometimes called disks) and magnetic drums with considerable variety in operating characteristics. These devices permit reference to and retrieval of required information without having to pass over all preceding information. Some of these devices permit retrieval and storage of information simultaneously, again without having to pass over other information. How are such devices useful? Consider the operating system with a whole set of modular functions, not all of which are in memory at one time, with the requirement to retrieve any one of these functions in any order. Consider the multiprogramming problem, in which jobs are constantly being remixed to ensure highest utilization of the computer, in which again jobs must be quickly accessible to the main memory as functional requirements change. Consider a multiprocessing configuration in which the administrative computer is preparing jobs for execution in the computational computer, in which there may be 5, 10, 20, or more jobs queued up waiting for service by the computational computer, and in which jobs are handled on a priority basis not necessarily in the order of entry into the queue. All these application areas have greater service as their major objective: greater service not only in terms of the facilities existing within the computer installation, but in terms of increased assistance to the users—which is why there are computers.

Some Final Words

It is difficult to describe the experience of encountering the computer for the first time. There is a mixture of awe and terrific challenge. One cannot help but feel exhilarated from the contact. To see a beautiful piece of equipment operate, to feel its sense of power, to know that your creation is controlling this equipment is not easily matched in normal experience. It takes some time before the programmer considers the computer for what it is, as simply a tool . . . and more so . . . as an extension of his own thoughts and actions—an artist's tool.

It has been our purpose to make the reader aware of the general truths and purposes of computers rather than to become expert in one particular area of programming. We have openly attacked the problem of error, for this phase of computer operation has been sorely neglected. We believe that the reader must now understand why we have emphasized this most elusive and difficult area. Further we have emphasized production and its many problems. Here too proper understanding with its rewards of efficient operation is sadly neglected in too many installations.

It has been a primary purpose of this book to make management and the computer users more aware of how to recognize what applications should be placed on the computer. We have aimed at expanding the computer-application area by making the reader understand the tool without misusing it. We cannot overemphasize the increasingly dominant role the computer must play in our daily business activity and our daily life. It would be difficult to imagine national defense without the aid of computers. In today's highly competitive market where decisions must be made rapidly, where the volumes of information gathered must be reduced and correlated and squeezed for their vital kernels, we must use computers. But we must use these computers properly. Good installations must develop from their inception if they are to be obtained cheaply. Since this has not happened for so many of our going installations, it is the responsibility of the people in and about them to recover—however dear the price—from the burdens that history and expediency have thrust upon them. It is likewise the responsibility of those people involved in starting new installations not to ignore the ever-increasing wisdom of other installations—often gained through such bitter experience.

BIBLIOGRAPHY

The reader who has come all this way with us should now be prepared for explorations on his own into more specialized areas of computers and their applications. To help him get started, we have compiled and annotated a short list of books and periodicals to which he may refer for at least the first stages.

Reviews and Periodicals

It is quite impossible for a bibliography to keep up with the constant flow of new and significant computer literature. Consequently, the first and best service a bibliography can render to its readers is to tell them how to find things it cannot or did not cover. Unfortunately, the task of finding the publications is complicated because articles about computers are likely to appear almost anywhere. One article may appear in the *Harvard Business Review,* the next in the *Scientific American.* Fortunately, there is a way to keep track of what is being published, and that is through *Computing Reviews,* the very useful journal published six times a year by the Association for Computing Machinery (ACM).

Computing Reviews attempts to obtain a one- or two-paragraph review of every publication—good or bad—relating in any way to computers and their uses. To do this, it covers journals, books, newspapers, and magazines published all over the world and in many languages. To some extent, this breadth of coverage tends to cause extraneous material to be included, but the generally accurate classification of the reviews helps the reader to get around those things of no interest to him. There may be delays of a year or more before an article or book gets reviewed in *Computing Reviews,* but anything important enough to read is probably still important a year later.

Computing Reviews should be available in most technical libraries, and the thousands of reviews in its back issues represent a sort of computer education by themselves. A subscription to *Computing Reviews* may be obtained by writing to the ACM. Members of the ACM receive a subscription as part of their membership, along with subscriptions to the *Journal of the ACM* and the *Communications of the ACM*. Membership information and information about other computer societies and journals can be found in most issues of the *Communications*.

General Topics

1. Lewis, Arthur O., Jr. (ed.): "Of Men and Machines," E. P. Dutton & Co., New York, 1963 (paperback).

A sometimes brilliant collection of thought and polemic about the role of machines in human life, going back as far as Francis Bacon (1624), and passing forward through Robert Frost, Walt Whitman, Carl Sandburg, Adam Smith, Isaac Asimov, Emily Dickinson, Stephen Spender, Samuel Butler, Stephen Vincent Benét, Stephen Crane, Mark Twain, Sherwood Anderson, W. H. Auden, Aldous Huxley, Edgar Allan Poe, George Orwell, E. E. Cummings, E. M. Forster, C. P. Snow, Ray Bradbury, and many others. This is a thoroughly stimulating book which has no practical value whatsoever and is thus to be recommended for anyone working with computers.

2. Morrison, Philip, and Emily Morrison (eds.): "Charles Babbage and His Calculating Engines: Selected Writings by Charles Babbage and Others," Dover Publications, Inc., New York, 1961 (paperback).

Charles Babbage might have been the father of the modern computing machine, for he enunciated all the logical principles on which modern computers are based. Unfortunately, he was born in 1792, probably a hundred years before his time. The nineteenth century just did not seem ready for him, though he fought hard and did succeed in building some calculating engines which are marvels even today. An extremely interesting book just as pure biography and autobiography, *Calculating Engines* also stands as a monument to the difficulty in getting really new innovations into the mainstream of technological and scientific life.

3. Phillipson, Morris (ed.): "Automation—Implications for the Future," Vintage Books, Random House, Inc., New York, 1962 (paperback).

This collection of 18 articles brings together under one cover the thinking of many of the fine minds of our time on what machines—particularly computers—may mean for our future. Among the authors are Arthur J. Goldberg, Norbert Wiener, Peter Drucker, Walter Reuther, and Paul Goodman, which perhaps will indicate the diversity of views presented.

Applications of Computers

1. Brandon, Dick H.: "Management Standards for Data Processing," D. Van Nostrand Company, Inc., Princeton, N.J., 1963, 404 pages.

This is one of the few books that have been written on the subject of administering a computing center. Although it has many shortcomings, at present it is the best of the lot in a most important field.

2. Freiberger, Walter, and William Prager (eds.): "Applications of Digital Computers," Blaisdell Publishing Company, New York, 1963, 256 pages.

This book might be a good place to start investigating applications of computers, if only because it covers such a wide variety of topics. The chapter headings are as follows: Computers and Operations Research; How Computers Can Learn from Experience; Recent Developments in the Science of Diagnosis; Recent Trends in Computer Programming and Numerical Analysis; Using Computers to Solve Problems in Physics; Computers and Brains; Sorting on Computers; Role of Computers in Astronomy; Computers in Fluid Mechanics; Use of Digital Computers in Civil Engineering; Information Theory and Numerical Analysis; Educational Implications of the Computer Revolution; Analysis and Design of Experiments with the Help of Computers; Automatic Data Processing for the Legal Profession; Automation and Pure Mathematics.

3. Garvin, Paul L., and others: "Natural Language and the Computer," McGraw-Hill Book Company, New York, 1963, 398 pages.

Among the most interesting areas of computer application is the host of possibilities connected with the processing of human languages by computers. Machine translation from one language to another is only one of many enticing possibilities, a number of which are covered in a sound, introductory way in the articles in this book.

4. Gass, Saul: "Linear Programming Methods and Applications," 2d ed., McGraw-Hill Book Company, New York, 1964, 280 pages.

Linear programming is a mathematical technique finding great application in modern industrial problems. Because of its name and the fact that computers are usually required to perform linear programming calculations, people often think that *linear* programming has something to do with *computer* programming. For those who have rid themselves of that particular misconception and who would like to know more about this technique as used on modern computers, Gass's book is a good place to begin. It is not, however, for mathematical novices (nor is any book on linear programming).

5. Hearle, Edward F. R., and Raymond J. Mason: "A Data Processing System for State and Local Governments," Prentice Hall, Inc., Englewood Cliffs, N.J., 1963, 150 pages.

By confining itself to the special problems in the very extensive area of data processing in governmental agencies, this book is able to achieve a depth which will be useful to people concerned with the paper-work problems of state and local governments.

6. Tocher, K. D.: "The Art of Simulation," D. Van Nostrand Company, Inc., Princeton, N.J., 1963, 182 pages.

Simulation is an ever-growing application of computers, and though this book is somewhat deficient in presenting simulation from a modern computing point of view, its basic soundness as an introduction to the problems and methods of simulation makes it a good place to begin one's studies in such a complex field.

Programming

1. Galler, Bernard: "The Language of Computers," McGraw-Hill Book Company, New York, 1962, 220 pages.

The Language of Computers is an introduction to computers from the point of view of the basic character, design, and operation of a computer language. This somewhat narrower point of view than that of *Computer Programming Fundamentals* enables the author to develop computer language ideas to a deeper level.

2. Iverson, Kenneth E.: "A Programming Language," John Wiley & Sons, Inc., New York, 1962, 286 pages.

The purpose of this book is twofold. First, it aims to develop and teach a concise and extremely helpful notation for thinking about and working out computer programming problems. Second, it applies that language to teach both elementary and advanced concepts and techniques in such programming areas as microprogramming, data representation, search techniques, metaprograms, and sorting. Iverson's book forms the ideal sequel to *Computer Programming Fundamentals* for the reader who intends to become a professional programmer. It is not an easy book, but it will reward many, many times over the effort put into reading it and working the numerous exercises.

3. Wegner, Peter (ed.): "Introduction to Systems Programming," Proceedings of a Symposium, London School of Economics, July, 1962, Academic Press Inc., New York, 1964, 316 pages.

Although this book suffers from being a collection of papers from a symposium rather than an integrated presentation, it will serve to give the reader the flavor of a number of different programming languages and systems and the techniques used in implementing them.

Mathematics of Computation

1. Hamming, R. W.: "Numerical Methods for Scientists and Engineers," McGraw-Hill Book Company, New York, 1962, 411 pages.

Hamming has certainly developed an outstanding, integrated, and unconventional introduction to numerical methods directed at the undergraduate scientist or engineer. The list of topics covered is quite comprehensive, but the outstanding features of this book are its integration of diverse numerical areas and its insightful philosophy, characterized by the book's motto: "The Purpose of Computing Is Insight, Not Numbers."

2. Ralston, Anthony, and Herbert S. Wolf (eds.): "Mathematical Methods for Digital Computers," John Wiley & Sons, Inc., New York, 1960, 293 pages.

This is really an outstanding book for the person who has a computational problem in one of the areas (Matrices and Linear Equations; General Elementary Functions; Ordinary and Partial Differential Equations; Statistics; and a number of miscellaneous topics) which the book covers. Each chapter of the book is devoted to a single mathematical technique, developed to the level of a specific flow chart from which coding for particular machines could be done. Each chapter has a description of the function of the method, a mathematical discussion, a summary of the calculation procedure, a flow chart, a description of the flow chart, subroutines required, a sample problem worked step by step, memory requirements and estimates of running times, and references.

3. Stiefel, Eduard L.: "An Introduction to Numerical Mathematics," Academic Press Inc., New York, 1963, 286 pages.

This book, translated from the German, introduces in varying detail the more important techniques employed in the solution of problems in linear algebra; linear programming; least squares and Tchebycheff approximation; nonlinear algebra, including the eigenvalue problem and general root finding; differential equations, both ordinary and partial; and aspects of interpolation. The book is directed at the junior or senior college level in mathematics, and the subjects are presented with simplicity, with emphasis on the computational aspect.

Design and Construction of Computers

1. Bucholz, Werner (ed.): "Planning a Computer System," McGraw-Hill Book Company, New York, 1962, 336 pages.

Planning a Computer System undoubtedly is the finest available book on how a computer is designed (or ought to be designed). It traces, in the words of the people who actually did the work, the design of the STRETCH computer, or IBM 7030, which was at the time the largest computer ever built. It discusses in great detail the problems of choosing such things as data units, a number base, a character set, formats of various kinds of data and instructions, instruction sequencing, indexing, input-output control, and multiprogramming; but it never loses sight of the over-all philosophy behind the machine's design.

2. Ware, Willis H.: "Digital Computer Technology and Design, Volume II: Circuits and Machine Design," John Wiley & Sons, Inc., New York, 1963, 560 pages.

The author, obviously a man with experience at teaching his material, takes up the design and construction of computers about at the level where Bucholz leaves off. Topics covered include reliability, toggle circuits, gates, and miscellaneous circuits, as well as higher level discussions of some of the larger logical units of a computer.

Theory of Computation

1. Davis, Martin: "Computability and Unsolvability," McGraw-Hill Book Company, New York, 1958, 210 pages.

Although the author claims that his reader need have no special training, this excellent book is on a much more sophisticated level than Trakhtenbrot's book, listed below, and should not be attempted by any reader without a well-developed ability to move about in mathematical notation. Nevertheless, those who do have the interest and the background will find Davis's presentation of such topics as computable functions, Turing machines, and unsolvable decision problems, well worth studying.

2. Trakhtenbrot, B. A.: "Algorithms and Automatic Computing Machines" (translated from the Russian), D. C. Heath and Company, Boston, 1963, 101 pages.

Although many people feel that the mathematic theory of computation has little if anything to do with practical computing, Trakhtenbrot has succeeded better than anyone else in bridging the gap between the two fields in his readable little book. The book requires no more mathematical training than does *Computer Programming Fundamentals* and is a good starting place in this often too difficult subject.

Analog Computers

Ashley, J. R.: "Introduction to Analog Computation," John Wiley & Sons, Inc., New York, 1963, 294 pages.

Based on interesting examples, this book is intended to overcome the "hardest part of learning analog computation," namely, getting started. This book has been called "one of the two or three best introductions to analog computation."

Specific Machines

.Generally, detailed information about specific computers is available only through the manufacturer. Often, a great deal of information may be had free for the asking, though there may be a charge for more expensive manuals. Also, of course, certain proprietary information may not be available at all; but generally, manufacturers are quite anxious to be helpful to anyone interested in their products.

Manuals particularly relevant to the 7090 family and the systems covered in this book are the following:

IBM 7090 Data Processing System Reference Manual . A22-6528
IBM 7094 Data Processing System Reference Manual . A22-6703
IBM 729, 7330, and 727 Magnetic Tape Units . . . A22-6589
IBM 7090/7094 Programming Systems: Macro Assembly
    Program Language (MAP) C28-6311
IBM 7090/7094 Programming Systems: FORTRAN IV
    Language C28-6274
IBM 7090/7094 Direct Couple System: Preliminary
    Spec. C28-6372

IBM 7090/7094 IBSYS Operating System: System
Monitor C28-6248
IBM 7090/7094 IBSYS Operating System: IBJOB
Processor C28-6275
IBM 7090/7094 IBSYS Operating System: Specifications
for IBJOB Processor Debugging Package C28-6362
FORTRAN—General Information Manual F28-8074
1301 and 1302 Disk Storage, Models 1 and 2, with the
7090, 7094, and 7094 Model II Data Processing Systems . A22-6785
7320 Drum Storage with the 7090/7094 Systems . . . A22-6747

Glossaries

Much of the terminology surrounding computers has not found (and some should not find) its way into standard dictionaries or even the specialized dictionaries in such fields as mathematics. Thus, the uninitiated reader attempting to understand an article in some new area cannot turn to the standard sources when he encounters unfamiliar words. A good glossary can help to overcome these difficulties.

We considered including such a glossary in this book, but thought better of it when we recognized that any effort we could make would be inferior to work that has already been done. Thus, we recommend instead that any reader intending to continue working in any area of computing spend 40 cents and obtain the following glossary from the U.S. Bureau of the Budget, Washington 25, D.C.: "Automatic Data Processing," 1962, 62 pages. It contains approximately 2,000 words, each of which has been carefully chosen and screened by several professionals in the field. It is particularly oriented to accounting and business data-processing terminology, but extends quite a bit into scientific computing terminology.

Other glossaries which have received some acclaim (but which may not be so readily available to the reader) include the following:

1. Grems, M., R. W. Bemer, and F. A. Williams: "IBM Glossary for Information Processing," preliminary ed., IBM, August, 1961.

2. "Standard EDP Reports Glossary," Auerbach Corporation, May, 1962.

3. Weik, Martin H.: "A Revised Glossary of Computer Engineering and Programming Terminology," Ballistic Research Laboratories, March, 1961.

In addition, of course, many of the books listed in this bibliography have short glossaries particularly oriented to their own material.

List of 7090 Instructions and Commands Used

List of SOS Pseudo-operations and Macro-operations Used

List of FORTRAN Statements

List of FORTRAN Debugging Statements

INDEX

454

SOCIAL SCIENCE LIBRARY

Manor Road Building
Manor Road
Oxford OX1 3UQ
Tel: (2)71093 (enquiries and renewals)
http://www.ssl.ox.ac.uk

This is a NORMAL LOAN item.

We will email you a reminder before this item is due.

Please see http://www.ssl.ox.ac.uk/lending.html
for details on:

- loan policies; these are also displayed on the notice boards and in our library guide.

- how to check when your books are due back.

- how to renew your books, including information on the maximum number of renewals.
Items may be renewed if not reserved by another reader. Items must be renewed before the library closes on the due date.

- level of fines; fines are charged on overdue books.

Please note that this item may be recalled during Term.